Blockchain for Distributed Systems Security

About IEEE Computer Society

IEEE Computer Society is the world's leading computing membership organization and the trusted information and career-development source for a global workforce of technology leaders including: professors, researchers, software engineers, IT professionals, employers, and students. The unmatched source for technology information, inspiration, and collaboration, the IEEE Computer Society is the source that computing professionals trust to provide high-quality, state-of-the-art information on an on-demand basis. The Computer Society provides a wide range of forums for top minds to come together, including technical conferences, publications, and a comprehensive digital library, unique training webinars, professional training, and the TechLeader Training Partner Program to help organizations increase their staff's technical knowledge and expertise, as well as the personalized information tool myComputer. To find out more about the community for technology leaders, visit http://www.computer.org.

IEEE/Wiley Partnership

The IEEE Computer Society and Wiley partnership allows the CS Press authored book program to produce a number of exciting new titles in areas of computer science, computing, and networking with a special focus on software engineering. IEEE Computer Society members continue to receive a 15% discount on these titles when purchased through Wiley or at wiley.com/ieeecs.

To submit questions about the program or send proposals, please contact Mary Hatcher, Editor, Wiley-IEEE Press: Email: mhatcher@wiley.com, Telephone: 201-748-6903, John Wiley & Sons, Inc., 111 River Street, Hoboken, NJ 07030-5774.

Blockchain for Distributed Systems Security

Edited by

Sachin S. Shetty
Charles A. Kamhoua
Laurent L. Njilla

Published by John Wiley & Sons, Inc., Hoboken, New Jersey.
Published simultaneously in Canada.

Library of Congress Cataloging-in-Publication Data is available.

ISBN: 978-1-119-51960-7

Printed in the United States of America.

V10009218_040419

Contents

Foreword

The success of the United States Department of Defense (DoD) in the future battlefield will hinge on the ability to protect the cyber infrastructure from loss of personal identifiable information, tampering of sensitive data, and interruption of services. Although all cyber risks are critical and need to be addressed, issues related to data integrity are most acute, as data tampering can have a huge impact on mission critical services that depend upon reliable data. The current cyber defense solutions are unable to combat data breaches effectively and are typically reactive in nature, and cannot keep up with the exponentially increasing cyber threats. Cyber defense solutions should be able to protect data despite attempts by adversaries to derail their effectiveness.

There is a pressing need for a paradigm shift in the development of next generation cyber defense strategies. Blockchain is an emerging technology that could address cyber security challenges, such as identity management and data provenance for distributed systems. Blockchain technology provides several advantages in building resilient cyber defense solutions. First, blockchains are shared, distributed, and fault-tolerant databases that every participant in the network can share, but no entity can control, and is resilient to single point of failure. Second, data integrity is ensured as tampering of blockchains is extremely challenging due to the use of a cryptographic data structure and lack of reliance on secrets. Third, blockchains assume the presence of adversaries in the network, making compromise by adversaries significantly expensive. Blockchain solutions for cyber security could represent a paradigm shift in how data manipulation will be defended by creating a trusted system in a trustless environment. Cloud, the Internet of Things (IoT), and the Internet of Battlefield Things (IoBT) are being used as distributed platforms. However, these platforms are plagued by numerous vulnerabilities that allow adversaries to gain access to sensitive information and disrupt services. A blockchain-empowered security platform will ensure the integrity of the data exchanged in these systems and reduce risks from data breach attacks.

Under the 2018 National Defense Authorization Act, the DoD will conduct a comprehensive study of blockchain, particularly in the context of cybersecurity. There have been DoD investments (research grants, SBIR/STTR awards, etc.)

in the investigation of blockchain for secure message delivery in tactical scenarios, additive manufacturing, and the protection of supply chains. On the flip side, there is growing concern that malware or other illicit content, once introduced into a blockchain, would be very hard to remove. There is also growing concern about the threat to blockchain posed by quantum computing.

The focus of the book is on providing blockchain-based solutions to distributed systems to ensure a resilient and reliable cyberinfrastructure for operations and missions. Most current books on blockchain only focus on impacts in the financial sector. There is a need for books to understand how the blockchain's impact goes beyond cryptocurrency, and to address security and privacy issues in cloud and IoT/IoBT platforms. The topics in the book provide blockchain-empowered solutions to protect cloud and IoT/IoBT platforms. The book also presents security challenges that must be addressed for blockchain technologies to reach their full potential.

Dr. Ananthram Swami
Senior Research Scientist (ST) for Network Science,
ARL Fellow, IEEE Fellow
US Army Research Laboratory, Adelphi, MD

Preface

Cyberattacks have increasingly targeted commercial, government, and military enterprises with the goal to steal sensitive information and/or disrupt service. There is an urgent need for cyber defense solutions to ensure traceable and tamper-evident accountability and auditability of command and control, logistics, and other critical mission data as future operations will involve the convergence of multiple domains and a heavily contested cyberspace. Thus, the emphasis needs to be on cyber defense solutions that can ensure resilient operation during adversarial attempts to thwart normal operation. The existing cyber defense solutions are reactive and are not able to combat the impact of the exponential rise in cyber threats. Centralized or homogenous information assurance systems and databases must evolve to possess distributed, disintermediated, and secure capabilities.

The cyber warfare strategy will come down to the ability to conduct operations on data in a secure and trusted environment. In order to win the cyber warfare, the military needs to protect data operations by (i) preventing adversarial access to networks housing critical data, (ii) ensuring the integrity of data despite the presence of the adversary on the network, and (iii) being resilient to the adversary's efforts to manipulate data. At the same time, the emergence of cloud and the Internet of Things to support on-demand computing, dynamic provisioning, and management of autonomous systems has increased the need to improve their security. Security assurance of intracloud and intercloud data management and transfer is a key issue. Cloud auditing can only be effective if all operations on the data can be tracked reliably. Assured provenance data can help detect access violations within the cloud computing infrastructure. The Internet of Things (IoT) in the military context interconnects warfighting resources, such as sensors, munitions, weapons, vehicles, robots, and wearable devices, to perform tasks such as sensing, communicating, acting, and collaborating with human warfighters. The massive scale and distributed nature of IoT devices will create several security and privacy challenges. Firstly, the underlying IoT networking and communication infrastructure needs to be flexible and adaptive to support dynamics military missions. This dynamic change to the communication infrastructure needs to happen in an autonomous fashion without reliance on centralized maintenance services. Second, there is a need to ensure the veracity of the information made available through the IoT devices. There is a need for a trusted platform to ensure the information consumed by the human warfighters are accurate.

Blockchain and distributed ledger technologies as a whole demonstrate the potential of a truly distributed and disintermediated mechanism for accountability and auditability. Blockchains are shared, distributed, and fault-tolerant databases that every participant in the network can share, but no entity can control. Blockchains assume the presence of adversaries in the network and nullify adversarial strategies by harnessing the computational capabilities of the honest nodes, and the information exchanged is resilient to manipulation and destruction. This ability allows leaders to continue military operations despite adversarial attempts to cause disruption. Blockchain solutions for cyber security will represent a paradigm shift in how data manipulation will be defended. Blockchain has the ability to create a trusted system in a trustless environment.

Tampering of blockchains is extremely challenging due to the use of a cryptographic data structure and no reliability of secrets. Blockchain has the potential to enhance cyber defense with its ability to prevent unauthorized actions through distributed consensus mechanisms and provision of data integrity through its immutability, auditability, and operational resilience (ability to withstand a single point of failure) mechanisms. Though blockchain is not a panacea for all cyber security challenges, the technology does have the ability to help organizations tackle cyber security risk issues such as identity management, provenance, and data integrity.

The focus of the book is on providing blockchain-based solutions to distributed systems to ensure a resilient and reliable cyberinfrastructure for operations and missions. There is a need to understand how blockchain's impact goes beyond cryptocurrency and can address distributed security and privacy issues in cloud and IoT platforms. The topics in the book describe the properties underlying formal foundations of blockchain technologies and practical issues for deployment in cloud and IoT platforms. In addition, the book also presents security and privacy issues that must be solved for blockchain technologies to reach full potential. Three book chapters (Chapters 4,5, and 8) are based on research articles that were voted as Top Blockchain papers at the 2019 Blockchain Connect Conference.[1]

This material is based on research sponsored by the Air Force Research Laboratory (AFRL) under agreement number FA8750-16-0301, and we would like to thank AFRL for their financial support, collaboration, and guidance. The US Government is authorized to reproduce and distribute reprints for governmental purposes notwithstanding any copyright notation thereon. The work

1 https://medium.com/blockchain-connect-conference/top-50-blockchainpapers-and-research-team-lead-you-to-the-frontier-of-blockchainacademic-277b0358b784

described in this book was also partially supported by other sources acknowledged in individual chapters.

The editors would like to acknowledge the contributions of the following individuals (in alphabetical order): Abdulhamid Adebayo, Philip Asuquom, Shihan Bao, Yue Cao, Haitham Cruickshank, Ali Dorri, Peter Foytik, Arash Golchubian, Y. Thomas Hou, Raja Jurdak, Salil S. Kanhere, Kevin Kwiat, Adriaan Larmuseau, Ao Lei, Jin Li, Xueping Liang, Wenjing Lou, Andrew Miller, Aziz Mohaisen, Mehrdad Nojoumian, DaeHun Nyang, Danda B. Rawat, Muhammad Saad, Devu Manikantan Shila, Jeffrey Spaulding, Marco Steger, Zhili Sun, Deepak Tosh, Yang Xiao, and Ning Zhang. We would like to extend our thanks to Misty Blowers, Jerry Clarke, Jim Perretta, and Val Red for their valuable support and guidance. We would like to thank Paul Ratazzi, Robert Reschly, and Michael Weisman for technical review support. Last, we would like to extend thanks and acknowledgment to Jovina E. Allen, Walter J. Bailey, Sandra B. Fletcher, Lisa M. Lacey, Sandra H. Montoya, Lorri E. Roth, and Jessica D. Schultheis, who helped edit and collect the text into its final form, and to Mary Hatcher and Vishnu Narayanan of Wiley for their kind assistance in guiding this book through the publication process.

List of Contributors

Abdulhamid Adebayo
Howard University

Philip Asuquom
University of Surrey

Shihan Bao
University of Surrey

Yue Cao
Northumbria University

Haitham Cruickshank
University of Surrey

Ali Dorri
University of New South Wales

Peter Foytik
Old Dominion University

Arash Golchubian
Florida Atlantic University

Y. Thomas Hou
Virginia Tech

Raja Jurdak
University of New South Wales

Salil S. Kanhere
University of New South Wales

Kevin Kwiat
CAESAR Group

Adriaan Larmuseau
United Technologies Research Center
China

Ao Lei
University of Surrey

Jin Li
Guangzhou University, Guangzhou,
China

Xueping Liang
Old Dominion University

Wenjing Lou
Virginia Tech

Andrew Miller
University of Illinois at
Urbana-Champaign

Aziz Mohaisen
University of Central Florida

Mehrdad Nojoumian
Florida Atlantic University

DaeHun Nyang
Inha University

Danda B. Rawat
Howard University

Muhammad Saad
University of Central Florida

Devu Manikantan Shila
United Technologies Research Center

Jeffrey Spaulding
University of Central Florida

Marco Steger
Virtual Vehicle Research Center, Graz, Styria, Austria

Zhili Sun
University of Surrey

Deepak Tosh
University of Texas at El Paso

Yang Xiao
Virginia Tech

Ning Zhang
Washington University in St. Louis

Part I

Introduction to Blockchain

1

Introduction

Sachin S. Shetty,[1] Laurent Njilla,[2] and Charles A. Kamhoua[3]

[1] *Old Dominion University, Virginia Modeling, Analysis and Simulation Center, Norfolk, VA, USA*
[2] *US Air Force Research Lab, Cyber Assurance Branch, Rome, NY, USA*
[3] *US Army Research Laboratory, Network Security Branch, Adelphi, MD, USA*

1.1 Blockchain Overview

Blockchain technology has attracted tremendous interest from a wide range of stakeholders, which include finance, healthcare, utilities, real estate, and government agencies [1–5]. Examples of potential applications of this technology are claims processing, transparency and auditing of operations, identity management, supply chain provenance to address the threat of counterfeit products, and integrity of the information acquired from Internet of Things (IoT) devices. Blockchains are a shared, distributed, and fault-tolerant database that every participant in the network can share, but no entity can control. The technology is designed to operate in a highly contested environment against adversaries who are determined to compromise. Blockchains assume the presence of adversaries in the network and nullify the adversarial strategies by harnessing the computational capabilities of the honest nodes, and the information exchanged is resilient to manipulation and destruction. Blockchains facilitate the development of trustworthy networks in a trustless environment.

The premise of blockchain is that applications do not need a trusted central authority to operate and can function in a decentralized fashion. Blockchain enables exchange of information among distrusting entities. Blockchain enables trustless networks and allows entities to engage in transactions in the absence of mutual trust. There is an assumption that a communication medium could be compromised by insiders or outsiders. The reconciliation process between entities is sped up due to the absence of a trusted central authority or intermediary. Tampering of blockchains is extremely challenging due to the use of a cryptographic data structure and no reliability of secrets. Blockchain networks are fault tolerant, which allows nodes to eliminate compromised nodes.

Blockchain for Distributed Systems Security, First Edition. Edited by Sachin S. Shetty, Charles A. Kamhoua, and Laurent L. Njilla.

Blockchains have the following advantages over centralized databases: (i) ability to directly share a database across diverse boundaries of trust in situations where it is difficult to identify a trusted, centralized arbitrator to enforce constraints of proof of authorization and validity. In a blockchain, transactions leverage their own proof of validity and authorization based on a verification process managed by multiple validating nodes and a consensus mechanism that ensures synchronization; and (ii) ability to provide robustness in an economical fashion without the need for expensive infrastructure for replication and disaster recovery. Blockchain requires no configuration to connect and synchronize nodes in a peer-to-peer (p2p) fashion, with built-in redundancy and no need for close monitoring. It can tolerate multiple communication link failures, allows external users to transmit transactions to any node, and ensures disconnected nodes will be caught up on missed transactions.

Blockchain's distributed database maintains a continuously growing list of records, called blocks, secured from tampering and revision by distributed storage and continuous verification. The blocks contain a temporal listing of transactions that are stored in a public ledger using a persistent, immutable, and append-only data structure that is globally viewable by every participant in the underlying p2p network. When such an elegant data structure is considered to track data transactions in a distributed environment, the block structure contains attributes such as the set of user transactions, a timestamp, a reference to a previous block in the blockchain, Merkle root of the transactions, and so on. In this manner, the blocks are linked together to form a chain, where the hash of the previous blocks helps to maintain the integrity of the whole blockchain (Figure 1.1).

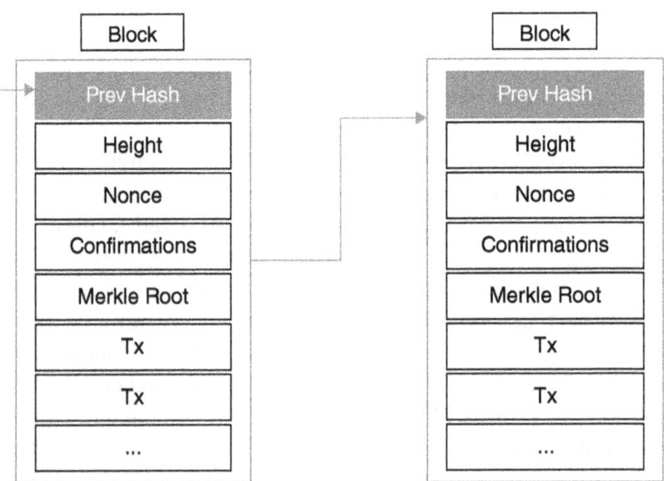

Figure 1.1 Block structure.

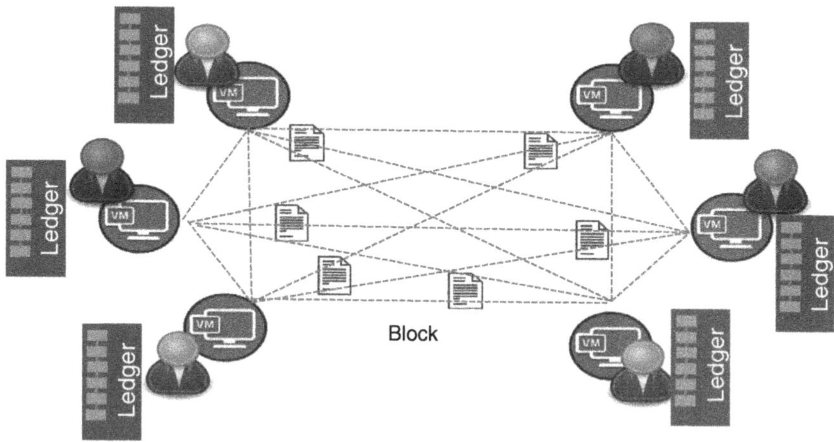

Figure 1.2 Blockchain architecture.

1.1.1 Blockchain Building Blocks

Blockchain technology's effectiveness hinges on the following three main components: a decentralized network, distributed consensus, and cryptographically secure algorithms. Figure 1.2 illustrates the basic blockchain architecture.

The key features of each of the components are as follows:

Decentralized Network—The function of the decentralized network is to ensure the propagation of transaction messages among the nodes responsible for maintaining the distributed ledger. The network protocol allows the transaction message to be broadcast from any node to all nodes in the decentralized network. However, the network is not a pure broadcast medium and allows nodes to propagate messages that represent valid transactions. The network can be part of a private or public blockchain that has ramifications on network performance and security. Irrespective of whether the blockchain is public or private, the decentralized network is based on a p2p architecture. The nodes can join and leave freely. There is no centralized arbitrator. The network has built-in redundancy and robustness to mitigate node and link failures.

Distributed Consensus—Blockchain uses consensus protocols over a decentralized p2p network for verification of transactions prior to adding blocks to the public ledger. The consensus protocol receives messages from the p2p network and inserts transactions in the distributed ledger. The consensus protocol is responsible for mining blocks and reaching consensus on their integration in the blockchain. The consensus protocol chooses the set of transactions that is accepted after passing a verification process. The verification process is determined by users and does not require a centralized administrator. The consensus protocols ensure that the newly added transactions are not at odds with the confirmed transactions in the blockchain and maintain the correct chronological order. The newly added transactions that are waiting to be confirmed are packed in a block and submitted to the blockchain network for validation.

Cryptographically Secure Algorithm—The foundational component of blockchain technology is the cryptosystem. State-of-the art blockchains' cryptography systems use public key algorithms such as Elliptic Curve Cryptography, and message digests such as SHA3-256. In a typical blockchain application, an Elliptic Curve key pair that contains a public key and private key is generated based on Secp256K1 curves. The private key has the traditional usage of being kept secret and utilized to sign transactions. For instance, in the case of bitcoin use, when a user exchanges bitcoins with another user, the user will sign the transaction with their private key prior to announcing to the network. Once the transaction is signed, the miners in the network will use consensus algorithms to verify the validity of the transaction signature, and validation is achieved.

1.1.2 Blockchain Commercial Use Cases

Home IoT—"Smart home" is an emerging Internet of Things (IoT) application that aims to provide higher accessibility to all home accessories and personalized user experience for the appliances. To operate efficiently, IoT hubs in smart homes collect and analyze a lot of sensible data from the home area network of all smart devices. With the gathered data, it is easy to derive usage patterns and user behaviors in the home environment, thus creating a digital trail of families in smart homes. However, this information could easily fall into the wrong hands, or the vendors could use the information to promote additional products. Therefore, when more smart technologies are added to smart homes, there is an increased possibility of a severe privacy breach. Conventional approaches may fail to achieve credible security and privacy in IoT because the IoT framework has particular characteristics. These characteristics include decentralized topology, resource-constrained devices, limited network performance, and minimal security standards for IoT devices. The introduction of blockchain technology could potentially address smart home challenges in an efficient manner because of the following facts: blockchain does not rely on a centralized control; instead, it works in a distributed network setting that is similar to IoT. As a result, blockchain avoids the problem of single-point failure and improves scalability. Moreover, blockchain inherently offers the anonymity that is required in the IoT environment, where identities must be kept private. Irrespective of the several advantages produced by blockchain technology, integration in the smart home environment may create the following obstacles: first, blockchain mining is computationally intensive in nature, and this requires decent computing capabilities in the participating devices; however, IoT devices have a heterogeneous computational power that may not be sufficient to mine blocks in a desirable amount of time. The second problem is that of data storage since blockchain is nothing but a distributed ledger stored locally to verify transactions; however, smart devices, such as various sensors, have a limited storage capacity. Finally, blockchain protocols also consume significant network capacity for internal communication, which may be undesirable for bandwidth-seeking smart devices.

Transportation Sector—In vehicle-to-vehicle (V2V) systems, vehicles communicate information with other vehicles. In vehicle-to-infrastructure (V2I) systems, vehicles communicate with the road network infrastructure to improve the safety and efficiency of the vehicle transportation infrastructure. Early examples of such systems are web-enabled tools such as Waze, a tool that provides real-time traffic conditions based on users, speed, and vehicle location. Even simple systems, such as automatic toll collection, stem from the idea of V2I. Futuristic examples are systems in which a car communicates its position on the road with other cars around it to prevent collisions, or for that vehicle to communicate with the transportation infrastructure, such as traffic signals, to provide better information on arriving vehicles to help it better manage traffic. In a global sense, each vehicle, traffic controller, and piece of road infrastructure can potentially become an IoT device, and each piece is connected to and can communicate through the Internet. The integrity of these devices must be ensured; the data that they produce will be critical. Blockchain technology can be applied to this area by confirming that a vehicle's ID is what it says it is, which is done by tracking its location on the road network. This would also prevent spoofed vehicles from tampering with or maliciously affecting automated systems. In 2014, Israeli students spoofed the Waze transportation application to report heavy congestion on a road when there was no traffic [6]. The students did this by reporting data on fake vehicles on the network at a particular road segment. A blockchain solution could have helped to autonomously manage vehicles IDs and their movements over the road network, and this would not allow systems such as Waze to account for vehicles that have just dropped onto particular segments. Moreover, the transportation infrastructure can ensure the integrity of vehicle data to help the autonomous systems make decisions based on a level of confidence in the data, backed by the knowledge of the valid history of the data.

Energy Sector—Blockchain technology has been proposed for use in the electric sector in the following application areas:

- Transactive energy—support distributed energy resource (DER) and its interaction with DER management systems (DERMS)
- eMobility—ability to transact energy charging at stations in multiple service territories
- Customer contracts—removing the middleman from the retail energy market

Blockchain technology can be used to provide supply chain security for the electric sector. Utilities are constantly installing new operations technology (OT) equipment and updating existing software and firmware in control system devices. One problem with this method is ensuring the integrity of the software and/or firmware. Some vendors use a digital signature when they distribute software and/or firmware updates, but this does not address the initial deployment. In addition, some vendors use a hash (typically MD5) as an integrity check. MD5 is not technically secure because it has a collision problem. That is, the same hash value can be computed on two different messages. Blockchain technology can be used to ensure software and/or firmware integrity in the electric sector security supply chain.

Consumer Electronics—Blockchain technology will impact the Consumer Electronics (CE) industry by providing cyber supply-chain provenance [7], where the customers as well as providers expect transparency for product information and delivery [8, 9]. Blockchain technology can mitigate cyber supply-chain risks for the CE industry by providing open access to the processes of planning, implementing, and controlling the movement of materials and finished goods to end users. Developing techniques and tools to provide provenance assurance are the top priority for addressing cyber supply-chain risks in the CE industry such as counterfeits, unauthorized production, tampering, theft, insertion of malicious software and hardware, as well as poor manufacturing and development practices. The globalization of the cyber supply chain has resulted in software and firmware being developed by offshore enterprises and has resulted in tremendous savings for the electronic data systems (EDS) sector. However, the dependency on third-party services has resulted in more maliciousness across the stages of the cyber supply chain. Specifically, there is a need for tools or technologies that can adequately address the risks involved in supply-chain processes, sourcing, third-party vendor management (every actor that has physical or virtual access to software code and/or systems), acquisition of compromised software or hardware purchases from suppliers, embedded malware in hardware or counterfeit hardware, and third-party data storage or data aggregators. Solutions exist, such as side-channel fingerprinting, reverse engineering, and formal methods, which are mostly deployed at the chip level to detect the presence of counterfeit chips. However, these methods cannot be scaled to protect the whole cyber supply chain. Thus, there is a need for blockchain-based methodology to maintain provenance across the supply-chain stages, as depicted in Figure 1.3. Radical evolution of IoT technology also attracts the majority of the CE industry to operate over cloud infrastructure [10]; thus, building a data provenance system will preserve transaction integrity and prevent malicious activities by alerting the users in real time.

Medical Sector—The recent influx of wearable medical devices promises to bring rich dividends to healthcare stakeholders. Wearable medical devices are networked computing devices equipped with sensors to track the patient's vital signs and physical activities. The data and the analytics can also be linked

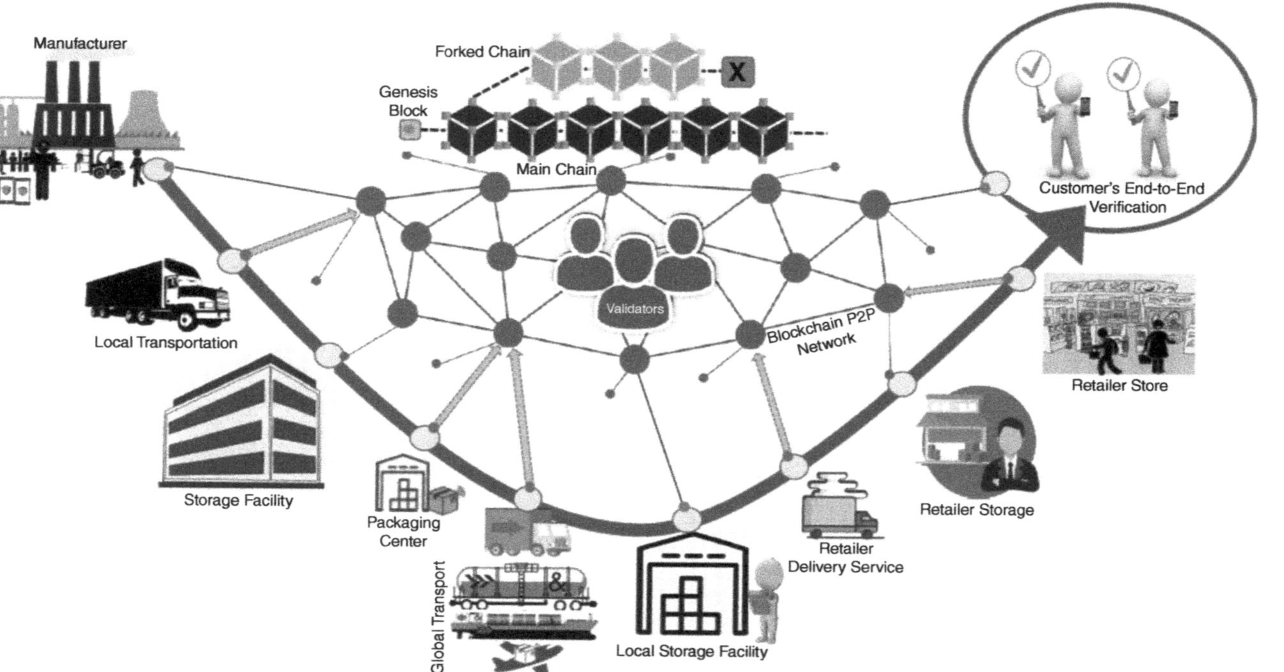

Figure 1.3 Supply-chain provenance overview.

to Electronic Health Records (EHR), which can benefit patients by helping them to monitor their personal health, aid doctors in prescribing personalized medicine, and allow insurance providers to gain insight into the cost of providing medical care.

However, due to security and privacy concerns, it has been reported that medical device manufacturers have only instrumented 20–30% of their networked devices to be used in hospitals. There have been several vulnerabilities reported with medical devices. For instance, ICS-CERT reported that Hospira's Symbiq drug infusion pump [11], used by medical facilities to automatically administer doses of medication to patients based on the amount specified by the caretaker, is vulnerable. The vulnerability allows an attacker to change doses of the prescribed medicine and impact patient safety. In 2017, the US Food and Drug Administration (FDA) reported vulnerabilities in St. Jude Medical's heart devices [12]. It is obvious that connected medical devices are here to stay, and the likelihood for compromising medical devices will grow exponentially. The current cyber-security solutions for identity management are inefficient and lack the ability to immediately track failure and accountability.

In addition to compromised medical devices, there are several privacy concerns with health data collected from both wearable devices and EHR systems. Patients are concerned about the lack of transparency in which a healthcare stakeholder has access to their data and how their data are used. Current healthcare cyber-security solutions focus on improving data providers' responsibilities to detect data disclosure activities; however, it is equally important to protect data access and provide immediate notifications of improper data disclosure risks. In addition, over 300 EHR systems use a centralized architecture that is prone to single point of failure and suffers from lack of interoperability that results in the absence of a holistic and thorough view of personal health. It is reported that 62% of insured adults rely on their doctors to manage their health records [13], which limits their ability to interact with healthcare providers other than their primary doctor. Moreover, even though health providers are supposed to follow rules or laws, such as HIPAA (Health Insurance Portability and Accountability Act of 1996), there are still many entities that are not covered by any laws. Therefore, it is crucial that any provider with access to data should be accountable for their operations on the data, and any operation on the data needs to be audited.

Blockchain's capability to capture data provenance will facilitate secure tracking of medical devices from production to ongoing use. The provenance information encoded in the blockchain provides immutable and reliable workflow with a trusted ground truth. The ground truth can be used for transparent traceability and accountability when any device malfunctions, accidentally or as a result of a security attack. The capability will also be useful for autonomous monitoring and preventive maintenance of medical devices. As compared to existing cyber-defense solutions, blockchain's distributed consensus protocols, cryptography techniques, and decentralized control will reduce cyber threat risks for medical devices. Other benefits include streamlining the secure tracking of medical devices, cost savings, and improving patient privacy by secure and targeted access to patient data.

Blockchain relies on pseudoanonymity (replacing names with identifiers) and public key infrastructure (PKI) to maintain the privacy of users. The workshop [14] co-conducted by the Office of the National Coordinator (ONC) for Health IT and the National Institute for Standards and Technology (NIST) focused on blockchain usage in healthcare and research, aiming to clarify the implications of blockchain as an infrastructure for healthcare use cases including privacy preservation for predictive modeling, increasing interoperability between institutions on a large scale, immutability of health records, health insurance claim process improvement, health information exchange, healthcare delivery models with artificial intelligence, identity management, monetization strategies, and data provenance requirements.

Data Provenance in the Cloud—Assured data provenance in cloud computing is needed to keep track of data transactions generated by data operations in the cloud and detect malicious activities. The current state-of-the-art data provenance technologies involve comparing logged data generated by execution of software on physical or virtual resources. However, they fail to detect integrity violations and are typically conducted in a private setting to allow better ownership of assets. Also, the process is not scalable to federated cloud environments, is costly, and lacks transparency. Hence, there is a strong need to develop a data provenance framework for the cloud computing environment, where multiple representatives or virtual stakeholders can participate in maintaining transparent and immutable provenance information. Blockchain technology, where data are stored in a public, distributed and immutable ledger and maintained by a decentralized network of computing nodes, provides a decentralized and permanent record-keeping capability, which is critical for data provenance and access control in cloud data protection.

1.1.3 Blockchain Military Cyber Operations Use Cases

Blockchain as a distributed ledger system provides many features and functionalities that are needed for cyber operations, such as auditing of historical information, assured data provenance, guaranteed variability of integrity violations of historical data, and auditing of contents from tampering. Besides, blockchain has both cost effectiveness merits as well as transparency features, making it an appealing system for military cyber operations.

- Generation of cyber assets—Blockchain can be utilized to generate cyber assets that will enable applications that rely on direct interaction between customers and assets. The blockchain system can aid in assuring the processes of issuance, transaction processing, and housing of cyber assets and identities.

- Transfer of ownership of cyber assets—The blockchain system allows transfer of cyber assets between owners by leveraging the property of blockchain so that once a transaction is guaranteed, it cannot be reversed. Any changes will have to be appended and will not result in change of an already validated transaction, thereby ensuring nonreversibility of transfer of ownership.
- Transparent and assured data provenance—Every operation on the cyber asset is encoded in the blockchain transaction using a publicly available and immutable ledger. The blockchain system ensures that provenance of every operation on the cyber asset is recorded and traceable.
- Verifiability and audit—The distributed ledger keeps track of transactions pertaining to creation and transfer of cyber assets. The tamper-resistant property of the ledger facilitates variability and audit of operations.

Military Cyber Operations—Ensuring traceable and tamper-evident accountability and auditability of command and control, logistics, and other critical mission data among international partners is paramount as our future operations involve the convergence of multiple domains and a heavily contested cyberspace. Centralized or homogenous information systems and databases must evolve distributed, disintermediated, and secure capabilities. As such, trust with respect to operations involving international entities must not be rooted in one single entity. Trust must be decentralized and built around robust, innovative cryptographic paradigms transcending the traditional PKI typically utilized in most homogenous enterprises.

An innovative, distributed trust and identity management mechanism is a crucial enabling technology assuring identification, authentication, and authorization in a way that would further allow disintermediated accountability and auditability. Emerging blockchain and distributed ledger technologies as a whole demonstrate the potential of a truly distributed and disintermediated mechanism for accountability and auditability. The current production application of cryptocurrencies has already created unprecedented accountability and auditability in a way that disrupts traditional fiat currencies and disintermediates the way people are able to transact internationally via pseudonymous identity management via wallets in permissionless and public blockchain implementations.

The nuances of disintermediated international partnerships and information exchange involve some mutually exclusive research and development challenges distinct from the permissionless and public implementations of blockchain. For the level of identification, authentication, authorization, accountability, and auditability challenges that encompasses overall integrity concerns for international operations, even more robust distributed identity management mechanisms must be investigated. Furthermore, the underlying practice of consensus must vary from the latency-tolerant and performance-heavy implementations observed in cryptocurrencies. Most importantly, the distributed ledger technology mechanism may be private and permissioned;

however, it must also not be vested in one single vendor's implementation in a way that inadvertently and ironically intermediates and centralizes information exchanges. We must thoroughly assess and demand interoperability and standardization among blockchain implementations for mission data, which further enables the disintermediated accountability and auditability required in our increasingly complex international operations in multiple domains.

1.1.4 Blockchain Challenges

Blockchain does have the potential to address cyber security issues in distributed systems. However, blockchain cannot be considered a panacea to address all cyber security concerns. Blockchain does have inherent capabilities to address integrity violations. However, assurance of confidentiality, availability, and authenticity is not guaranteed by blockchain and will require integration with several security solutions. Organizations that are considering blockchain to address cyber security issues should carefully assess whether the technology is a good fit. Specifically, the below outline is a good start to identify whether the organization does need blockchain to replace the existing solution [15]:

- Do you have concerns regarding the ability of the centralized database to withstand failures?
- Are there multiple stakeholders responsible for modifying the contents of the database?
- Do the multiple parties operate under differing trust domains?
- Are there clear defined rules to control data input?
- Is there a value proposition in having validators in the form of consensus?

Once the need for distributed blockchain has been justified, the next steps are to identify the blockchain solution that's a good fit for the organization. There are several aspects that need to be addressed, such as the type of data encoded in the blockchain transactions, frequency of transactions, the infrastructure used to store the blockchain (public or permissioned), key management system, number of validators, bootstrap time, ability of smart contracts to learn rules dynamically, attack surfaces in the blockchain solution, etc. For instance, for the healthcare sector, the type of data stored in the blockchain needs to be carefully identified as any sensitive information can be subjected to confidentiality attacks. Any organization that would like to ensure that activities of participants in the blockchain are compliant would prefer permissioned blockchain [16].

Below is a summary of key research challenges that need to be addressed for realizing a practical blockchain solution.

Scalability—Bitcoin's current implementations are not scalable due to the fact that it takes 10 minutes or longer to confirm transactions and seven transactions is the maximum throughput that can be achieved. There is a need for fundamental research to develop a scalable blockchain platform. Prior to developing a scalable blockchain platform, it is imperative to not only define scalability in the context of blockchain, but also identify metrics to quantify scalability. There have been efforts to improve the scalability in blockchain by modifying parameters such as block size and block intervals. However, these efforts to achieve scaling through reparameterization alone can only realize limited benefits and do not address network performance issues. Network performance is exacerbated due to blockchain's p2p overlay network protocol, degree of decentralization, and number of peers in the network. The throughput of blockchain depends on the throughput of the overlay network that determines the rate at which blocks propagate and the percentage of nodes involved in the exchange of blocks in a given time interval. For example, if the transaction rate reaches 80% of the throughput, it is quite possible that 10–20% of the p2p nodes will not be able to render services and reduce effective network mining power.

There is a need to develop new architectures for blockchain to ensure sufficient scalability without sacrificing decentralization. The architecture should involve protocol design strategies across several layers, namely network, consensus, and storage. There is also a need to identify and measure scalability metrics such as throughput, latency, bootstrap time, storage, cost of confirmed transaction, fairness, and network utilization. The architecture will also need to be designed to address issues such as, "Does exploitation of system parameters to improve scalability sacrifice security properties?" and "What is the degree of resilience of the system during a cyberattack?"

Network Layer—The objective of the network layer in the blockchain architecture is to provide an effective mechanism to propagate transaction messages. The network layer ensures that messages from any participant can be transmitted to all the nodes in the blockchain network. However, the network layer does not operate in full broadcast mode and nodes exchange messages that contain validated transactions. And, in most current implementations of the blockchain network, the network is heavily underutilized and limits throughput. Thus, the network layer in blockchain is a bottleneck in the processing of transactions.

Consensus Layer—The consensus layer is responsible for validating transactions and uses the network layer to deliver messages and record the transactions in the distributed ledger. The consensus protocols include proof of work (PoW), proof of stake (PoS), and byzantine fault tolerance. Traditional blockchain technology relies heavily on the underlying PoW mechanism to achieve consensus in the decentralized system where the miner has to spend its computational power to solve the cryptopuzzle so as to successfully include its block in the blockchain. With such an approach, miners opt for various specialized hardware to achieve their computational ability. The eventual goal of the miners is to win the block-adding race so that they can be rewarded, and a significant amount of energy is required to do so. For a simple example, if we consider the case of Bitcoin's blockchain, the miners compete to get the reward of 25 Bitcoin, which is worth approximately $20,000 and is freshly minted for the winning miner every 10 minutes. Thus, the amount of reward per second is $33.30, and if we assume the rate of industrial electricity is $0.01/KWhr, then we can approximately state that Bitcoin miners use energy of 1100 MW per second. This substantial quantity is spent to reach consensus using the PoW approach and most of it is used in computing the irreversible SHA256 hashing function. Since the value of direct incentives will diminish eventually, the critical question of "how will the PoW miners be motivated to mine?" has to be addressed so as to smoothly run the consensus process. PoS consensus protocol is interestingly attractive; it provides block inclusion decision-making power to those entities that have stakes in the system irrespective of the blockchain's length or history of the public ledger. The principal motivation behind this scheme is to place the power of leader election in the blockchain update process into the hands of the stakeholders. This is done to ensure that the security of the system will be maintained while the members' stakes are at risk. Roughly speaking, this approach is similar to the PoW consensus except the computational part. Hence, a stakeholder's chances to extend the blockchain by including its own block depend proportionately on the amount of stake it has in the system.

There is a need for developing a customized consensus engine that will not require participants to make significant investments in computation and will balance the tradeoff between the number of transactions processed, transaction validation time, incentives, and security rules set by participators. The customized consensus engine will choose the optimal combination of consensus protocols to achieve the aforementioned objectives.

Privacy—Permissioned blockchain platforms, such as Hyperledger Fabric and JP Morgan's Quorum, claim that privacy is a goal; but the way they achieve it is actually quite limited. These systems consist of several validating nodes, each of which sees the entire transaction log in plaintext. That is, while the systems are designed to provide availability/consistency even when some of the nodes fail, they cannot guarantee privacy if one of the nodes suffers a data breach. Some permissioned blockchain platforms offer a feature where you can create a "private channel" comprising just a subset of these nodes; however, among this subset, it is still the case that any data breach would leak the transaction data and then the private channel cannot interact with the other channels. With the existing systems, there is an inherent tradeoff between resilience and expressiveness on the one hand, and privacy on the other.

There are a variety of technical approaches that can provide better operating points. These include threshold cryptography/multi-party computation, zero knowledge proofs, and homomorphic encryption. The theory for these approaches is well established in general, but in concrete terms it is a great open challenge to (a) find efficient algorithms for applications of interest, and (b) integrate with existing systems. So, focusing on building better privacy mechanisms could be a well-motivated and technically interesting challenge to add.

Security—Despite the advantages of using blockchain for distributed systems security, there have been numerous instances of reported security risks associated with this technology [17–19]. In 2016, it was reported that an adversary was able to withdraw $50 million from "The DAO", a decentralized autonomous organization that operates on blockchain-based smart contracts [20]. In June 2017, Bitfinex reported a distributed denial-of-service (DDoS) attack that led to a temporary suspension. Several exchanges of Bitcoin and Ethereum (a blockchain-based distributed computing platform) have also suffered from DDoS attacks and Domain Name System (DNS) attacks frequently, hampering service availability to the users.

The attack surfaces in blockchain can be broadly classified into the following three main categories: (i) Threats associated with the techniques employed for creating/maintaining the distributed ledger (e.g. blockchain forks, stale blocks, orphaned blocks, etc.), (ii) threats to the blockchain system's underlying network infrastructures (e.g. attacks on consensus protocols that cause delays, decreased throughput, inconsistencies, DDoS attack, DNS attacks, Fork After Withholding [FAW] attacks, etc.), and (iii) threats associated with frontend/backend applications integrated with blockchain technology (stealing of private keys, attacks on certificate authorities, attacks on membership services in permissioned blockchain, blockchain ingestion, double spending, wallet theft, etc.).

1.2 Overview of the Book

The book has encompassing themes that drive the individual contributions including the broad theme of blockchain-based secure data management and storage for cloud and IoT; data provenance in cloud storage; secure IoT model, auditing architecture, and application of blockchain in military and healthcare domain; and empirical validation of permissioned blockchain platforms. It will synthesize a mix of earlier works (on topics including data provenance in blockcloud and blockcloud security analysis) as well as newer, cutting-edge research findings that promise to attract strong interest (on topics including invariant-based supply chain protection, information-sharing framework, and trustworthy information federation). The contributions address security and privacy concerns in blockchain in key areas, including the following: preventing digital currency miners from launching attacks against mining pools, empirical analysis of the attack surface of blockchain, countering double spending in blockchains, security analysis of blockchain consensus protocols, and privacy in permissioned blockchain platforms.

1.2.1 Chapter 2: Distributed Consensus Protocols and Algorithms

Fault-tolerant consensus has been extensively studied in the context of distributed computing. By regulating the dissemination of information within the network of distributed processors, a fault-tolerant consensus mechanism guarantees that all processors agree on common data values and perform the same course of action in response to a service request, in spite of faulty processors and unreliable communication links. This consensus guarantee is crucial to normal functioning of the distributed computing system. Similarly, as a realization of a distributed system, blockchain requires a consensus protocol that assures all nodes in the p2p network agree on a single chain of transaction history (or "public ledger") given the adverse effect of malfunctioning nodes and unpredictable network conditions. At the time of writing, there are more than a hundred blockchain primitives in the cryptocurrency market, embodying more than 10 classes of consensus protocols. Aiming at the fundamentals of distributed consensus, this chapter provides an overview of topics ranging from classic fault-tolerant consensus in distributed computing to the current stage of blockchain consensus protocols. Essentially, analysis of consensus performance will be aided by mathematical modeling. In this chapter, we first provide the basics of fault-tolerant consensus in distributed computing in a succinct manner. Next, we conduct formal analysis of the Nakamoto protocol—the pioneering PoW blockchain consensus protocol for Bitcoin. We will also present several emerging non-PoW blockchain consensus protocols and their application scenarios. We will provide a qualitative evaluation and comparison over the aforementioned blockchain consensus protocols.

1.2.2 Chapter 3: Overview of Attack Surfaces in Blockchain

In this chapter, we explore the attack surface of blockchains and the possible ways in which this technology can be compromised. Toward this goal, we attribute attack viability in the attack surface to (i) blockchain cryptographic constructs, (ii) the distributed architecture of the systems using blockchain, and (iii) the blockchain application context. For each of those contributing factors, we outline several attacks, including selfish mining and associated peer behaviors, 51% attack, DNS attacks, DDoS attacks, equivocation, consensus delay (due to selfish behavior or DDoS attacks), blockchain forking, orphaned and stale blocks, block ingestion, wallet thefts, and privacy attacks. We then explore the causal relationship between these attacks and show how one fraudulent activity can lead to the possibility of other attacks. A secondary contribution of this work is outlining effective defense measures taken by blockchain technology or proposed by researchers to mitigate the effects of these attacks and patching the vulnerabilities in blockchains.

1.2.3 Chapter 4: Data Provenance in Cloud Storage with Blockchain

This chapter broadly covers the topic of data provenance in cloud storage and key challenges. It presents ProvChain, a blockchain platform that provides assured data provenance, which achieves the following objectives: (i) real-time cloud data provenance, (ii) tamper-proof environment, (iii) enhanced privacy preservation, and (iv) provenance data validation. A detailed design to achieve the aforementioned objectives within ProvChain is given. An implementation of ProvChain on ownCloud, an open source cloud storage service, is provided. Then, it presents detailed evaluation results to demonstrate the effectiveness of ProvChain to provide assured data provenance with the desired privacy and availability in cloud storage platforms. Finally, it describes and offers some solutions to the challenge of processing graph data in the cloud.

1.2.4 Chapter 5: Blockchain-based Solution to Automotive Security and Privacy

Smart vehicles are increasingly being connected to other vehicles in close proximity and to roadside infrastructures, for example, traffic lights and overhead displays at motorways, and more generally to the internet, thus making the vehicles part of the IoT. This high degree of connectivity introduces new, sophisticated personalized services for smart vehicle owners as well as for vehicle manufacturers, suppliers, and service providers (SPs) such as insurance companies. However, this high degree of connectivity makes smart vehicles highly vulnerable to security threats and raises various privacy concerns.

In this chapter, we present a decentralized privacy-preserving and secure blockchain-based architecture for a smart vehicle ecosystem. Smart vehicles, Original Equipment Manufacturer (OEM) (i.e. car manufacturers), and other SPs jointly form an overlay network where they can communicate with each other. Nodes in the overlay are clustered and only the cluster heads are responsible for managing the blockchain and performing its core functions. These nodes are known as overlay block managers (OBMs). Transactions are broadcast to and verified by the OBMs, thus eliminating the need for a central broker. To protect user privacy, each vehicle is equipped with in-vehicle storage to store privacy-sensitive data, for example, location traces. The vehicle owner defines which data (and the granularity) is traded to third parties for beneficial services and which data should be stored in the in-vehicle storage. Consequently, the owner has greater control over the exchanged data.

All transactions (i.e. communications) in the network are encrypted using asymmetric encryption. Nodes are authenticated using their Private Keys (PKs). Strong communication security and authentication introduced by blockchain mitigates the risk of the vehicle being remotely hacked and thus increases the safety of the passengers. We undertake a qualitative analysis on the security and privacy of the proposed architecture. Multiple possible attacks and the protection methods employed by our framework are discussed to show the resilience of our framework against them. We develop an implementation as a proof of concept to demonstrate the applicability of our approach and to analyze its packet and delay overheads.

1.2.5 Chapter 6: Blockchain-based Dynamic Key Management for IoT-Transportation Security Protection

IoT is the next generation platform that aims to maximize the connection between the cyber platform and the physical world including, but not limited to, vehicles, infrastructures, home sensors, smart medical systems, and wearable electronics. However, security is still the main concern in IoT environments. Even though significant developments in security assurance schemes have taken place over the past few years in the area of communication engineering, application layer security, especially cross-domain and cross-scenario (heterogeneity) security schemes, are still an open topic for research. Moreover, blockchain technology provides a feasible solution for these security challenges. This chapter describes a blockchain-based IoT platform for transportation security, specifically, a blockchain-based solution that suits one of the emerging IoT use cases—Vehicular Communication Systems (VCS), one of the most important IoT components and a subsystem of Intelligent Transportation Systems (ITS). The solution mainly adapts to simplify the distributed key management in heterogeneous VCS domains. A dynamic transaction collection period is proposed to minimize the key transfer time during vehicle handover. Furthermore, potential developments in the privacy prevention area are demonstrated.

1.2.6 Chapter 7: Blockchain-enabled Information Sharing Framework for Cybersecurity

This chapter examines the design, development, and evaluation process established for a blockchain-based information sharing (BIS) framework. The BIS at its core offers a mechanism for confidential information and infrastructure protection from future cyberattacks leveraging on blockchain technology. Blockchain is the concept used in the Bitcoin system, currently explored to provide transparent p2p transactions in multiple domains. In BIS, multiple organizations share security-related information, while preserving their privacy, in a bid to jointly protect their cyberspace. The bigger picture here is to collect high-resolution cyberattack information from multiple organizations with the organizations having no specific knowledge about the usage of other organizations' data or exposure of information about a particular company's cybersecurity attacks. BIS offers a decentralized approach for blockchain with transactions being digitally signed to ensure identification of legitimate organizations. This allows the detection of adversaries posing as legitimate users to learn from the public ledger with hashed pointers. Furthermore, the activities of nonparticipating users of BIS for security attacks and defenses are analyzed using a Stackelberg game.

Also included in the chapter is blockchain-based protocol for cyber threat information sharing, an overview of integrated information-sharing framework (iShare), blockchain protocol that protects confidential information from adversarial threats, and a game-theoretic approach to analyze security attacks on iShare.

1.2.7 Chapter 8: Blockcloud Security Analysis

In this chapter, we focus on security analysis of blockchain-based data provenance in cloud. Blockchain's public and distributed p2p ledger capability benefits cloud computing services, which require functions such as assured data provenance, auditing, management of digital assets, and distributed consensus. Blockchain's underlying consensus mechanism allows the building of a tamper-proof environment where transactions on any digital assets are verified by a set of authentic participants or miners. However, achieving consensus demands computational power from the miners in exchange for a handsome reward. Therefore, greedy miners always try to exploit the system by augmenting their mining power. In this chapter, we first discuss blockchain's capability in providing assured data provenance in cloud and present vulnerabilities in blockchain cloud. We model the block withholding (BWH) attack in a blockchain cloud considering distinct pool reward mechanisms. BWH attack provides a rogue miner ample resources in the blockchain cloud for disrupting honest miners' mining efforts, which was verified through simulations.

1.2.8 Chapter 9: Security and Privacy of Permissioned and Permissionless Blockchain

Most analysis of blockchain protocols we have seen so far, ranging from traditional consensus protocols like Paxos and PBFT to Nakamoto consensus, all rely on the "majority honest" assumption, where we assume a majority of the parties follow the protocol correctly. But why should we be willing to assume that any of the peers will be honest and run the protocol exactly? In this chapter, we discuss two security design considerations and apply them to both permissioned and permissionless models. The first design approach is committee selection, by which a large population of participants are winnowed down into a small, fairly sampled subset, where the attacker does not have much presence in the committee. This design approach applies equally well in both permissionless and permissioned blockchains since it can improve performance versus having the entire population active. The second issue we discuss is privacy. Blockchain applications often need to provide privacy guarantees for users, for example, if they involve sensitive information about financial transactions or about the real-time location of Internet of Things devices. Here, cryptography can be employed. If we have a high degree of trust in the peers, as in a permissioned setting, secret sharing is a natural approach since we assume a majority of the peers will not be breached. On the other hand, in a context with less trust, zero-knowledge proofs allow clients to prevent any of the peers from seeing protected data.

1.2.9 Chapter 10: Shocking Public Blockchains' Memory with Unconfirmed Transactions—New DDoS Attacks and Countermeasures

In 2017, blockchain-based systems have seen a rise in their value. Consequently, they have attracted several forms of denial-of-service attacks, and their attack surface is being widely explored in the fields of security and distributed systems. In this chapter, we present a new form of attack that can be carried out on the memory pools (mempools) of blockchain systems in general. Towards that end, we study such an attack and explore its effects on transaction fee structures of legitimate users. We also propose countermeasures to contain such an attack. Our countermeasures include fee-based and age-based designs, which optimize the mempool size and help in countering the effects of this attack. We further evaluate our designs by simulations and analyze their usefulness in varying attack conditions. Our analyses can be extended to a wide variety of blockchain systems using proof concepts, where fees are provided as an incentive for participation.

1.2.10 Chapter 11: Preventing Digital Currency Miners From Launching Attacks Against Mining Pools by a Reputation-Based Paradigm

The mining process in blockchain is very resource intensive; therefore, miners form coalitions to verify each block of transactions in return for a reward where only the first coalition that accomplishes the PoW will be rewarded. This leads to intense competitions among miners and, consequently, dishonest mining strategies such as BWH attack, selfish mining, eclipse attack, and stubborn mining, to name a few. As a result, it is necessary to regulate the mining process to make miners accountable for any dishonest mining behavior. In this chapter, we propose a new reputation-based framework for PoW computation in blockchain in which miners are not only incentivized to conduct honest mining, but also disincentivized for committing any malicious activities against other mining pools. We first illustrate the architecture of our reputation-based paradigm, explain how the miners are rewarded or penalized in our model, and subsequently, we provide game-theoretical analyses to show how this new framework encourages the miners to avoid dishonest mining strategies. In our setting, a mining game is repeatedly played among a set of pool managers and miners where the reputation of each miner or mining ally is continuously measured. At each round of the game, the pool managers send invitations only to a subset of miners based on a nonuniform probability distribution defined by the miners' reputation values. We show that by using our proposed solution concept, honest mining attains Nash equilibrium in our setting. In other words, it will not be in the best interest of the miners to employ dishonest mining strategies even by gaining a short-term utility. This is due to the consideration of a long-term utility in our model and its impact on the miners' utilities over time.

1.2.11 Chapter 12: Private Blockchain Configurations for Improved IoT Security

Blockchain has the potential to provide secure device authentication, trusted event logs, and interoperability for IoT. There are several blockchain platforms to realize the aforementioned requirements; however, there is no consensus on the optimal blockchain platform and the necessary configuration that is applicable to IoT deployments. In this chapter, we focus on the methodology to configure the blockchain technology to meet the security requirements of IoT.

We describe, implement, and compare two possible private blockchain configuration strategies—blockchain-enabled gateways and blockchain-enabled end devices. Test use cases for both strategies are implemented on a network of Raspberry Pi devices using the popular Ethereum and Hyperledger Fabric blockchain frameworks, respectively. We show that while the more popular blockchain gateway approach is better suited to the current architecture and computational requirements of leading blockchain frameworks, the blockchain-enabled end device approach is technically feasible and highly promising, enabling more trustworthy data collection and complex device management strategies. The chapter focuses on the different roles that IoT devices can play within a blockchain deployment as well as the security guarantees that the blockchain can provide an IoT device in a certain role. We also identify system functionality and cyber security guarantees in scenarios wherein IoT devices are configured as full nodes of the blockchain.

1.2.12 Chapter 13: Blockchain Evaluation Platform

In the final chapter, we provide a systematic methodology to simulate, test, and evaluate blockchain platforms. The methodology described in this chapter will provide empirical means to evaluate the efficacy of the approaches presented in preceding chapters. This chapter strives to provide some insight into how blockchain theoretical models can be simulated and tested on a practical platform. The chapter will describe the development of a blockchain simulator that can be used to conduct performance and security evaluation. We will also provide insights into blockchain implementation within a Hyperledger Fabric, an open-sourced blockchain application and toolset managed by the Linux Foundation. The Hyperledger Fabric example is a fully capable blockchain platform that can be modified to work in a real environment. Both examples can be scaled to test the performance of protocols and theories as needed, which makes them both good examples to use. The software code will be available to the reader via an online repository and can be downloaded and run generally on any system with some open-sourced software requirements.

References

1 J. Kelly and A. Williams, "Forty big banks test blockchain-based bond trading system." [Online]. Reuters, March 3, 2016. Available: https://www.reuters.com/article/banking-blockchain-bonds/forty-big-banks-test-blockchain-based-bond-trading-system-idUSL8N16A30H.

2 I. Kar, "Estonian citizens will soon have the world's most hack-proof health-care records." [Online]. Quartz, March 3, 2016. Available:https://qz.com/628889/this-eastern-european-country-is-moving-its-health-records-to-the-blockchain/.

3 S. Lacey, "The energy blockchain: How bitcoin could be a catalyst for the distributed grid." [Online]. Green Tech Media, February 26, 2016. Available: https://www.greentechmedia.com/articles/read/the-energy-blockchain-could-bitcoin-be-a-catalyst-for-the-distributed-grid#gs.4cTkNvw.

4 D. Oparah, "3 ways that the blockchain will change the real estate market." [Online]. TechCrunch, February 7, 2016. Available: https://techcrunch.com/2016/02/06/3-ways-that-blockchain-will-change-the-real-estate-market/.

5 A. Mizrahi, "A blockchain-based property ownership recording system." [Online]. 2015. Available: https://chromaway.com/papers/A-blockchain-based-property-registry.pdf.

6 N. Tufnell, "Students hack Waze, send in army of traffic bots." [Online]. Wired, March 25, 2014. Available: http://www.wired.co.uk/article/waze-hacked-fake-traffic-jam.

7 K. Toyoda, P. T. Mathiopoulos, I. Sasase, and T. Ohtsuki, "A novel blockchain-based product ownership management system (POMS) for anti-counterfeits in the post supply chain," *IEEE Access*, vol. 5, no. 99, pp. 17465–17477, 2017.

8 J. H. Lee and M. Pilkington, "How the blockchain revolution will reshape the consumer electronics industry [future directions]," *IEEE Consumer Electronics Magazine*, vol. 6, no. 3, pp. 19–23, July 2017.

9 D. Puthal, N. Malik, S. P. Mohanty, E. Kougianos, and C. Yang, "The blockchain as a decentralized security framework," *IEEE Consumer Electronics Magazine*, vol. 7, no. 2, pp. 18–21, 2018.

10 J. Gubbi, R. Buyya, S. Marusic, and M. Palaniswami, "Internet of things (IoT): A vision, architectural elements, and future directions," *Future Generation Computer Systems*, vol. 29, no. 7, pp. 1645–1660, 2013.

11 M. Mellen, "Tip of the Iceberg: FDA's alert to unplug Hospira's drug infusion pumps from clinical networks." [Online]. August 4, 2015. Available: https://researchcenter.paloaltonetworks.com/2015/08/tip-of-the-iceberg-fdas-alert-to-unplug-hospiras-drug-infusion-pumps-from-clinical-networks/.

12 A. Stark, "FDA issues safety communication on availability of firmware update to address cybersecurity vulnerabilities identified in Abbott's (formerly St. Jude Medical's) implantable cardiac pacemakers." [Online]. 2018. Available: https://www.fda.gov/NewsEvents/Newsroom/FDAInBrief/ucm573853.htm.

13 2016 connected patient report, https://www.salesforce.com/assets/pdf/industries/2016-state-of-the-connected-patient-pr.pdf.

14 C. Ryan, "Use of blockchain in healthcare and research workshop." [Online]. The Office of the National Coordinator (ONC) for Health IT, the National Institute for Standards and Technology (NIST), November 2016. Available: https://oncprojectracking.healthit.gov/wiki/display/TechLabI/Use+of+Blockchain+in+Healthcare+and+Research+Workshop.

15 G. Greenspan, "Avoiding the pointless blockchain project." [Online]. November 22, 2015. Available: http://www.multichain.com/blog/2015/11/avoiding-pointless-blockchain-project/.

16 S. Friedman, "Before the blockchain: 4 questions to answer." [Online]. June 25, 2018. Available: https://gcn.com/articles/2018/06/25/blockchain-questions.aspx.

17 X. Li, P. Jiang, T. Chen, X. Luo, and Q. Wen, "A survey on the security of blockchain systems." [Online]. 2018. Available: http://arxiv.org/abs/1802.06993.

18 I.-C. Lin and T.-C. Liao, "A survey of blockchain security issues and challenges." *IJ Network Security*, vol. 19, no. 5, pp. 653–659, 2017.

19 N. Atzei, M. Bartoletti, and T. Cimoli, "A survey of attacks on Ethereum smart contracts (SoK)," in Proceedings of the 6th International Conference on Principles of Security and Trust—volume 10204, Sweden, 2017, pp. 164–186.

20 D. Siegel, "Understanding the DAO attack." [Online]. June 25, 2016. Available: https://www.coindesk.com/understanding-dao-hack-journalists/.

2

Distributed Consensus Protocols and Algorithms

Yang Xiao,[1] Ning Zhang,[2] Jin Li,[3] Wenjing Lou,[1] and Y. Thomas Hou[1]

[1] *Virginia Polytechnic Institute and State University, Blacksburg, VA, USA*
[2] *Washington University in St. Louis, St. Louis, MO, USA*
[3] *Guangzhou University, Guangzhou, China*

2.1 Introduction

Fault-tolerant consensus has been extensively studied in the context of distributed systems. By regulating the dissemination of information within the network of distributed components, a fault-tolerant consensus algorithm guarantees all components agree on common data values and perform the same course of action in response to a service request, in spite of the presence of faulty components and unreliable communication links. This consensus guarantee is crucial to the normal functioning of a distributed system.

Being a realization of a distributed system, a blockchain system relies on a consensus protocol for ensuring all nodes in the network agree on a single chain of transaction history, given the adverse influence of malfunctioning and malicious nodes. At the time of writing, there are over a thousand initiatives in the cryptocurrency plethora, embodying more than 10 classes of consensus protocols. This chapter provides an overview of the basics of classic fault-tolerant consensus in distributed computing and introduces several popular blockchain consensus protocols.

We organize the chapter as follows: Section 2.2 introduces the basics of fault-tolerant consensus in a distributed system and two practical consensus protocols for distributed computing. Section 2.3 presents the Nakamoto consensus protocol, a pioneering proof-of-work (PoW) based consensus protocol first used by Bitcoin. Section 2.4 presents several emerging non-PoW blockchain consensus protocols and their application scenarios. Section 2.5 gives a qualitative evaluation and comparison over the mentioned blockchain consensus protocols. Section 2.6 concludes this chapter and summarizes the design philosophy for blockchain consensus protocols.

Blockchain for Distributed Systems Security, First Edition. Edited by Sachin S. Shetty, Charles A. Kamhoua, and Laurent L. Njilla.

2.2 Fault-tolerant Consensus in a Distributed System

In a distributed system, all components strive to achieve a common goal in spite of being separated geographically. Consensus, in the simplest form, means these components reach agreement on certain data values. In an actual system, the system components and their communication channels are prone to unpredictable faults and adversarial influence. In this section, we discuss the consensus problem of message-passing systems[1] in the presence of two types of component failures—*crash failure* and *Byzantine failure*. We then study two practical consensus algorithms that tolerate these component failures in distributed computing. For convenience, the terms processor, node, and component are used interchangeably in this section.

2.2.1 The System Model

There are three major factors of consensus in a distributed system—network synchrony, component faults, and the consensus protocol.

2.2.1.1 Network Synchrony

Network synchrony is a basic concept in distributed systems. It defines the degree of coordination of all system components. We need to assume a certain network synchrony condition before any protocol development or performance analysis. Specifically, there are three network synchrony conditions:

- *Synchronous*—operations of components are coordinated in rounds. This is often achieved by a centralized clock synchronization service. In each round, all components perform the same type of operations. For example, in round r, all components broadcast messages to others and in round $(r + 1)$, all components process the received messages and broadcast the outputs.
- *Asynchronous*—operations of components are not coordinated at all. This is often the result of no clock synchronization service or the drifting effect of component clocks. Each component is not bound by any coordination rules and performs its own routine in an opportunistic fashion. There is no guarantee on message delivery or an upper bound of message transmission delay between components.
- *Partially synchronous*—operations of components are not coordinated, but there is an upper bound of message transmission delay. In other words, message delivery is guaranteed, though it may not be in a timely manner. This is the network condition assumed for most practical distributed systems.

In most application scenarios, we assume the system is either synchronous or partially synchronous. For example, the voting process of a democratic

1 There is another type of distributed system called shared-memory system. Please refer to [1] for more details. In this chapter, we adhere to the message-passing system because of its resemblance to blockchain.

congress is considered synchronous while the Bitcoin network is considered partially synchronous.[2]

2.2.1.2 Faulty Component

A component is faulty if it suffers a failure that stops it from normal functioning. We consider two types of faulty behaviors that a component may suffer:

- **Crash failure**—the component abruptly stops functioning and does not resume. The other components can detect the crash and adjust their local decisions in time.
- **Byzantine failure**—the component acts arbitrarily with no absolute condition. It can send contradictory messages to the other components or simply remain silent. It may look normal from outside and not incur suspicion from others throughout the history of the network.

Byzantine failure got its name from Lamport, Shostak, and Pease's work on the Byzantine generals problem [2], which we will discuss later along with the Oral Messaging algorithm (OM). A Byzantine failure is often the result of a malfunctioning system process or the manipulation of a malicious actor. When there are multiple Byzantine components in the network, they may collude to deal even more damage to the network. Byzantine failure is considered the worst case of component failure and crash failure is often seen as a benign case of Byzantine failure.

2.2.1.3 Consensus Protocol

A consensus protocol defines a set of rules for message passing and processing for all networked components to reach agreement on a common subject. A message passing rule regulates how a component broadcasts and relays messages while a processing rule defines how a component changes its internal state in response of received messages. As a rule of thumb, we say consensus is reached when all no-faulty components agree on the same subject.

From security's perspective, the strength of a consensus protocol is usually measured by the number of faulty components it can tolerate. Specially, if a consensus protocol can tolerate at least one crash failure, we call it crash-fault tolerant (CFT). Similarly, if a consensus protocol can tolerate at least one Byzantine failure, we call it Byzantine-fault tolerant (BFT). Because of the inclusive relationship between Byzantine failure and crash failure, a BFT consensus is naturally CFT. Moreover, consensus can never be guaranteed in an asynchronous network with even just one crash failure, let alone Byzantine failures. Interested readers may refer to [3] for the impossibility proof.

In the remainder of this chapter, we focus on the Byzantine fault tolerance of consensus protocols in synchronous or partially synchronous networks.

---

2 Many research papers refer to the Bitcoin network as "asynchronous". Since Bitcoin is based upon the Internet, which guarantees message delivery, we follow the above taxonomy and consider the Bitcoin network partially synchronous.

2.2.2 BFT Consensus

Formally, we consider a distributed message-passing system with N components $C_1, C_2, ..., C_N$. Each component C_i has an input x_i and an output y_i that is not assigned until the first round of consensus execution. Components are interconnected by communication links that deliver output messages across the network.

Consensus goal—the BFT consensus for the above system must satisfy the following conditions [4]:

- **Termination**—every nonfaulty component decides an output.
- **Agreement**—all nonfaulty components eventually decide the same output $\hat{y}$.
- **Validity**—if all components begin with the same input $\hat{x}$, then $\hat{y} = \hat{x}$.
- **Integrity**—Every nonfaulty component's decision and eventually $\hat{y}$ must have been proposed by some nonfaulty component.

The integrity condition ensures that the consensus result $\hat{y}$ should not originate from an adversary. In many older textbooks and research papers, it is often not included for the reason that the origin of $\hat{y}$ is not important, as long as $\hat{y}$ is a legal result of the consensus process (validity) and accepted by all nonfaulty components (agreement). Here, we value a correct origin of the consensus result and consider integrity as an essential part of the consensus goal.

For an algorithm to achieve BFT consensus, the super majority (more than two thirds) of the components must be nonfaulty. A more precise statement is given in Theorem 1.

Theorem 1: In a message-passing system with n components, if f components are Byzantine and $n \leq 3f$, then it is impossible for the system to reach the consensus goal.

Theorem 1 can be conveniently proved by contradiction in a scenario where components are partitioned into three groups, with one group consisting of all the Byzantine components. Interested readers may refer to [1,5,6] for different flavors of proofs, all of which are based on the partitioning scheme.

To better illustrate Theorem 1, a three-component system example is shown in Figure 2.1. In this system component, C_1, C_2 are honest while component C_3 is Byzantine. All input/decision values are taken from the bivalent set $\{v_0, v_1\}$.

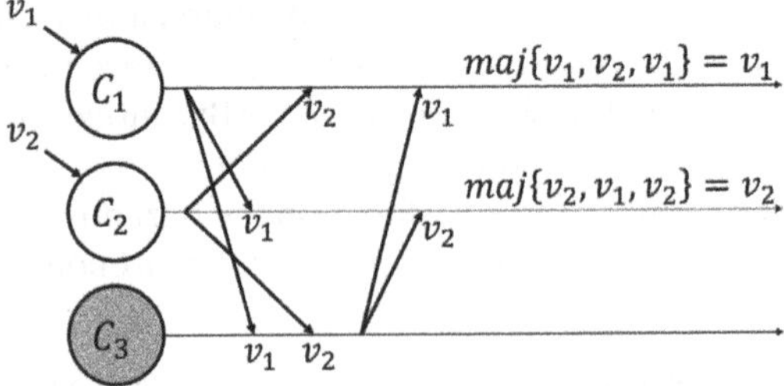

Figure 2.1 Example for Theorem 1—a three-component message-passing system with one component being Byzantine.

Assume the initial input values for C_1 and C_2 are v_1 and v_2, respectively, and the consensus algorithm is as simple as choosing the majority value of all the values received. After C_1, C_2 broadcast their values, C_3 sends v_1 to C_1 and v_2 to C_2. As a result, C_1 decides v_1 while C_2 decides v_2, violating the agreement condition of the consensus goal. Therefore, in order to tolerate one Byzantine component, the network size should be at least four. In a general case, for any distributed system with N components and f being Byzantine, $N \geq 3f + 1$ is required to ensure consensus.

2.2.3 The OM Algorithm

First we describe the Byzantine generals problem. N Byzantine generals, each commanding an equal-sized army, have encircled an enemy city. They are geographically separated and can communicate only through messengers. To break the stalemate, each general votes to attack or retreat by sending messengers to other generals. Each general makes his/her decision locally based on the votes received. To complicate the situation, there are traitors within the generals who will sabotage the consensus by sending contradicting votes to different generals. The ultimate goal is for all loyal generals to agree on the same action, as a halfhearted attack or retreat will result in a debacle.

The Oral Messaging (OM) algorithm was proposed as a solution in the original Byzantine generals problem paper [2]. It assumes that within the N generals, there is a "commander" who starts the algorithm and the other $N - 1$ called "lieutenants" who orally pass around the messages they received. The network is synchronous and the protocol proceeds in rounds. Specially, we assume the commander knows at most f generals will be faulty (including him/herself) and starts the consensus process by executing the *OM(f)* algorithm. Note that DEFAULT is a predetermined value, either "retreat" or "attack".

Algorithm 1: $OM(f), f > 0$

```
Commander sends its value to every lieutenant;
for i = 1 : N-1 do
    Lieutenant i stores the value received from Commander as v_{i,i};
      v_{i,i} =DEFAULT if no value received;
    Lieutenant i performs OM(f − 1) as Commander to send the value v_{i,i}
      to the other N − 2 lieutenants;
end
for i = 1 : N-1 do
    for j = 1 : N-1 and j ≠ i do
        Lieutenant i stores the value received from lieutenant j as v_{i,j};
          v_{i,j} =DEFAULT if no value received;
    end
    Lieutenant i uses majority{v_{i,1}, v_{i,2}, ..., v_{i,N−1}};
end
```

Algorithm 2: $OM(0)$ (The base case for $OM[f]$)

Commander sends its value to every lieutenant;
for $i = 1 : N\text{-}1$ **do**
  Lieutenant i stores the value received from Commander as $v_{i,i}$;
   $v_{i,i}$ =DEFAULT if no value received;
  Lieutenant i uses $v_{i,i}$;
end

Since the OM algorithm is executed in a recursive fashion in which the recursion ends at $OM(0)$, it requires $f + 1$ rounds of executions. Essentially, as long as $N \geq 3f + 1$, the $f + 1$ rounds of recursive executions guarantee that at the end of the algorithm, every general has exactly the same set of votes, from which the *majority* function then produces the same result—consensus is achieved. Due to its recursive fashion, the $OM(f)$ algorithm has $O(N^{f+1})$ message complexity, which is impractical when N is large.

2.2.4 Practical Consensus Protocols in Distributed Computing

Now we have discussed single-value consensus in a synchronous network. In a typically distributed computing system, the clients spontaneously issue computing requests while the distributed servers work as a consortium to provide correct and reliable computing service in response to these requests. The correctness requirement means not only every single request should be processed correctly, but also the sequence of requests from a client (or a group of clients) should be processed in the correct order, which is called the total ordering requirement. The combination of the two requirements makes distributed computing a significantly harder task than the single-value consensus problem we have seen so far. Moreover, the asynchronous nature of real-world networks further complicates the problem. In practice, we assume the real-world distributed computing network is partially synchronous with bounded communication delay between two nonfaulty servers.

Replication—in actual distributed computing systems, replication is the de facto choice for ensuring the availability and the integrity of the service in the face of faulty servers. A replication-based distributed system maintains a number of redundant servers in case the primary server crashes or malfunctions. The redundant servers are also called *backups* or *replicas*. There are two major types of replication schemes—primary-backup and state-machine replication.

- **Primary Backup (PB)**—PB is also known as passive replication. It was first proposed in [7]. In a PB-based system of n replicas, one replica is designated as the primary and the others are backups. The primary interacts with clients and processes clients' operation requests. After the primary finishes one task, it sends to the backups what it has done. If the primary crashes, a replica will be selected to assume the role of the primary. PB only tolerates crash failures; it does not tolerate any number of Byzantine failures.

- **State-Machine Replication (SMR)**—SMR is also known as active replication. It was proposed in [8]. In an SMR-based system, the consensus protocol is instantiated at each server that runs a deterministic state machine that receives inputs, changes states, and produces outputs in an "organized" manner. This enables the distributed network to provide fault-tolerant service by replicating the state machine across server replicas and processing clients' operation requests in a coordinated way. A good SMR protocol should guarantee two basic service requirements—*safety*, i.e. all processors execute the same sequence of requests, and *liveness*, i.e. all valid requests are executed.

Next we introduce two well-known SMR-based consensus protocols for distributed computing: **Viewstamped Replication** and **Practical Byzantine Fault Tolerance.**

2.2.4.1 Viewstamped Replication (VSR)

VSR is an early protocol developed for distributed replication systems. Here, we present an updated version of VSR proposed by Liskov and Cowling in 2012 [9]. Interested readers may refer to [10] for Oki and Liskov's original design. In a VSR system with N replicas, there is one *primary* and $N - 1$ backups. Each replica operates a local state machine with the state variables listed in Table 2.1. The "viewstamp" refers to the $\langle v, n \rangle$ pair, which essentially enables the replication network to process clients' operation requests in the correct order.

Table 2.1 State variables at replica *i* in VSR.

Variable	Description
i	Self index
rep-list	List of all replicas in the network
status	Operation status: either NORMAL, VIEW-CHANGE, or RECOVERING
v	Current view number
m	The most recent request message from a client
n	Sequence number of m
e	$=$ EXECUTE(m), the execution result of m
c	Sequence number of the most recently committed client request
log	Record of operation requests received so far
client-table	Record of the most recent operation for all clients

Table 2.2 Messages in VSR.

Message	From	To	Format
Request	Cient	Primary	$\langle$REQUEST, $m\rangle$
Prepare	Primary	All backups	$\langle$PREPARE, $m, v, n, c\rangle$
PrepareOK	Replica i	Primary	$\langle$PREPAREOK, $v, i\rangle$
Reply	Primary	Client	$\langle$REPLY, $v, e\rangle$
Commit	Primary	All backups	$\langle$COMMIT, $v, c\rangle$
StartViewChange	Replica i	All replicas	$\langle$STARTVIEWCHANGE, $v + 1, i\rangle$
DoTheViewChange	Replica i	New primary	$\langle$DOTHEVIEWCHANGE, $v + 1, i\rangle$
StartView	Primary	All replicas	$\langle$STARTVIEW, $v + 1, log\rangle$
Recovery	Replica i	All replicas	$\langle$RECOVERY, $i\rangle$
RecoveryResponse	Replica i	The recoverer	$\langle$RECOVERYRESPONSE, $v, n, c, i\rangle$

VSR consists of three subprotocols; each is designed specially for one of the three status cases. The messages involved are listed in Table 2.2. We will leave out the message details and focus on the high-level work flow of these protocols.

(1) Normal operation protocol—the normal operation runs from session to session when all functioning replicas hold the same view and the primary is in a good condition. A session includes the client sending a request and the replicas processing this request. A diagram of the normal operation protocol for a three-replica system is shown in Figure 2.2. At the beginning of a session, the client sends to the primary a *Request* message indicating a new operation request.

(a) **Prepare**—upon receiving a request message, the primary updates its n, *log*, and *client-table* and then passes this request to all backups using *Prepare* messages, which also include its n and c that were updated in the previous session. Each backup executes the primary-committed operations if there are any and updates its state accordingly.
(b) **PrepareOK**—each backup sends a *PrepareOK* message to the primary showing its state is up to date. After receiving f *PrepareOK* messages, the

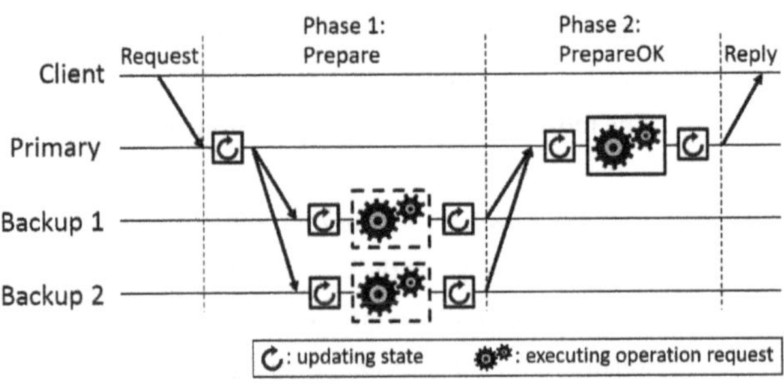

Figure 2.2 The normal operation protocol of VSR for a three-replica system.

primary executes the requested operation and then updates c, *log*, and *client-table.*

The primary then sends a *Reply* message to the client. Specifically, if the primary hasn't received a client request for a long time, it sends a *Commit* message to the backups indicating the updated c, as an alternative to the *Prepare* message.

(2) View-change protocol—a view change is needed in the event of primary failure, which can be detected by a backup replica if no *Prepare* or *Commit* message has been received for a long time. After detecting the need for a view change, a replica updates its status to VIEW-CHANGE and advances the view number to $v + 1$. It then sends a *StartViewChange* message including the new view number $v + 1$ to other replicas. When a replica receives at least f *StartViewChange* messages with the new view number $v + 1$, it sends a *DoTheViewChange* message to the backup that will become the primary. When the new primary receives at least $f + 1$ *DoTheViewChange* messages, it updates its state accordingly, sends to other replicas a *StartView* message with the updated *log* and the new view number $v + 1$, and starts processing operation requests from clients. In the meantime, backup replicas receive the *StartView* message and update their state according to the *log* in the message, and finally change the status to *normal.*

(3) Recovering protocol—when a replica recovers from a crash, it has to go through the recovering protocol before participating in normal operation and view change. It first sends a *Recovery* message to all other replicas. Each replica responds with a *RecoveryResponse* message indicating the current v. The primary needs to respond with additional state information including *log*, n, and c. The recovering replica waits until it has received at lease $f + 1$ *RecoveryResponse* messages, and then updates its state accordingly.

Fault tolerance—note that VSR can tolerate f crash failures if the total number of replicas (including the primary) $N \geq 2f + 1$. However, it has zero tolerance of Byzantine failures. For example, if the primary is Byzantine faulty due to adversarial manipulation, it can simply deny all client operation requests while pretending to work normally with the backups. If a backup is Byzantine on the other hand, it may maliciously initiate a view-change session to oust the current primary.

Complexity analysis—we analyze the message complexity of the normal operation. The communication overhead is primarily contributed by two phases—the Prepare phase, in which the primary broadcasts a *Prepare* message to all replicas; and the PrepareOK phase, in which all replicas send a *PrepareOK* message to the primary. Therefore, the message complexity for VSR's normal operation is $O(N)$.

2.2.4.2 Practical Byzantine Fault Tolerance (PBFT)

In the practical scenario where the distributed computing system may be compromised by malicious actors, both the primary and the backups are subject to

Table 2.3 State variables at replica *i* in PBFT.

Variable	Description
i	Self index (0 for primary)
rep-list	List of all replicas in the network
σ_i	Replica *i*'s key for signing messages
status	Operation status—NORMAL or VIEW-CHANGE
v	Current view number
m	The most recent request message from a client
n	Sequence number of m
d	= DIGEST(m), the digest of m
e	= EXECUTE(m), the execution result of m
s	The latest checkpoint
h	Low-water mark, i.e. the sequence number of s
H	High-water mark; $\langle h, H\rangle$ form a sliding window of length K.
$\mathcal{C}$	Set of all valid *Checkpoint* messages proving the correctness of s
$\mathcal{P}_t$	Set of a valid *Pre-prepare* message and all matching *Prepare* messages for a request with the sequence number t
$\mathcal{P}$	Set of the $\mathcal{P}_t$ for every request t that is higher than n
$\mathcal{V}$	Set of all valid *View-Change* and *View-Change* messages
$\mathcal{O}$	Set of specially chosen *Pre-Prepare* messages
log	Record of operation requests received so far

adversary manipulation, which falls into the realm of Byzantine failures. Proposed by Castro and Liskov in 1999 [11], PBFT advances VSR for tolerating Byzantine failures.

PBFT consists of three subprotocols—normal operation, checkpoint, and view-change. The state variables at a replica are listed in Table 2.3 and the messages involved are listed in Table 2.4. As an additional security measure, each message is signed by the sender and verified by the receiver. In the following part, we assume there are at most f faulty replicas and the network size $N = 3f + 1$. Later, we will show that $N \geq 3f + 1$ guarantees the protocol's Byzantine fault tolerance.

(1) Normal operation protocol—similar to VSR, PBFT runs its normal operation from session to session. A diagram of normal operation for a four-replica system is shown in Figure 2.3. A session starts with a client operation request and goes through three sequential phases of replica interaction, namely Pre-Prepare, Prepare, and Commit, before replying to the client.

Table 2.4 Messages in PBFT.

Message	From	To	Format (signed)
Request	Client	Primary	$\langle \text{REQUEST}, m\rangle_{\sigma_c}$
Pre-Prepare	Primary	All backups	$\langle \text{PRE-PREPARE}, v, n, d\rangle_{\sigma_0}$
Prepare	Replica i	All replicas	$\langle \text{PREPARE}, v, n, d, i\rangle_{\sigma_i}$
Commit	Replica i	All replicas	$\langle \text{COMMIT}, v, n, d, i\rangle_{\sigma_i}$
Reply	Replica i	Client	$\langle \text{REPLY}, e, i\rangle_{\sigma_i}$
View-Change	Replica i	All replicas	$\langle \text{VIEW-CHANGE}, v+1, n, C, \mathcal{P}, i\rangle_{\sigma_i}$
New-View	Primary	All replicas	$\langle \text{NEW-VIEW}, v+1, \mathcal{V}, \mathcal{O}\rangle_{\sigma_0}$
Checkpoint	Replica i	All replicas	$\langle \text{CHECKPOINT}, n, d, i\rangle_{\sigma_i}$

(a) **Pre-Prepare**—when the primary receives an operation request message m, it assigns a sequence number n to the request and sends a *Pre-Prepare* message along with the message m to all backups. After receiving a *Pre-Prepare* message, a backup checks the associated signatures and the validity of v, n, and d. If everything is valid and n is within the water marked range $\langle h, H\rangle$, the backup accepts this message, updates its state accordingly, and proceeds to the Prepare phase.

(b) **Prepare**—each backup sends a *Prepare* message to all other replicas. A replica that has received at least $2f + 1$ *Prepare* messages with the same v, n, and d values updates its state accordingly and proceeds to the Commit phase.

(c) **Commit**—each replica sends a *Commit* message to all other replicas. When a replica receives at least $2f + 1$ *Commit* messages with the same v, n, and d values, it first finishes executing the old requests with sequence numbers lower than n, then executes the current request m to produce the result e, and finally updates its state accordingly.

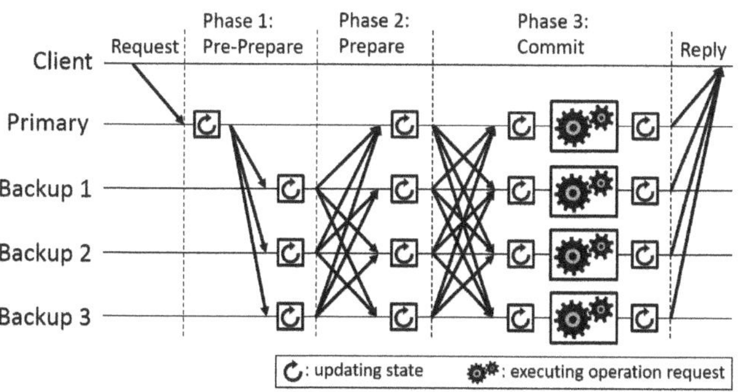

Figure 2.3 The normal operation protocol of PBFT for a four-replica system.

When a replica finishes the Commit phase, it sends the execution result e in a *Reply* message to the client. The client accepts an execution result only after it receives at least $2f + 1$ *Reply* messages containing the same result e.

(2) Checkpoint protocol—the checkpoint protocol is used by the replicas to safely discard old items in *log* and agree on a stable checkpoint that provides essential service state info for the view-change process. Each replica periodically marks an executed client request as a checkpoint in *log* and records its sequence number as h, which is called the low-water mark. It multicasts the checkpoint to other replicas in the form of a *Checkpoint* message. When a replica collects at least $2f + 1$ *Checkpoint* messages with the same n and d, it marks this checkpoint *stable* by assigning n to the variable h, and saves these *Checkpoint* messages as the proof from the stable checkpoint. After that, the replica can safely discard from its *log* all *Pre-Prepare, Prepare,* and *Commit* messages with sequence numbers prior to h. In addition to h, each replica also updates the high-water mark H so that the pair $\langle h, H \rangle$ form sliding window of length K. Note K is user-defined.

(3) View-change protocol—since a view is bound to a known primary, when the primary is suspected faulty, the backups carry out the view-change protocol to choose a new primary. When a backup, received a request but has not executed it for a certain timeout (for example, it stays in Phase2 of normal operation for too long), it stops receiving further messages related to the current view v and updates the status to VIEW-CHANGE before sending a *View-Change* message for view $v + 1$ to all replicas. When the new primary receives at least $2f$ *View-Change* messages for view $v + 1$, it multicasts a *New-View* message to all backups, updates its *log* and $\langle h, H \rangle$ pair, and proceeds into normal operation. A replica validates the received *New-View* message, updates its state, and proceeds to normal operation as well.

Fault tolerance—in the normal operation, the separation of the pre-prepare phase and prepare phase is essential to the correct ordering of request execution and faulty primary detection. When a primary sends a *Pre-Prepare* message with an out-of-order request or stays silent for a long time, the backups will consider the primary faulty and initiate the view-change protocol for a new primary, as long as the majority of backups are nonfaulty. Now, we discuss the condition for PBFT to tolerate f Byzantine replicas. In the normal operation, a replica needs to receive $2f + 1$ *Prepare* messages with the same state to proceed to the Commit phase; it then needs to receive $2f + 1$ *Commit* messages with the same state to proceed to request execution. This is equivalent to the scenario we discussed in the OM algorithm for the Byzantine generals problem—in a fully connected network, consensus can be reached if more than two thirds of components are nonfaulty. The same consensus routine is applied in the checkpoint protocol and view-change protocol as well to guarantee the safety of the new primary election. As we have assumed $N = 3f + 1$ in the beginning, messages from $2f + 1$ nonfaulty replicas are just enough to tolerate f Byzantine replicas. In a general case where f is unknown (but $N \geq 3f + 1$ is assumed), this number

Table 2.5 A comparison between VSR and PBFT for partially asynchronous distributed computing systems.

	VSR	PBFT
Year proposed	1988	1999
CFT condition	$N \geq 2f + 1$	$N \geq 2f + 1$
BFT condition	Not supported	$N \geq 3f + 1$
Message complexity	$O(N)$	$O(N^2)$

should be updated to $\lfloor \frac{2N}{3} \rfloor + 1$ from $2f + 1$ in the protocol to tolerate at least f Byzantine failures.

Complexity analysis—we analyze the message complexity of the normal operation. The communication overhead is primarily contributed by three phases; in the Pre-Prepare phase, the primary broadcasts a message to all backups $[O(N)]$; in the Prepare phase, every backup broadcasts a message to all other replicas $[O(N^2)]$; in the Commit phase, every replica broadcasts a message to all other replicas $[O(N^2)]$. Therefore, the overall message complexity of PBFT's normal operation is $O(N^2)$. This is acceptable for a network that is fully or near-fully connected unless N is huge.

2.2.4.3 Comparison between VSR and PBFT

VSR and PBFT are compared in Table 2.5. To summarize, PBFT achieves Byzantine fault tolerance with a more complex protocol scheme and higher communication overhead. To date, PBFT has gained considerable interest in the blockchain community for its application in blockchains with small network size and permissioned access. We will introduce it in Section 2.3.

2.3 The Nakamoto Consensus

Since its inception in 2008, Bitcoin has become the leading figure in the cryptocurrency plethora. As of the first quarter of 2018, the Bitcoin network has about 10,000 mining nodes and market capitalization of more than 100 billion dollars. The popularity of Bitcoin and other cryptocurrencies has brought huge academic and industrial interest to blockchain, the enabling technology behind the cryptocurrencies and many emerging distributed ledger systems.

Out of various aspects of Bitcoin, the celebrated Nakamoto consensus [12] is the key innovation to its security and performance. Similar to distributed computing systems, the consensus target for blockchain is the network's entire transaction history—not only the transactions' content, but also their chronological order. In a practical blockchain system such as Bitcoin and Ethereum, the consensus protocol also needs to consider various physical factors such as network connectivity, network size, and adversarial influence. In this section, we introduce the Nakamoto consensus protocol from a distributed system point of view.

2.3.1 The Consensus Problem

Consensus goal—the goal of the Nakamoto consensus is for all nodes to form a unified view on the network's transaction history. Similar to the four conditions for BFT consensus in the previous section, the following are the adapted conditions for the Nakamoto consensus:

- **Finality (Probabilistic)**—for every block that has been attached to the blockchain, its drop-off probability asymptotically decreases to zero.
- **Agreement**—every block is either accepted or dropped off by all honest nodes. If accepted, it should have the same block number in all blockchain replicas. In other words, all honest nodes agree on the same blockchain.
- **Validity**—if all nodes receive the same valid block, then this block should be accepted into the blockchain. The genesis block is a good example.
- **Hash-chain integrity**—the blockchain contains all blocks up to the current block number. For block B with block number t and block B' with block number $t + 1$, the hash value of the previous block in B' is the hash of B.

2.3.2 Network Model

Like most public blockchain networks, the Bitcoin network is a peer-to-peer overlay network based upon the Internet. Every node runs an instance of the Nakamoto protocol and maintains a replica of the blockchain. We model the network as an a partially synchronous message-passing system with bounded transmission delay between two honest nodes, the same network model we assumed for the distributed computing systems in Section 2.1. In addition to network synchrony, the Bitcoin network also features permissionless access and gossip-fashion information propagation.

Permissionless access—the Bitcoin system is the first permissionless blockchain system and no authentication is required for a new player to instantiate a node and participate in the network. Specifically, to join the network, a fresh node needs to be set up in three steps:

1. Fetch a list of initial peers from several known DNS servers.
2. Search for new peers by asking its current peers and listening for spontaneous advertisements from other peers. Make sure the number of peers does not go below a minimum value (currently 8 for Bitcoin).
3. Retrieve a blockchain replica from peers and start normal operation.

To leave the network, a node simply disconnects. It will gradually be purged from the peer lists of its peers. Since the transactions containing the node's public addresses have been written in the blockchain, the node can reclaim the

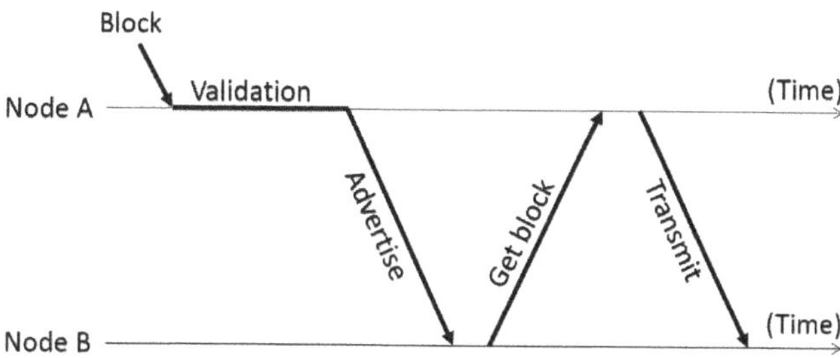

Figure 2.4 One-hop block propagation between two nodes.

same public address and hence its unspent transaction outputs when it rejoins the network using the same private key.

Information propagation—the information propagation and message passing dynamics were first analyzed in [13]. There are two types of messages contributing to the consensus process—*transaction* and *block*. Figure 2.4 shows the diagram of one-hop propagation of a block. The propagation of transactions is in the same manner. The *validation* of a block consists of the validation of all transactions in the block and the verification of the hash value of the block header. The *advertise* message contains the hash of the validated block (or a list of hashes of validated blocks). If node B sees a block that is new to its blockchain replica, it sends to node A a *get block* message containing the hash of the desired block. Finally, node A *transmits* the desired block to node B, which then repeats this process with its own peers, except node A.

Note that once node B has an economic incentive to pass the block around. When other nodes know this block, they are less likely to create conflicting blocks (which will cause a fork) and more likely to accept the later block created by B, which eventually helps B make better use of its computation power and harvest more block benefits.

2.3.3 The Consensus Protocol

The Nakamoto consensus protocol is executed in a distributed fashion. Each node runs the same protocol and manages its own blockchain replica independently. The security of the consensus depends on the majority of nodes being honest, i.e. running the correct version of the Nakamoto protocol. The protocol can be summarized into the following four rules for a single node:

1. **Message passing rule**—all newly received or locally generated blocks and transactions should be broadcast to peers in a timely manner.
2. **Validation rule**—blocks and transactions need to be validated before being broadcast to peers or appended to the blockchain. Invalid blocks and transaction are discarded.
3. **Longest-chain rule**—the longest chain is always the desired chain. Mining should be aimed at extending the longest chain by appending new blocks to

it. If the node receives a valid block B^* with the same height as the block B that it is still working on, it discards B and appends B^* to the blockchain and starts working on the new chain.

4. **Proof of Work (PoW)**—the generation of a block includes inserting a nonce into the block header. The hash of the header should be less than a particular value, which is also called the PoW difficulty. Higher PoW difficulty yields more hashing operations expected for finding such a nonce. For security reasons, the PoW difficulty is automatically adjusted so that the average block generation interval of the network remains a constant value as the gross hashing power fluctuates (currently 10 minutes for Bitcoin).

As a result, the majority decision of the network is represented by the longest chain, which embodies the greatest amount of PoW computation effort.

Probabilistic finality—according to the longest-chain rule, blocks that end up in a chain branch that is not the suffix of the longest chain shall be discarded or "orphaned". This means any block in the blockchain (except the genesis block) can be revoked, since it is possible for a powerful attacker to start from an early block and redo the proof of works all the way up to the current blockchain height so that the network will acknowledge this new chain as the longest. On the bright side, if the attacker has less than 50% of the network's gross hashing power, it will produce blocks slower than the rest of the network. Let p denote the hashing power percentage controlled by the attacker and $p < 50\%$. Then the probability that the attack will eventually catch up from behind m blocks is:

$$P\{\text{Catch-up}\} = \left(\frac{p}{1-p}\right)^m. \tag{2.1}$$

Since $p < 50\%$, this probability drops exponentially as m increases. In other words, revoking such block from the blockchain is computationally impossible if more than half of the hashing power is owned by honest nodes and m is large. Currently in Bitcoin, $m = 6$ is used as the transaction confirmation time. All blocks that have at least six descendants are considered probabilistically finalized.

2.4 Emerging Blockchain Consensus Algorithms

Due to the inherently tight trade-off between security and scalability in PoW-based blockchains, researchers and developers have been exploring new blockchain schemes to support higher transaction volume and larger network size with lower energy consumption. This section introduces several promising non-PoW consensus algorithms—proof of stake (PoS), PBFT-based consensus protocols, Ripple consensus protocol, proof of elapsed time (PoET). These algorithms are proposed either as alternatives to PoW for public blockchains (PoS, PoET) or for domain-specific applications (PBFT-based, Ripple). We will go through their consensus protocols and briefly analyze their fault-tolerance limits and security concerns.

2.4.1 Proof of Stake

Proof of Stake (PoS) was proposed by the Bitcoin community as an alternative to PoW. Compared to PoW, in which miners race for the next block with brute computing force, PoS resembles a new philosophy of blockchain design, according to which the race should be carried out in a "civilized" manner that saves energy and maintains security. PoS maintains a set of validators who participate in the block generation process by depositing an amount of currency (stake) in the competition, which is designed in such a way that a bigger stakeholder has a higher chance to win the competition.

There two major types of PoS are *Chain-based* PoS and *BFT-style* PoS. Chain-based PoS is the original design of PoS and got its name from retaining the longest-chain rule of the Nakamoto consensus. It was first implemented in the cryptocurrency Ppcoin, later known as Peercoin [14]. In comparison, BFT-style PoS leverages the established results of BFT consensus for finalizing new blocks. In this section, we introduce the basics of chain-based PoS. BFT-style PoS will be introduced along with other BFT consensus protocols in Section 2.4.2.

Chain-based PoS—in chain-based PoS, the blockchain maintains a set of validators who participate in the competition for the right to generate the next block. For every block generation cycle, chain-based PoS runs in two steps:

- **Step 1**—every validator invests a stake in the competition for block generation. The deposited stakes are kept frozen until the end of this block generation cycle.
- **Step 2**—after a validator deposits its stake, it starts to generate new blocks similar to Nakamoto's proof of work, but with a limited difficulty which is further discounted by its stake value. The first block produced is immediately appended to the longest chain and the corresponding validator claims the block reward.

Fault tolerance—analogous to PoW in the Nakamoto consensus, as long as all honest validators follow the protocol and own more than half of the total stake value, the probability of a block being revoked from the blockchain drops exponentially as the chain grows. From an economical perspective, attackers should be more reluctant to perform 51% attack in a PoS system than in a PoW system. In most PoS blockchain systems any fraudulent behavior of a validator is punishable by forfeiting its stake while in a PoW system only electricity is wasted. Therefore for most attackers, losing all stakes is more economically devastating than wasting computing power.

Other security concerns—nonetheless, there are many other practical issues concerning the stability and security of chain-based PoS. Here we identify two of them.

1. **Time value of the stake** PoS strongly resembles of capitalism, where a dominant stakeholder can invest-profit-reinvest its capital and profit till it attains a monopoly status. To alleviate the monopoly problem and encourage small stakeholders to participate in the game, a practical method is to let the unused stakes (of which the validators have not been a generator since the initial deposit) appreciate in value with time. Once a validator is chosen as the generator, its stake value returns to the default value at time zero. In the meantime, the stakes of unchosen validators continue appreciating. In Peercoin for example, a validator's stake value is measured by *coin age*, which is the product of the deposited currency amount and the time elapsed since the initial stake deposit. The winning probabilities for small stakeholders grow in time as long as their stakes are kept unused. On the other hand, to prevent a stake from accumulating too much time value, which can be exploited by a malicious validator to lock in a future block, the time value of a stake is limited by an upper bounded, for example 100 block generation cycles.
2. **Double-bet problem**—this is also known as the *nothing-at-stake* problem. Since the longest-chain rule is still observed, when there are multiple parallel chain branches (forks), a PoS validator has the incentive to generate blocks on top of every branch at once without additional cost. In PoW, however, a miner has to do that by divesting its precious computing power to each additional branch. Therefore, the chain-based PoS system needs to incorporate a penalty scheme against those who place double bets. Possible choices include forfeiting the frozen stake and nullifying the block benefit for the correct bet. However, these penalty schemes will be ineffective if a group of validators with more than 50% of the network's total stake value collude to maintain parallel chains.

2.4.2 BFT-based Consensus

BFT-based consensus protocols typically require high network connectivity and all nodes to reveal their true identities to others—a good fit for permissioned blockchains where the network size is small and the consortium of participants are known a priori. Similar to that of the Nakamoto consensus, the goal of BFT-based consensus is to ensure all participants agree on a common history of blocks, which requires the correctness of block content and block order. However, there is a major difference between them: the *finality* condition for BFT-based consensus is deterministic. In other words, blocks will never be tampered with once written into the blockchain.

2.4.2.1 PBFT for Blockchain

As we discussed in the previous section, PBFT is a classic consensus protocol for distributed computing based on state machine replication. To be used in a blockchain scenario, PBFT needs to adapt in the following ways:

1. **Parallelism**—in PBFT, replicas are separated into a primary and backups for every view. However, the decentralized nature of blockchain requires that all nodes should be able to process client transactions as a primary and relay other's transactions. More specifically, when any node is ready to broadcast its new block, it initiates a new instance of PBFT by broadcasting a *Pre-Prepare* message containing this block. To deal with *Pre-Prepare* messages from different sources, the Prepare phase and Commit phase need to be modified in the way that the received blocks should be processed, in chronological order. In other words, there can be multiple parallel protocol instances running and interacting in the Prepare and Commit phase.
2. **Dynamic view change**—as there is only one primary in the original PBFT for each view, the view-change protocol can be executed in a rather orderly manner. In blockchain, since every node can act as the primary, the view-change protocol should be able to update multiple primaries in a single execution.

Theoretically, PBFT is able to tolerate f Byzantine nodes if the network size $N \geq 3f + 1$. In practical scenarios, there can be many implementation-related issues preventing PBFT from realizing its full potential, with network connectivity being the major bottleneck. The operational messages in PBFT are time sensitive and a lowly connected network may not be able to execute PBFT in the correct manner. To make PBFT work most reliably, a fully connected network is required.

There are a handful of blockchain initiatives using an adapted version of PBFT for consensus. Examples include Hyperledger Fabric[3] [15] and Stellar [16]. Interested readers may refer to their specific implementations of PBFT.

BFT-style PoS—BFT-style PoS has been used in Tendermint [17], EOS [18], and Ethereum's Casper initiative[4] [19]. Instead of following Nakomoto's contention-based blockchain generation process, BFT-style PoS embraces a more radical design in which the set of validators periodically finalize blocks in the main chain through BFT consensus. Here, we use Ethereum Casper as an example. Similar to PBFT, Casper finalizes blocks from checkpoint to checkpoint. Each validator keeps a replica of the blockchain as well as a checkpoint tree. In every checkpoint cycle, Casper runs in following steps:

- **Step 1**—every validator deposits an amount of currency (stake). The deposited stakes are kept frozen until the end of this checkpoint cycle.
- **Step 2**—every validator grows new blocks from a justified checkpoint using a block proposal mechanism and then broadcasts them in a timely manner. No consensus is needed between validators at this time.

3 Although PBFT is used currently, Hyperledger Fabric is designed to support an arbitrary consensus module in a plug-in fashion.

4 The Ethereum Foundation plans to partially convert the Ethereum main net from PoW to Casper PoS by 2019.

- **Step 3**—after a checkpoint interval is reached (100 blocks in Casper), the validators begin to form a consensus on a new checkpoint. Every validator casts a vote for a checkpoint block and broadcasts its vote to the network. The vote message contains five fields—hash of the source checkpoint *s*, hash of the voted target checkpoint *t*, height of *s*, height of *t*, and the validator's signature.
- **Step 4**—when a validator receive all the votes, it reweighs the votes by the sender's stake value and then computes the stake-weighted votes for each proposed checkpoint block. If a checkpoint *t* has a 2/3 approval rate (super majority), then the validator marks *t justified* the source checkpoint *s finalized*. All blocks before *s* are also finalized.

A fundamental difference between chain-based PoS and BFT-style PoS is that the latter offers deterministic finality. In other words, BFT-style PoS guarantees a finalized block will never be revoked in the future, while chain-based PoS and PoW don't rule out this possibility. Importantly, the deterministic finality also enables the punishment for double-betting validators (i.e. solving a nothing-at-stake problem). Because every finalized block comes with the proposer's public address, a validator is accountable for all the finalized blocks it had proposed. Once it is found double betting, the consensus protocol can legally forfeit the frozen stake of the double-betting validator and revoke the conflicting blocks.

Fault tolerance—since a proposed checkpoint needs a 2/3 approval rate to be justified, this algorithm can tolerate up to 1/3 faulty validators ideally. Nonetheless, due to the immaturity of PoS, specially Casper PoS, there are many security and performance concerns that haven't been addressed. For example, what is the optimal checkpoint interval for the trade-off between security and communication efficiency, how to design a reliable and efficient block proposal mechanism without consensus until the next checkpoint, etc. The authors of this book will keep following the progress of Casper and other BFT-style PoS blockchains.

2.4.3 Proof of Elapsed Time (PoET)

The concept of PoET was proposed by Intel in 2016 as an alternative to PoW. It is currently used in Hyperledger's Sawtooth project [20]. Compared to competing with computing power in PoW or currency ownership in PoS, PoET implemented a contention scheme based on a random back-off mechanism, which has widely been used in medium access control protocols for local area networks. For a single block generation cycle, PoET is as simple as the following two steps:

- **Step 1**—each validator waits a random length of time (back-off).
- **Step 2**—the first validator finishing the back-off becomes the generator.

Trusted random back-off—to ensure the back-off time of each validator is truly random and fully elapsed, the back-off mechanism in each validator should be verified and trusted by all others. In practice, this can be achieved with a specially designed microprocessor that can execute sensitive programs in a trusted execution environment (TEE) or simply an "enclave". As as 2018, Intel and ARM are the market leaders for such microprocessors. Take Intel for example; some of its six-plus generation Core-series microprocessors are able to run Intel's Software Guard Extensions (SGX), which enables certain security services such as isolation and attestation [21]. In a PoET-based blockchain, when a validator joins the network, it acquires the trusted back-off program from peers or a trusted server and runs it in an SGX-enabled enclave. If required by the trusted server, the validator can send its enclave measurement in an attestation report to the network indicating the authentic back-off program is loaded in its enclave. After successfully finishing a back-off, the validator proceeds to generate the new block; meanwhile, the trusted back-off program in the enclave generates a certificate of completion along with the enclave measurement, which will be broadcast along with the new block.

Fault tolerance—theoretically, the PoET scheme can tolerate any number of faulty validators, as long as the back-off program running in a validator's enclave can be remotely attested by others, even if the hosting validator is not trustworthy. However, since each enclave runs the same back-off program independently, a rich validator can invest in multiple enclave instances to shorten its expected back-off time. This resembles PoW's economic model, with the only difference that miners invest in TEE hardwares instead of mining devices. Therefore, PoET needs to make sure more than 50% of enclaves are in the hands of honest validators.

Hardware vendor dependency—another major drawback of PoET is its dependence on TEE platform providers, namely Intel and ARM, for providing TEE-enabled hardware and remote attestation services. Take Intel SGX for example; the security of the PoET system is bounded by the security of Intel's microprocessors and the reliability of Intel's attestation server. This explicit attack surface to some extent contradicts the blockchain's robustness-through-decentralization ideal.

2.4.4 Ripple

Operated by the Ripple company, Ripple is a real-time gross settlement network (RTGS) providing currency exchange and remittance services. Unlike public blockchain systems where anyone can participate in the validation process, Ripple regulates a set of known validators that mainly consist of companies and institutions. They run the Ripple server program and accept transaction requests from clients. A Ripple client only needs to submit transactions to their designated validator and the validator network will fulfill this transaction through consensus. Essentially, validators run the Ripple consensus protocol [22] in a distributed manner and form consensus on a common ledger of transactions.

Ripple consensus protocol—we will use "node" and "validator" interchangeably subsequently. In the validator network, each node p maintains a Unique Node List (UNL) of nodes, which is the only subnetwork p needs to trust partially (for not colluding). The Ripple consensus protocol is applied by each node for every consensus cycle. For each cycle, the protocol proceeds in four steps:

- **Step 1**—each node prepares a *candidate set* containing all the valid transactions it has seen, which may include new transactions submitted by clients and old transactions held over from the previous consensus cycle.
- **Step 2**—each node combines its candidate set with the candidate sets of its UNL peers, votes "yes/no" on the validity of each transaction in the combined set, and sends votes to its UNL nodes.
- **Step 3**—each node, upon receiving votes from its UNL nodes, discards from its candidate set the transactions with a "yes" rate below a minimum threshold. The discarded transactions may be reused in the next consensus cycle.
- **Step 4**—repeat steps 2 and 3 for several rounds. In the final round, the threshold is increased to 80%. Each node appends the remaining transactions to its ledger and ends the consensus cycle.

Fault tolerance—a transaction is finalized if it is approved by at least 80% of the nodes of the UNL. As long as $f \leq \frac{1}{5}(m-1)$ where m is the size of a UNL and f is the number of Byzantine nodes in the UNL, the Ripple consensus protocol is BFT. This is a rather strong security assumption as it should be satisfied by every UNL clique. In practice, this is fulfilled by Ripple's validator authentication scheme, which ensures the true identity of any validator is known to others.

Connectivity requirement—since every node only keeps communication links with its UNL peers, different nodes may have disparate or even disjoint UNLs, which leads to the network partitioning problem, as discussed previously. In a simple scenario, a group of nodes connected by UNL relationships can form a clique which is fully connected; however, two UNL cliques may agree on two conflicting ledgers in parallel if there is little communication between them. To prevent this problem, the Ripple network puts the following connectivity requirement for any two UNL cliques S_i and S_j:

$$|S_i \cap S_j| \geq \frac{1}{5}\max\{|S_i|, |S_j|\}, \forall i, j \tag{2.2}$$

This requirement literally means any pair of UNL cliques should share at least 25% of nodes. This level of inter-clique connectivity guarantees that no two UNL cliques can agree on two conflicting transactions, because otherwise they would not pass the 80% approval requirement in the Ripple consensus protocol.

Note that this connectivity requirement relies on the Ripple company's supervision and thus is not realistic for public blockchains such as Bitcoin where there are more than 10,000 pseudonymous validators (miners).

Complexity analysis—we assume every message has a fixed size, which is approximately the size of all transactions in the candidate set. Since a node only needs to communicate with its UNL peers, the message complexity of the Ripple consensus protocol is $O(Km^2)$, where m is the size of the UNL and K is the number of UNL cliques in the network.

2.5 Evaluation and Comparison

Table 2.6 qualitatively evaluates all the consensus protocols mentioned in this chapter. Specifically, we consider the following aspects:

- **Permission needed**—*yes* means the blockchain participants need to be authenticated at joining and reveal true identities to others. *No* means any one can join the network freely and pseudonymously.
- **Trusted third party needed**—whether the network needs a trust third party for a common service.
- **Consensus finality**—the finality of blocks in the blockchain. *Probabilistic* means all written blocks (except the genesis block) are prone to revocation, although with small probabilities. *Deterministic* means all written blocks will never be revoked.
- **Connectivity requirement**—*low* means a node only needs to maintain a minimum number of connections to peers. *High* means a node needs to connect with a significant percentage of the network.
- **Fault tolerance**—what percentage of faulty participants the protocol can tolerate. Different protocols have different adversarial models. For example, hashing rate matters in PoW while stake value matters in PoS.

2.6 Summary

Consensus is a core function of a distributed system. We introduced the basics of distributed consensus, two practical consensus protocols for distributed computing, the basics of the Nakamoto consensus, and several emerging blockchain consensus protocols. These consensus protocols are evaluated qualitatively and compared based on security and complexity aspects. As of the year 2018, some of the protocols are still under development, such as Ethereum's Casper PoS, Hyperledger Sawtooth, and Hyperledger Fabric, and we will see more of them come out.

Generally, we need to take into account two models when designing a blockchain consensus protocol—the network model and the trust model. A

Table 2.6 A comparison of blockchain consensus algorithms.

	PoW	Chain based PoS	BFT-style PoS	PoET	PBFT	Ripple Protocol
Permission needed	No	No	No	No	Yes	Yes
Third party needed	No	No	No	TEE platform vendor	Identity manager	Identity manager (Ripple company)
Consensus finality	Probabilistic	Probabilistic	Deterministic	Probabilistic	Deterministic	Deterministic
Connectivity requirement	Low	Low	Low	Low	High	High
Fault tolerance	50% hashing rate	50% stake value	33.3% stake value	50% enclave instances	33.3% voting power	20% nodes in UNL
Example	Bitcoin, Ethereum, Litecoin	Peercoin, Blackcoin	Ethereum Casper, Tendermint	Hyperledger Sawtooth	Hyperledger Fabric, Stellar	Ripple

highly connected and amenable network allows the participants to propagate transactions and blocks in a timely manner, which enables the use of message-heavy consensus protocols with high security guarantees. On the other hand, a benign trust model enables the utilization of highly efficient consensus protocols with focus on performance rather than security. The Nakamoto consensus protocol and PoW consensus algorithms in general have limited transaction capacity because they are deigned to endure uncertain network conditions and permissionless access scenarios with near-zero trust. In comparison, BFT-based protocols and the Ripple consensus protocol are highly efficient and support high transaction capacity because they are deigned for domain-specific applications in which high network connectivity is guaranteed and permissioned access is enforced.

In conclusion, the consensus protocol is vital to the balance between security, performance, and efficiency for a blockchain system. A protocol designer needs to carefully consider the security requirement and performance target, as well as the level of communication complexity the network can undertake.

Acknowledgment

This work was supported in part by the US National Science Foundation under grants CNS-1446478 and CNS-1443889.

References

1 H. Attiya and J. Welch, *Distributed Computing: Fundamentals, Simulations, and Advanced Topics*, vol. 19. John Wiley & Sons, 2004.

2 L. Lamport, R. Shostak, and M. Pease, "The byzantine generals problem," *ACM Transactions on Programming Languages and Systems (TOPLAS)*, vol. 4, no. 3, pp. 382–401, 1982.

3 M. J. Fischer, N. A. Lynch, and M. S. Paterson, "Impossibility of distributed consensus with one faulty process," *Journal of the ACM (JACM)*, vol. 32, no. 2, pp. 374–382, 1985.

4 G. F. Coulouris, J. Dollimore, and T. Kindberg, *Distributed Systems: Concepts and Design*. Pearson Education, 2005.

5 M. Pease, R. Shostak, and L. Lamport, "Reaching agreement in the presence of faults," *Journal of the ACM (JACM)*, vol. 27, no. 2, pp. 228–234, 1980.

6 G. Bracha and S. Toueg, "Asynchronous consensus and broadcast protocols," *Journal of the ACM (JACM)*, vol. 32, no. 4, pp. 824–840, 1985.

7 P. A. Alsberg and J. D. Day, "A principle for resilient sharing of distributed resources," in *Proceedings of the 2nd International Conference on Software Engineering*, IEEE Computer Society Press, San Francisco, 1976, pp. 562–570.

8 F. B. Schneider, "Implementing fault-tolerant services using the state machine approach: A tutorial," *ACM Computing Surveys (CSUR)*, vol. 22, no. 4, pp. 299–319, 1990.

9 B. Liskov and J. Cowling, "Viewstamped replication revisited," Computer Science and Artificial Intelligence Laboratory Technical Report, Massachusetts Institute of Technology, 2012.

10 B. M. Oki and B. H. Liskov, "Viewstamped replication: A new primary copy method to support highly-available distributed systems," in *Proceedings of the Seventh Annual ACM Symposium on Principles of Distributed Computing*, 1988, pp. 8–17.

11 M. Castro and B. Liskov, "Practical Byzantine fault tolerance," in *OSDI '99 Proceedings of the Third Symposium on Operating Systems Design and Implementation*, 1999, pp. 173–186.

12 S. Nakamoto, "Bitcoin: A peer-to-peer electronic cash system." [Online]. 2008. Available: https://bitcoin.org/bitcoin.pdf.

13 C. Decker and R. Wattenhofer, "Information propagation in the Bitcoin network," in *2013 IEEE Thirteenth International Conference on Peer-to-Peer Computing (P2P)*, IEEE, 2013, pp. 1–10.

14 S. King and S. Nadal, "PPCoin: Peer-to-peer crypto-currency with proof-of-stake." [Online]. Self-published Paper, August 19, 2012. Available: https://pdfs.semanticscholar.org/0db3/8d32069f3341d34c35085dc009a85ba13c13.pdf.

15 E. Androulaki, A. Barger, V. Bortnikov, C. Cachin, K. Christidis, A. De Caro, D. Enyeart, C. Ferris, G. Laventman, Y. Manevich, S. Muralidharan, C. Murthy, B. Nguyen, M. Sethi, G. Singh, K. Smith, A. Sorniotti, C. Stathakopoulou, M. Vukolić, S. W. Cocco, and J. Yellick, "Hyperledger Fabric: A distributed operating system for permissioned blockchains." arXiv preprint arXiv:1801.10228. 2018.

16 D. Mazieres, "The Stellar Consensus Protocol: A federated model for internet-level consensus." [Online]. Stellar Development Foundation, 2015. Available: https://www.stellar.org/papers/stellar-consensus-protocol.pdf.

17 J. Kwon, "Tendermint: Consensus without mining." [Online]. 2014. Retrieved May 18, 2017. Available: https://tendermint.com/static/docs/tendermint.pdf.

18 EOS.IO, "EOS.IO Technical White Paper v2", 2018. Available: https://github.com/EOSIO/Documentation/blob/master/TechnicalWhitePaper.md

19 V. Buterin and V. Griffith, "Casper the friendly finality gadget." arXiv preprint arXiv:1710.09437. 2017.

20 The Linux Foundation, "Hyperledger Sawtooth project." [Online]. 2016. Available: https://www.hyperledger.org/projects/sawtooth.

21 V. Costan and S. Devadas, "Intel SGX explained." [Online]. IACR Cryptology ePrint Archive, 2016. Available: https://eprint.iacr.org/2016/086.pdf.

22 D. Schwartz, N. Youngs, and A. Britto, "The Ripple Protocol consensus algorithm," Ripple Labs Inc. White Paper, 2014.

3

Overview of Attack Surfaces in Blockchain

Muhammad Saad,[1] Jeffrey Spaulding,[1] Laurent Njilla,[2] Charles A. Kamhoua,[3] DaeHun Nyang,[4] and Aziz Mohaisen[1]

[1] *University of Central Florida, Department of Computer Science, Florida, USA*
[2] *U.S. Air Force Research Lab, Cyber Assurance Branch, Rome, NY, USA*
[3] *U.S. Army Research Laboratory, Network Security Branch, Adelphi, MD, USA*
[4] *Inha University, Department of Computer Engineering, Incheon, Republic of Korea*

3.1 Introduction

In this chapter, we explore the attack surface of Blockchains and possible ways in which this technology can be compromised. Towards this goal, we attribute attack viability in the attack surface to (i) Blockchain cryptographic constructs, (ii) the distributed architecture of the systems using Blockchain, and (iii) the Blockchain application context. For each of those contributing factors, we outline several attacks, including selfish mining and associated peer behaviors, 51% attack, Domain Name System (DNS) attacks, distributed denial-of-service attacks, equivocation, consensus delay (due to selfish behavior or distributed denial-of-service attacks), Blockchain forking, orphaned and stale blocks, block ingestion, wallet thefts, and privacy attacks. We then explore the causal relationship between these attacks and show how one fraudulent activity can lead to the possibility of other attacks. A secondary contribution of this work is outlining effective defense measures taken by the Blockchain technology or proposed by researchers to mitigate the effects of these attacks and patch vulnerabilities in Blockchains.

Blockchain has recently stimulated many applications in the digital world, such as cryptocurrency, smart contracts, ledger maintenance, and distributed provenance, among others. Using Blockchain's transparent and fully distributed peer-to-peer design, those applications can benefit from an append-only model in which "transactions" accepted in the Blockchain cannot be modified. The transparency of the Blockchain enables storing publicly verifiable and undeniable records. Furthermore, the Blockchain's peer-to-peer

Blockchain for Distributed Systems Security, First Edition. Edited by Sachin S. Shetty, Charles A. Kamhoua, and Laurent L. Njilla.

system provides verifiable ledger maintenance without a centralized authority, thus addressing the single point of failure and single point of trust. For example, Bitcoin (a popular cryptocurrency using Blockchain technology) takes advantage of the aforementioned properties, making it easy to verify the history of financial transactions.

Despite the functional features that Blockchain brings to those applications, recent reports have highlighted the security risks associated with the technology. For example, in June 2016, an unknown attacker managed to drain US$50 million from "The DAO", a decentralized autonomous organization that is running through rules on Blockchain-based smart contracts [1]. In August 2016, bitcoins worth US$72 million were stolen from the exchange platform Bitfinex in Hong Kong [2]. In June 2017, Bitfinex also experienced a distributed denial-of-service (DDoS) attack that led to its temporary suspension. Several exchanges of Bitcoin and Ethereum (a Blockchain-based distributed computing platform) have also suffered from DDoS attacks frequently, hampering service availability to users. Those attacks have application-specific consequences. For example, with Bitcoin, and due to the capital involved in its operation, those attacks can cause devaluation of the cryptocurrency.

The security of Blockchain systems is paramount for their acceptability by their potential users. For example, investors take the security of Bitcoin into account when studying the risks associated with their investments and use of this technology. Understanding the threats associated with Blockchain systems in general is the first step towards realizing the potential of applications built on Bitcoin. To this end, this work is dedicated to an in-depth look at the attack surface of Blockchain.

We envision that Blockchain will be used in many applications, and we report on the attacks that could jeopardize those applications. Namely, we classify those attacks into three broad types: (i) attacks associated with the mathematical techniques used for creating the ledger (e.g. Blockchain forks, stale blocks, and orphaned blocks), (i) attacks associated with the peer-to-peer architecture used in the Blockchain system, (e.g. selfish mining, 51% attack, consensus delay, DDoS attack, and DNS attack), and (iii) attacks associated with the application context that uses the Blockchain technology (e.g. Blockchain ingestion, double spending, and wallet theft). Our motivation is to highlight the key threats associated with Blockchain technology by investigating its attack surface and also potential remedies for the various attacks.

Contributions—our first contribution is the survey of possible attacks related to design constructs of Blockchains, the peer-to-peer architecture, and the application-oriented use of Blockchains. We highlight the nature of attacks and the ways in which they affect Bitcoin. We also show the causal relationship between sequences of attacks to outline how one attack can facilitate the possibility of another one. Understanding these links can help devise a common cure that can fix multiple problems at the same time. Finally, for every attack, we explore the defense strategies that are found in the literature.

Organization—in Section 3.2, we review the design constructs of Blockchain that enable various attacks, such as Blockchain forks, stale blocks, and orphan blocks. In Section 3.4, we look into the features of distributed networks that create possibilities for selfish mining, majority attack, DNS attacks, DDoS attacks, consensus delays, etc. We go on to describe the aspects of peer-to-peer architecture that enable the possibility of their potential misuse in Blockchain applications. In Section 3.5, we outline the application-specific vulnerabilities found in Blockchain and assess the threats that they face. That is followed by the conclusion and future work in Section 3.7.

3.2 Overview of Blockchain and its Operations

Conceptually, a Blockchain can be viewed as a database of public transactions (ledger) that is tamper-evident due to its replication on a large number of peers in a peer-to-peer system. Having a single ledger in a Blockchain means that all peers in the system that make the network must have a consensus on the state of the Blockchain and the data it contains. To achieve consensus, all blocks in the Blockchain require a proof of work (PoW) [3, 4], which is a function that is computationally expensive to generate but easy to verify.

In the case of Bitcoin, for example, a PoW involves solving a mathematical challenge that is performed by special nodes in the network called miners. Miners collect application-specific events (e.g. transactions in the case of Bitcoin) and add them into a block. The process of "mining" is essentially solving challenges and verifying transactions; blocks are created by using computational power. The challenge in Bitcoin is to come up with a *nonce* (i.e. a number used once) that when hashed with a block, produces a hash value that is less than the target threshold set by the system. The target threshold is a 256-bit unsigned integer that is encoded in a 32-bit "compact" form (called the *nBit*), which is stored in the block header. In the process of solving the challenge, miners spend time and computational effort and, in return, get rewarded for solving a block and adding it to the Blockchain. As of October 2017, the reward for solving a block is 12.5 bitcoins. For more details about mining a block in Bitcoin, we refer the reader to Reference [5].

As mentioned earlier, several attacks against Blockchain technology are to do with the Blockchain itself, and how it is affected by the behavior of certain miners and the peer-to-peer architecture it is built upon. In the subsequent three sections, we explore the possible attacks associated with the Blockchain structure, attacks associated with the peer-to-peer architecture used in the Blockchain system, and attacks associated with the application services that use Blockchain technology (i.e. Bitcoin). We supplement each section with possible defenses, countermeasures, and remedies to address those attacks.

3.3 Blockchain Attacks

3.3.1 Blockchain Fork

A fork represents a condition in which nodes in the network have diverging views about that state of the Blockchain persisting over long periods of time or even indefinitely. These forks can be created unintentionally through protocol malfunctions or incompatibilities in client software upgrades. Forks can also be caused by malicious intents such as implanting "Sybil nodes" that follow conflicting validation rules or by carrying out "selfish mining", as discussed further in Section 3.4.1. Furthermore, intentional forks can either be soft or hard forks, the latter of which occur when new blocks that the network accepts appear invalid to prefork nodes. On the other hand, soft forks occur when some blocks appear invalid to postfork nodes. In either case, a Blockchain fork represents an inconsistent state that can be exploited by adversaries to cause confusion, fraudulent transactions, and distrust within the network [6]. Figure 3.1 demonstrates a hard fork example that results from peers following conflicting rules about the state of the Blockchain.

When "The DAO" was drained by more than one-third of its digital cash by attackers [1], Ethereum used a hard fork to roll back transactions and retrieve millions of dollars' worth of ether (the "fuel" for the Ethereum network). However, this required consensus by the majority of nodes in the network. In such a scenario, if a consensus delay happens due to a majority attack or DDoS event, fraudulent activities become somewhat difficult to deal with and prolonged delays can ultimately cause devaluation of cryptocurrency.

3.3.2 Stale Blocks and Orphaned Blocks

Two forms of inconsistencies can occur with the consensus process that can leave valid blocks out of the Blockchain. The first form is a "stale block", which is a block that was successfully mined but is not accepted in the current best Blockchain (i.e. the most-difficult-to-recreate chain). We will see in Section 3.4.1 that a form of Blockchain attack known as "selfish mining" can lead to the creation of stale blocks in the network, which deprives an honest miner of its reward.

The other form of inconsistency is an "orphan block"—a block whose previous (parent) hash field points to an unauthentic block that is detached from the

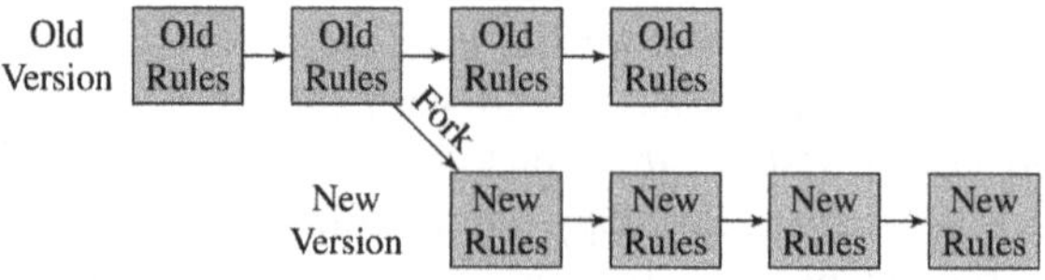

Figure 3.1 Hard fork resulting from a set of peers following conflicting rules.

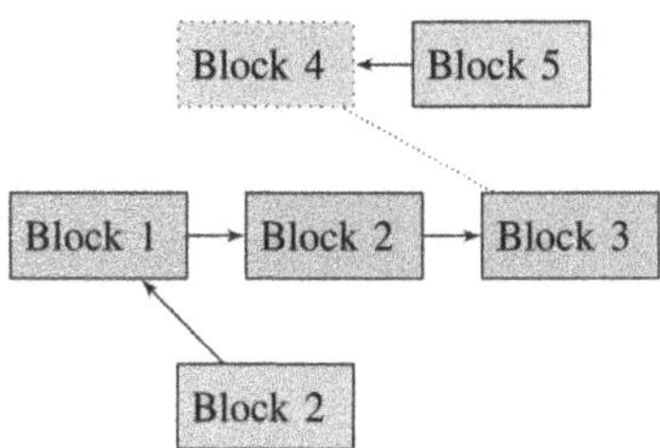

Figure 3.2 Stale vs. orphan blocks. Note that the stale block (block 2, bottom, and block 4) are valid but they are not part of the Blockchain. Orphan block (block 5) does not have a parent belonging to the Blockchain.

Blockchain and thus cannot be validated. These inconsistencies can be introduced by an attacker or caused by race conditions in the work of the miners. Stale blocks may be initially accepted by the majority of the network, but they can be rejected later when proof of a longer Blockchain (i.e. the current best) is received that does not include that particular block. Figure 3.2 demonstrates a chain where stale and orphan blocks can be found. The first orphaned block in Bitcoin was found on March 18, 2015, and that was the beginning of a period in which the most orphaned blocks were created. The trend saw a decline in 2016, and from June 14, 2017 to the date of this chapter, no orphaned block has been added to the list [7].

3.3.3 Countering Blockchain Structure Attacks

Resolving soft forks in a Blockchain network is a relatively easy process. All peers in the network can come to a consensus about the true state of the Blockchain and resume activities from there. Resolving hard forks can be challenging because conflicting chains can be lengthy with transaction activities dating back to the time of the conflict. Although the stakes of rolling back from a hard fork are high, they can be resolved by the same principle of consensus that was discussed earlier. As was the case with Ethereum, a hard fork was used to retrieve money for the investors after The DAO was attacked. Ultimately, the process of solving a fork depends upon the agreement of peers in the network.

In Ethereum, stale blocks are actually rewarded and become part of the Blockchain (as so-called uncle blocks) [8]. Recently, the number of orphan blocks in Bitcoin has decreased due to the shift towards highly centralized mining networks, thus reducing the high probability of orphan blocks prevalent in decentralized mining networks.

3.4 Blockchain's Peer-to-Peer System

The underlying peer-to-peer architecture is the primary reason why certain guarantees are provided by Blockchain, including security. Counterintuitively,

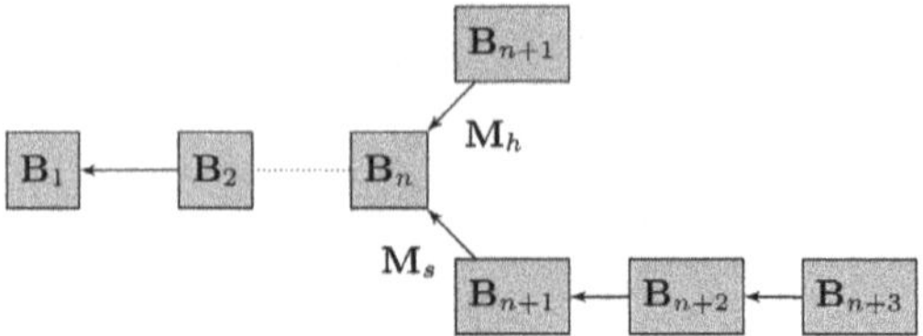

Figure 3.3 Illustration of selfish mining.

this peer-to-peer architecture that the Blockchain resides on actually contributes to several attacks, which we explore in this section.

3.4.1 Selfish Mining

As introduced by [9], the selfish mining attack is a strategy opted for by certain miners who attempt to increase their rewards by deliberately keeping their blocks private. Rather than releasing them to the public upon discovery, these selfish miners continue to mine their own private blocks to obtain a longer chain than the public Blockchain. Once the public Blockchain starts approaching the length of their private chain, the selfish miners finally release their blocks to the public to ultimately claim the reward. Figure 3.3 demonstrates how a selfish mining attack is carried out.

Consider a Blockchain with blocks **B1**, **B2**,…,**B*n***. Suppose an honest miner **M*h*** has successfully mined the next block **Bn** + 1 and in the same network, a selfish miner **M*s*** has also solved **B*n*** + 1. Instead of releasing his/her block, **M*s*** chooses not to publish it and successfully mines two more blocks, **B*n*** + 2 and **B*n*** + 3. Assuming favorable situations for **M*h***, we show that **M*h*** can still be cheated despite having a majority of the network's confidence in their work. Let the hash value of **M*h***'s block **B*n*** + 1 be lower than both the target threshold and **M*s***'s block **B*n*** + 1. If only these two blocks were presented to the network, **M*h***'s block would be chosen (due to its greater computational complexity) over **M*s***'s block and appended to the public Blockchain. After some time, **M*s*** releases all of his/her blocks **B*n*** + 1, **B*n*** + 2, and **B*n*** + 3. Due to the design protocols of Blockchain, the network will invariably shift to **M*s***'s blocks and discard block **B*n*** + 1 of **M*h***. The effort put forth by **M*h*** in computing its block will be wasted entirely due to the selfish behavior of **M*s***. The incentive in adopting this selfish mining strategy is maximizing block rewards by publishing a longer chain. It should be noted that excluding **M*h***'s block **B*n*** + 1 from the Blockchain does not destroy the block; rather, it leads to another significant problem in the network, known as "stale blocks" (Section 3.3.2).

Selfish mining attacks can produce undesirable results for the rest of the network by invalidating the blocks of honest miners who contribute to the Blockchain. In a case where two selfish miners compete to add their chains to the network, the chances of a "Blockchain fork" arise (Section 3.3.1). These forks can cause a delay of consensus in the network, which can further lead to other potential attacks such as "double spending", as discussed in Section 3.5.2. One selfish activity in the network has the potential to disrupt the overall network, and therefore it is imperative to study their relationship with one another.

3.4.2 The 51% Attack

The 51% attack happens when a single attacker, a group of sybil nodes, or a mining pool in the network attains the majority of the network's mining hash rate to manipulate the Blockchain. As such, the attackers would be able to (i) prevent transactions or blocks from being verified (thus making them invalid), (ii) reverse transactions during the time they are in control to allow double spending, and (iii) prevent other miners (verifiers) from finding any blocks for a short period of time. Having a majority of the hashing power at their disposal, the attacker's blocks will be appended to the Blockchain with higher probability, compared to others [10]. Also, these blocks can possibly have fraudulent or double-spent transactions. For example, if an attacker performs a transaction in exchange for any product with Alice, it can replicate the same transaction with Bob and put it on the block. Transactions on Blockchains are not reversible, and only one transaction can be considered valid among the two.

A 51% attack is not beyond the realm of possibilities. In July 2014, the mining pool "GHash.IO" held over 51% of the hash rate for a day in Bitcoin [11], which raised many concerns in the press and media about Bitcoin and its vulnerabilities. "GHash.IO" later shrunk in size when miners left its pool and eventually closed in October 2016. It should be noted that mining pools do not always need 51% of the network's hashing power to carry out the fraudulent activities mentioned previously [48]. Even with less hashing power, similar targets can be achieved with a significant probability of success. As shown by Bahack [12], majority attacks are possible with one-quarter of the network's hashing power.

3.4.3 DNS Attacks

When a node joins the Bitcoin network for the first time, it will be unaware of the active peers in the network. To discover the active peers (identified by their IP addresses) in the network, a bootstrapping step is required. The DNS can be used as a bootstrapping mechanism, and DNS seeds are queried by nodes upon joining the network to obtain further information about other active peers. As pointed out in the developer's guide of Bitcoin [13], DNS opens a wide attack surface to the Bitcoin network; i.e. the DNS resolution is vulnerable to man-in-the-middle attacks (resolver), cache poisoning, etc. As a result, by using the attack surface of the DNS, an adversary can potentially isolate Blockchain peers (by feeding them with an invalid list of peers), feed the peers with fake blocks, invalidate transactions, etc. For more on DNS security in general, the reader may refer to the work in Reference [14].

3.4.4 DDoS Attacks

One of the most common attacks on online services is the DDoS attack [15,16]. Blockchain technology, despite being a peer-to-peer system, is still prone to DDoS attacks. Blockchain-based applications, such as Bitcoin and Ethereum, have repeatedly suffered from these attacks [8,17–20]. DDoS attacks manifest themselves in a number of ways, depending on the application nature, network architecture, and peer behavior. For example, in the Bitcoin network, the 51% attack can lead to denial of service. Specifically, if a group of miners acquire a significant hashing power, they can prevent other miners from adding their mined blocks to the Blockchain, invalidate ongoing transactions, and cause service failure in the network. Intentional forks—forks that are the result of malicious behavior—can turn into hard forks, resulting in similar outcomes of denial of service.

Another possibility for the attack is due to the limited number of transactions per block the Bitcoin network can process in a given time. For example, on average, it takes the Bitcoin network 10 minutes to mine a block, which has a maximum size of 1 MB. Although the size of transactions in Bitcoin varies, the average size of a transaction in Bitcoin is approximately 500 bytes, allowing approximately 2000 transactions per block on average—the maximum number of transactions added to a block in Bitcoin is reported to be 2210 [7]. Furthermore, the average time needed to mine one block, based on the predefined difficulty, is approximately 10 minutes. As such, for all current transactions in the network to be successfully included in the Blockchain, their number may not exceed 200 transactions per minute. Taking that into account, and the fact that each transaction requires a minimum of two peers (identified by two different public identifiers) to be involved in a transaction, the total active peers served by the network per minute (i.e. where a block containing their transaction will be mined) will not exceed 200 peers.

An adversary may exploit the aforementioned operational reality of the Bitcoin system by introducing Sybil identities; the same adversary may also control multiple wallets. Furthermore, using those identities, the adversary may issue several dust transactions (e.g. 0.001 BTC per transaction) between the various Sybil identities under his/her control. By introducing a large number of transactions of a small value over a short period of time, the network will be congested by creating blocks containing those transactions, and service to legitimate users in the network will be denied. As a result of this congestion, the adversary may as well launch other attacks, e.g. double spending of tokens not mined due to the congestion.

One may argue that miners may choose which transactions are to be included in a block. However, this is discouraged by design in Bitcoin, as outlined by Satoshi [13]. Blocks today even include transactions of values as low as 0.0001 BTC, which makes flooding the network with low-value transactions possible.

3.4.5 Consensus Delay

Another attack associated with the peer-to-peer nature of the network is consensus delay. In this attack, an attacker may inject false blocks to delay or prevent peers from reaching consensus in the Blockchain. Such delays can be introduced by either forcing the network to mine small blocks with a small coin base, or by forcing it to spend time to reach consensus on corrupted blocks. In particular, because accepting or rejecting false blocks can be time consuming, this process allows misbehaving nodes to game the system. The problem is further exacerbated for time-critical applications, where resolution needs to be achieved within a short period of time.

3.4.6 Countering Peer-to-Peer Attacks

Prior research has been conducted to address the problem of selfish mining, and researchers have suggested several possible solutions [9, 21–24]. Solat and Potop-Butucaru [25] proposed a "lifetime" for blocks that prevents *block withholding* by selfish miners. If the expected lifetime of a block expires (calculated by the honest miners), it is rejected by the network. Heilman [22], impedes the profitability of selfish miners by introducing a defense scheme called "Freshness Preferred." Heilman [22] builds on top of previous work by Eyal and Sirer [9], by adding unforgeable timestamps to blocks and prefers blocks with more recent timestamps compared to older ones. Their work reduces the incentive for selfish miners to withhold their blocks for long periods of time.

Majority attacks have also been widely discussed with countermeasures proposed to overcome a monopoly in Blockchain networks. Bastiaan [11] introduced the concept of "two phase proof-of-work" (2P-PoW) to counter 51% attacks. 2P-PoW is a continuous-time Markov chain (CTMC) model that incorporates two challenges for miners to solve instead of one. The states of the CTMCs prevent the pool from increasing beyond an alarming size by shrinking the incentive for miners in the pool. 2P-PoW prevents large pools from creating a hegemony.

Johnson et al. [26] proposed a game theory model to address DDoS attacks against mining pools. Other countermeasures include putting a cap on the minimum amount in the transaction that a sender can have or increasing the block size to accommodate more transactions. Yet another approach is to reduce the target difficulty in mining blocks so that more blocks can be mined with no transactions going to waste. Each of these propositions has its own caveats. To prevent DNS-based attacks, there is an enormous amount of literature that can be used to equip the Blockchain system with DNS attack defenses [27–29]. The dimensions we explored in this chapter encourage additional research in Blockchain technology in the areas regarding DNS and DDoS attacks.

3.5 Application Oriented Attacks

The Blockchain and the associated peer-to-peer system are separate from the application services using them. Based on the nature of the applications, they will have their own shortcomings. Thus, we expect a significant number of attacks based on the application, which we address in this section.

3.5.1 Blockchain Ingestion

Blockchain is a public ledger, making it accessible to anyone who wants to mine it. As such, the analysis of public Blockchain can reveal useful information to an adversary. This process is known as Blockchain ingestion and it might not be desirable to the Blockchain application or its users. For example, a credit card company in the open market can use data analytics to delve into public information on the Blockchain and optimize its own schemes to compete with the digital currency. To demonstrate the potential exploitation of public data, Fleder et al. [30] used graph analysis to create links between Blockchain data of Bitcoin and associated identities of the users.

3.5.2 Double Spending

To illustrate double spending with an example, consider the following scenario. In cryptocurrency operations, a transaction transfers the ownership of asset from a sender's address to the receiver's public address, and the value of the transaction is signed by the signer with a private key. Once the transaction is signed, it is broadcasted to the network upon which the receiver validates the transaction. The validation at the recipient's end happens when the receiver looks up the unspent transaction output of the sender, verifies the sender's signature, and waits for the transaction to be mined into a valid block. The process takes a few minutes, and in Bitcoin, the average time of block mining is 10 minutes.

In an environment of fast transactions [31] or if a receiver is optimistic, he/she may release the product to the sender before the transaction gets mined into the Blockchain. As such, this gives the sender an opportunity to sign the same transaction and send it to another recipient. This phenomenon of signing the same transaction with a private key and sending it to two different receivers is known as double spending. In double spending, there are two transactions derived from the same unspent transaction output of the sender, and only one of them gets incorporated into the Blockchain. Consensus delay in the network (Section 3.4.5) or 51% attack (Section 3.4.2) can cause additional delays in the verification process, which increase the chances of an adversary to carry out the double spending.

3.5.3 Wallet Theft

Where credentials, such as keys, associated with peers in the system are stored in a digital wallet, the "wallet theft" attack arises with certain implications on the application. For example, in Bitcoin, the wallet is stored unencrypted by default, allowing an adversary to learn the credentials associated with it and the nature of transactions issued by it. Even when a wallet is safely guarded on a host, launching a malware attack on the host will allow the adversary to steal the wallet. Finally, with many third-party services enabling storage of wallets, those services can also be compromised and the wallets can be leaked to an adversary [1].

3.5.4 Countering Application Oriented Attacks

Application-oriented attacks have various possible countermeasures. For example, to secure blocks, it is advised to keep backups of the wallet and secure the keys used for signing transactions. Passwords are easy to compromise, and using a strong password is required. However, changing passwords does not change the keys secured by them, making those keys vulnerable due to a previous compromise of the password. Wallet encryption, a standard practice in the original Bitcoin design, is highly recommended to cope with vulnerable keys. Another mechanism to cope with wallet security is insurance, which technically does not address the problem by remedying its consequences.

New models of cryptocurrency, such as "Zcash", hide transactions and maintain anonymity on the Blockchain, thus preventing a block ingestion attack. The double-spending attack is easily addressed in fast networks, but not when the network is characterized by high latency. One possible approach to deal with the problem is utilizing one-time (or a few time) signatures, such as Extended Merkle Signature Scheme (XMSS) [32, 33]. However, this requires change in the current signature algorithms that Blockchain applications have used. Other proposals include reducing the difficulty parameter of Blockchain to enable swift block mining, which is a reasonable approach, except that it would further facilitate selfish mining.

3.6 Related Work

Blockchains are used in cryptocurrencies [34], smart contracts [35, 36], electronic voting [37], cloud computing [38–40], online gaming [41, 42], and supply chain provenance [43]. All of these applications use the cryptographic constructs of Blockchains for ledger maintenance and the decentralized peer-to-peer model for information flows. Therefore, they can possibly encounter similar attacks and problems, as outlined in this chapter.

Kwon et al. [6], presented a new attack called Fork After Withholding (FAW). Through an empirical analysis, they found it to be more rewarding for the attacker than selfish mining and block withholding. Apostolaki et al. [44] studied routing attacks on cryptocurrency and analyzed the hijacking of Border Gateway Protocol (BGP) announcements. Empirically, they show that an attacker can isolate up to 50% of the hashing power of the network. Bradbury [45] reviewed various attacks on Bitcoin, namely the 51% attack, code-based attacks, double-spending, and dust transactions.

Eyal and Sirer [9], addressed selfish mining and its deterrence. Sapirshtein et al. [21] analyzed optimal selfish mining strategies. Thwarting selfish mining has been addressed by Heilman [22] and Solat and Potop-Butucaru [25]. Bastiaan [11] studied the 51% attack by a stochastic analysis of 2P-PoW [46]. Eyal et al. [47], introduced Bitcoin-NG, a scalable Bitcoin protocol. Their work can be used to equip most Blockchain networks with better consensus mechanisms to avoid unnecessary delays and block forks.

DDoS and DNS-related attacks have not been not investigated yet in the context of Blockchain systems. Since DDoS attacks manifest themselves in a different way in the peer-to-peer architecture, as opposed to a centralized system, their prevention also requires nonconventional approaches.

3.7 Conclusion and Future Work

In this chapter, we explored the attack surface of Blockchain technology. We attribute attacks to the cryptographic constructs of the Blockchain, the underlying communication architecture, and the context in which they are applied. In doing so, we highlight major threats and ongoing defense research activities. We believe that various attacks against Blockchain can be still launched, notwithstanding the current and existing defenses, and that some of those attacks can be used to facilitate several others. In the future, we will explore exact parameters and settings to empirically understand the cost of launching those attacks, under various defense capabilities.

References

1 D. Siegel, "Understanding the DAO attack." [Online]. 2016. Available: https://www.coindesk.com/understanding-dao-hack-journalists/.

2 C. Baldwin, "Bitcoin worth 72 million stolen from Bitfinex exchange in Hong Kong." [Online]. *Reuters*, 2016. Available: http://reut.rs/2gc7iQ9.

3 M. Bellare and P. Rogaway, "Random oracles are practical: A paradigm for designing efficient protocols," in *Proceedings of the 1st Acm Conference on Computer and Communications Security*, Fairfax, 1993, pp. 62–73.

4 A. Juels and J. G. Brainard, "Client puzzles: A cryptographic countermeasure against connection depletion attacks," in *Proceedings of the Network and Distributed System Security Symposium, NDSS 1999*, 1999, pp. 151–65.

5 J. A. Kroll, I. C. Davey, and E. W. Felten, "The economics of Bitcoin mining, or Bitcoin in the presence of adversaries," in *Proceedings of The Twelfth Workshop on the Economics of Information Security (WEIS 2013)*, Washington, 2013.

6 Y. Kwon, D. Kim, Y. Son, E. Vasserman, and Y. Kim, "Be selfish and avoid dilemmas: Fork after withholding (FAW) attacks on Bitcoin," in *CCS '17: Proceeding of the 2017 ACM SIGSAC Conference on Computer and Communications Security*, 2017, pp. 195–209.

7 I. Eyal and E. G. Sirer, "How to disincentivize large Bitcoin mining pools." *Bitcoin Block Explorer—Blockchain*, 2014. [Online]. Available: https://www.blockchain.com/charts.

8 M. Vasek, M. Thornton, and T. Moore, "Empirical analysis of Denial-of-Service attacks in the Bitcoin ecosystem," in *Financial Cryptography and Data Security*. Springer, 2014, pp. 57–71.

9 I. Eyal and E. G. Sirer, "Majority is not enough: Bitcoin mining is vulnerable," in *Proceedings of the Eighteenth International Conference on Financial Cryptography and Data Security*, 2014, pp. 436–54.

10 Bitcoin Community, "51% Attack." 2017. [Online]. Available: https://learncryptography.com/cryptocurrency/51-attack.

11 M. Bastiaan, "Preventing the 51%-attack: A stochastic analysis of two phase proof of work in Bitcoin." [Online]. 2015. Available: https://goo.gl/nJsMzV.

12 L. Bahack, "Theoretical Bitcoin attacks with less than half of the computational power (draft)." *arXiv Preprint arXiv:1312.7013*. 2013.

13 Bitcoin, "Bitcoin developer guide." [Online]. 2017. Available: https://bitcoin.org/en/developer-guide.

14 A. R. Kang, J. Spaulding, and A. Mohaisen, "Domain name system security and privacy: Old problems and new challenges." [Online]. *CoRR*, 2016. Available: http://arxiv.org/abs/1606.07080.

15 A. Wang, A. Mohaisen, and S. Chen, "An adversary-centric behavior modeling of DDoS attacks," in *37th IEEE International Conference on Distributed Computing Systems, ICDCS 2017*, Atlanta, Georgia, June 5–8, 2017, pp. 1126–36.

16 M. Saad, M. T. Thai, and A. Mohaisen, "POSTER: Deterring DDoS attacks on blockchain-based cryptocurrencies through mempool optimization" in *Proceedings of 13th ACM ASIA Conference on Information, Computer and Communications Security, ASIACCS 2018*, 2018, pp. 809–811.

17 P. Muncaster, "World's largest Bitcoin exchange Bitfinex crippled by DDoS." [Online]. 2017. Available: http://bit.ly/2kqo6HU.

18 C. Cimpanu, "Bitcoin trader hit by 'severe DDoS attack' as Bitcoin price nears all-time high." [Online]. 2017. Available: http://bit.ly/2lA5iT6.

19 V. Buterin, "Ethereum responds to recent DDoS attack." [Online]. 2016. Available: http://bit.ly/2gcrn9d.

20 J. Wilcke, "The Ethereum network is currently undergoing a DoS attack." [Online]. 2016. Available: http://bit.ly/2cwlB0D.

21 A. Sapirshtein, Y. Sompolinsky, and A. Zohar, "Optimal selfish mining strategies in Bitcoin," in *Financial Cryptography and Data Security*. Springer, 2016, pp. 515–32.

22 E. Heilman, "One weird trick to stop selfish miners: fresh Bitcoins, a solution for the honest miner," in *Financial Cryptography and Data Security*. Springer, 2014, pp. 161–62.

23 N. T. Courtois and L. Bahack, "On subversive miner strategies and block withholding attack in Bitcoin digital currency." *arXiv Preprint arXiv:1402.1718*. 2014.

24 M. Nojoumian, A. Golchubian, L. Njilla, K. Kwiat, and C. A. Kamhoua, "Incentivizing blockchain miners to avoid dishonest mining strategies using a reputation-based paradigm," in *Proceedings of the 2018 Computing Conference*, London, United Kingdom, July 2018.

25 S. Solat and M. Potop-Butucaru, "ZeroBlock: Preventing selfish mining in Bitcoin." *arXiv Preprint arXiv:1605.02435*. 2016.

26 B. Johnson, A. Laszka, J. Grossklags, M. Vasek, and T. Moore, "Game-theoretic analysis of DDoS attacks against Bitcoin mining pools," in *Financial Cryptography and Data Security*. Springer, 2014, pp. 72–86.

27 P. Silva, "DNSSEC: The antidote to DNS cache poisoning and other DNS attacks." An F5 Networks, Inc. Technical Brief, 2009.

28 T. Peng, C. Leckie, and K. Ramamohanarao, "Survey of network-based defense mechanisms countering the DoS and DDoS problems," *ACM Computing Surveys (CSUR)*, vol. 39, no. 1, pp. 3, 2007.

29 J. Etheridge and R. Anton, "System and method for detecting and countering a network attack," US Patent Appl. 7904959B2, April 18, 2005.

30 M. Fleder, M. S. Kester, and S. Pillai, "Bitcoin transaction graph analysis." *arXiv Preprint arXiv:1502.01657*. 2015.

31 G. O. Karame, E. Androulaki, and S. Capkun, "Double-spending fast payments in Bitcoin," in *Proceedings of the 2012 ACM Conference on Computer and Communications Security—CCS 12*, 2012, pp. 906–917.

32 A. Hülsing, D. Butin, S. Gazdag, and A. Mohaisen, "XMSS: Extended hash-based signatures." [Online]. 2015. Available: https://www.ietf.org/id/draft-irtf-cfrg-xmss-hash-based-signatures-10.txt.

33 M. Saad, A. Mohaisen, C. Kamhoua, K. Kwiat, and L. Njilla, "Countering double spending in next-generation blockchains," in *2018 IEEE International Conference on Communications*, Kansas City, 2018.

34 M. Saad and A. Mohaisen, "Towards characterizing blockchain-based cryptocurrencies for highly-accurate predictions," in *Proceedings of 10th International Workshop on Hot Topics in Pervasive Mobile and Online Social Networking, HotPOST 2018*, Honolulu, 2018.

35 A. Kosba, A. Miller, E. Shi, Z. Wen, and C. Papamanthou, "Hawk: The blockchain model of cryptography and privacy-preserving smart contracts." in *2016 IEEE Symposium on Security and Privacy (Sp)*, 2016, pp. 839–58.

36 G. Wood, "Ethereum: A secure decentralised generalised transaction ledger," Ethereum Project Yellow Paper 151, 2014.

37 Lee, Kibin, Joshua I James, Tekachew Gobena Ejeta, and Hyoungjoong Kim. 2016. "Electronic Voting Service Using Block-Chain." *The Journal of Digital Forensics, Security and Law: JDFSL* 11 (2). Association of Digital Forensics, Security; Law:123.

38 D. Tosh, S. Shetty, P. Foytik, C. A. Kamhoua, and L. Njilla, "CloudPoS: A proof of stake consensus design for blockchain integrated cloud" in *Proceedings of the 2018 IEEE International Conference on Cloud Computing, (IEEE CLOUD 2018)*, San Francisco, CA, July 2018.

39 X. Liang, S. Shetty, D. Tosh, C. A. Kamhoua, K. Kwiat, and L. Njilla, "ProvChain: A blockchain-based data provenance architecture in cloud environment with enhanced privacy and availability" in *Proceedings of the 2017 IEEE/ACM International Symposium on Cluster, Cloud and Grid Computing (CCGrid)*, Madrid, Spain, May 2017.

40 D. Tosh, S. Shetty, X. Liang, C. A. Kamhoua, K. Kwiat, and L. Njilla, "Security implications of blockchain cloud with analysis of block withholding attack" in *Proceedings of the 2017 IEEE/ACM International Symposium on Cluster, Cloud and Grid Computing (CCGrid)*, Madrid, Spain, May 2017.

41 T. I. Ron and S. Attias, "The effect of blockchain technology in the gaming regulatory environment," *Gaming Law Review*, vol. 21, no. 6, pp. 459–460, 2017.

42 D. B. Rawat, L. Njilla, K. Kwiat, and C. A. Kamhoua, "iShare: Blockchain based privacy-aware multi-agent information sharing games for cybersecurity" in *Proceedings of the 2018 IEEE International Conference on Computing, Networking and Communications (ICNC)*, Maui, Hawaii, March 2018.

43 H. M. Kim and M. Laskowski. 2016. "Towards an Ontology-Driven Blockchain Design for Supply Chain Provenance," *SSRN Electronic Journal*, 2016. https://doi.org/10.2139/ssrn.2828369.

44 M. Apostolaki, A. Zohar, and L. Vanbever, "Hijacking Bitcoin: Routing attacks on cryptocurrencies," in *2017 IEEE Symposium on Security and Privacy (Sp)*, San Jose, 2017, pp. 375–92.

45 D. Bradbury, "The problem with Bitcoin," *Computer Fraud & Security*, vol. 2013, no. 11, pp. 5–8, 2013.

46 I. Eyal and E. G. Sirer, "How to disincentivize large Bitcoin mining pools." [Online]. 2014. Available: http://bit.ly/1srPhPs.

47 I. Eyal, A. E. Gencer, E. G. Sirer, and R. Van Renesse, "Bitcoin-NG: A scalable blockchain protocol," in *NSDI'16 Proceedings of the 13th Usenix Conference on Networked Systems Design and Implementation*, Santa Clara, 2016, pp. 45–59.

48 Y. Velner, J. Teutsch, and L. Luu, "Smart contracts make Bitcoin mining pools vulnerable." [Online]. IACR Cryptology ePrint Archive, 2017. Available: https://eprint.iacr.org/2017/230.pdf.

Part II

Blockchain Solutions for Distributed Systems Security

4

ProvChain: Blockchain-based Cloud Data Provenance

Xueping Liang,[1] Sachin S. Shetty,[1] Deepak Tosh,[2] Laurent Njilla,[3] Charles A. Kamhoua,[4] and Kevin Kwiat[5]

[1] *Old Dominion University, Virginia Modeling, Analysis and Simulation Center, Norfolk, VA, USA*
[2] *University of Texas at El Paso, Department of Computer Science, El Paso, TX, USA*
[3] *US Air Force Research Lab, Cyber Assurance Branch, Rome, NY, USA*
[4] *US Army Research Lab, Network Security Branch, Adelphi, MD, USA*
[5] *Haloed Sun TEK, LLC, CAESAR Group, Sarasota, Fl, USA*

4.1 Introduction

Cloud computing is widely adopted by the commercial and military environment to support data storage, on demand computing, and dynamic provisioning. Cloud computing environments are distributed and heterogeneous with a diversity of software and hardware components that are provided by different vendors, possibly introducing risks of vulnerabilities and incompatibility. The security assurance of intracloud and intercloud data management and transfer arises as a key issue. Cloud auditing can only be effective if all operations on the data can be tracked reliably. Provenance is a process that determines the history of a data product, starting from its original sources [1]. Assured provenance data can help detect access violations within the cloud computing infrastructure. However, developing assured data provenance remains a critical issue for cloud storage applications. Besides, provenance data may contain sensitive information about the original data and the data owners. Hence, there is a need to not only secure the cloud data but also ensure integrity and trustworthiness of provenance data. State-of-the-art cloud based provenance services are vulnerable to accidental corruption or malicious forgery of provenance data [2].

Blockchain technology has attracted interest due to a shared, distributed, and fault-tolerant database through which every participant in the network can share the ability to nullify adversaries by harnessing the computational capabilities of the honest nodes; the information exchanged is resilient to manipulation. Blockchain network is a distributed public ledger where any single transaction is witnessed and verified by network nodes. Blockchain's decentralized

Blockchain for Distributed Systems Security, First Edition. Edited by Sachin S. Shetty, Charles A. Kamhoua, and Laurent L. Njilla.

architecture can be leveraged to develop an assured data provenance capability for the cloud computing environment. In a decentralized architecture, every node participates in the network for providing services, thereby providing better efficiency. Availability is also ensured because of blockchain's distributed characteristics. Since a centralized authority is frequently used in cloud services, there is a need to safeguard personal data while maintaining privacy. With blockchain-based cloud data provenance service, all data operations are transparently and permanently recorded. Thus, the trust between users and cloud service providers can easily be established. Furthermore, maintaining provenance can assist in improving the trust of cloud users toward cyber-threat information sharing [3, 4] to enable proactive cyber defense at a reduced security investment [5,6].

In this paper, we present ProvChain, a blockchain-based data provenance architecture to provide assurance of data operations in a cloud storage application, while enhancing privacy and availability at the same time. ProvChain records the operation history as provenance data that will be hashed into Merkle tree nodes [7]. A list of hashes of provenance data will constitute a Merkle tree and the tree root node will be anchored to a blockchain transaction. A list of blockchain transactions will be used to form a block and the block needs to be confirmed by a set of nodes in order to be included in the blockchain. An attempt to modify a provenance data record will require an adversary to locate the transaction and the block. Blockchain's underlying cryptographic theory will allow to modify a block record only if the adversary can present a longer chain of blocks than the rest of the miners' blockchain, which is quite difficult to achieve. By leveraging the global-scale computing power of the blockchain network, blockchain-based data provenance can provide integrity and trustworthiness. In our architecture, we keep the hashed identity of users in order to protect their privacy from the rest of the nodes in the blockchain network.

The rest of the paper is organized as follows. Section 4.2 provides an overview of state-of-the art data provenance efforts and blockchain technology. Section 4.3 describes the design of ProvChain, our blockchain-based data provenance architecture. The detailed implementation is given in Section 4.4. Performance evaluation of ProvChain is presented in Section 4.5. Finally, we conclude in Section 4.6.

4.2 Background and Related Work

4.2.1 Data Provenance

The origins of the word provenance can be traced back to the French "provenir", which means "to come from". So provenance describes the custodial chronology of an object. From an information security perspective, data provenance refers to an auditing process that maintains a record of all operations conducted on data generated by a workflow. In the context of a blockchain, data provenance can be found in the distributed public ledger that catalogs all operations on data related to an asset. The owner of an asset can authenticate a transaction and facilitate transfer to another owner without the need for an arbitrator. Data provenance in a blockchain can take advantage of capabilities such as verifiable audit trail, creation and ownership transfer of digital assets, consensus agreement, and crypto-based identities.

4.2.2 Data Provenance in the Cloud

Cloud computing environments are dynamic and heterogeneous and involve several diverse and disparate software and hardware components that are manufactured by different vendors and require interoperation. As businesses, irrespective of whether they are private or public, have been adopting cloud computing as a platform for data storage, processing, service provisioning, etc., protection of data in cloud has become the top priority for cloud providers. For many, confidentiality reigns supreme; therefore, assurance of data transfer within intracloud and intercloud environments is oftentimes a mandatory requirement. Typical assurance of data focuses on ensuring the confidentiality, integrity, and availability of the contents of the data. However, assurance of the ancestry of the data (where the data came from) is a challenge in cloud environments. Keeping track of each critical data object in the cloud environment could potential ensure confidentiality, integrity, and availability of the data content. This process, called data provenance, would record every transaction on cloud data so that their ancestry information can be derived at any time to prove their authenticity. Data provenance has the potential to prevent insider attack and network intrusion scenarios by identifying the exact sources that lead the state of data object to an abnormal state. Data provenance addresses the ancestry of the data based on detailed derivation of the data object. If true data provenance existed in the cloud for all data stored on cloud storage, distributed data computations, data exchanges and transactions, detecting insider attacks, reproducing research results, and identifying the exact source of system or network intrusions would be achievable. Unfortunately, the state of the art in data provenance in cloud does not provide such assurances and there is a need to develop techniques to address this challenge.

Data provenance is very critical for cloud computing system administrators to debug break-ins to the system or network. Cloud computing environments are typically characterized by data transfers between diverse system and network components. These data exchanges could take place within a data center or across federated data centers. The data does not usually follow the same path due to multiple copies of the data and diversity of paths taken to ensure resilience. This design adds a degree of difficulty for administrators to accurately identify the origin of the attack, what software and/or hardware components caused the attack, and the impacts of the attack. Security violations need to be identified at a fine granularity and provenance can assist. Current state of the art provenance systems in the cloud support the above tasks through logging and auditing technologies. These technologies are not effective in cloud computing systems, which are complex in nature, due to several layers of interoperating software and hardware components spread across geographical and organizational boundaries. To identify the origin, cause, and impact of security violations in cloud infrastructures, collection of forensics and logs from the diverse and disparate sources is required, which is an insurmountable task. At the same time, logs only provide a sequential history of actions related to every application. The provenance data provides the history of the origins of all changes to a data object, the list of components that have either forwarded or processed the object, and users who have viewed and/or modified the object and have enhanced requirements for assurance.

Cloud computing platforms are comprised of geographically distributed and disparate physical machines, each of which hosts one or more virtual resource (virtual machines [VM]). Each VM is owned by a cloud user and comprises an operating system, software, data, etc. An executing VM creates dynamic data that are key for provenance. As such, and in cloud computing today, provenance is provided on cloud through the linking of log data (data that is generated through the execution of software on the given physical, virtual, or application resource) and audit data (data that is created for the sole purpose of provenance assurance). Provenance in the cloud is limited. Besides the limited functionality of comparing logs to audit data, today's provenance functions are done in a private manner to establish ownership of digital assets. This, in turn, has a few limitations. First, the cost of provenance is high and prohibitive, in the sense that a provenance assurance should be established for each individual cloud service. Second, the process of provenance assurance, when multiple players are involved as is typical in cloud computing, lacks transparency. As such, moving to a more transparent, open, and public system is desirable.

Researchers have presented several data provenance related efforts. PASS is the first scheme to address the collection and maintenance of provenance data at the operation system level [8]. A file provenance system [9] is proposed to collect provenance data by intercepting file system calls below the virtual file system, which requires changes to operating systems. For cloud data provenance, S2Logger [10] was developed as an end-to-end data tracking tool that provides both file-level and block-level provenance in kernel space. In addition to data provenance techniques and tools, the security of provenance data and user privacy has also been explored. Asghar et al. [11] proposed a secure data provenance solution in the cloud, which adopts the two-folder encryption method to enhance privacy albeit at a higher computation cost. SPROVE [12] protects provenance data confidentiality and integrity using encryption and digital signature. However, SPROVE does not possess provenance data querying capability. Progger [13] is a kernel-level logging tool that can provide log tamper evidence at the expense of user privacy. There are also efforts that use provenance data for managing the cloud environment, such as discovery of usage patterns for cloud resources, popularized resource reuse, and fault management [14].

4.2.3 Blockchain

Blockchain technology has attracted tremendous interest from a wide range of stakeholders, which includes finance, healthcare, utilities, real estate, and government agencies. Blockchains are a shared, distributed, and fault-tolerant database that every participant in the network can share, but no entity can control. The technology is designed to operate in a highly contested environment against adversaries who are determined to compromise. Blockchains assume the presence of adversaries in the network and nullify adversarial strategies by harnessing the computational capabilities of the honest nodes; the information exchanged is resilient to manipulation and destruction. The reconciliation process between entities is sped up due to the absence of a trusted central authority or intermediary. Tampering with blockchains is extremely challenging due to the use of a cryptographic data structure and no reliability of secrets. Blockchain networks are fault tolerant, which allows nodes to eliminate compromised nodes. Despite this, there are several vulnerabilities that exist [15], which could potentially disrupt the integrity of the blockchain. However, it requires the malicious node to have enormous computational power to conduct attacks, which may not even be cost worthy.

The decentralization and security characteristics of blockchain have attracted researchers to develop various applications such as smart contracts, distributed DNS, and identity management. Besides Bitcoin, Ethereum [16] is also designed on top of public blockchain for simple and quick development of decentralized applications. To implement the value transmitting function and reward participants, Ethereum adopts a new type of cryptocurrency named Ether, with a value unit called Wei. Ethereum can provide the function of a smart contract, which can be supported and implemented by Solidity and other high-level languages. On blockchain networks, those contracts will be compiled into a binary format and be able to run on Ethereum Virtual Machine (EVM). The Ethereum platform adopts a per-address transaction model and each transaction is independent, which means a transaction is simply transfering assets between participating nodes.

Multichain [17] provides an open-source permissioned blockchain network, where developers can host their blockchain on a private cloud architecture. Multichain uses the per-output transaction model and can handle high throughput [18]. The per-output transaction model means each transaction's input has some relationship with the previous transaction's output. By using different addresses for the same user, this model provides a higher degree of privacy. Multicurrency is supported by Multichain so that developers can utilize different kinds of assets for different transaction types. Futher, Multichain project will add two features—blockchain messaging and database synchronization—that will definitely benefit developers and other blockchain users. By contrast, Ethereum is designed for simple and quick development of blockchain applications, which is one of the most outstanding features of the per-address transaction model. Besides, there is a great saving of space since each transaction only requires one signature, one reference, and one output.

Hyperledger [19] is an open source permissioned blockchain project hosted by The Linux Foundation, including leaders in finance, banking, the IoT, supply chain, manufacturing, and technology. Hyperledger Fabric [20] is an architecture delivering high degrees of confidentiality, resiliency, flexibility, and scalability potentials on top of the Hyperledger platform, supporting pluggable implementations of different customized components. Developers can benefit from the Fabric framework by integrating customized and desired techniques on the open platform.

Tierion [21] provides a platform for uploading and publishing data records into the Blockchain network. With public application programming interfaces (APIs) available, Tierion is convenient for integrating applications that demand the need of blockchain. Developers can post metadata using an HTTP request into the Tierion data store and fetch record information. Each data record has a record ID that can be used to retrieve the blockchain receipt generated based on blockchain transactions. The blockchain receipt contains the transaction ID, which will be used to locate a transaction and the block that hosts the transaction. In this way, the data record posted on the blockchain cannot be tampered with and integrity is assured.

The Blockstack Labs from Princeton University proposed a decentralized Public key infrastructure (PKI) service on top of Namecoin and a blockchain-based naming and storage system [22]. Blockchain application in information-centric networks for name-based security of content distribution has also been proposed [23]. Enigma is a decentralized computation platform with guaranteed privacy, which uses the blockchain network to control the network, manage access control and identity, and create a tamper-proof log of events [24]. Guardtime provides industrial-scale blockchain services using Keyless Signature Infrastructure (KSI) and secure one-way hash function, which is quantumimmune in contrast to asymmetric cryptographic algorithm (RSA) [25]. Guardtime also proposed a blockchain standard for digital identity and a protocol for authentication and digital signature that provides a simplified mechanism for revocation management and long-term validity [26].

4.2.4 Blockchain and Data Provenance

Blockchain technology provides such capability and resolves many needed functionalities and properties for effective provenance in the cloud. In essence, blockchain is a peer-to-peer ledger system, where information that constitutes provenance for physical, virtual, and application resources can be stored publicly for transparent verifiability and audit. As such, both transparency and cost effectiveness are provided, while access control and privacy for individual users of the ledger are ensured through encryption techniques, where individuals can see only parts of the ledger that are related to them. Thus, blending blockchain technology into the cloud environment can lead to achievement of the task of data provenance, where the cloud nodes implicitly create a distributed network to record provenance data in the distributed and fault-tolerant ledger that is secured with a strong cryptographic notion. This distributed ledger of the blockchain is to be updated by all the nodes in the cloud environment, but this depends on a certain rule that every node agrees upon. Designing such a consensus mechanism that ensures consistency in the blockchain is challenging.

4.3 ProvChain Architecture

ProvChain is a data provenance architecture built on a blockchain, which will provide the ability to audit data operations for cloud storage. ProvChain achieves the following four objectives.

- **Real-time cloud data provenance**—User operations are monitored in real time to collect provenance data, which will further support access control policy enforcement [27] and intrusion detection.
- **Tamper-proof environment**—Data provenance record is collected and then published to the blockchain network, which protects the provenance data. All data on the blockchain is shared among the nodes. ProvChain builds a public time-stamped log of all user operations on cloud data without the presence of a trusted third party. Every provenance entry is assigned a blockchain receipt for future validation.
- **Enhanced privacy preservation**—Data provenance record is associated with a hashed user ID to preserve privacy so that a blockchain network node cannot correlate data records associated with a specific user. A provenance auditor can access provenance data owned by the user but can never identify the true owner. Only the service provider can link each record with the owner of the record data.
- **Provenance data validation**—Data provenance record is published globally on the blockchain network, where a number of blockchain nodes provide confirmation for every block. ProvChain uses blockchain receipt to validate every provenance data entry.

To achieve the above objectives, we adopt the below methods to design ProvChain's architecture.

- Monitor user activities in real time using hooks and listeners so that every user operation on files will be collected and recorded for generating provenance data.

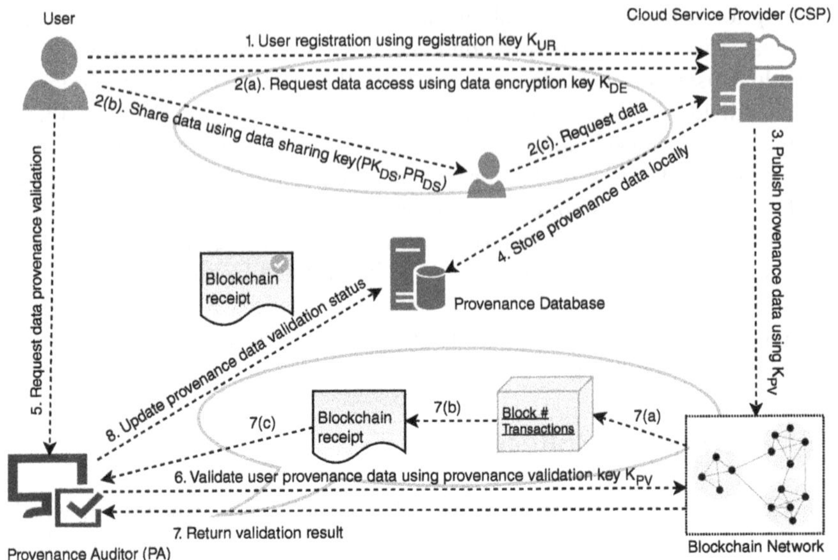

Figure 4.1 ProvChain system interaction.

- Store all hashed data operations in the form of blocks in the blockchain. Every node on the blockchain can verify the operations by mining the block so that data provenance is authentic and tamper proof.
- Hash the user ID while publishing provenance data so that the blockchain network and the provenance auditor cannot determine user identity and the data operations.
- The provenance auditor validates provenance data by retrieving transactions from the blockchain network by using the blockchain receipt that contains block and transaction information.

4.3.1 Architecture Overview

An overview of ProvChain architecture is illustrated in Figure 4.1. The following are the critical components of ProvChain:

- **Cloud user**—A user, who owns its data and has a sharing relationship with other users' data, may opt for the provenance service, where the provenance data is stored on the public blockchain. Data changes made by the user can be monitored and validated by blockchain nodes, but the nodes may not know about details of other users' activities. The provenance data will not expose real user identity.
- **Cloud Service Provider (CSP)**—The cloud service provider offers a cloud storage service and is responsible for user registration. A CSP can benefit from our system in the following aspects: First, they can audit data changes

all the time, and they can learn a lot about data operations performed by all the users to better improve their service. Through provenance data, they can also detect intrusion from anomalous behaviours. Besides, they can protect their own daily records just like normal users. As far as business aspects are concerned, they can gain brand reputation from using blockchain provenance services since they provide trustworthiness.

- **Provenance database**—The provenance database records all provenance data on the blockchain network, which is used for detecting malicious behaviors. All data records are anonymized.
- **Provenance Auditor (PA)**—The PA can retrieve all the provenance data from the blockchain, into the provenance database, and validate the blockchain receipt. The PA maintains the provenance database but cannot correlate the provenance entry to the data owner.
- **Blockchain network**—The blockchain network consists of globally participating nodes. All the provenance data will be recorded in the form of blocks and verified by blockchain nodes.

4.3.2 Preliminaries and Concepts

ProvChain uses cloud file as the data unit and monitors file operations to provide data provenance service. After each file operation is detected, a provenance entry will be generated. The cloud service provider will upload the provenance entry onto the blockchain network. In this section, we describe the details on file provenance use case and block structure.

File provenance use case—For each file provenance, we can record activities, such as file creation, file modification, file copy, file share, and file delete. A file can be created by user A, which refers to the origin of file X. Then user A copies file X to another location, probably for backup or other reasons. The read and write operation of user A on file X can also be recorded. If user B asks user A to share file X, there will also be a record both on user A and user B. User A shares file X at a predefined location and user B creates a new file Y from the shared file X. Then user B can operate on file Y just the same as user A did on file X, such as read and write operations. If user B deletes the file, there will be a record for deletion. At some point of time, user A decides to make file X public so that file access is changed. Anyone who accesses it will also create a new file at their own respective location. The history of files (different versions of the file) can be backed up for future use.

Block structure—ProvChain uses blockchain network to provide data record verification and resist tampering. The block structure is composed of two parts—a block header and a list of transactions. The main attributes in the header are block hash, height, confirmations, nonce, and Merkle root. Block hash is computed using the previous block hash and a nonce. The height represents the block index in the global blockchain network. The confirmation number of the block indicates the number of nodes that have mined this block and the nonce is used by blockchain nodes to check the integrity of the block. The Merkle root is the root of the binary hash tree created out of all the transactions in a block. Transaction lists come after the block header. Each transaction has a hash, with inputs and outputs. In ProvChain, each data record is hashed into a Merkle tree node. The Merkle tree root node will be anchored to one transaction in a certain block.

4.3.3 Threat Model

Here, we analyze the potential vulnerabilities in ProvChain. The cloud service provider offers data provenance service as well as cloud storage service, which allow users to store data on the cloud platform and provide the option to enable the data provenance service. The cloud service provider cannot guarantee that data records will remain unchanged due to known vulnerabilities in hypervisors and cloud operating systems. Once the data provenance service is enabled, the user will be able to trace the data and the PA is allowed to access all the provenance data. However, the PA cannot be completely trusted. The adversary can potentially access or modify user data and/or user provenance data. Since ProvChain's main objective is to protect provenance data, we assume that user data stored on the cloud are encrypted and are not accessible to anyone without the decryption key.

4.3.4 Key Establishment

To use ProvChain, users are required to register the service and create their credentials. For cloud storage applications, users generate data encryption key pairs to encrypt their cloud data for confidentiality. If the user wants to share a file, a data sharing key will be provided. For provenance data, the cloud service provider generates key pairs to encrypt provenance data for privacy considerations, because provenance data will further be uploaded and published to the blockchain network. We describe each key as follows:

- **User registration key K_{UR}**—In ProvChain, the user needs to register the cloud storage service to store data on the cloud. We denote the key as K_{UR}. Every time the user wants to operate on cloud data, the registration key is needed.
- **Data encryption key K_{DE}**—After registration, the user generates an encryption key K_{DE}, for encrypting all the data stored in the cloud. When a file is created, the user has the option to encrypt the file, which limits file access to only key holders.
- **Data sharing public/private key pair (PK_{DS}, PR_{DS})**—For data sharing, a public/private key pair will be generated, denoted as (PK_{DS}, PR_{DS}). For common cases, the private key is used to generate a signature from the owner, while the public key is used by others to verify data ownership. When users

share the data with others, they share the private key for data ownership changes.

- **Provenance verification key K_{PV}**—Each block on the blockchain holds several provenance data entries; and provenance data entry is produced upon detection of a file operation. Every data operation will trigger the cloud service provider to generate a key K_{PV} to encrypt the provenance data. The key will be shared with the PA if the user assigns a PA to audit the provenance data.

4.4 ProvChain Implementation

The implementation of ProvChain is conducted using a three-layer architecture, comprising of a data storage layer, a blockchain layer, and a provenance database layer, as in Figure 4.2. The functions for each layer are described as follows:

- **Data storage layer**—ProvChain is implemented to support cloud storage applications. Here we use one cloud service provider but our architecture can be scaled to multiple providers.
- **Blockchain network layer**—We use the blockchain network to record each provenance data entry. Each block can record multiple data operations. Here we use the file as a data unit, so we record each file operation with a username and file name. File access operations include Create, Share, Change, and Delete.
- **Provenance database layer**—We build an extended database locally for recording file operation as well as querying. In ProvChain, the service provider can assign a PA to verify the data from the blockchain network.

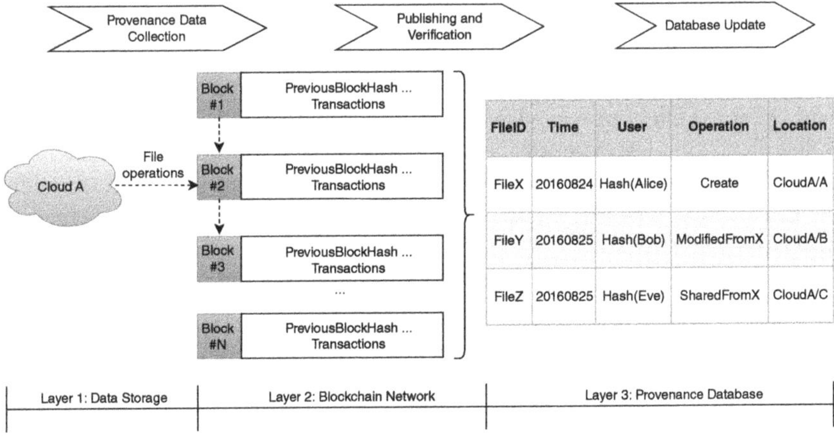

Figure 4.2 ProvChain system architecture.

The response is a blockchain receipt that gets validated and appended in the database.

There are three phases in the life cycle of data provenance for ProvChain, namely provenance data collection, provenance data storage, and provenance data validation.

4.4.1 Provenance Data Collection and Storage

Once a user performs actions on the data files stored in the cloud, the corresponding operations get recorded. The operation can be denoted in a metadata, including all the file attributes. Note that for this phase, only RecordID, Date and Time, Username, Filename, AffectedUser, and Action attributes are recorded. The transaction hash, block hash, and validation field will be collected after the PA queries the blockchain network. The AffectedUser attribute is considered in two cases. One is data modification in which the same user is operating on the data, using the data encryption key, where there are no affected users other than the user itself. The other case is data sharing, where user shares a file with someone else. In the second case, the attribute, AffectedUser, in the file operation metadata, will include all the users in the sharing group.

We build ProvChain on top of an open source application called ownCloud [28] to collect the provenance data. ownCloud is a self-hosted file synchronization and sharing server. OwnCloud provides both web-based cloud storage services and a desktop client, similar to Dropbox and Google Drive, which provide user control of personal data and universal file access to all of the data seamlessly. Besides, ownCloud is flexible and developers can utilize their functions to develop various applications on top of it, allowing authorized users to enable and disable features, set policies, create backups, and manage users. The server also manages and secures API access to ownCloud client and developers, while providing the internal processing engine needed to deliver high-performance file-sharing services.

In order to collect provenance data, we use hooks to listen to file operations in the ownCloud web interface. After an operation is monitored, a record will be generated, which is then uploaded to the blockchain network and stored in the provenance database. Figure 4.3 shows the architecture of our provenance data collection and storage.

We take the file change operation as an example to demonstrate the original provenance data in JSON format as follows:


```
{
"app":"files",
"type":"file_changed",
```

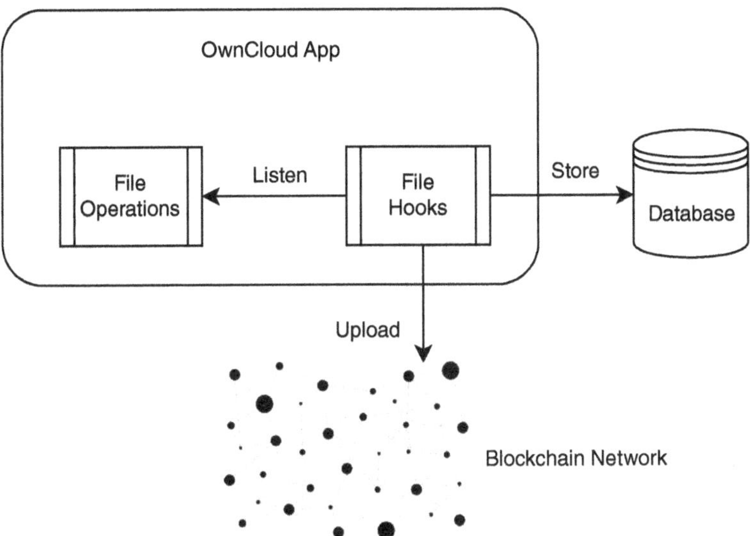

Figure 4.3 Provenance data collection and storage.

```
"affecteduser":"test",
"user":"test",
"timestamp":"1475679929",
"subject":"changed_self",
"message":"",
"messageparams":"[]",
"priority":"30",
"object_type":"files",
"object_id":"142",
"object_name":"66.txt",
"link":"/apps/files/"
}
```

For provenance data storage after data collection, we use Tierion API [21] to publish data records to the blockchain network. Tierion provides data API primarily for collecting data, and for managing Datastores and Records in a personal account. Accessing Tierion's Data API requires an API Key, which is required in every request to the Data API. The submission of credentials should contain the headers X-Username and X-Api-Key for each data store owned by the account. In addition to using the data API to create a record, we can choose the option to submit an HTML form directly to Tierion, since our ownCloud application is web based and the provenance data is coming from a web site, which is easier to implement. The following URL is used to submit a data record to the blockchain network, by the POST method:

```
https://tierion.com/form/submit
```

For privacy consideration, ProvChain hashes user name. In that case, the PA cannot know which user each provenance data belongs to. Only the service provider can relate each user with the hashed user name since the provider keeps a list of user names. ProvChain also keeps the provenance data in a local provenance database for further update and validation.

For publishing data records to the blockchain network, the Chainpoint standard [29] is adopted. Chainpoint is an open standard for creating a timestamp proof of any data, file, or series of events, which proposes a scalable protocol for publishing data records on the blockchain and generating blockchain receipts. By anchoring an unlimited amount of data to multiple blockchains and verifying the integrity and existence of data without relying on a trusted third party, the Chainpoint standard is widely used in blockchain applications. According to Chainpoint 2.0, data records are hashed so that each Merkle tree can host a large number of records, as is shown in Figure 4.4. The target hash of the specific record and the path to the Merkle root constitute the Merkle proof of the provenance data, which is a JSON-LD document that contains the information to cryptographically verify that a piece of data is anchored to a blockchain. It proves the data existed at the time it was anchored. The Merkle root for each Merkle tree is related to one transaction in the blockchain network.

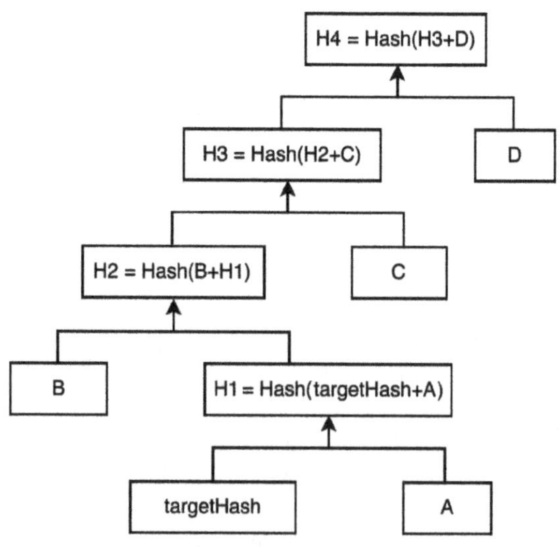

Figure 4.4 Merkle tree.

4.4.2 Provenance Data Validation

To validate the data records that are published in the blockchain network, the PA requests the blockchain receipt via Tierion API. The Data API offers a way to validate blockchain receipts. Before validating the blockchain receipt, we use Data API to request the record along with the blockchain receipt, using the following URL and the GET method:

```
https://api.tierion.com/v1/records/<id>
```

The request header should include *Content-Type: application/x-www-form-urlencoded* or *Content-Type: application/json* to set the data format to be received. The requests to the Data API are made over HTTPS. The blockchain receipt contains information of the blockchain transaction and the Merkle proof used to validate the transaction. Figure 4.5 is a sample blockchain receipt.

We can reconstruct the Merkle tree from the blockchain receipt. Each provenance record is stored along with other records in the blockchain network as a transaction, which is accessible in blockchain Block Explorer [30]. Since the transaction attribute height represents the block index, we can find the exact block information as well (Figure 4.6). To validate the format and contents of a blockchain receipt, and to confirm that the Merkle root of one record is stored in the blockchain, we use the following URL and POST method, provided by Tierion API:

```
https://api.tierion.com/v1/validatereceipt
```


```
{
 "@context": "https://w3id.org/chainpoint/v2",
 "type": "ChainpointSHA256v2",
 "targetHash": "82e46ffd212d680b3e1a169e6a8b59472985ac55398b8740832fe94fd5e5fd63",
 "merkleRoot": "9f0100055a430539796817ce626d84ccb5485453e4d558cf3353e4d4a7e59031",
 "proof": [
    {
       "right": "0f6117e8bddd7fdc713aa5365e74aafe34f5cc31fd654ed84ea37976d873c087"   A
    },
    {
       "left": "f860e7697ba57d944d925f311cce786e6d20833071d1c16e6e5fef3fc4749c96"    B
    },
    {
       "right": "de4b5b29183d193b95905ae9741a928ab056cbbbefb9a537ac9282fe180c78bd"   C
    },
    {
       "right": "e75da94bc44a3a9778b2ec7a5ffd58e4a622d4ce4c20676215eb88a4764bb335"   D
    }
  ],
 "anchors": [
    {
       "type": "BTCOpReturn",
       "sourceId": "0b956b057330591cd63c90e5572ba364c6f9f08299c3e8ee0c893411db1c30a6"
    }
  ]
}
```


Figure 4.5 Blockchain receipt.

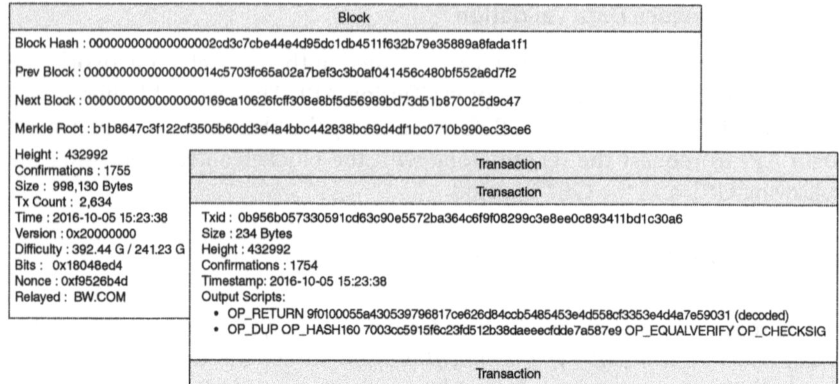

Figure 4.6 Transaction and block information.

Algorithm 1: Blockchain Receipt Validation Algorithm

Validate(proof, merkleRoot, targetHash)
    nodeNum ← number of Merkle tree nodes in *proof*
h ← *targetHash*;
i ← *0*;
while *i* < *nodeNum* **do**
    if *proof(i).key* = *right* **then**
        h ← *hash(h + proof(i).value).*
    end
    else
        h ← *hash(proof(i).value + h).*
    end
    $i \leftarrow i + 1$
end
if *h* = *merkleRoot* **then**
    return
end
true
return false

Algorithm 1 is used to validate the blockchain receipt by the PA. In the algorithm, the proof, merkleRoot, and targetHash in the blockchain receipt are inputs and the output is a validation result. If true is returned, then the data record is validated based on the fact that the transaction and block are authentic. If false is returned, it means the block has been tampered with and the data record is forged. Note that all the hashes used in building Merkle trees and proofs are handled in the binary format, according to the Chainpoint requirement. The anchors in the receipt indicate how the data record is anchored. Blockchain receipt validation confirms that a receipt's content is valid and true. Specifically, the validation process will confirm the following four elements: the receipt is a well formatted JSON document; all required fields are present; the targetHash, merkleRoot, and proof values are valid; and the merkleRoot value is anchored at the specified location(s).

After the validation of the blockchain receipt, the PA can update the data record in the provenance database by filling in the remaining attributes, including transaction hash, block hash, and validation result. If the validation result is true, then the PA can make sure that the provenance data is authentic. If the result is false, then the PA will report to the service provider that tampering has happened.

4.5 Evaluation

4.5.1 Summary of ProvChain's Capabilities

Prior to providing the performance evaluation of ProvChain, we summarize the capabilities.

- ProvChain provides a real-time auditing for all data access in the cloud storage application. We use a file as a data unit, and all the operations on the cloud data objects are audited as well as recorded using blockchain. In this way, evidence for all cloud data access events can be collected and monitored.
- For each of the access records, we transform the provenance data and upload the record to the blockchain network. By doing so, we create an unalterable fingerprint of file operations, with secure and permanent record keeping as well as a tamper-proof timestamp. Any changes to the blockchain will be detected by validating the blockchain receipt. Once the data record is published, no one can maliciously rewrite or alter the records without exposure.
- By utilizing the blockchain network, we reduce the need for trust. There is no need to trust the owner of the remote computers involved in the blockchain network, thus removing the requirement for a trusted third party. Even the cloud service provider is not trusted for keeping the provenance data record. With decentralization, data records are confirmed and validated by continual system cross checking among computing nodes. Besides, the decentralized method ensures the integrity of data records and each of the data record has a copy with each node in the blockchain network, thereby resisting any DDoS attack. Besides, there is no single point failure problem since no single machine holds all the data records.
- Users can subscribe to the data provenance service while preserving their privacy. User access records are anonymized in the blockchain network. The PA cannot learn user activities. Anonymity is preserved in two aspects. On

Table 4.1 Evaluation environment specification.

Software	Name	Version
Server operating system	Ubuntu	14.04
Web server	Apache server	2.4.6
Database	MariaDB	5.5.44
Cloud storage	OwnCloud	9.0
Performance benchmarking	Apache JMeter	3.2

one hand, user identity will not be linked to provenance data entries since the user ID is hashed. On the other hand, unlinkability between each user is also achieved, especially for provenance of shared data.

4.5.2 Performance and Overhead

The evaluation environment setup includes three categories—the server side software, the ownCloud application configuration, and a benchmarking tool. For provenance collection, we use Apache Jmeter [31] as a benchmarking tool to assess the performance of the provenance-enabled ownCloud application. The specifications of the software and the version used are listed in Table 4.1.

Apache Jmeter is an open source and Java-based software designed to test functions and behaviors on a large scale, with various performance measures such as transaction time, response time, and throughput. Web applications are the main cases where Jmeter plays an important role. Jemter uses test plans to describe a series of steps that will execute when we run the test plan. A complete test plan usually consists of one or more thread groups, logic controllers, sample generating controllers, listeners, timers, scripts, and configuration elements. Jmeter provides data analysis and visualization plugins, allowing great extensibility as well as personalization. User-defined functions can be used to provide dynamic input to a test or handle data manipulation.

We build a test plan to measure the performance of file create using both provenance-enabled ownCloud and nonprovenance ownCloud. Our test plan aims to simulate the action of a user who logsin to ownCloud and then creates a file using a filename. The simulation also uses random strings to represent the file content to be stored when the user closes the file.

The test plan contains two controllers. One is for user login and the other is for file create. When simulating user login, we use HTTP Get to request the ownCloud server at our experimental server path */owncloud/index.php/login* for a request token. Using the request token, we use HTTP POST to send the user credentials as well as the request token to the same path in exchange for the access token. Here, we use a regular expression to extract the access token from the returned HTML files. After acquiring the access token, we are able to create random files. Using HTTP POST, we can send the filename and file content at the same time to the path */owncloud/index.php/apps/files/ajax/upload.php*. The following BeanShell Preprocessor script is used to simulate the file content:

```
import org.apache.commons.io.FileUtils;
import org.apache.commons.lang3.Random
StringUtils;
import org.apache.commons.lang3.Random
Utils;
// create a temp file
File f = File.createTempFile("f-", "");
// generate random string
// and write to file
FileUtils.writeStringToFile(f,
RandomStringUtils.random(RandomUtils.
nextInt(1000, 10000)), "UTF-8");
// store file name
vars.put("fname", f.getCanonicalPath());
```

We perform file create with random file names and file contents for 500 repetitions in Jmeter [32]. The file size ranges from 1KB to 2MB. Figure 4.7 shows the average response time of both provenance-enabled ownCloud and non provenance ownCloud. From Figure 4.7, we can conclude that the provenance service brings an average of 6.49% of total overhead against the original ownCloud application in terms of the response time, which is

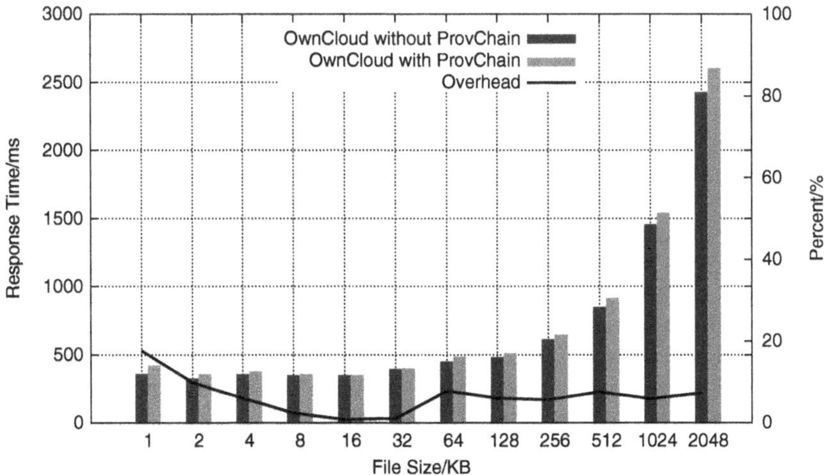

Figure 4.7 Average response time with different file size.

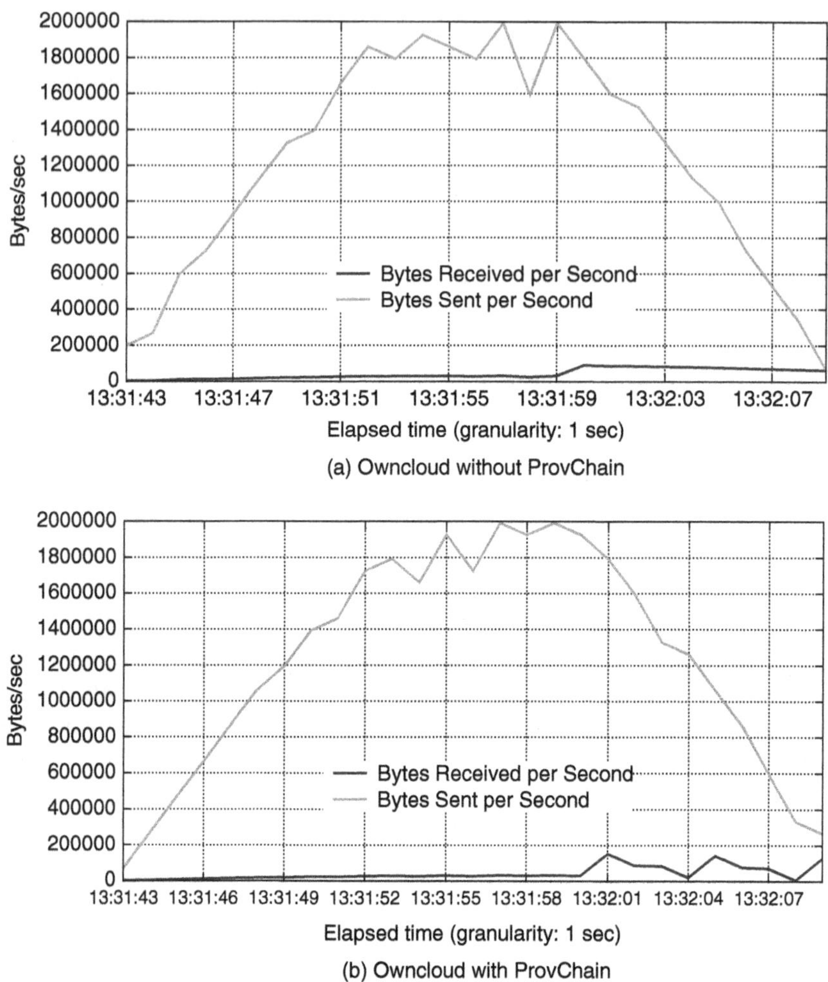

(a) Owncloud without ProvChain

(b) Owncloud with ProvChain

Figure 4.8 Bytes throughput over time.

acceptable considering the security features it provides. Besides, with the file size increases, the overhead is generally not as much as it is when the file size is smaller, since the larger the file size is, the more is the time that will be spent on transmitting the file itself and the less is the time for provenance service.

Figure 4.8 shows the throughput for both original ownCloud 4.8(a) and provenance-enabled ownCloud 4.8(b). We choose 64KB as the file size to assess the performance where only one server is responsible for the provenance service regardless of the production environment, which is comprised of a web server and services for load balancing and network flow optimization. The results show that both systems have the same amount of traffic received; however, there is a difference in the amount of traffic sent.

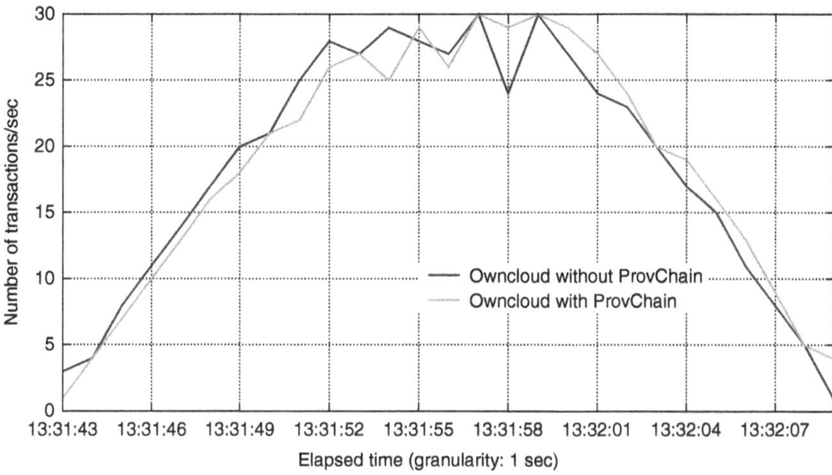

Figure 4.9 Number of transactions per second.

The provenance-enabled ownCloud has a comparable transaction rate, as depicted in Figure 4.9. Overall, the transaction time distribution is considered acceptable, as shown in Figure 4.10. More evaluations can be conducted with varying file types, operations, and file sharing statuses.

We use file create operation as a use case for our performance evaluation of provenance data collection. The evaluation for other file operations follows the same procedures.

For provenance retrieval, we focus on the efficiency of requesting blockchain receipt for each of the provenance data entries. In our experiment, we query 10 records each time with a total size of 1.004KB, which uses an average time of 221ms. For each retrieval of blockchain receipt, we record the retrieval time for different file operations. Performance test for provenance data storage follows the same way. Table 4.2 is the provenance retrieval overhead, from which we can conclude that our retrieval methods have a low overhead for the cloud storage system.

Table 4.2 Overhead for provenance data retrieval.

Record Type	Size of Data Transferred	Average Time Cost
File create	1.07KB	0.838s
File change	1.06KB	0.676s
File delete	1.07KB	0.675s
File share	1.07KB	0.790s

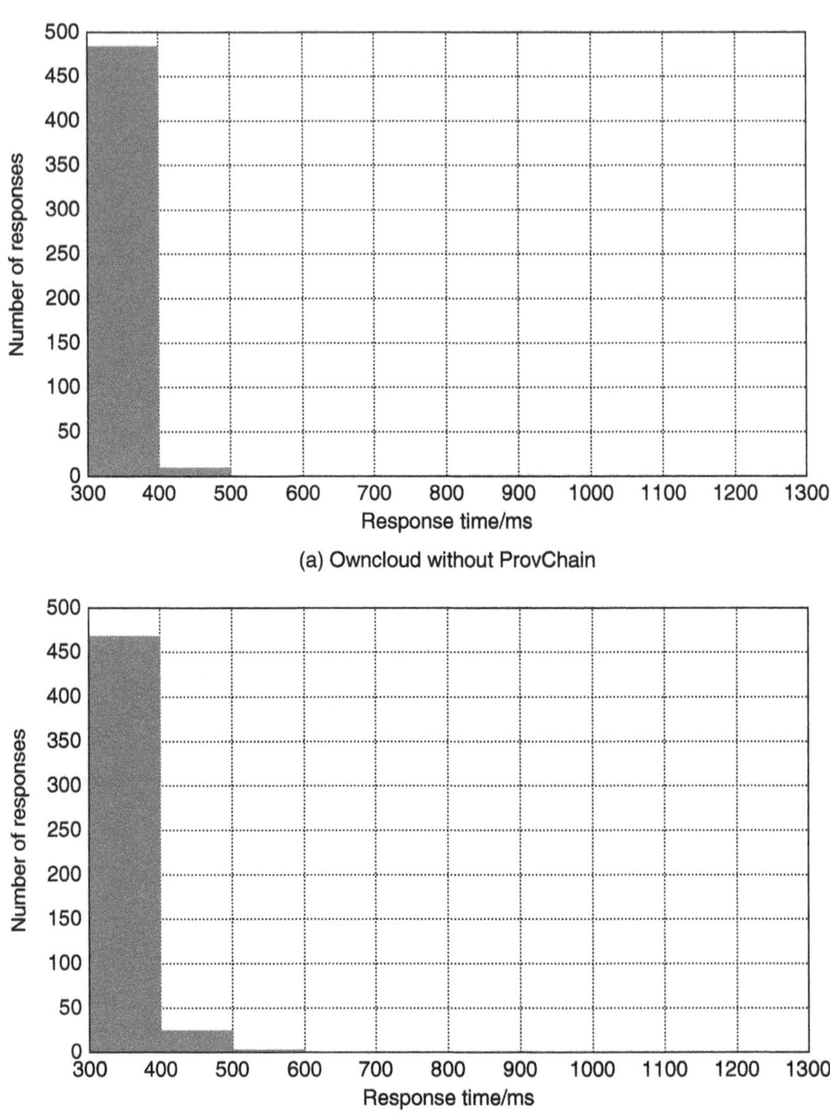

Figure 4.10 Response time distribution.

4.6 Conclusions and Future Work

In this paper, we present the design and implementation of ProvChain, a blockchain-based data provenance system for cloud auditing, with preserved user privacy and increased availability. Using blockchain technology, we make the record with unalterable timestamping and generate blockchain receipt for each of the data records for validation. With each data provenance record provided with a blockchain receipt, our system performs functions with stability and scalability. Based on the current work, we can extend the system to various use cases where globally verified proof is needed. Our evaluation of cloud storage performance shows that provenance-enabled ownCloud brings a low overhead. Instead of a file as the data unit, in the future we can also use other granularity such as data chunk in cloud storage, at a finer-grain level.

As for the rewards of blockchain miners, cloud users may have to pay a fee to enable data provenance services by a cloud service provider. The service provider can then pay for the blockchain network. In this way, miners can be paid for continuous mining on blocks and validation of block authenticity. The fee can be determined depending on the different level of data usage of each user.

Currently, we collect provenance data inside one cloud service provider and one cloud application. For future work, we plan to develop ProvChain for federated cloud service providers. Cloud storage applications on federated cloud providers will require the need to address interoperability, cross-provider data sharing, and management. We will collect data provenance across different cloud providers and different cloud storage applications to provide better provenance services and enhance data security. For provenance validation, we currently use the Tierion API to validate the blockchain receipt, which is effective and flexible regarding the way of API implementation and usage.

For future work, we will implement the validation on top of an open source architecture that will improve not only overall performance but also security and reliability. The actual cost for each blockchain receipt should be analyzed and calculated for business scenarios. We can also define the data attributes to be recorded according to client user needs to prevent sensitive information leakage, thus preserving privacy. We will use the collected provenance data to check for access control violations [33] by way of machine learning strategies. The automatically generated access control rules will better serve the purpose of malicious behavior detection and intrusion prevention, which will in return provide better protection for the cloud storage application. Meanwhile, the same architecture can be applied to IoT scenarios where large a number of mobile devices are responsible for data collection and processing.

Acknowledgment

This work is supported by Air Force Material Command award FA8750-16-0301 and Office of the Assistant Secretary of Defense for Research and Engineering (OASD [R&E]) agreement FA8750-15-2-0120.

References

1 Y. L. Simmhan, B. Plale, and D. Gannon, "A survey of data provenance in e-science," *ACM Sigmod Record*, vol. 34, no. 3, pp. 31–36, 2005.
2 B. Lee, A. Awad, and M. Awad, "Towards secure provenance in the cloud: A survey," in *2015 IEEE/ACM 8th International Conference on Utility and Cloud Computing (UCC)*, IEEE, 2015, pp. 577–582.
3 D. Tosh, S. Sengupta, C. A. Kamhoua, and K. A. Kwiat, "Establishing evolutionary game models for CYB security information Exchange (CYBEX)," *Journal of Computer and System Sciences*, vol. 98, pp. 27–52, 2018.
4 C. Kamhoua, A. Martin, D. K. Tosh, K. Kwiat, C. Heitzenrater, and S. Sengupta, "Cyber-threats information sharing in cloud computing: A game theoretic approach," in *IEEE 2nd International Conference on Cyber Security and Cloud Computing (CSCloud)*, 2015, pp. 382–389.
5 D. K. Tosh, S. Sengupta, S. Mukhopadhyay, C. Kamhoua, and K. Kwiat, "Game theoretic modeling to enforce security information sharing among firms," in *IEEE 2nd International Conference on Cyber Security and Cloud Computing (CSCloud)*, 2015, pp. 7–12.
6 D. K. Tosh, M. Molloy, S. Sengupta, C. A. Kamhoua, and K. A. Kwiat, "Cyber-investment and cyber-information exchange decision modeling," in *IEEE 7th International Symposium on Cyberspace Safety and Security*, 2015, pp. 1219–1224.
7 R. C. Merkle, "Protocols for public key cryptosystems," in *1980 IEEE Symposium on Security and Privacy*, April 1980, p. 122.
8 K.-K. Muniswamy-Reddy, D. A. Holland, U. Braun, and M. I. Seltzer, "Provenance-aware storage systems," in *USENIX Annual Technical Conference, General Track*, 2006, pp. 43–56.
9 S. Sultana and E. Bertino, "A file provenance system," in *Proceedings of the Third ACM Conference on Data and Application Security and Privacy*, ACM, 2013, pp. 153–156.
10 C. H. Suen, R. K. Ko, Y. S. Tan, P. Jagadpramana, and B. S. Lee, "S2logger: End-to-end data tracking mechanism for cloud data provenance," in *2013 12th IEEE International Conference on Trust, Security and Privacy in Computing and Communications*, IEEE, 2013, pp. 594–602.
11 M. R. Asghar, M. Ion, G. Russello, and B. Crispo, "Securing data provenance in the cloud," in *Open Problems in Network Security*. Springer, 2012, pp. 145–160.
12 R. Hasan, R. Sion, and M. Winslett, "Sprov 2.0: A highly-configurable platform-independent library for secure provenance," *ACM, CCS, Chicago, IL, USA*, 2009.
13 R. K. Ko and M. A. Will, "Progger: An efficient, tamper-evident kernel-space logger for cloud data provenance tracking," in *2014 IEEE 7th International Conference on Cloud Computing*, IEEE, 2014, pp. 881–889.

14 M. Imran and H. Hlavacs, "Applications of provenance data for cloud infrastructure," in *2012 Eighth International Conference on Semantics, Knowledge and Grids (SKG)*, IEEE, 2012, pp. 16–23.

15 D. K. Tosh, S. Shetty, X. Liang, C. Kamhoua, K. Kwiat, and L. Njilla, "Security implications of blockchain cloud with analysis of block withholding attack," in *International Symposium on Cluster, Cloud and Grid Computing*, IEEE/ACM, Madrid, 2017.

16 Ethereum, "Ethereum project." [Online]. 2018. Available: https://www.ethereum.org/.

17 G. Greenspan, "Multichain private blockchain white paper." [Online]. 2015. Available: http://www.multichain.com/download/MultiChain-White-Paper.pdf.

18 A. Sharif, "Design rationale." [Online]. 2018. Available: https://github.com/ethereum/wiki/wiki/Design-Rationale.

19 The Linux Foundation, "Hyperledger-blockchain technologies for business." [Online]. 2018. Available: https://www.hyperledger.org/.

20 C. Cachin, "Architecture of the Hyperledger blockchain fabric," in *Workshop on Distributed Cryptocurrencies and Consensus Ledgers*, 2016.

21 Tierion, "Tierion api." [Online]. Available: https://github.com/chainpoint/chainpoint-node/wiki/Chainpoint-Node-API:-How-to-Create-a-Chainpoint-Proof.

22 M. Ali, J. Nelson, R. Shea, and M. J. Freedman, "Blockstack: A global naming and storage system secured by blockchains," in *2016 USENIX Annual Technical Conference (USENIX ATC 16)*, 2016.

23 N. Fotiou and G. C. Polyzos, "Decentralized name-based security for content distribution using blockchains," in *2016 IEEE Conference on Computer Communications Workshops (INFOCOM WKSHPS)*, IEEE, 2016, pp. 415–420.

24 G. Zyskind, O. Nathan, and A. Pentland, "Enigma: Decentralized computation platform with guaranteed privacy." arXiv preprint arXiv:1506.03471. 2015.

25 A. Buldas, A. Kroonmaa, and R. Laanoja, "Keyless signatures infrastructure: How to build global distributed hash-trees," in *Nordic Conference on Secure IT Systems*. Springer, 2013, pp. 313–320.

26 A. Buldas, R. Laanoja, and A. Truu, "Efficient implementation of keyless signatures with hash sequence authentication." [Online]. IACR Cryptology ePrint Archive, vol. 2014, p. 689, 2014. Available: https://eprint.iacr.org/2014/689.pdf.

27 D. Nguyen, J. Park, and R. Sandhu, "Dependency path patterns as the foundation of access control in provenance-aware systems." [Online]. *TaPP*, 2012. Available: https://www.usenix.org/system/files/conference/tapp12/tapp12-final23.pdf.

28 ownCloud, "ownCloud." [Online]. 2018. Available: https://owncloud.org/.

29 Chainpoint, "Chainpoint: A scalable protocol for anchoring data in the blockchain and generating blockchain receipts." [Online]. 2018. Available: http://www.chainpoint.org/.

30 BTC.com, "Bitcoin block explorer." [Online]. 2018. Available: https://btc.com/.

31 Apache Software Foundation, "Apache JMeter." [Online]. 2018. Available: jmeter.apache.org/.

32 ownCloud, "ownCloud enterprise edition on IBM elastic storage server: A performance and sizing study for large user number scenarios." [Online]. March 10, 2016. Available: https://www.slideshare.net/ownCloud/own-cloud-on-ibm-infrastructure.

33 T. Ma, H. Wang, J. Cao, J. Yong, and Y. Zhao, "Access control management with provenance in healthcare environments," in *2016 IEEE 20th International Conference on Computer Supported Cooperative Work in Design (CSCWD)*, IEEE, 2016, pp. 545–550.

5

A Blockchain-based Solution to Automotive Security and Privacy

Ali Dorri,[1] Marco Steger,[2] Salil S. Kanhere,[1] and Raja Jurdak[3]

[1] *University of New South Wales, Sydney, Australia*
[2] *Virtual Vehicle Research Center, Graz, Styria, Austria*
[3] *Commonwealth Scientific and Industrial Research Organisation Data61, Brisbane, Australia*

5.1 Introduction

Smart vehicles use wireless communication networks to connect to the roadside infrastructure and traffic management systems, to other vehicles in close proximity, and, more generally, to the Internet. Thus, connected vehicles are becoming an essential part of the Internet of Things (IoT), and offer a plethora of beneficial services and applications to the drivers, vehicle manufacturers (i.e. OEM), service centers, insurance companies, and to a wide range of other Service Providers (SP). Alongside the benefits of highly connected vehicles is their increased vulnerability to a new range of security threats as well as serious privacy concerns.

Malicious entities can compromise a vehicle, which endangers not only the security of the vehicle but also the safety of the passengers and even other road users. In [1], the authors presented a sophisticated attack on a Jeep Cherokee using the wireless interface of the infotainment system. In the worst case, this attack allowed an attacker to remotely control the core functions of the vehicle such as steering and braking.

Smart connected vehicles are equipped with a number of sensors and devices (such as Global Positioning System [GPS]), dashboard cameras, and Light Detection and Ranging [LIDAR]), allowing better perception of the environment and facilitating independent decision making to avert accidents. Resulting from this wide range of devices, a smart vehicle will produce a large volume of data, which is predicted to be up to 4 TB per day [2]. This data can be used by smart urban infrastructure to offer services, e.g. available parking spots or green light assistance. However, this data, which is exchanged

Blockchain for Distributed Systems Security, First Edition. Edited by Sachin S. Shetty, Charles A. Kamhoua, and Laurent L. Njilla.

with other vehicles, and the infrastructure may contain privacy sensitive information about the vehicle owner, e.g. the location of the vehicle. This could be construed as a serious breach of personal privacy.

Conventional security and privacy methods used in smart vehicles tend to be ineffective due to the following challenges:

- **Centralization**—Conventional smart vehicle architectures rely on centralized brokered communication models where all vehicles are identified, authenticated, authorized, and connected through central cloud servers. This model is unlikely to scale when a large number of vehicles are connected. Additionally, the cloud servers will remain a bottleneck and a single point of failure that can disrupt the entire network.
- **Lack of privacy**—Most of the current secure communication architectures either do not consider the user's privacy, e.g. they resort to exchanging all data of the vehicle without the owner's permission, or reveal noisy or summarized data to the requester. However, in several smart vehicle applications, the requester needs precise vehicle data to provide personalized services.
- **Safety threats**—Smart vehicles have an increasing number of autonomous driving functions. A malfunction due to a security breach (e.g. by installing malicious software) could lead to serious accidents, thereby endangering the safety of the passengers and also of other road users in close proximity.

Blockchain (BC), an immutable, auditable, and timestamped ledger of blocks, has attracted tremendous attention from academia and practitioners as a distributed, private, and secure solution to tackle the aforementioned challenges in the automotive domain. In BC, the basic communication primitive between participants is known as a *transaction*. All transactions are broadcast in the network and verified by all participating nodes, thus eliminating the need for central brokers. Particular nodes, known as miners, choose to form blocks consisting of newly generated transactions and append blocks to the BC, a process known as mining, by solving a computationally demanding, hard-to-solve, and easy-to-verify puzzle. This puzzle underpins a trustless consensus algorithm among untrusted nodes. The computation resources required to participate in the consensus algorithm are typically large. This limits the number of blocks that each miner can mine and thus offers protection against malicious mining of blocks. Solving the puzzle involves a process that introduces randomness among miners, thus increasing the BC security. Two widely used consensus algorithms in BC are (i) Proof of Work (POW), which demands high computational resources to solve the puzzle [3], and (ii) Proof of Stake (POS), which demands both computational and memory resources to solve the cryptographic puzzle [4]. The blockchain is formed by linking together timestamped blocks. Each block includes the hash of the previous block in the ledger. Any modifications to a block (and its transactions) can be readily detected as the hash maintained in the subsequent block will differ. This inherent immutability offered by blockchains is a highly desirable property.

BC users employ a changeable Public Key (PK) as their identity, which offers some degree of anonymity, and thus helps in protecting the user's privacy. Storing all transactions in the ledger in an immutable manner provides the ability to audit any transaction at a later time. BC was first introduced in a cryptocurrency known as Bitcoin and since then has been widely used in other cryptocurrencies known as altcoins [5]. Despite its advantages, the existing instantiations of BC cannot be readily adopted in the automotive industry due to the following reasons:

Scalability and overhead—All new transactions and blocks are broadcast to and verified by all participating nodes in BC. The broadcast traffic and processing overhead would increase quadratically with the number of nodes in the network, which limits BC scalability. Verifying all new blocks and transactions is far beyond the capabilities of smart connected vehicles due to limited bandwidth and processing resources.

Complex consensus algorithms—The consensus algorithms employed in traditional BC systems (POW or POS) require significant computational resources, which are far beyond the capabilities of smart connected vehicles.

Latency—Mining and verifying a transaction is associated with a nontrivial delay, e.g. 30 minutes in Bitcoin. However, smart connected vehicles have stricter delay requirements, e.g. the vehicles in close proximity should not wait for several minutes to receive transactions, which may contain congestion information from other vehicles.

Throughput—BC throughput is defined as the number of transactions that can be mined per second. Conventional BC instantiations have limited throughput. For example, Bitcoin throughput is 7 transactions per second. However, smart connected vehicles will generate a large number of transactions to communicate with close-proximity vehicles, roadside infrastructure, and SPs that offer personalized services, thus requiring higher throughput.

In this chapter, we present a BC-based framework to address the outlined security and privacy challenges in smart vehicles. To reduce the associated overhead of conventional BCs, we base our framework on our previously designed BC instantiation known as Lightweight Scalable BC (LSB) [6]. Smart vehicles, OEMs, roadside infrastructure, service centers, and SPs jointly form an overlay network where they can exchange transactions, i.e. communicate. To ensure scalability, the overlay participants are clustered and only selected nodes known as Cluster Heads (CHs) perform the core BC functions. New transactions and blocks are broadcast to and verified by these CHs. CHs collate new transactions and form blocks by following a lightweight consensus algorithm, thus reducing the processing overhead and delay in mining new blocks. Privacy-sensitive data, e.g. location traces, of each vehicle are stored in an in-vehicle storage unit, which further enhances the user's privacy. After defining our framework, we discuss multiple applications, including wireless remote software updates, flexible insurance, charging of electric vehicles, and car sharing.

The rest of the chapter is organized as follows. An introduction to Blockchain is provided in Section 5.2. Details of the proposed framework are outlined in Section 5.3. Section 5.4 presents multiple applications of the proposed framework. Detailed security analysis and performance evaluations are presented in Section 5.5. Section 5.6 discusses related work, and finally Section 5.7 concludes the chapter.

5.2 An Introduction to Blockchain

This section presents a brief overview of BC and outlines details of LSB. As outlined in Section 5.1, in BC the basic communication primitive between participants is known as a transaction. The basic structure of a transaction in BC is represented below:

$$T_{\mathrm{ID}}||P.T_{\mathrm{ID}}||Input||Output||PK||Sign$$

Depending on the BC instantiation, the transactions can have additional fields. T_{ID} represents the unique identifier of the transaction, which is the hash of all other fields of the transaction. $P.T_{ID}$ refers to the ID of the previous transaction of the same node (or entity), which forms a ledger of transactions of the same node. Each user requires a *genesis transaction*, which serves as the first transaction in the ledger to which subsequent transactions can be chained. The process of creating the genesis transaction depends on the BC instantiation. There may exist dependences between transactions whereby certain fields generated in one transaction (outputs) are referenced as inputs in another transaction. The inputs and outputs are stored in the *Input* and *Output* fields, respectively. Recall that in BC, each node is known by a PK. Participating nodes might decide to change their PK for each transaction that they create as a way to increase anonymity, and thus enhance their privacy. The hash of this PK is stored in the PK field. Storing the hash of the PK reduces the size of the transaction and secures the transaction against possible future attacks where malicious nodes reconstruct the private key associated with the PK. Finally, the *Sign* field contains the signature of the transaction generator, created using the private key corresponding to the PK.

New transactions are broadcast to the network. Each miner verifies every received transaction and adds it to a pending pool of transactions, i.e. received transactions that are not yet mined in the BC. To verify a transaction, first the miner validates the embedded signature using the corresponding private key. Next, the miner checks whether the $P.T_{ID}$ exists in the BC. Once the number of pending transactions equals a predefined *block size*, the miner collates them to form a block. The miner generates a Merkle tree [7] by recursively hashing the constituted transactions of the block, which are stored as the leaves of the tree, as shown in Figure 5.1. The root of the Merkle tree is stored in the block

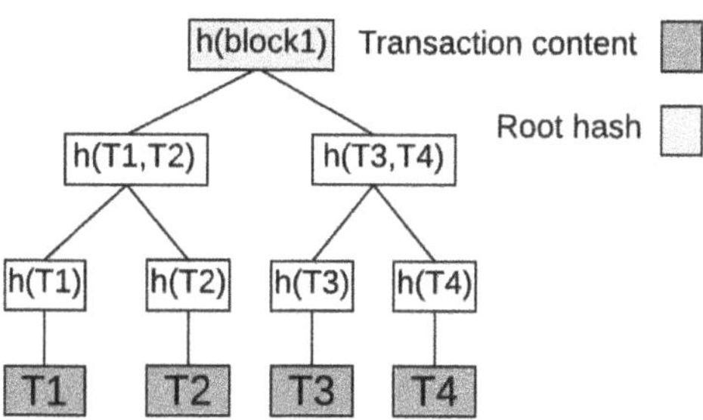

Figure 5.1 The structure of a Merkle tree.

header to speed up the process of verifying the membership of a transaction in the block. A key feature of the Merkle tree is that the existence (or not) of a leaf can be checked with a small overhead. As an illustrative example, to prove the existence of 'T1' in the Merkle tree shown in Figure 5.1, one must store *h(T2)* and *h(T3,T4)* locally. To verify T1's existence, *h(T1)* is hashed with *h(T2)*, and the result is then hashed with *h(T3,T4)*. If the final hash equals *h(block1)*, then the existence of 'T1' is proved.

The miner appends the block into the BC by following a consensus algorithm, as outlined earlier in Section 5.1. The mined block is broadcast to all nodes. Each node appends the new block to its local copy of the BC after validating all constituent transactions.

As outlined in Section 5.1, the existing BC instantiations have limitations including high (processing and packet) overhead and low scalability and throughput. To address these challenges, we employ our previously designed BC instantiation known as LSB [6], which is optimized for the IoT and large-scale low-resource networks. LSB introduces a Distributed Time-based Consensus (DTC) algorithm that replaces the demand for solving a computational puzzle with a scheduled block generation process, thus eliminating the significant processing overhead of conventional consensus algorithms. Each miner is permitted to store one block during a specific time period known as *consensus_period*. To decrease the number of duplicate blocks resulting from simultaneously mined blocks, each miner waits for a random *waiting_time* prior to storing the block in the BC. To address the scalability challenge, LSB clusters the network and only the CHs manage the BC by verifying new transactions and forming blocks. LSB dynamically adjusts the throughput using a Distributed Throughput Management (DTM) method to ensure that the BC throughput does not significantly deviate from the transaction load generated by the nodes in the network. To achieve this, the CHs first try to adjust the consensus_period, and if the consensus_period hits the predefined thresholds, then the network is reclustered to change the number of CHs. The latter incurs significantly higher overhead compared to the former as it requires reconfiguration of the overlay network; thus, CHs prioritize the former. DTM ensures that LSB is self-scaling,

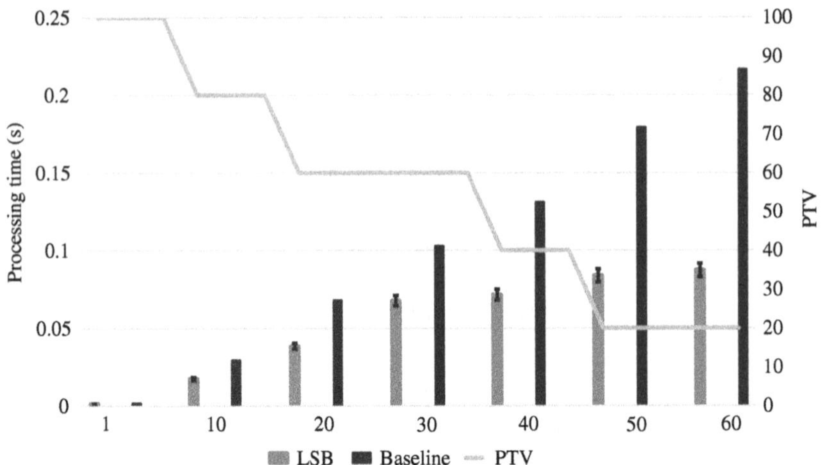

Figure 5.2 An evaluation of the processing time for validating new blocks [6].

meaning that as the number of transactions increases, the BC throughput will also increase.

In conventional BCs, all transactions of a new block must be validated by all participating nodes that receive the block, which incurs significant processing overhead on the miners. To reduce the associated overhead, LSB uses a distributed trust algorithm that gradually reduces the number of transactions that need to be verified in each new block as CHs build up trust in one another. Each CH maintains a list that records the total number of validated blocks that other CHs have generated. As shown in Figure 5.2, as more blocks are stored in BC, the Percentage of Transactions to be Verified (PTV) decreases. Thus, the processing time for validating new blocks in LSB is significantly lower compared to Bitcoin BC, which always validates every transaction in a block. This is also supported by the simulation results presented in Figure 5.2. The processing time of LSB for 60 blocks is roughly half of that of conventional BCs. In LSB, the data of IoT devices is stored off-the-chain, i.e. in local or cloud storage, and only the hash of the data is stored in the BC, which reduces the BC memory footprint as well as the packet overhead on the network. LSB creates a clear distinction between data and transaction flows. Data packets are routed in the overlay toward destination using conventional routing protocols, e.g. Open Shortest Path First (OSPF), while transactions are broadcast in the network.

Nodes use transactions to communicate with other nodes in the overlay. In LSB, there are two types of transactions based on the number of signatures that must be validated:

- **Single signature**—A single signature transaction requires one signature, which is the signature of the transaction generator, to be considered valid.

The structure of this type of transaction is similar to that of conventional BC transactions; however, there is no input/output field in the transactions. Thus, the single signature transaction can be shown as follows:

$$T_{ID}||P.T_{ID}||PK||Sign$$

- **Multisig**—A multisig transaction requires two signatures, which are the signatures of the transaction generator and recipient, to be considered valid. The structure of this transaction is as follows:

  $$T_{ID}||P.T_{ID}||PK.1||Sig.1||PK.2||Sig.2$$

  The first two fields are as discussed in the beginning of Section 5.2. The subsequent fields contain the PK and signatures (Sign) of the transaction generator and recipient, respectively.

All transactions are broadcast to all CHs. A multisig transaction that arrives at the CH may not be valid as it may not yet have been signed by the recipient, particularly when the recipient belongs to the cluster of that CH. Each CH maintains a list of PK pairs (essentially an access control list), which identifies the nodes that are allowed to communicated with each other. The cluster members (i.e. the overlay nodes) upload key pairs to the key list of their CH to allow other overlay nodes to access them. If the CH finds a PK pair in its list that matches with the PKs in the transaction (PK.1/PK.2), then it forwards the transaction to the corresponding node that uploaded the key pair. Otherwise, the transaction is broadcast to other CHs.

5.3 The Proposed Framework

In this section, we discuss the details of the proposed BC-based architecture for automotive security and privacy. We use LSB as the underlying BC due to its salient features, outlined in Section 5.2. This design is based on our previous architectures proposed in [8, 9].

The proposed BC-based architecture is comprised of the following entities: smart vehicles, roadside infrastructure, SPs, OEMs, service centers, cloud storage providers, and mobile devices of the users such as smart phones, laptops, or tablets. The vehicles are connected to the overlay by utilizing a Wireless Vehicle Interface (WVI). Recall from Section 5.2 that only the CHs manage the BC by adding new blocks and verifying new transactions and blocks. Thus, the CHs must be selected from participants with low mobility and high resource availability, e.g. OEMs, software providers, and roadside infrastructure. Figure 5.3 shows an example of an overlay network.

Each vehicle is equipped with an in-vehicle storage unit, e.g. a portable backup drive, that is used to store privacy-sensitive data, e.g. location and maintenance history, to protect the privacy of the user. The vehicle shares such

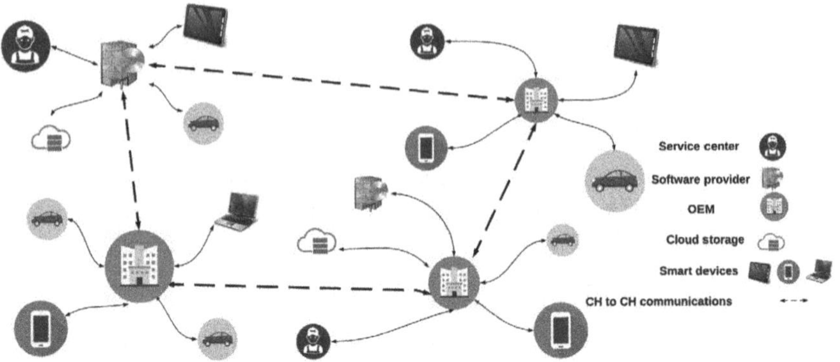

Figure 5.3 An overview of the proposed method.

privacy-sensitive data with SPs only in case of necessity; e.g. in the event of an accident, the vehicle may share data with the insurance company. Meanwhile, the SP needs to ensure that the data has not been changed since generation. To address this challenge, the vehicle generates single signature transactions in predefined time intervals containing the signed hash of the data stored in the in-vehicle storage unit during the corresponding time interval. The vehicle then sends the transaction to its CH to be stored in the BC. Utilizing this transaction, other participants in the BC can trust the data source (i.e. the vehicle creating the data). As the in-vehicle storage has limited capacity, a back-up storage can be considered in the smart home of the vehicle owner. The vehicle periodically transfers data from the in-vehicle storage unit to the backup storage. In this instance, the hash of the backup storage is stored in the BC.

Recall that in BC, each node is known by a changeable PK. Changing the PK for each transaction introduces some level of anonymity, thus enhancing user privacy. However, in some instances, other participating nodes may need to know the real-world identity of a PK owner; e.g. the vehicles must identify the owner of transactions introducing a new software update. To address this challenge, the participating nodes whose identity must be known, including OEMs, insurance companies, and cloud storage, use third party Certificate Authorities (CAs) to certify their PK. Other participating nodes can verify the CA's certificate to confirm the identity of these nodes. Note that we rely on a centralized approach, i.e. the existing public key infrastructure for this aspect of identity verification. However, the rest of the functionality is achieved by our proposed distributed architecture. It is worth noting that the aforementioned nodes can also use changeable PKs for transactions where their identity is to be kept private.

Recall that participating nodes send and receive transactions through their CH. The mobility of the vehicles causes extended delays in receiving responses from their CH due to increased communication delays. To address this challenge, we propose a solution based on the soft handover method [10].

Moving vehicles measure the communication delay with multiple CHs in their neighborhood. The CH with the lowest delay is selected as the new CH. Then, the vehicle updates the key list in this new CH with a set of key pairs that allows other nodes to send transactions to this vehicle. Finally, the vehicle clears the entries within the key list of the previous CH for the vehicle, and thus disconnects from that CH. The vehicle experiences no delay or interruption in receiving transactions from the overlay as all transactions are broadcast to all participating nodes in BC; thus, the new CH will receive the transactions of the new vehicle. As the vehicle has updated the key list of the new CH, the CH will forward transactions to the vehicle. In case the vehicle fails to find a suitable new CH, e.g. if the CHs are sparsely distributed, the vehicle remains associated with the original CH.

5.4 Applications

In this section, we discuss various applications that can leverage the proposed architecture.

5.4.1 Remote Software Updates

The process of upgrading the functionality of Electronic Control Units (ECUs) of a vehicle, or fixing a bug in the software installed on one of the ECUs requires a software update where the currently installed software is replaced by a new software version. Traditionally, such updates are performed in local environments, such as service centers, using wired connections between the vehicle and a dedicated diagnostic device. However, in the future, Wireless Software Update (WSU) systems will see increased adoption. WSU will thereby provide efficient update mechanisms within the entire lifecycle of a vehicle—in the vehicle development and assembly phase, as well as for maintenance of the vehicle in a service center. The automotive industry is investigating Wireless Remote Software Update (WRSU), where the software update is performed while the vehicle is out in the field. Securing WRSU is one of the most critical challenges in the automotive domain, as it requires full access to the vehicle and its ECUs. The current security architectures are centralized, e.g. Tesla utilizes a VPN to perform remote software updates, which would not necessarily scale for a very large number of vehicles. Furthermore, these architectures do not address the privacy issues outlined in Section 5.1. Thus, WRSU demands a distributed security method while maintaining the vehicle owner's privacy.

The entire software update process based on our architecture is sketched in Figure 5.4 and described below. Each OEM uses a cloud storage to store new available software, and uses this storage to start the software distribution step. An account is created in the cloud storage for each vehicle by the OEM, and the account is associated with a public/private key pair. The keys are used to authorize and authenticate nodes that request to download the software update.

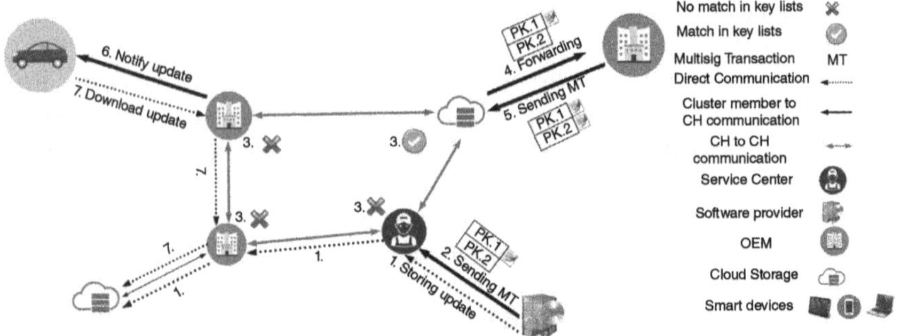

Figure 5.4 WRSU process utilizing the BC architecture.

First, the software provider, which can be a specific department of the OEM or a supplier providing the ECU with the embedded software, creates a new software version and stores it in the cloud storage provided by the OEM (step 1 in Figure 5.4). Then, the software provider creates a multisig transaction (Section 5.2) and populates its own PK in the PK.1 field. The signed hash of the stored software binary in the cloud is added to the Sig.1 field. As the binary is stored in the cloud, the hash can be verified by other overlay nodes, thereby ensuring data integrity. Following this, the software provider populates the PK of the OEM in the PK.2 field. Recall that CHs use a key list to decide on how to forward a transaction. The software provider sends the resulting multisig transaction to its CH (step 2).

CHs broadcast the transaction (step 3). The CH of the cluster containing the concerned OEM finds the match in its key list and thus forwards the transaction to the OEM (step 4). The OEM verifies the new software version and signs the received transaction, by populating the Sig.2 field. The OEM sends the transaction to its CH (step 5), which is then broadcast to all CHs. The CHs verify the multisig transaction by checking the signature of both the software provider and the OEM using the PKs included in the transaction. Next, the CHs notify their cluster members, i.e. vehicles, about the latest available software update (step 6).

On receiving the transaction from the CH, the smart vehicle verifies it by ensuring that the PK.2 field in the transaction equates with the PK of its OEM. The vehicle subsequently downloads the software directly from the cloud storage (step 7). Recall that each vehicle has a public/private key pair to authenticate itself to the cloud. Next, the vehicle verifies the integrity of the downloaded binary by comparing the signed hash of the software binary in the received transaction, from the OEM and software provider, with the hash of the downloaded version. This ensures integrity during WRSU.

Using the outlined steps enhances the security and privacy of WRSU. We will further elaborate on security and performance of the WRSU using our framework in Section 5.5.

5.4.2 Insurance

Insurance companies are beginning to use vehicular data (e.g. braking patterns and speed) collected by in-vehicle systems or an additional device such as an OBD (i.e. On-board Diagnostics) dongle connected to the vehicle, to record driving behavior. This information is then used for a flexible insurance rate scheme where responsible and hence safe drivers pay less than others. These Pay As You Drive (PAYD) approaches can be beneficial for both the insurance company as well as the driver. In this subsection, we discuss the suitability and advantages of our architecture for the PAYD application.

To be able to communicate with the insurance company, the vehicle requires a PK. This PK must be known by the insurance company so that the company can associate the received data or transactions with the particular customer to offer a flexible insurance. Once the customer chooses such a PAYD model, the insurance company creates a public/private key pair for the car along with an account in a cloud storage. The cloud storage account is used by the vehicle to store data, as storing data in the BC incurs huge packet overhead. The vehicle uses the key pair to secure communications with the insurance company. Using the PK in each transaction, the insurance company can identify the real identity of each account holder.

The data sent by the vehicle may contain privacy-sensitive data, e.g. the location of the vehicle. This may compromise the privacy of the vehicle owner as the insurance company knows the real identity associated with each key pair. In the proposed architecture, such privacy-sensitive data is stored in the in-vehicle storage unit and is not sent to the cloud to enhance the privacy of the customer. When privacy-sensitive data is requested by the insurance company, e.g. when an accident happens, the vehicle sends the data stored in the in-vehicle storage unit to the insurance company to file an accident claim. Recall that the signed hash of the in-vehicle storage unit is periodically stored in the BC. This hash can be used by the insurance company to ensure that the data has not been modified since the time when the hash is stored in BC.

At the end of the contract period or if the vehicle owner discontinues his/her contract, the insurance company marks the associated keys, used for authentication and authorization, of the vehicle in the cloud as expired. Consequently, further requests by the vehicle either for receiving personalized services or to store data in the cloud storage are denied.

5.4.3 Electric Vehicles and Smart Charging Services

The number of electric vehicles is constantly growing due to their noticeable advantages, including reduced environmental footprint. Thus, there is a growing trend in the demand for fast and efficient charging infrastructure. The charging infrastructure may endanger the privacy of the vehicle owner as one may track the frequency and the locations where the user charges his/her vehicle to build a profile of the user's activities. The vehicles can be interconnected with the mobile devices of the vehicle owner and more generally to the IoT to offer sophisticated services to the user. For example, the charging process can become more personalized if information about the travel habits of the user are made available (e.g. through their calendar). This information can be used to guarantee that the vehicle is fully charged when the user needs it. By interconnecting with the smart grid, the vehicles can not only be charged by avoiding peak load times and thus with cheapest price, but can also sell the excess energy with the highest price to increase user profit. However, ensuring the privacy of the user is highly challenging.

Using the proposed architecture, the vehicles can communicate with other participants, including IoT devices, the smart home of the user, and the smart grid, in a secure and private manner. The user may employ multiple PKs to enhance its privacy in the BC. Existing cryptocurrencies, e.g. Bitcoin, can be used along with our architecture to pay the charging fee. This protects the privacy of the user as there is no link between the current and the previous payments of the user. To ensure user control over the exchanged data, the user (i.e. the vehicle owner) defines which information can be shared between his/her vehicle and other participants in the BC.

5.4.4 Car-sharing Services

Car-sharing services such as Car Next Door [11] are growing rapidly. These services require the interconnection of smart vehicles, car-sharing SPs, and the users of the services in a secure, private, and reliable way. The exchanged data between these parties include privacy sensitive data, e.g. the location of the vehicle, and confidential data, e.g. the keys to unlock the car and payment details of the user.

Using the proposed architecture, multiple participants can communicate or exchange messages or data in a secure, private manner. For example, the car sharing SP can share the location of the vehicle with the user and authorize the user to unlock the vehicle. All interactions between the participants are stored (i.e. logged) in BC in an immutable manner, making the BC a trusted party to solve disputes between the participants. For example, consider a situation when the user is unable to unlock the vehicle for the period he/she booked the car as the SP has not yet shared the key or shared a wrong key. The user can request a refund of his/her money and BC can serve as the trusted evidence that the user was unable to unlock the vehicle.

5.4.5 Supply Chain

Sustainable Supply Chain Management (SSCM) for smart connected vehicles has received significant attention from consumers, OEMs, and governments as it considers three important dimensions of sustainable development, namely economic, environmental, and social [12]. The consumers are increasingly demanding that the parts installed on their vehicle be genuine to ensure their safety. The OEMs purchase raw materials, parts, or sensors and devices installed on smart vehicles from other manufacturers or suppliers distributed around the globe. A supplier may supply parts or raw material for more than one OEM and vice versa. The OEMs collaborate with each other or suppliers to reduce the final cost of a vehicle. As outlined by the authors in [13], the supply chain of smart vehicles should also consider vehicle recycling as some parts of the vehicle can be reused to prevent environmental hazards.

The supply chain contains privacy-sensitive information about the participants, e.g. the total number of parts produced by a supplier. Some information in the supply chain, e.g. the type of devices installed in a vehicle, have to remain confidential as an attacker might attempt to break into a vehicle by using the vulnerabilities of the installed parts or devices. Thus, it is important to consider privacy and security in supply chain solutions for smart connected vehicles.

The proposed BC-based framework has the potential to serve as a secure, trusted, private, and distributed solution to SSCM. All involved parties in the vehicle supply chain join the distributed BC and store all their communications in the BC. The provider of raw materials or parts creates a ledger for each material/part that is used to record all trade history of that material/part. As all transactions are stored in the BC, all participants, including consumers, can check whether the parts they purchased are genuine using the PK of the supplier. The latter is known to the BC participants using CA. By employing existing cryptocurrencies along with our architecture, the participants can trade distributedly, and thus eliminate the demand for central banks.

5.4.6 Liability

As the vehicles are being increasingly connected to other vehicles and roadside infrastructure as well as the Internet, identifying the party that should be blamed for an accident is getting more complicated. This issue is highly critical for insurance companies to pay the compensation and is referred to as the *liability* challenge in the literature. Liability can be attributed to different parties, e.g. the OEM if the accident happens when the vehicle is in autonomous mode, the software provider when the software program is deemed to have led to an accident, or the service center when the accident happens due to the action that the service technician conducted on the vehicle. The authors in [14] outlined six fundamental requirements for liability frameworks in smart connected vehicles, namely evidence integrity, secure storage, nonrepudiation, decentralization, authorization, and privacy. Due to its salient features, BC can serve as an effective solution to address the outlined challenges in liability.

Recall that in the proposed framework, all interactions between participants are stored in the BC as transactions. The stored transactions are immutable, so any change to the transactions can be readily detected. Thus, the proposed framework can serve as a trusted party to facilitate the collection of comprehensive evidence for making liability decisions. The collected evidence includes interactions between the vehicle and other parties. The stored transactions might also contain the hash of the exchanged data between parties; thus, modifications to data can also be readily detected.

5.5 Evaluation and Discussion

In this section, we provide qualitative discussions on the security and privacy of the proposed framework as well as qualitative performance evaluations.

5.5.1 Security and Privacy Analysis

This section provides an analysis of the security and privacy of the proposed framework.

Privacy—In the proposed method, each participating node employs a PK as its identity, which introduces some level of anonymity and thus enhances user privacy. An attacker might attempt to deanonymize a user by either tracking multiple identities of a user and linking them together or monitoring the frequency with which the transactions are generated. This attack is known as a linking attack in the literature. In the proposed framework, each user employs a fresh PK for communicating with different parties in the network. Each participant can have multiple ledgers in the BC, enabling them to have PKs that are known by the transaction receiver. This reduces the chance of a successful linking attack and thus enhances user privacy.

The vehicles generate privacy-sensitive data, e.g. the vehicle location. To enhance the privacy of the vehicle owner, in the proposed framework, such privacy-sensitive data are stored in an in-vehicle data storage unit. The hash of the data is stored periodically in the BC; thus, other parties can trust that the data received by the vehicle is not modified by matching the hash of the received data with the hash of the stored transaction in the BC.

Each vehicle is equipped with a wide range of sensors and devices that collect data from the vehicle. These devices exchange the produced data with multiple parties to receive service. To ensure user privacy, the user must be able to identify which participants can access his/her devices or data and with what frequency. Using the proposed framework, the user can authorize other participants to access the vehicle using the key lists in the CHs (Section 5.2). All interactions between participants is stored in the BC; thus, the user can monitor the frequency with which his/her devices are accessed.

Security—The security of the proposed architecture is inherited from the BC. The transactions (and data) are encrypted using asymmetric encryption, which ensures confidentiality. The signed hash of each transaction is stored in the BC, which ensures integrity. Each CH maintains a key list that enables the associated participants to authorize other participants to access them, which ensures authorization.

In the following paragraphs, we evaluate the resilience of the proposed architecture to selected security attacks. We define different attack scenarios that allow the attacker to control a smart vehicle:

Data manipulation—In this attack, the attacker changes the data stored in a cloud storage. The aim of this attack varies based on the entity that performs the attack. For example, an attacker may manipulate the software binary in a cloud to install malware in vehicles, or an insurance company may alter the data sent by a vehicle to falsely make the vehicle owner responsible for an accident and thus not pay the compensation. Recall that the signed hash of the exchanged data between participants is stored in the BC. Thus, any modification of the data can be readily detected as the singed hash in the BC does not match with the hash of the modified data.

Masking attack—In this attack, the attacker pretends to be another node and performs action on behalf of that node; e.g. a malicious node may pretend to be an OEM and distribute malicious software updates. Recall that in the proposed architecture, all participating nodes are anonymous. Thus, the attack is only possible in cases where a node is known by other overlay nodes. The PKs of such nodes are known by all participants and can be verified using CA. Thus, the attacker cannot claim to be another node as it will require the private key associated with the PK of the relevant node.

Distributed Denial of Service (DDoS) attack—To perform a DDoS attack, the attacker first compromises a large number of participating nodes in the overlay. These compromised nodes are then orchestrated to send a large number of transactions to a targeted overlay node in order to overwhelm it. Recall that a CH forwards a transaction to one of its cluster members only if the keys in the transaction (i.e. PK.1 and PK.2) match with a key pair in its key list. The transactions generated by the compromised nodes participating in the DDOS attack will not match with any key pair in the key list, and thus are eventually dropped and do not impact the target node. However, this large number of transactions incur packet overhead on CHs. Since the transactions require the signature of the target node to be considered valid, none of them are stored in the BC.

5.5.2 Performance Evaluation

In order to evaluate the performance of the proposed method with a particular focus on the WSU case (see [15] for more information), we implement our BC infrastructure using BeagleBone Black boards (BBB) and an additional communication cape that allows a BBB to connect to a vehicle via CAN/OBD. Figure 5.5a depicts the devices used in our implementation. We implement the overlay nodes in Java in the same host, except for those that are placed in devices, e.g. BBB. We store the software update in the storage and distribute

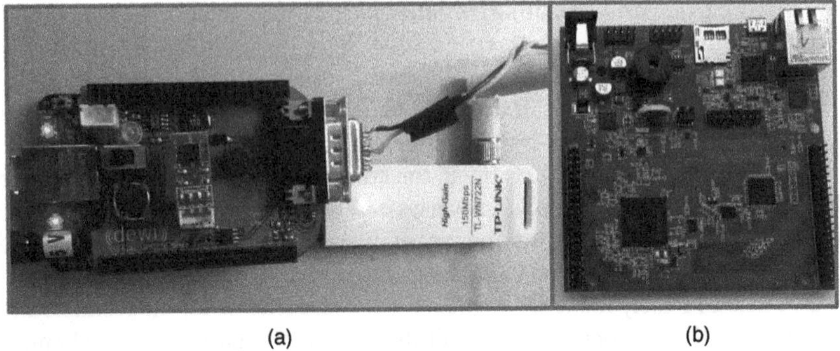

(a) (b)

Figure 5.5 (a) The WVI prototype based on a BeagleBone Black and our developed communication cape; (b) target ECU: Infineon AURIX ECU in the AURIX application kit TC277 TFT.

it using the proposed framework to evaluate the performance of the vehicles. As target ECU for the software update, we use an Infineon AURIX ECU, an automotive multi-core ECU, assembled in the AURIX application kit TC277 (Figure 5.5b).

The WVI, the vehicle, and the Diagnostic Tester (DT) are interconnected using an IEEE 802.11s mesh network. We chose this protocol as the mesh characteristics of an IEEE 802.11s network increases the flexibility as well as the reliability of the network due to its multihop capability and the resulting redundancy.

To compare our method, we have implemented a baseline that is similar to the state-of-the-art method where the software is distributed by the OEM to all the vehicles and the vehicles use a digital certificate to verify the identity of the OEM and the authenticity of the software. We measured two metrics, which are as follows:

- Packet overhead—This refers to the total number of packets generated to distribute the new software.
- Latency—Herein we measure the incurred processing overhead by BC for distributing new software.

In the following, we discuss the evaluation results.

Packet overhead—To evaluate the packet overhead, we first evaluate the incurred overhead resulting from using BC for distributing new software. We collect the exchanged packets in the overlay and group them into data-related (i.e. packets that contain the new software itself), BC-related, and initialization packets that are required to initialize the network. The packet overhead is affected by the number of vehicles, the size of the software binary, and the total number of performed updates, which are 20 vehicles, 32KB, and 100 software updates, respectively, in our evaluation. The corresponding results demonstrate an incurred overhead of 3.4%, which is increased to 7.3% when only one

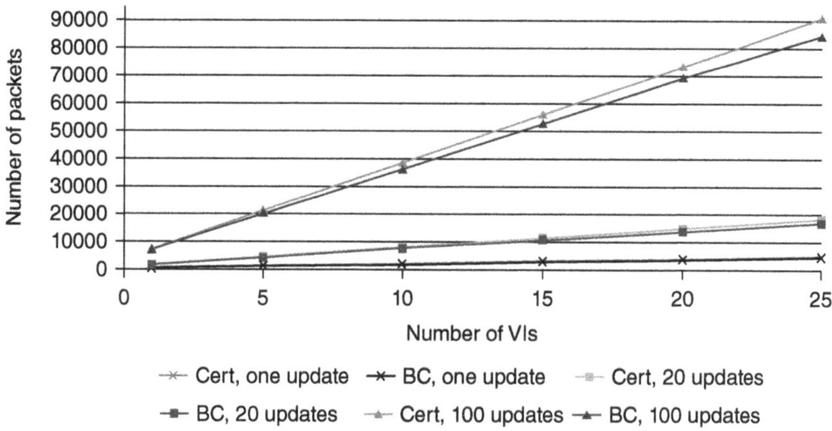

Figure 5.6 A comparison of the packet overhead of BC-based and certificate-based frameworks.

of the vehicles performs the update. As evident from the results, by increasing the number of vehicles in the overlay, the total ratio of the packet overhead for software update is reduced.

Next, we measure the packet overhead incurred by the proposed framework compared to conventional certificate-based software updates. We implement both the studied methods in a network formed by 10 devices (including BBBs, Raspberry Pi3's, and a laptop). We study the packet overhead as a function of the total number of vehicles, the number of packets, and the total number of updates per vehicle. Figure 5.6 outlines the implementation results. As is evident, BC sligthly reduces the packet overhead for software updates compared to a certificate-based method.

Latency—In this part, we evaluate the delay incurred by the proposed framework. We first measure the latency to install and distribute the software update. For this, we measure the following: (i) the latency required for distributing the software using our LSB infrastructure and (ii) the latency for installing the software itself. This is essentially the last step in the proposed framework where the new received software is installed on an ECU, as described in [15] in more detail. Table 5.1 summarizes the implementation results.

The implementation results demonstrate that the installation of a new software binary on an ECU using a wired in-vehicle bus takes more than five times

Table 5.1 Study on the latency of software update.

Software Distribution	Wireless Local Update	WVI Installation
2682.3 ± 8.3 ms	16271.0 ± 323.4 ms	13831.7 ± 228.3 ms

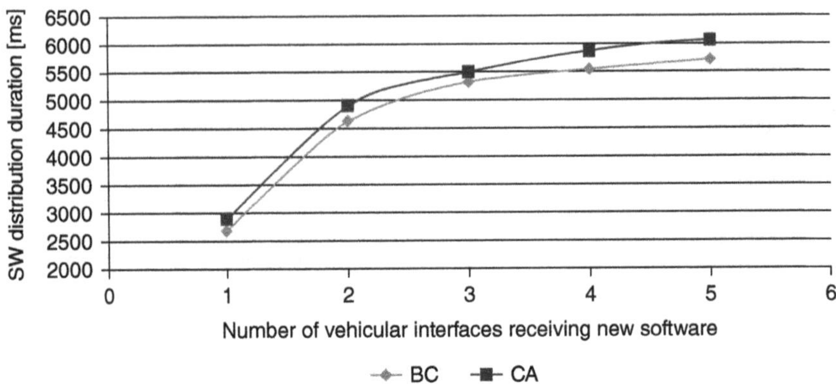

Figure 5.7 A comparison of the latency of BC-based and certificate-based frameworks.

longer than the software distribution from an emulated software provider to the vehicle using the proposed BC-based framework. The software update distribution in the proposed framework is six times faster than the local software update process (such as that performed in a service center). It is worth noting that the software distribution does not include delay resulting from the verification of new software performed by the OEM.

We next compare the latency in the proposed method with conventional certificate-based software updates. We implement both studied methods in a network formed by 10 devices (including BBBs, Raspberry Pi3's, and a laptop). As is evident from the implementation results shown in Figure 5.7, the proposed framework reduces the latency for software update compared to conventional certificate-based methods.

5.6 Related Works

In this section, we provide a brief literature review on using blockchain for smart connected vehicles.

The authors in [16] proposed a BC-based framework to ensure trust and security for communications between vehicles. To ensure trust, the vehicle manufacturer generates and stores an Intelligent Vehicle-Trust Point (IV-TP) in each vehicle it produces. The IV-TP is used between the communications of the vehicles to ensure trust. However, this method does not consider the privacy of the vehicle owner as transactions generated by a single IV-TP can be tracked, which reveals privacy-sensitive information about the vehicle owner.

The authors in [17] proposed a BC-based layered interconnection model for Intelligence Transportation Systems (ITS). The proposed model consists of seven layers, namely physical, data, network, consensus, incentive, contract, and the application layer. Utilizing these layers, ITS participants can communicate using multiple BC instantiations. However, the framework is yet to be applied in real scenarios.

A BC-based framework to ensure security and privacy in smart cities is proposed by the authors in [18]. The proposed method utilizes a permissoned blockchain where a revocation authority controls the identity of the vehicles joining the BC network and specifies which vehicles can serve as miners. Although the proposed method can ensure security in communications due to the usage of BC, the associated (processing and packet) overheads are significant, which would limit the applicability of the proposed method.

The authors in [19] studied the usability of consortium BC (which is essentially a permissioned blockchain) to secure communications between smart vehicles. Using the proposed framework enables the vehicles to exchange data with other participants. The exchanged data can be vehicle maintenance records or the data produced by the sensors and devices of the vehicle. The identity of each vehicle is verified using a central identity database. However, the proposed framework does not consider user privacy and the associated packet overhead to exchange data through BC.

The authors in [20] proposed a BC-based framework, known as block4forensic, to address the liability challenge in smart vehicles. In block4forensic, multiple participants in the vehicle life cycle manage the BC. All interactions between these participants are stored in the BC to be used later as evidence for liability. The data of the sensors embedded in the vehicle are shared with the insurance company by a forensic daemon and the hash of all exchanged data is stored in the BC to protect data integrity. In a similar attempt, the authors in [14] have proposed a liability framework for smart vehicles. The proposed framework is based on a permissioned blockchain where only authorized participants can join the BC. Different transactions are introduced to facilitate the collection of evidence for liability decision.

The authors in [21] proposed a reliable privacy-preserving framework that selects the charging infrastructure for the vehicle without revealing privacy sensitive data, e.g. the vehicle location or payment information. The proposed framework selects the best charging infrastructure based on the price and location.

5.7 Conclusion

In this chapter, we proposed a BC-based solution to automotive security and privacy. The proposed framework incorporates all entities in the vehicle life cycle, including, but no limited to, insurance companies, software or hardware suppliers, and roadside infrastructure. The interactions, i.e. transactions, between these parties are recorded in BC, which provides high auditability. Each participant is known by a changeable PK, which introduces a level of anonymity.

We studied the applicability of several automotive use cases in our framework. We described possible attack scenarios and discussed how the proposed architecture is able to mitigate and inhibit these attacks. Implementation results demonstrated that the BC-based solution reduces delay and packet overhead in remote software update compared to conventional centralized methods.

References

1 C. Miller and C. Valasek, "Remote exploitation of an unaltered passenger vehicle," *Black Hat USA*, vol. 2015, 2015.
2 Intel, "Intel." [Online]. 2018. Available: https://www.networkworld.com/article/3147892/internet/one-autonomous-car-will-use-4000-gb-of-dataday.html.
3 M. Vukolić, "The quest for scalable blockchain fabric: Proof-of-work vs. BFT replication," in International Workshop on Open Problems in Network Security. Springer, 2015, pp. 112–125.
4 G. Wood, "Ethereum: A secure decentralised generalised transaction ledger," Ethereum Project Yellow Paper, vol. 151, 2014.
5 Altcoin, "Altcoin." [Online]. 2017. Available: http://altcoins.com [Accessed July, 2017.
6 A. Dorri, S. S. Kanhere, and, R. Jurdak, (2017, April). Towards an optimized blockchain for IoT. In Proceedings of the Second International Conference on Internet-of-Things Design and Implementation (pp. 173–178). ACM.
7 R. C. Merkle, "A digital signature based on a conventional encryption function," in *Conference on the Theory and Application of Cryptographic Techniques*. Springer, 1987, pp. 369–378.
8 A. Dorri, M. Steger, S. S. Kanhere, and R. Jurdak, "Blockchain: A distributed solution to automotive security and privacy," *IEEE Communications Magazine*, vol. 55, no. 12, pp. 119–125, 2017.
9 M. Steger, A. Dorri, S. S. Kanhere, K. Römer, R. Jurdak, and M. Karner, "Secure wireless automotive software updates using blockchains: A proof of concept," in *Advanced Microsystems for Automotive Applications 2017*. Springer, 2018, pp. 137–149.
10 S. J. Koh, M. J. Chang, and M. Lee, "mSCTP for soft handover in transport layer," *IEEE Communications Letters*, vol. 8, no. 3, pp. 189–191, 2004.
11 Car Next Door, "Car Next Door." [Online]. 2018. Available: https://www.carnextdoor.com.au/ [Accessed May, 2018].
12 B. Mota, M. I. Gomes, A. Carvalho, and A. P. Barbosa-Povoa, "Towards supply chain sustainability: Economic, environmental and social design and planning," *Journal of Cleaner Production*, vol. 105, pp. 14–27, 2015.
13 H.-O. Günther, M. Kannegiesser, and N. Autenrieb, "The role of electric vehicles for supply chain sustainability in the automotive industry," *Journal of Cleaner Production*, vol. 90, pp. 220–233, 2015.

14 C. Oham, R. Jurdak, S. Kanhere, A. Dorri, S. Jha, "B-FICA: BlockChain based Framework for auto-Insurance Claim and Adjudication," In proceedings of The IEEE International Conference on Blockchain (Blockchain 2018), Halifax, Canada, July, 2018.
15 M. Steger, T. Niedermayr, C. Boano, K. Roemer, M. Karner, J. Hillebrand, and W. Rom, "An efficient and secure automotive wireless software update framework," *IEEE Transactions on Industrial Informatics (TII)*, vol. 14, no. 5, pp. 2181–2193, December 2017.
16 M. Singh and S. Kim, "Intelligent vehicle-trust point: Reward based intelligent vehicle communication using blockchain." arXiv preprint arXiv:1707.07442. 2017.
17 Y. Yuan and F.-Y. Wang, "Towards blockchain-based intelligent transportation systems," in *2016 IEEE 19th International Conference on Intelligent Transportation Systems (ITSC)*, IEEE, 2016, pp. 2663–2668.
18 P. K. Sharma, S. Y. Moon, and J. H. Park, "Block-VN: A distributed blockchain based vehicular network architecture in smart city," *Journal of Information Processing Systems*, vol. 13, no. 1, p. 84, 2017.
19 K. L. Brousmiche, T. Heno, C. Poulain, A. Dalmieres, and E. B. Hamida, "Digitizing, securing and sharing vehicles life-cycle over a consortium blockchain: Lessons learned," in *2018 9th IFIP International Conference on New Technologies, Mobility and Security (NTMS)*, IEEE, 2018, pp. 1–5.
20 M. Cebe, E. Erdin, K. Akkaya, H. Aksu, and S. Uluagac, "Block4Forensic: An integrated lightweight blockchain framework for forensics applications of connected vehicles." arXiv preprint arXiv:1802.00561. 2018.
21 F. Knirsch, A. Unterweger, and D. Engel, "Privacy-preserving blockchain-based electric vehicle charging with dynamic tariff decisions," *Computer Science–Research and Development*, vol. 33, no. 1-2, pp. 71–79, 2018.

6

Blockchain-based Dynamic Key Management for IoT-Transportation Security Protection

Ao Lei,[1] Yue Cao,[2] Shihan Bao,[1] Philip Asuquom,[1] Haitham Cruickshank,[1] and Zhili Sun[1]

[1]University of Surrey, Institute for Communication Systems, Guildford,UK
[2]Northumbria University, Computer and Information Sciences, Newcastle-upon-Tyne,UK

6.1 Introduction

A recent report from the US Department of Transport (DoT) indicates that nearly 82% of traffic accidents can be prevented by introducing intelligent transportation system (ITS) into the existing traffic systems [1]. ITS is proposed as the only candidate to solve the current problems within transportation systems, such as road safety, navigation, and congestion control. As a submodule of the ITS, Vehicular Communication System (VCS) supports the exchange of messages between vehicles and also with infrastructural facilities [2]. One of the most well-known VCS structures is called Vehicular Ad Hoc Network (VANET). As an extension of Mobile Ad Hoc Network (MANET), VANET offers a platform among ITS for vehicles to exchange messages with different functions, such as safety notification messages. In addition to the message exchange among multiple vehicles, VCS supports message communications between vehicles and infrastructure as well. Moreover, VCS is one of the most important use cases of the Internet of Things (IoT). As shown in Figure 6.1, VCS plays the overlap part between ITS and IoT.

VCS security highly relies on the trustworthiness of the information inside exchanged messages. These messages are known as safety messages. The correctness of the vehicle status information in these safety messages (e.g. speed, direction, position, and vehicle size) determines whether ITS runs in a regular and sustainable manner as it enables vehicles and infrastructures to be aware of the status of the surrounding environment; vehicles can obtain a better understanding of current road situation and accident report based on the information contained in safety messages from nearby ITS communication nodes. To

Blockchain for Distributed Systems Security, First Edition. Edited by Sachin S. Shetty, Charles A. Kamhoua, and Laurent L. Njilla.

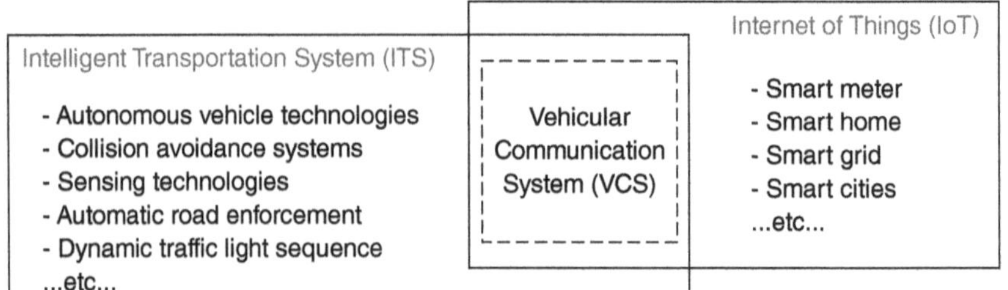

Figure 6.1 The relationship between ITS, VCS, and IoT.

guarantee the trustfulness and legality of safety messages, the messages are supposed to be encrypted with a pre-agreed secret key. Thus, the problem of providing VCS application layer security can be mapped into the problem of how to reliably distribute or update secret keys among all the communicating participants, especially how to timely deliver the secret key to another security domain to finish the node handover progress. Moreover, high mobility, a massive number of devices, and a wide range of vehicle activities pose extra challenges to VCS-centralized management and Access Point (AP) deployment. For this reason, distributed VCS management structures are considered as a possible method to achieve higher network management efficiency, mild network manager burden, and lower infrastructure building cost.

The current solution to achieve trusted safety message exchange among the VCS area is to encrypt and authenticate the message [3] before broadcasting the message to VCS. The encrypted safety message exchange is achieved on the premise that secret keys be distributed in a safe manner using key management schemes. Even though significant developments have taken place over the past few years in the area of VCS, security issues, especially in the area of key management schemes, are still an important topic of research. With this in mind, Blockchain is considered as a feasible solution to achieve the goal. Consensus algorithms and state replication in distributed databases are historically confined to closed, distributed systems. In open systems, trust, security, and acceptability require different solutions. In 2008, Nakamoto launched the digital currency Bitcoin [4] and its key technology, Blockchain, in which distributed ledgers of verified transactions are created with no central control, where trust is a self-emerging property based on a subtle interplay between incentives, cryptographic puzzle solving, and peer-to-peer consensus creation.

However, with most of the Blockchain researchers focusing on the financial area, other characteristics of Blockchain are neglected, which are distributed authentication and information propagation. Blockchain is a synchronized and distributed ledger that stores a list of blocks. Blocks record user information and a receipt to link to the previous block. Some approaches have already examined the feasibility of Blockchain-based IoT solutions. In a paper [5], it was proposed to use blockchain in line with a decentralized system to manage personal data over IoT devices. The access control of personal data is monitored by blockchain. The authors in [6] focus on a cutting-edge secure transaction exchange system using blockchain for decentralized energy trading in two different IoT scenarios—smart grids and smart medical systems. Despite the fact that there are several solutions for using blockchain in IoT, blockchain-proposed security schemes, especially in the VCS scenario, still need to be designed and examined.

6.2 Use Case

The use case should be addressed based on the technical challenges within the IoT networks. The security research work aims to establish a novel key management scheme based on the use case, which contains a large volume of VCS service participants. Two barriers that exist in the IoT use cases are the high expense of the network overheads and computation inefficiency. In fact, these two aspects are the major difficulties of the key management research, especially in VCS. Thus, the first aim of key management research is to reduce the overall broadcast messages, also known as the communication overhead, whereas the second aim is to speed up the key management processing time. For these reasons, the node handover is considered as the major use case.

The wireless network allows nodes to move freely without the restriction of cable connections. The wireless network achieves coverage by deploying multiple cellular subnetworks. The aim of handover in the wireless mobile network is to enable mobile nodes to seamlessly roam from previous subnetworks to another one. Handover authentication appears to become a new barrier because of the unavoidable authentication processing time upon network shift. The identity and validity of the joining user are verified by the new cellular subnetwork in order to assure security, also known as key handover. Figure 6.2(a) illustrates a typical key handover scenario in a mobile network. Apart from mobile nodes (mobile phones or vehicles), the handover procedures involve collaboration between four entities—Mobile Nodes (MN), Home Agent (HA), Foreign Agent (FA) and Authentication Server. The authentication server is

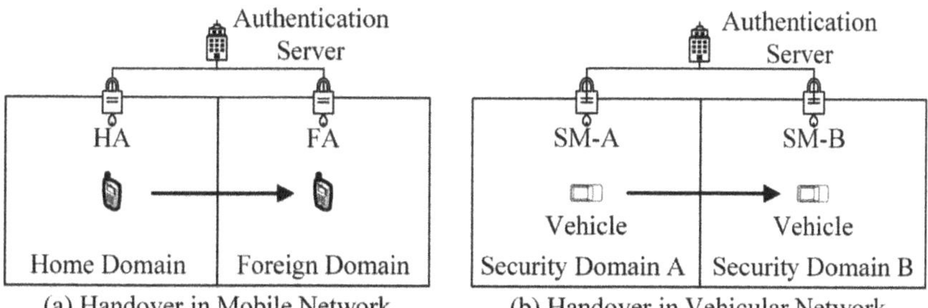

Figure 6.2 The conventional mobile node handover process.

located at the top level of the system architecture and is responsible for the management, issuance, and initialization of cryptographic materials, such as secret keys and certificates. The middle layer contains subnetwork cells, namely HA and FA. The MN current registers with HA, while a key handover happens when the MN roams into the coverage area of FA. MNs occupy the end branches of the architecture. They are the end users who require access to network services. The MN demands network access within the entire network and it has network connection via HA. No mutual trust relationship is established between MN and any non-HA subnetwork; this means that the MN can not trust the information from any non-HA server without verifying, and vice versa. The current connection is achieved after successfully authenticating with HA. Compulsory authentication steps are required if MN wants to enable network access outside the coverage area of HA. At the same time, FA uses cryptography-based messages to prove its identity and legality. Thus, the handover starts with the MN joining and ends with the completion of authentication. Identity and legality are checked during the authentication steps. The identity is checked by verifying the signature, which can be linked to the current pseudonym related key pairs of MN. Legality is shown in a specific field inside the certificate. The field is dedicated to indicate the legality-valid period of the MN.

The existing key handover schemes are based on mobile phone networks or general Wireless Sensor Networks (WSNs), such as schemes in [7, 8]. MN in these scenarios have unpredictable trajectories; therefore, the message handover authentication is triggered by MN and multiple handshakes are required between FA and HA. While in the VCS scenario, the trajectories are easily predicted due to the fact that the vehicle sends safety messages and SM knows the driving status of all the vehicles under its coverage area. Figure 6.2(b) shows that HA and FA are replaced by Security Managers (SM). Here, we assume Security Manager A (SM-A) plays the role of HA and SM-B acts as FA. In VCS, SM-A knows the vehicle is about to join the coverage area of SM-B according to the driving direction, speed, position, and all the cryptographic materials. Thus, SM-A informs SM-B about the message handover action in order to let SM-B update keys to the vehicle. To sum up, the handover schemes in the mobile network need a round trip between three entities (MN, FA, and HA) to finish, while only a one-way communication is needed in VCS. A more detailed introduction about message handover in VCS is illustrated below, starting with a brief description of the proposed VCS network structure.

6.2.1 Message Handover in VCS

Nodes in VCS are hierarchically classified into four layers, based on responsibilities. Three layers are on the side of service providers, while the service user occupies a single layer. As shown in Figure 6.3, the service provider comprises RSUs, SMs, and Public Key Infrastructures (PKIs). SMs and Road Side Units

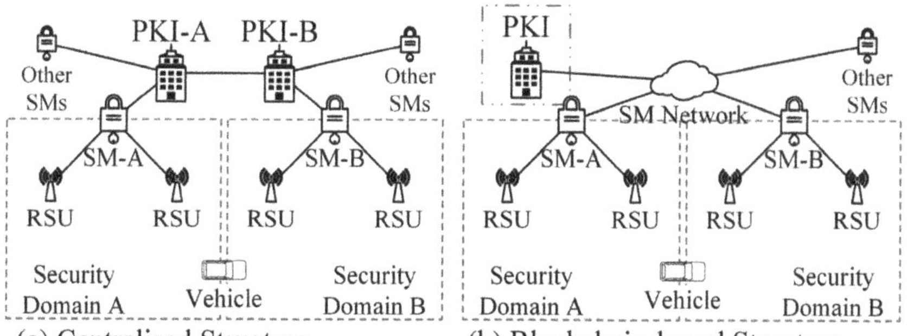

Figure 6.3 VCS network structure; (a) traditional structure; (b) blockchain-based structure.

(RSUs) have wireless communication devices using VCS standards. Meanwhile, vehicles are required to equip communication devices to support the corresponding VCS standards. Safety messages are periodically sent by vehicles, which are collected by RSUs that are built along the road at regular intervals in order to provide maximum network coverage. A PKI contains Certificate Authority (CA), anonymity server, and other central management infrastructures to support applications. All the cryptographic materials are managed by the PKI, which plays the central manager of the network. Permanent identities, certificates, and pseudonyms of vehicles are calculated and authenticated at PKI in order to issue legal user identities in VCS. Each SM has its own logical coverage area, which is called security domain. SMs help PKI to manage cryptography materials of security domains, which are logically placed below the PKI layer. It is proposed to install SMs in a geographically sparse manner, one for each security domain. RSUs act as APs that offer interfaces to bridge messages between the service provider and users.

Traditional structure—The traditional structure strictly follows the aforementioned hierarchy. We assume SMs take the job of HA, FA, and RSUs only for improving the network coverage area. The current registered SM acts as HA, while the SM in the about-to-join domain is the FA. Additionally, malicious behaviours in VCS can easily endanger human life; it requires top-level security to deliver trusted service. The requirement is fulfilled by equipping the server that supervises user data. Thus, the handshakes between SMs are checked by the infrastructure inside PKI in a mandatory manner. As shown in Figure 6.3(a), security domains are areas managed by different SMs and PKIs supervise the network at the top level. Each PKI manages multiple numbers of SMs; the number depends on the geographical topology of the area. This, however, makes the network an inefficient key exchange, and will require unnecessary handshakes if a car passes from one security domain to another.

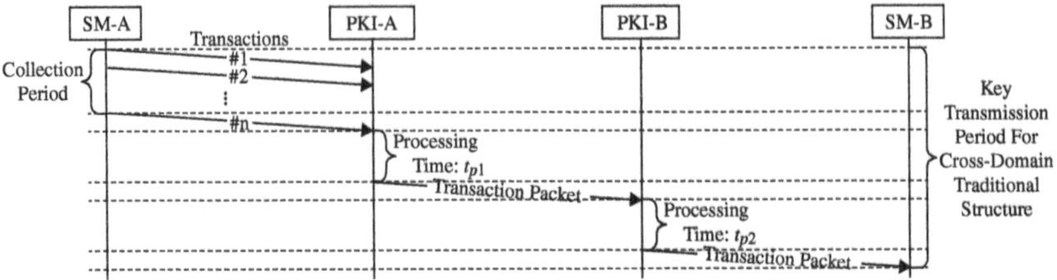

Figure 6.4 Cross-domain key handover handshake procedures in traditional structure.

The cross-domain handshake procedures in the traditional network are shown in Figure 6.4. Before the key management scheme runs, the network sets a collection period based on the traffic level. When a vehicle attempts to join Security Domain B from Security Domain A, it keeps sending safety messages that contain speed and position information. SM-A picks up the safety messages and recognizes the border crossing request from the information inside the safety messages. SM-A (the previous SM) picks up all the border crossing requests from safety messages within a transaction period. These requests and information related to the vehicle are encapsulated into transactions. SM-A sends these transactions one by one to PKI-A. To assure security, the digital signature and certificate within the requests are checked for proof of authenticity and integrity. The message format is shown in step 1 below. The ciphertext is decrypted using PKI-A's private key and re-encrypted using PKI-B's public key. That's because the original ciphertext is secured using PKI-A's public key and PKI-B doesn't have the corresponding key to decrypt. During proofreading, the proved transactions are translated into a new version, which is readable by PKI-B. The above message format is shown in step 2. In step 3, PKI-B repeats the checking steps after receiving the transaction packet and converts them into an SM-B readable version. Finally, all the cross-border requests arrive at SM-B, packed in the transaction packet. A handshake message flow is shown below for details, where $En\{*\}$ stands for the encryption activities using the Elliptic Curve Integrated Encryption Scheme (ECIES) [9], and $Sig\{*\}$ is the signing conducted using the Elliptic Curve Digital Signature Algorithm (ECDSA) [10]. PK_* and SK_* are elliptic curve based public and private key pairs, respectively.

1. **SM-A** *sends* **transactions** *to* **PKI-A** :

$En\{info\}_{PK_{PKI-A}} + dest_{SM} + Sig\{Cipher + dest_{SM}\}_{SK_{SM-A}}$

2. **PKI-A** *forwards the* **transaction packet** *to* **PKI-B** :

$En\{info\}_{PK_{PKI-B}} + dest_{SM} + Sig\{Cipher + dest_{SM}\}_{SK_{PKI-A}}$

3. **PKI-B** *forwards the* **transaction packet** *to* **SM-B** :

$En\{info\}_{PK_{SM-B}} + dest_{SM} + Sig\{Cipher + dest_{SM}\}_{SK_{PKI-B}}$

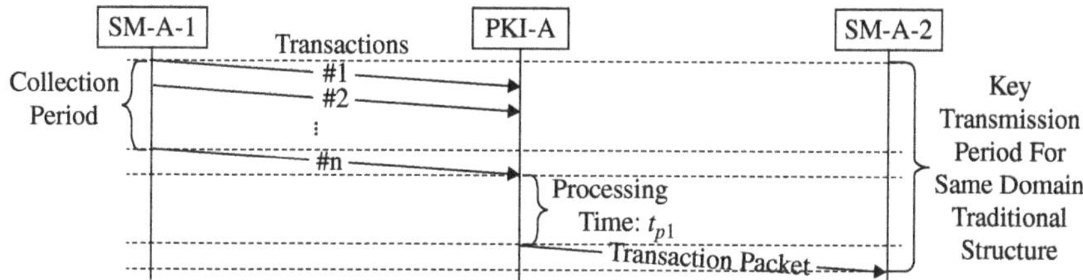

Figure 6.5 Same-domain key handover handshake procedures in traditional structure.

The handshake steps are simplified if SMs at both sides are in the same security domain. The formats of the handshake messages are presented below. In step 1, SM-A-1 forwards transactions to PKI-A to prove the authenticity and integrity. In this same domain scenario, both SMs are undermanaged by the same PKI. Therefore, there is no need to translate transactions into another version that is dedicated to other PKIs. Similar to the cross-domain version above, SM-A-2 receives transactions from the transaction packet in the end. The aforementioned steps are presented in Figure 6.5.

1. **SM-A-1** *sends* **transactions** *to* **PKI-A** :
$En\{info\}_{PK_{PKI-A}} + dest_{SM} + Sig\{Cipher + dest_{SM}\}_{SK_{SM-A}}$
2. **PKI-A** *forwards the* **transaction packet** *to* **SM-A-2** :
$En\{info\}_{PK_{SM-A-2}} + dest_{SM} + Sig\{Cipher + dest_{SM}\}_{SK_{PKI-A}}$

Blockchain-based structure—It is tedious to force the key handover messages passing PKI as key transferring between security domains is delayed due to multiple handshakes within PKIs. The key handover handshake could thus be simplified by introducing a Blockchain decentralized structure. The Blockchain structure helps to minimise the network structure, which helps the messages to be verified by the SM network but not the PKI. A part of the functions of the PKI is diverted to the SM network, such as processing the key transferring. Similar to the Bitcoin network, the function of Blockchain enables nodes to share information without the need for centralized supervision of this ledger by a central manager. SMs are linked to the SM network, which connects other SMs within different security domains. The SM network uses the peer-to-peer (P2P) structure and operates in the manner of a cloud network. As presented in Figure 6.3(b), the central manager (PKI) is placed in an isolated environment to dedicatedly generate cryptographic materials for all the nodes. Cryptographic materials, such as vehicle identities, pseudonyms, and pseudonym certificates, are supposed to be kept in a secured facility for privacy and security purposes [11]. Thus, the central managers are accessed under the following two situations: **(i)** *Initial registration*—New vehicles need to apply for the

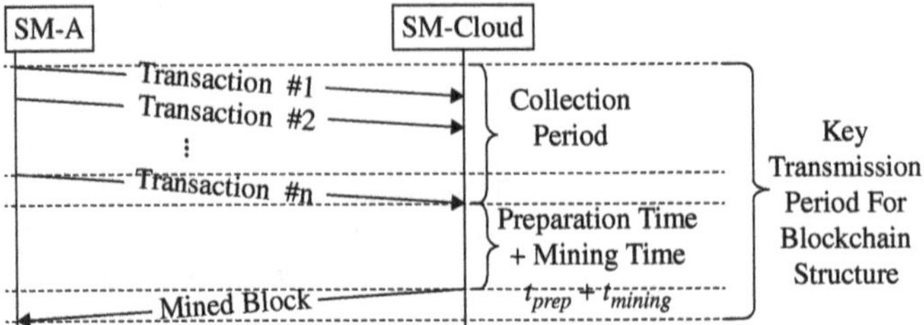

Figure 6.6 Handshake procedures of cross-domain handover in distributed ledger technology based structure.

initial registration when they leave the manufacturer and first participate in a new security domain. **(ii)** *Adversary revocation*—In the blockchain based structure, malicious behaviours are recognized by using blockchain look-up. Identity (including pseudonyms) of the adversary is publicized once the malicious behaviours have been confirmed.

A simplified handshake graph is shown in Figure 6.6 and the message handshakes with message formats are shown below. The collection period allows several transactions to be broadcasted into the SM network and picked up by SMs in the network. Digital signatures and certificates in the transactions are processed to verify whether the information in the transactions is trustworthy. Ciphertext in transactions is kept from decryption until they reach the destination SM since the ciphertext is encrypted using the public key of the destination SM. According to the nature of blockchain mining, transactions are inserted into the block in random order, which is decided by SMs. Last but not the least, the above block will be mined using mining algorithm and the mined block will be broadcasted back to the network. The above procedures are presented as follows:

1. **SM-A** *sends* **transactions** *to* **SM-Cloud** :

   $En\{info\}_{PK_{SM-dest}} + dest_{SM} + Sig\{Cipher + dest_{SM}\}_{SK_{SM-A}}$
2. **SM-Cloud** *returns the* **mined block** *to* **SM-A** :

6.3 Blockchain-based Dynamic Key Management Scheme

In this approach, Blockchain is used to simplify the network structure so that the key handover proccesses experience fewer message handshakes and delay. Based on the description of the simplified structure in the previous section, information propagation between security domains can be accelerated since the information is directly sent to the destination rather than passing the messages through PKIs. Moreover, the distributed structure of the Blockchain network shows better robustness under the single point of failure. Here, we propose our Blockchain-based key management scheme based on the following assumptions:

Assumption 1: ***(role of miners)***—Generally speaking, nodes are classified into two roles according to different responsibilities among the Blockchain network, namely service user and miners. The miners are nodes with powerful computation power that use their computation power to maintain the Blockchain. In the Bitcoin network, a portion of nodes chooses to play the role of a miner by their own accord. The miners are paid Bitcoins as reward if they successfully mine a block. In our Blockchain-based scheme, we assume all the block mining tasks are carried out by all the SMs in a mandatory manner. As a reward, the SMs are granted permission of access to the key management services. All the SMs take the roles of service user and miner at the same time.

Assumption 2: ***(mining synchrony)***—It is necessary to assume that all the SMs start mining tasks at the same time or approximately the same time. As the navigation service is contained in the ITS applications, each vehicle should have a synchronized clock. This helps to limit the deadline for each transaction collection interval.

Assumption 3: ***(consensus)***—The most famous consensus method is Proof of Work (PoW), which is calculated by trying multiple hashes. The PoW is a piece of digital receipt that is hard to generate and easy to verify. The nature of consensus in Blockchain is a distributed way to establish an agreement between a group of nodes, instead of relying on the central manager's decision. The PoW with low difficulty is proposed in this approach as all the SMs have identical processing modules inside and they are assumed to link with highly secured wire connections. The low difficulty allows a short PoW computation time, resulting in efficient consensus.

6.4 Dynamic Transaction Collection Algorithm

6.4.1 Transaction Format

Transactions are designed to encapsulate key transfer materials from the source SM to the destination SM. Seven fields are proposed to contain useful information inside the transaction header of our previous papers, which follow the basic transaction template of blockchain applications (Table 6.1) [12, 13]. The first field shows the results of the remaining five fields, which are calculated through the hash function. A type field is inserted into the transaction in order

Table 6.1 The format of transaction.

	Transaction Header
1.	Hashed result of the transaction
2.	Transaction type
3.	Number of this transaction in the block
4.	Current security domain number *SM-this*
5.	Destination security domain number *SM-dest*
6.	Vehicle identity materials including the encrypted vehicle pseudonym and certificate
7.	Signature of this transaction to ensure integrity and authentication; the Signature is generated using private key of SM: $SK_{SM-this}$
	Payload field: (encrypted transaction information)
	$Cipher = En\{info\}_{PK_{SM-dest}}$

to further extend the transaction function to privacy applications. The transaction number shows the position of this transaction in the block. The value of this field varies depending on how SM organises the transaction sequence. The current and the destination SM numbers are equivalent to the currency input and output of Bitcoin applications, respectively [4]. The identity materials, including the pseudonym and the certificate of the handover vehicle, are encrypted using the public key of the destination SM. The signature occupies the last position of the transaction to maintain the authentication, integrity, and nonrepudiation of the key transfer information.

Table 6.1 shows the payload field, which attaches behind the transaction header. Here, *info* is the identity and vehicle status materials in the transaction, including the certificate, pseudonym, speed, heading, and other status data. To keep the confidentiality of the information in transactions, identity materials and vehicle status data are encrypted using the destination SM's public key. As a result, the information stays unreadable to the SM network except for the destination SM. Privacy-related information is encrypted into ciphertext $En\{info\}_{PK-dest}$ using the destination SM's public key PK_{dest}. The signature is computed using both ciphertext and the number of the destination SM, and signed using the source SM's private key SK_{this}. Encrypting the privacy-related information combined with digitally signed transaction contents ensures that an adversary cannot act as a normal node, or amend and eavesdrop cross-domain requests, as that would require the adversary to forge a signature. Simultaneously, other SMs are able to examine whether this transaction is legitimate or not. Similarly, a malicious user cannot read anything from the encrypted message, as only the destination SM has the key to decrypt the message.

Table 6.2 The format of block.

Block Header		
No.	**Field**	**Description**
1.	Version	Block version number
2.	Previous block hash	Hash of the previous block in the chain
3.	Merkle tree root	Hash of the Merkle tree root $Root_M$
4.	Timestamp	Creation time of this block
5.	Targeted difficulty	The proof of work difficulty target
6.	Nonce	A counter for the proof of work
Block Payload (transactions)		
Transaction no. 1 $\cdots$ Transaction no. n		

6.4.2 Block Format

The block header is constructed by six fields, as illustrated in Table 6.2, similar to the Bitcoin block structure [12]. In this security purpose application, all the blocks have the same block version value in the first field since all the blocks are used to transfer handover requests. However, the field can further be developed to indicate other Distributed Ledger Technology (DLT) applications, such as pseudonym shuffling for privacy purposes. The second field links the block to the previous blocks. This field helps blocks to link to each other and creates a chain structure to generate the ledger. All the transactions and their sequence in the block are represented in the block header in the form of Merkle tree root [14]. Merkle tree root assures the integrity of transactions since even a single alteration in transactions can cause a totally different value of Merkle root value. Time tampering is prevented by checking the timestamp field. The PoW algorithm defines a 256-bit target mining solution with a number of zeros at the start of the hash result of the block header [6]. The number of zeros is denoted as n_{zeros} and it also the targeted difficulty in the PoW mining algorithm. SM collects all the transactions within a pre-agreed period (transaction collection period) of time and sorts these transactions in an arbitrary order into a block. In this way, blocks are able to aggregate multiple cross-border requests.

The payload field of a block is comprised of verified transactions that SMs collect within the transaction collection period, denoted by t_{CP}. These transactions are marked in sequence and packed into the same block. The theoretical number of transactions is decided by t_{CP} and the number of passing vehicles in each hour (n_H). The number of transactions n_T can be calculated by using the equation $n_T = \dfrac{n_H}{3600s/hour} \times t_{CP}$.

Table 6.3 The time elements of processing procedures.

Parent Field	Description of Parent Field
t_{prep}	The time cost to prepare block, which will be mined later
$t_{transfer}$	Transmission time cost in SM network including CSMA back-off time
$t_{processing}$	Processing time for message **encryption, decryption, signing**, and **verification**
Child Field	**Description of Child Field**
t_{rand}	Calculation time to generate random transaction sequence
t_{fill}	Time cost to insert transactions into the block message
t_{merkle}	Calculation time to get Merkle tree root
t_{header}	Processing time to prepare block header
t_{BO}	Average CSMA back-off time
t_P	Propagation time in network cable
t_E	Processing time to encrypt plain text (ECIES)
t_D	Processing time to decrypt cipher text (ECIES)
t_S	Processing time to sign messages (ECDSA)
t_V	Processing time to verify signature (ECDSA)

6.5 Time Composition

Table 6.3 shows all the time elements that compose the key transfer time. For a traditional structure, all the time variables in $t_{processing}$ are taken into account, while t_V is the only one to be considered in a blockchain structure. Message transfer time $t_{transfer}$ includes the information propagation time in cable, as well as the random back-off time in the Carrier Sense Multiple Access with Collision Avoidance (CSMA/CA) protocol that is specified in SAE J2735 [15]. The variable t_{prep} is dedicated to blockchain applications, containing time cost variables to create a new block.

As described above, processing times for three situations are summarized in Eq. 6.1–6.3, where n_T is the average number of transactions in a single collection period. Variables t_{TC}, t_{TS}, and t_B are processing times of key transfer procedures in the cross-domain traditional structure, same-domain traditional structure, and blockchain structure, respectively.

$$t_{TC} = n_T \times (t_V + t_D + t_E + t_S) \times 2 + (t_{BO} + t_P) \times 3. \tag{6.1}$$

$$t_{TS} = n_T \times (t_V + t_D + t_E + t_S) + (t_{BO} + t_P) \times 2. \tag{6.2}$$

Eq. 6.1 and 6.2 describe the time components in the traditional structure. PKIs in the traditional structure must verify and translate transactions to the neighbour PKIs or SMs. Both situations take all the elements in $t_{processing}$ into calculation. For the cross-domain scenario, the above processes are designed to be implemented twice.

$$t_B = n_T \times t_V + (t_{BO} + t_P) \times 2 + t_{prep} + t_M. \tag{6.3}$$

Eq. 6.3 expresses that only signature verification is required in transaction checking. However, mining time t_M and block preparation steps are attached to overall processing time in order to extend the blockchain.

6.5.1 Dynamic Transaction Collection Algorithm

As mentioned in the above subsection, the number of transactions n_T is decided by the length of the transaction collection period t_{CP}. The key handover time varies depending on the overall number of transactions to be proceeded. Therefore, it is necessary to consider a dynamic transaction collection algorithm to control the number of transactions, and further adapt the key handover time according to the dynamic traffic situations.

In order to have a reasonable metric to measure the results, a time period of 1 second is selected as the standard metric to measure the performances of various collection periods. Here, assume that n_{T-All} is a sum-up number of transactions that contains all the key handover activities on all the roads. t_{B-1} is the average processing time measured in 1 second under various collection periods. n_R is the number of roads that are taken into calculation. Based on the transaction number n_T and Eq. 6.3, the number of transactions coming from the overall number of n_R roads and average processing time t_{B-1} can be derived as follows:

$$n_{T\text{-}All} = \frac{traffic\ amount}{3600s/hour} \times t_{CP} \times n_R. \tag{6.4}$$

$$t_{B-1} = [n_{T\text{-}All} \times t_V + (t_{BO} + t_P) \times 2 + t_{prep} + t_M]/t_{CP}. \tag{6.5}$$

To find the most suitable transaction collection time, several candidates are prepared within a range with regular intervals, such as five candidates from 0.5 seconds to 1.0 second with spacing of 0.1 seconds. The estimated key transfer time is calculated using various collection periods as inputs. The optimized transaction collection time is selected according to the minimum key transfer time:

$$\underset{t_{CP}}{\operatorname{argmin}}\ t_{B-1}\ subject\ to:\ t_{CP} \in [t_{CP}^{\mathbf{1}}, t_{CP}^{\mathbf{n}}]$$

To sum up, a transaction collection period optimization algorithm is demonstrated using the pseudo-algorithm in Algorithm 1.

Algorithm 1: Optimize the transaction collection period

Input: : Traffic amount on each road n_H, n optional transaction collection periods $(t^{\mathbf{1}}_{CP} \cdots t^{\mathbf{n}}_{CP})$
Output: : Optimized transaction collection period $t^{\mathbf{m}}_{CP}$

Initialise a data sink $\mathbf{t}_{B-1} = [t^{\mathbf{1}}_{CP} \cdots t^{\mathbf{n}}_{CP}]$
for $(i = 1; i \leqslant n; i{+}{+})$ **do**
  Call **Equation**(6), calculate $t^{\mathbf{i}}_{B-1}$ when $t_{CP} = t^{\mathbf{i}}_{CP}$ and traffic amount on each road is equal to n_H;
  $\mathbf{t}_{B-1}[i] \leftarrow t^{\mathbf{i}}_{B-1}$, record $t^{\mathbf{i}}_{B-1}$ into the result sink;
end for
$t^{\mathbf{m}}_{CP} = \min(\mathbf{t}_{B-1})$, Find the minimum key transfer timeïijŻ
return $t^{\mathbf{m}}_{CP}$;
End Algorithm

6.6 Performance Evaluation

The performance evaluation of the Blockchain-based key management scheme is carried out using network simulations. Performance evaluation is broken into two parts. The first part studies the processing time of cryptographic schemes and mining algorithms, namely encryption, decryption, signing, verification, block mining, and block preparation. The second part further studies the processing time in the blockchain network against different transaction collection periods.

6.6.1 Experimental Assumptions and Setup

The assumed parametersare shown in Table 6.4. The simulations aim to test key transmission time under different traffic levels and transaction collection periods. Here, assume that the system calculates the overall number of cross-border activities at the end of the collection periods. The vehicle cross-border activities follow the exponential distribution. The cross-border events, occurrence rate follows the quantile function of exponential distribution [17]. The simulation uses OMNeT++ 4.5 [18] with the dedicated traffic simulator (Veins) packet [19]. The network structure setup follows the Blockchain-based structure, which isolates the central manager away from major key management tasks. The central managers like PKIs are only responsible to generate cryptographic materials and pseudonyms. This aims to improve the key management efficiency in a large scale geographical area. The middle layer infrastructures, SMs, are introduced into the network to support most of the key management job. SMs in this scenario act as the key manager and a relay between the local

Table 6.4 Assumption of scenario parameters.

Parameter Name	Parameter Value
Distance between SMs	5000 meters
Mining difficulty (number of zeros)	3
Traffic amount per hour	15,000, 12,000, 9000, 6000, 3000
Length of transaction collection time	0.5s, 0.6s, 0.7s, 0.8s, 0.9s, 1.0s
Vehicle joining event's distribution	Exponential distribution [16]
Mining speed	250 K-hashes (thousands of Hashes) per second
Maximum transaction range	
For large scale simulation:	1000 transactions
Block preparation	
Maximum transaction range	
For large scale simulation:	2000 transactions
Key handover processing time	

security domain and foreign domains. Dynamic transaction collection periods are proposed to provide better key management flexibility. For each SM, cross border is collected and picked into a transaction packet from every half second to 1 second in order to test the performance regarding different transaction collection lengths. The results depend only on the overall number of transactions as it focuses on the processing time in terms of transaction numbers. Thus, the simulation setup is comprized of the following steps:

(i) At the end of each t_{CP}, a certain number of transactions flood into the SM network. The movement of vehicles is not considered in these two parts.
(ii) Each SM records the processing time results of cryptography schemes and block preparation. The results are recorded by averaging the results from SMs.
(iii) Transactions ranging from 0 to 200 are set for test cryptographic schemes to get a zoom-in view of results.

An average distance of 5000 meters is assumed between SMs. The low level is considered as a relatively mild traffic level. Higher traffic level is the stress testing under heavy traffic conditions to examine scalability properties. The heavy traffic condition test aims to study performance within a big city. One purpose is to test scalability. Another purpose is to examine the future development space of the scheme as the large scale deployment of VCS leads to a large number of transactions with the network. The upper and the lower amounts of vehicle traffic are considered under a saturated traffic condition and off-peak traffic of big cities. The off-peak time has 3,000 vehicles per hour, while the saturated traffic is set to have 15,000 vehicles passing a road in an hour, aiming to examine our scheme under the worst case as well as the heaviest burden of VCS. The topology of the scenario here is assumed in the biggest cities in the world, such as Beijing. The city topology is assumed as a 3-by-3 topology and this is based on Beijing, which has eight urban districts. Here, we assume that districts are connected to each other by five two-way highways (overall 120 highways). For each SM, t_{CP} is ranged from 0.5 seconds to 1 second in order to test the performance regarding different transaction collection lengths. For the large-scale simulation, up to 1000 transactions are introduced in block preparation simulations so that the exponential growth of results can be demonstrated. A maximum of 2000 transactions are simulated to test time value differences between blockchain and tradition structures. The benchmark is selected as the key handover schemes in the traditional VCS structure. They are both used for conventional handover handshake procedures. This helps to clarify the improvement of the Blockchain-based scheme over the traditional scheme. The specifications of hardware and cryptographic schemes are specified as follows: Blocks are mined by our laptop with Intel Core i5 and 8GB RAM and display card GeForce 920M. This device can finish 250K hash calculations per second. ECIES with elliptic curve secp160r1 in Crypto++ [20] is selected not only for the cryptographic scheme ECIES, but also for the digital signature scheme ECDSA as well. The cipher block has a length of 75 bytes, which is because ECIES provides a much better security level.

6.6.2 Processing Time of Cryptographic Schemes

The performance evaluation first studies the processing time cost for cryptographic schemes. It aims to obtain the accurate data of elements in Table 6.3 and further complete the result of Eq. 6.1–6.3. The key handover time is built up with the computation time data of cryptographic schemes. Figure 6.7 shows the performance of different cryptographic schemes that are used in key transfer procedures. Except for the mining time cost, the processing time increases linearly with the growth of transaction numbers. The mining algorithm is always single mining progress and the mining processing time is an average value of multiple simulations. The practice value is highly likely to have a value below this average value as only the fastest mined block is accepted by the network. The encryption and decryption schemes cost similar processing times. Signature verification costs the longest computation time among schemes. According to Eq. 6.1–6.3, signature verification is a key component in key transfer time. Table 6.5 records the average processing time for each cryptographic scheme.

Figure 6.8 plots the block preparation time in terms of various transaction numbers. The preparation time increases nonlinearly with respect to the growth of transaction numbers. The processing time slowly increases quasi-linearly before 300 transactions. Processing time is over 0.1 seconds when there are more than 400 transactions. Finally, preparation time reaches 0.95

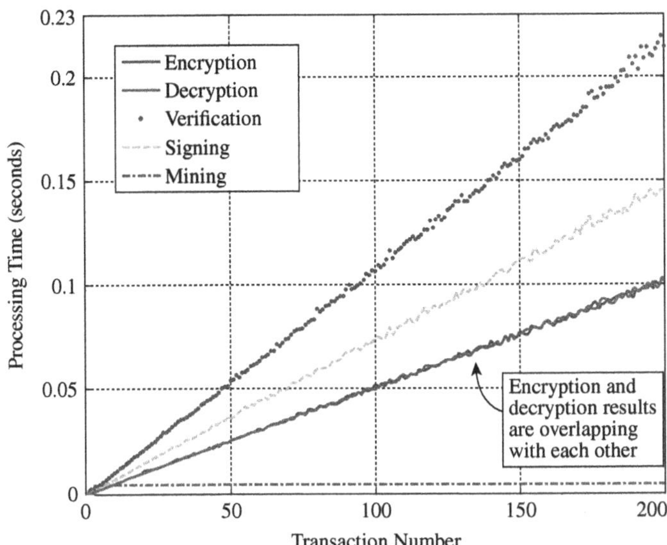

Figure 6.7 Computation time of cryptographic schemes with respect to the transaction number.

seconds when there are 1000 transactions. The nonlinear curve is caused by exponential increasing of t_{rand}, while the rest of the preparation time components increase linearly in proportion to the transaction number.

6.6.3 Handover Time

Figure 6.9 depicts the key handover performances of the blockchain scheme and the traditional scheme with respect to varying the number of transactions. The handover procedures in traditional structures are used as the benchmark of the simulation, which aims to show the performance improvement by using

Table 6.5 Average cryptography processing time.

Cryptography Scheme	Processing Time (milliseconds)
ECIES encryption	0.51027
ECIES decryption	0.73996
ECDSA signing	0.51011
ECDSA verifying	1.10171
Block mining	4.11046

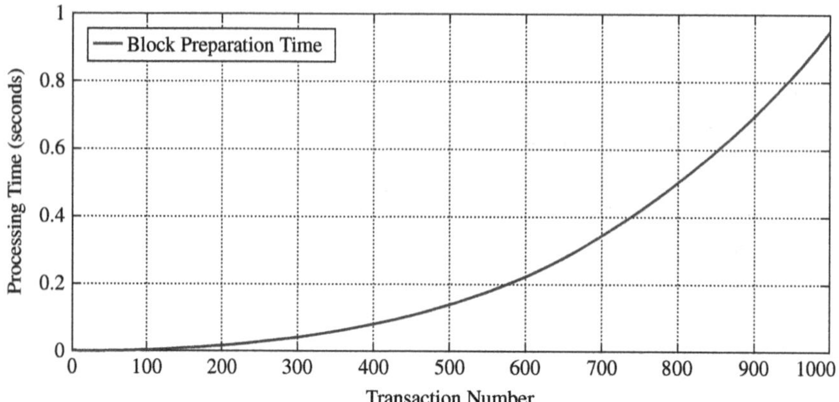

Figure 6.8 The block preparation time with respect to the transaction number.

our scheme, referring to the traditional structure results on the figure. Comparison of the different performances of key handover within the same security domain is shown in Figure 6.9(a). All the results have zero processing time when border-acrossing action does not appear in the network. It takes approximately 0.8 seconds to finish the transfer of 500 transactions, while nearly double the time is taken to handle the same amount of transactions in the traditional structure. However, two curves have an intersection at around 1300 transactions due to the nonlinear increase of blockchain key transfer time.

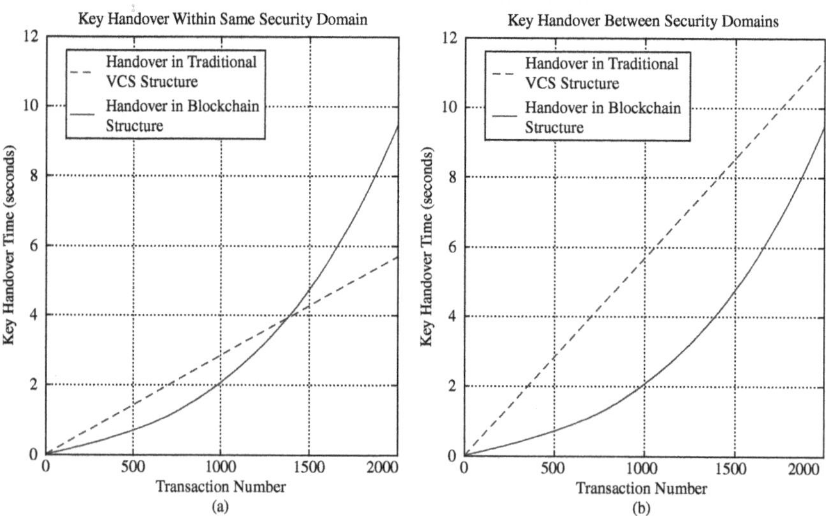

Figure 6.9 Key handover processing time comparison between structures and schemes; (a) time cost values when hand over within same security domain; (b) time cost values when hand over across different security domains.

Although our scheme costs more processing time due to the growing number of transactions, our schemes provide better scalability against the traditional structure when transaction number less than 1300. Additionally, our blockchain-based scheme saves nearly half of the processing time at transaction number equalling 1300 and the time results are always below those of the traditional scheme when transaction number is no less than 2000. According to the saturated traffic level in Beijing, the rush hour has 15,000 vehicles passing a road. This means approximately four vehicles pass a road per second. Thus, 1000 transactions can support the key handover on up to 250 roads, which is enough for most city scenarios. Similar contradistinction is demonstrated in the Figure 6.9(b) to show the results of key handover between two security domains that are managed by different PKIs. The PKIs translate messages from one security domain to another in the traditional structure. Two PKIs need to communicate with each other in order to finish the key handover. Thus, extra handshakes between PKIs result in tedious handover time in the traditional structure. Handover time cost of the traditional structure exceeds 10 seconds when the transaction number is more than 1750. The Blockchain scheme costs much less time. To summarise, the Blockchain structure has better scalability performance against the traditional structure upon message handover due to less processing time cost.

6.6.4 Performance of the Dynamic Transaction Collection Algorithm

The various transaction collection period provides an interface to allow SMs to control the number of picked transactions. A longer collection period collects more transactions, and vice versa. Therefore, different period lengths decide the number of transactions flooding into the SM network. According to the assumptions in Section 6.6.1, two-way highways support two traffic flows on the road. Here, take a single traffic flow as a standard metric unit and simulate the average transactions in a single traffic flow. Figure 6.10 plots the average transactions as a function of traffic levels and transaction collection periods. The appeared transactions are generated from a single-direction road. From the results in the figure, the appeared transaction number is directly proportional to the traffic level. Moreover, the longer the t_{CP}, the more are the transactions that are caught by SMs. The average number of transactions per t_{CP} from each traffic flow is calculated as follows: $\lambda = n_{T/CP} = \frac{n_H}{3600} \times t_{CP}$, where $n_{T/CP}$ is the average number of key handover requests (also known as transactions) within each t_{CP} and n_H is the average number of vehicles (the traffic level) passing on a road in each hour. The parameter n_R is multiplied by $n_{T/CP}$ to get the average transaction number on all the roads; here, n_R is the number of roads that are taken into calculation on the assumed topology.

Figure 6.11 Illustrates the key handover performances under various collection periods. Here, the results consider all the transactions within the highways

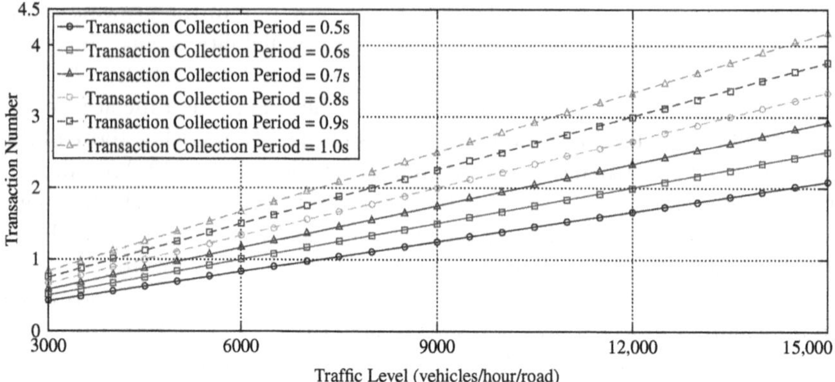

Figure 6.10 Average transaction number under various traffic levels.

based on the Beijing topology. The result of 0.5–0.7 seconds increases steadily when other results increase nonlinearly. It can be seen that mild exponential growth appears on the transaction collection period from 0.5 to 0.8 seconds. A marked nonlinear rise trend appears when the collection period is longer than 0.8 seconds. The above results indicate that a longer collection period lets SMs collect more transactions, leading to heavier processing burden and tedious computation time. According to the peak-time traffic results in Figure 6.10, an average of 4.2 transactions are captured within a 1 second collection period when the traffic level is equal to 15,000 vehicles/hour/road, while an average of 3.3 transactions are captured within 1 second's time under the lower traffic level of 12,000 vehicles/hour/road. This causes a transaction difference of $120 \times (4.2 - 3.3) = 108$ transactions, resulting in a huge difference of key handover time. Based on the result in Figure 6.7 and Figure 6.8, the key handover

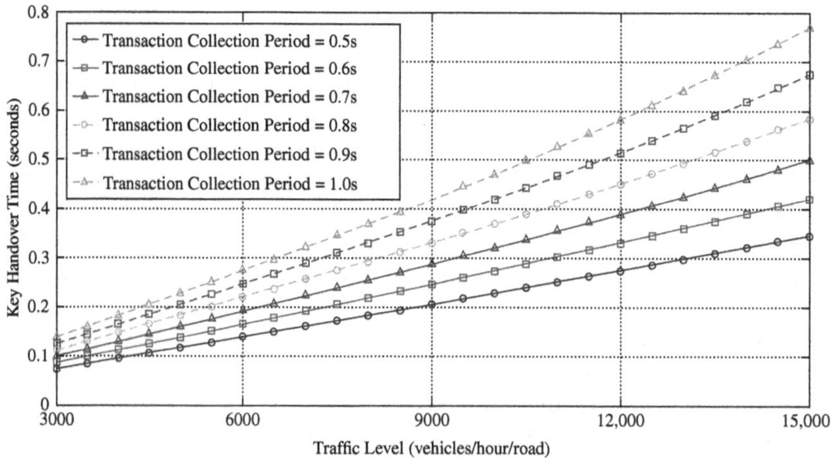

Figure 6.11 Key handover time under the transaction collection periods.

processing time increases exponentially with respect to the growth of the transaction number. Therefore, the nonlinear growth in the above figure is caused by the increasing number of collected transactions.

As mentioned in the description of dynamic transaction collection algorithm, in order to measure performance more accurately, it is necessary to have a unified measurement standard. To confirm the effectiveness of the dynamic transaction collection period, the scheme has carried out a simulation experiment to investigate the average processing time of key transfer in 1 second. The running time of the dynamic transaction collection period simulation is set to be 1 hour, and multiple key transfer procedures under various collection periods are recorded. The results are divided by 3600 seconds to measure the performance in 1 second.

The results of the dynamic collection period scheme are shown in Figure 6.12(a). The figure not only shows the time data of key handover procedures under different collection periods, but also demonstrates results using the dynamic transaction collection period scheme. From the figure, it can be seen that the dynamic scheme always occupies the minimum key transfer time among results. This is because the optimal choice of collection

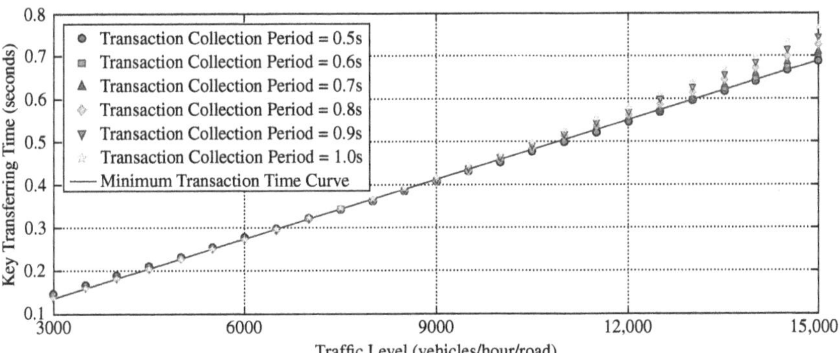

(a) Key handover time comparison—fixed and dynamic collection period schemes

	Traffic Level											
	4500	5000	5500	6000	6500	7000	7500	8000	8500	9000	9500	10,000
$t_{cp} = 0.5s$	0.211	0.233	0.255	0.279	0.298	0.323	0.344	0.365	0.387	0.409	0.433	0.455
$t_{cp} = 0.6s$	0.209	0.231	0.253	0.276	0.296	0.321	0.343	0.364	0.387	0.409	0.434	0.455
$t_{cp} = 0.7s$	0.207	0.229	0.252	0.275	0.295	0.320	0.342	0.364	0.387	0.410	0.435	0.457
$t_{cp} = 0.8s$	0.206	0.228	0.251	0.275	0.295	0.320	0.343	0.365	0.389	0.412	0.438	0.461
$t_{cp} = 0.9s$	0.205	0.228	0.251	0.275	0.296	0.321	0.344	0.366	0.391	0.415	0.442	0.466
$t_{cp} = 1.0s$	0.205	0.227	0.251	0.275	0.296	0.322	0.346	0.369	0.394	0.419	0.447	0.471

(Shaded cells: Minimum Processing Time)

(b) Key handover time from traffic level of 4500 to 10,000 vehicles/hour/road

Figure 6.12 Key handover time results measured in one second; (a) key handover time comparison—fixed and dynamic collection period schemes; (b) key handover time from traffic level of 4500 to 10,000 vehicles/hour/road.

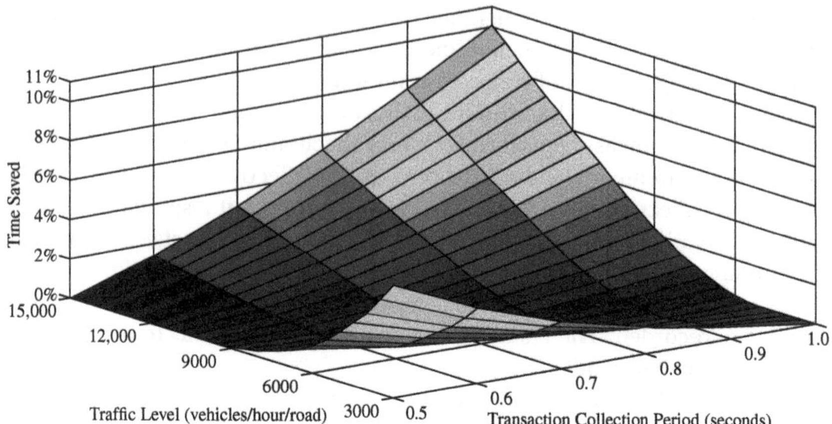

Figure 6.13 Decreased key handover time in percentage.

periods are computed using Algorithm 1. The algorithm forces SMs to select a t_{CP} that forces the system to transfer keys with the minimum time cost. A more intuitive demonstration of the simulated results is expressed in a numerical version, as shown in Figure 6.12(b). Along with the growth of traffic levels, the minimum time results occur in different t_{CP} values; a longer collection period gives less key handover process time under mild traffic conditions. However, rapid collection frequency and shorter collection intervals perform better under heavy traffic burden. That means the length of the collection period can be adjusted in terms of the traffic so that the key handover processing time can be minimized. Figure 6.13 plots the average decreased time as a function of various traffic levels and transaction collection periods ranging from 0.5 to 1 second. Under the heavier traffic level, more frequently transaction collection causes lower proportion of decreased time. While infrequent transaction collection guides to a larger proportion of decreased time at off-peak traffic level. Albeit fewer handshakes, longer collection period takes more than 10% of time cost to finish key transfer at peak traffic level. Thus, for higher traffic levels, using a shorter transaction collection period becomes an economic selection to release the computation burden and improve system efficiency. Shorter collection period, on the other hand, consumes more time to transfer transactions at low traffic situations.

6.7 Conclusion and Future Work

A decentralized VCS network structure has been proposed and implemented in this chapter. Blockchain technology is utilized to simplify the structure. The simplified structure avoids the handover procedures from passing the third party central authorities. This helps to reduce the key handover time. Dynamic transaction collection algorithm is introduced in order to further shorten the key handover time. The optimized scheme is capable of dynamically adjusting various traffic levels.

The trustworthiness of an algorithm is proved by comparison with benchmark schemes. Here, the benchmark is selected as the Blockchain-based static key management scheme. The result comparison between traditional and Blockchain schemes proves that the Blockchain-based structure can provide better key handover performance over the traditional structure. The simulation results show that the Blockchain structure gives a steady key handover time cost, which means better scalability. The Blockchain-based scheme costs lesser same-domain handover time than that of the traditional scheme when the transaction number is less than 1300. Moreover, the Blockchain-based scheme produces better cross-domain handover results compared to the results of the traditional structure if the transaction number is no more than 2000.

The effectiveness and trustworthiness of the dynamic collection periods can be further confirmed by showing better performance over the static collection period scheme. For this reason, the time-saving performances of the dynamic scheme are studied. The transaction collection period t_{CP} ranges from half to 1 second at 0.1 seconds intervals. The higher transaction collection frequency results in a lower proportion of decreased time under the heavier traffic level. In contrast, infrequent transaction collection times lead to a larger proportion of decreased time at mild traffic levels. A longer collection period takes more than 10% of the time cost to finish key transfer at peak traffic level, albeit with fewer handshakes. Thus, for higher traffic levels, using a shorter t_{CP} becomes an economic selection to release the computation burden and improve system efficiency. A shorter collection period, on the other hand, consumes more time to transfer transactions in low traffic situations. To sum up, 10% and 5% of the key handover time are saved by employing dynamic transaction collections periods under heavy and mild traffic levels, respectively.

In addition to security, another issue that matters in the VCS is privacy problems. The future blueprint of the IoT assumes that everything will be connected, including the details of human life. For this reason, people's private information is threatened by malicious users in the IoT environment. Moreover, privacy protection helps an IoT device to avoid concentrated attacks, as the adversaries are unable to focus their attack on a specific device. In order to address the privacy problem, future work will focus to further take privacy issues into consideration, including the investigation of a system that provides both security and privacy. The future work will be developed as an extension of the current contributions. The extension of the work aims at pseudonym management using a Blockchain structure, based on the current scheme. Specifically speaking, the planned future work aims at pseudonym management using a blockchain based on the current system. Moreover, users are able to decide the trade-off between security and privacy. Additionally, blockchain can support message propagation, as well as store the message history in the public ledger. These attributes have potential benefits to the accountability function, as the accountability purpose can be realized by looking back at the public ledger. To sum up, the future direction of a Blockchain-based structure in the VCS scenario will focus on how to merge security, privacy, and accountability purposes and use a single Blockchain to support them. Furthermore, the blockchain-based structure can be extended to other IoT scenarios to achieve better and stronger integrity of IoT system security.

References

1 J. B. Kenney, "Dedicated short-range communications (DSRC) standards in the United States," *Proceedings of the IEEE*, vol. 99, no. 7, pp. 1162–1182, 2011.

2 P. Papadimitratos, L. Buttyan, T. Holczer, E. Schoch, J. Freudiger, M. Raya, Z. Ma, F. Kargl, A. Kung, and J.-P. Hubaux, "Secure vehicular communication systems: Design and architecture," *IEEE Communications Magazine*, vol. 46, no. 11, pp. 100–109, November 2008.

3 C. K. Wong, M. Gouda, and S. Lam, "Secure group communications using key graphs," *IEEE/ACM Transactions on Networking*, vol. 8, no. 1, pp. 16–30, February 2000.

4 S. Nakamoto, "Bitcoin: A peer-to-peer electronic cash system." [Online]. 2008. Available: https://bitcoin.org/bitcoin.pdf.

5 G. Zyskind, O. Nathan, and A. Pentland, "Decentralizing privacy: Using blockchain to protect personal data," in *2015 IEEE Security and Privacy Workshops (SPW)*, May 2015, pp. 180–184.

6 N. Z. Aitzhan and D. Svetinovic, "Security and privacy in decentralized energy trading through multi-signatures, blockchain and anonymous messaging streams," *IEEE Transactions on Dependable and Secure Computing*, vol. 15, no. 5, pp. 840–852, 2016.

7 D. He, C. Chen, S. Chan, and J. Bu, "Secure and efficient handover authentication based on bilinear pairing functions," *IEEE Transactions on Wireless Communications*, vol. 11, no. 1, pp. 48–53, January 2012.

8 D. He, S. Chan, and M. Guizani, "Handover authentication for mobile networks: Security and efficiency aspects," *IEEE Network*, vol. 29, no. 3, pp. 96–103, May 2015.

9 D. Hankerson, A. J. Menezes, and S. Vanstone, *Guide to Elliptic Curve Cryptography*. Springer Science & Business Media, 2006.

10 D. Johnson, A. Menezes, and S. Vanstone, "The elliptic curve digital signature algorithm (ECDSA)," *International Journal of Information Security*, vol. 1, no. 1, pp. 36–63, 2001.

11 R. Schlegel, C. Y. Chow, Q. Huang, and D. S. Wong, "User-defined privacy grid system for continuous location-based services," *IEEE Transactions on Mobile Computing*, vol. 14, no. 10, pp. 2158–2172, October 2015.

12 A. Lei, C. Ogah, P. Asuquo, H. Cruickshank, and Z. Sun, "A secure key management scheme for heterogeneous secure vehicular communication systems," *ZTE Communications*, vol. 21, p. 1, 2016.

13 A. Lei, H. Cruickshank, Y. Cao, P. Asuquo, C. P. A. Ogah, and Z. Sun, "Blockchain-based dynamic key management for heterogeneous intelligent transportation systems," *IEEE Internet of Things Journal*, vol. 4, no. 6, pp. 1832–1843, 2017.

14 R. C. Merkle, "A digital signature based on a conventional encryption function," in *Advances in Cryptology, CRYPTO87*. Springer, 1987, pp. 369–378.

15 SAEJ2735, "Dedicated Short Range Communications (DSRC) Message Set Dictionary", J2735_201603, March 2016. [Online]. Available: http://doi.org/10.4271/J2735_201603.

16 R. T. Luttinen, *Statistical Analysis of Vehicle Time Headways*. Helsinki University of Technology, 1996.

17 J. Rice, *Mathematical Statistics and Data Analysis*. Brooks/Cole Pub. Co., 1988.

18 A. Varga, "The OMNeT++ discrete event simulation system," in *Proceedings of the European Simulation Multiconference (ESM2001)*, 2001, pp. 1–7.

19 C. Sommer, R. German, and F. Dressler, "Bidirectionally coupled network and road traffic simulation for improved IVC analysis," *IEEE Transactions on Mobile Computing*, vol. 10, no. 1, pp. 3–15, 2011.

20 W. Dai, "Crypto++ library 5.6.0." [Online]. 2009. Available: http://www.cryptopp.com.

7

Blockchain-enabled Information Sharing Framework for Cybersecurity

Abdulhamid Adebayo,[1] Danda B. Rawat,[1] Laurent Njilla,[2] and Charles A. Kamhoua[3]

[1] *Howard University, Department of Electrical Engineering and Computer Science, Washington DC, USA*
[2] *US Air Force Research Lab, Cyber Assurance Branch, Rome, NY, USA*
[3] *US Army Research Laboratory, Network Security Branch, Adelphi, MD, USA*

7.1 Introduction

Despite the attraction of interest in cyber defense, the proactive prevention and especially response to cyberattacks is a continuous challenge in a bid to protect critical infrastructures and private information [1–4]. Network systems exhibit heterogeneity, as do cyberattacks, which makes cybersecurity a more difficult job. Hence, the following questions are raised: Can organizations share information to help prevent cyberattacks? Can the threat information be shared in such a way that their privacy will be maintained? Today's frameworks have, however, failed to answer these questions in a low-cost and privacy-aware implementation [5].

Taking a cue from the popular national "if you see something, say/report something" campaign by the US Department of Homeland Security (and used by many nations in antigraft wars), the goal is to have participating organizations report cybersecurity-related incidents without revealing their private information to enable others to make informed decisions about security measures and solutions. As promising as this sounds, it has been found that several organizations are conservative about sharing information about their cyber threats with other (competitive or not) organizations. Investigations show that this hesitation is due to the following reasons:

- Having access to a company's threat information might provide their competition with a comparative advantage.
- There is no standardized format for information exchange about cybersecurity-related incidents [5].

Blockchain for Distributed Systems Security, First Edition. Edited by Sachin S. Shetty, Charles A. Kamhoua, and Laurent L. Njilla.

- The public perception that often accompanies the exposure of information about an organization's cyberattack can be devastating; previous breaches have resulted in the loss of millions of dollars in market value by shareholders [6].
- Benefits from threat information sharing are often not immediately visible.

Despite these constraints, several efforts have been made to make threat information sharing and intelligence gathering a reality. Notably, a group of cybersecurity experts and policy makers from the government and industry, known as ITU-T Study Group 17, developed a cybersecurity information exchange framework [5]. This system enables researchers to explore the information-sharing mechanisms.

One domain that could benefit immensely from information sharing is the health sector. A Fast Healthcare Interoperability Resources (FHIR) framework provides an application programming interface (API) for health record exchange [7, 8]. Other similar research has focused on the Internet of Things (IoT) [9], security in decentralized infrastructure models, and privacy-risk control in healthcare systems [10].

Blockchain as a concept has been successfully used in privacy-aware systems such as Bitcoin [11, 12]. Bitcoin has proven the correctness of having a trusted and auditable peer-to-peer communication system by using a public ledger that offers transaction transparency. However, the requirements for a threat information-sharing framework are unique. Any information identifiable should be anonymous. This is important in protecting the identity of the source organization of cyberattack intelligence. Also, the information shared through the framework should be restricted, with only the summary about the attack incident and the cyber-defense solutions shared with other participants.

Notable concerns with traditional information-sharing frameworks include the need to transfer huge data to other organizations or use a central unit to collect data, creating a pool from participating organizations. Multiple transfers of huge data could suffer from limited bandwidth. Also, the use of a central unit requires ownership of control by the central trusted authority. This poses a problem of ownership and privacy for organization data. The lack of a universal authoritative standard for such centralization plays a large role in the adoption (or lack of it) of threat-sharing frameworks.

The rest of the chapter is organized as follows: Section 7.2 provides an overview of the Blockchain-based Information Sharing (BIS) framework. In Section 7.3, the Blockchain and transaction process in the BIS framework is discussed. Section 7.4 discusses cyberattack detection and information sharing within BIS and deployment of cyber-defense solutions. A one-way cross-group attack game in the BIS framework is presented in Section 7.5 with the two-way attack presented in Section 7.6. In Section 7.7, a Stackelberg game for cyberattack and defense analysis is discussed. The chapter is concluded in Section 7.8.

7.2 The BIS Framework

Transfer of funds from one party to another traditionally requires trusted third parties such as banks or payment merchants. As a disruptive technology, Bitcoin is based on a cryptographic technique that uses peer-to-peer communication and does not require such third parties. Bitcoin uses a distributed ledger system where all transactions are published on a public ledger using the concept of Blockchain. A block in the chain is then executed using a consensus algorithm such as proof of work. Bitcoin requires that transactions are verified by other users in a decentralized network, making it practically impossible to generate illegitimate transactions.

Following the approach used in Bitcoin, BIS uses a Blockchain protocol over the public internet. The BIS framework is shown in Figure 7.1 and has three entities:

- *Organization*—this refers to the parties participating in the cyberattack information sharing with a collective goal to prevent future cyberattacks.
- *Services*—refers to the providers of the cyberattack-related information and applications that process data.

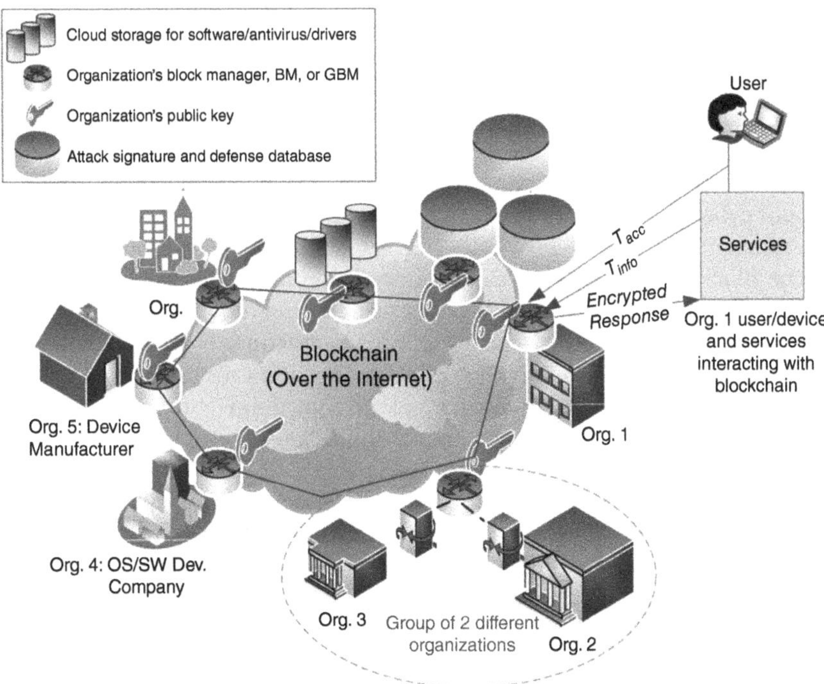

Figure 7.1 A typical Blockchain-based information-sharing framework among multiple organizations/agents [13].

- *Manager nodes*—trusted devices that are dedicated to maintaining the Blockchain as well as the distributed cryptographic keys. Even though organizations use dynamically changed public keys to conceal their identity, manager nodes maintain service profiles on the Blockchain and verify the identity of every participating organization.

7.3 Transactions on BIS

After a description of the BIS framework components, a detailed look into how transactions are handled in BIS is depicted in Figure 7.1. BIS typically accepts two types of transactions provided to organizations via the API:

1. transactions for access control management (Tacc)
2. transactions for information storage and retrieval (Tinfo)

While maintaining their privacy, each participating organization shares its cyberattack information using BIS over an interface, usually graphical. Upon signing up, each organization is assigned an identity with associated permissions, which are sent to the Blockchain using the Tacc transaction. As an integral part of BIS, shared information is sent to the Blockchain using the Tinfo transaction after being encrypted using a shared encryption key. Subsequently, when participating organizations retrieve such information either by querying with the Tinfo transaction or by a service, only a pointer to the data on the public ledger is used. Services and organizations are verified using the digital signature. As a means to address the conservation of organizations in adopting a cyberattack information sharing system, BIS only collects information about a cyberattack and not the details about its success or damage recorded by the attack.

The Blockchain in BIS consists of transaction blocks, as depicted in Figure 7.2. The blocks are chained together using a hash or numeric digest of the block content through which the integrity of transactions is verified, making it practically impossible to manipulate. By chaining, it means the hash of a block n depends on its predecessor block $n - 1$. As shown in Figure 7.2, that makes the Blockchain immune to malicious actions, as a change in one block would require change in subsequent predecessor blocks.

The Blockchain grows with every verified transaction by participating organizations in the BIS framework. The legitimacy of a transaction is verified using the digital signature of the organization (verification) and the existence of the previous transaction on the same ledger. In Section 7.4, a proof-of-attack-detection (PoAD) consensus algorithm is discussed for generating new blocks. The group block manager (GBM) or Block Manager (BM) then creates a new block and forwards it to other BMs for verification. This allows all BMs to contribute to verifying the correctness of the block by digitally signing it. A GBM can be nominated from a group of BMs based on their business memorandum

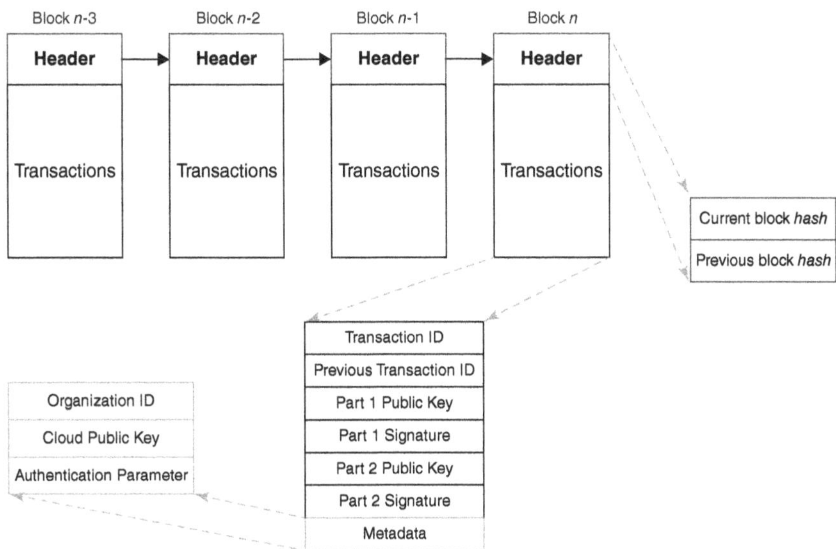

Figure 7.2 A typical structure of Blockchain for information sharing [13].

of understanding (MoU). The signed block is subsequently returned to the originating BM, which adds it to the Blockchain.

BIS allows a heterogeneous network of organizations including manufacturers, system/software providers, security service providers, as well as devices such as cell phones, cyber-physical systems, and IoT devices. In an occurrence of multiple similar devices belonging to the same organization, a BM is chosen to store BIS transactions. Also, each organization maintains a local copy of the transactions related to the organization (known as a private ledger), which is then linked to the BM by using a hash that contains the hash of the public Blockchain. Control is established in each organization with a trusted device known as local manager, which is responsible for maintaining the private ledger as well as connecting the organization to the BIS framework through an internet gateway. Similar to the analogy employed in Port Address Translation (PAT) and/or Network Address Translation (NAT) in IPv4 networks, all communications to and from the organization are routed through the local manager.

7.4 Cyberattack Detection and Information Sharing

In the previous section, we saw how each organization generates transactions and how the blocks are merged on the BIS framework. In this section, PoAD is described as a consensus algorithm. Based on the Evaluation Assurance Level

(EAL) used by the organization for its infrastructure (which includes security patches, operating systems, and firewalls), it is assumed that the organization is responsible for compliance with such a standard. Also, the sharing of cyberattack information or attack signatures (with possible countermeasures) through the BIS framework is the sole responsibility of each organization [3, 14, 15].

A malicious organization in BIS is, however, identified by its unwillingness to participate in a timely and positive manner. An example of a malicious organizations is an antivirus company that fails to develop security patches for known vulnerabilities or engages in the creation of new malware products themselves. Another example are operating system developers that provide backdoors to their systems without providing timely patches to fix them. Attack information sharing is done with the help of participating organizations on BIS in the verification of the shared information using Blockchain. For instance, attack information from an organization with Microsoft Windows 10 running on HP devices with a firewall and Avast antivirus should be verified through the Blockchain on BIS by HP, Avast, and Microsoft to reach a consensus. The source of the cyberattack information is declared as the initiator of this process.

In order to avoid unnecessary multiple entries of incident reports, which can occur with multiple organizations reporting the same attack at the same time, the cloud storage chooses the report with a countermeasure (if any) and discards the rest. Once the cyber-defense solution for a reported/shared cyberattack is available, it is published like software updates to all participating organizations for download and deployment.

Recall that the goal of BIS is to provide a robust framework to prevent cyberattacks in any networked system. Thus, providing cyber-defense solutions to participating organizations in BIS is a key functionality. Once a solution is available, it is stored in the cloud, where it is accessible to all participating organizations and shared using Blockchain. The source of this solution creates a multisignature transaction where its own key 1 and signature, which is generated using signed hash, are stored. Hence, the hash can be verified by other participating devices to ensure data integrity. In a case where the source is a software provider, the software binary file is assumed to be stored in the cloud for users to download. The part 2 field of the transaction is written by the manufacturer and must match the part 1 key and signature for updates to be forwarded to all devices/networks within the organization. Otherwise, it is forwarded to the gateways of other organizations who verify it by matching the key in the transaction with its manufacturer's key. The received multisignature transaction metadata contain authentication parameters from legitimate software updates. The integrity of the update is checked by comparing the signed hash of both the equipment manufacturer and the software provider. Note that verified attack information is also shared along with the cyber-defense solutions in BIS and then stored in the cloud-based information base of BIS.

7.5 Cross-group Attack Game in Blockchain-based BIS Framework: One-way Attack

Organizations with similar features or that belong to similar domains have similar requirements and interests. They can form a group and function together to achieve maximum profit for the group. Social networking companies like Twitter, Facebook, and Snapchat can combine to form groups.

Consider two groups, Group 1 and Group 2, with N1 and N2 number of organizations, respectively, sharing cyberattack information through BIS. The benefit achieved by the group is shared among the group members. Member organizations with bits of input are rewarded equally after the completion of work. BIS also allows for cross participation among group members. For instance, Group 2 members could form a subgroup and act as an organization to participate in Group 1. They can also choose not to participate in the legitimate block formation of their own group by not releasing detected cyberattack information or not developing cyber-defense solutions for reported security attacks.

A one-way attack aims to reduce the utility of Group 1 by using a subgroup of $X_{2\rightarrow1}$ ($\leq N_2$) members from Group 2, where $X_{2\rightarrow1}$ members of Group 2 could try to hinder the Blockchain-building process. The direct utilities of group k in BIS can be expressed as [13]:

$$U_k = \log(\sigma_k + \gamma_k), \quad k = 1, 2$$

where $\log(\sigma_k + \gamma_k)$ is a generic convex function of γ_k for each group k and typical value 1, $X_{2\rightarrow1}$ members of Group 2 are considered malicious in Group 1, as they do not participate in the Blockchain building of their own group. The quality factor of the Blockchain generation process for Group 1 can be expressed as:

$$\gamma_1 = \frac{N_1}{N - X_{2\rightarrow1}}.$$

Since $X_{2\rightarrow1}$ members do not participate in Group 2, leaving $N - X_{2\rightarrow1}$ active members, the quality factor of the Blockchain-generation process for Group 2 is expressed as:

$$\gamma_2 = \frac{N_2 - X_{2\rightarrow1}}{N - X_{2\rightarrow1}}.$$

Since there is no mechanism for selective rewarding of legitimate members in a group, all members are rewarded equally with the cross-participating members; i.e. Group 1 members share their utility with the Group 2 members

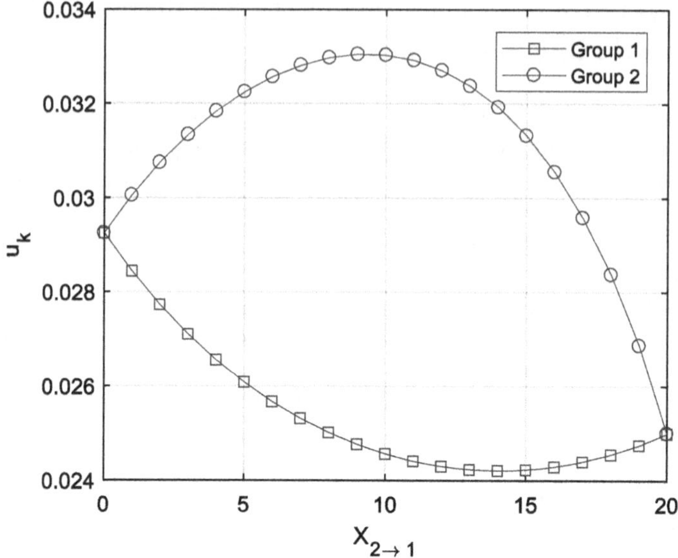

Figure 7.3 Variation of expected utility vs. the number of cross-group participants, where N = 40 organizations/users are equally divided into two groups.

that intruded it. The utility density functions for Groups 1 and 2 are then expressed as:

$$u_1 = \frac{\log\left(1 + \frac{N_1}{N - X_{2\to1}}\right)}{N_1 + X_{2\to1}}$$

$$u_2 = \frac{\log\left(\frac{N_2 - X_{2\to1}}{N - X_{2\to1}}\right) + X_{2\to1}\frac{\log\left(1 + \frac{N_1}{N - X_{2\to1}}\right)}{N_1 + X_{2\to1}}}{N_2}.$$

Evaluating the performance of the game with multiple simulations of different number of cross-group participants shows a decrease in Group 1 utility until 50% of the organizations cross participate. $N = 40$ organizations is equally halved to form groups. In this phase, $X_{2\to1}$ increases despite a corresponding utility increase in Group 2 over the same period. This is attributed to the fact that Group 2 participants get rewards from cross participation in addition to the rewards from the group, as shown in Figure 7.3.

At $X_{2\to1} = N_2$, indicating a full cross participation by members of Group 2, they get the contribution of the subgroup, which is only a fraction of what is obtainable from legitimate participation. It is then concluded that a dominant strategy of the game will have full cross participation of all members of the group. If not, then not participating in cross-group activities will be the best response.

7.6 Cross-group Attack Game in Blockchain-based BIS Framework: Two-way Attack

In this form of attack, a subgroup of Group 1 of size $X_{1\rightarrow2} < N_1$ participates in Group 2, and a subgroup of Group 2 of size $X_{2\rightarrow1} < N_2$ subsequently acts maliciously in Group 1. The direct utility of a group, k, is expressed as [13]:

$$U'_k = \log\left(1 + \gamma'_k\right), \quad k = 1, 2,$$

where γ'_k is calculated as

$$\gamma'_k = \frac{N_k - \sum_{\forall j} X_{k\rightarrow j}}{N - \sum_{\forall j} X_{k\rightarrow j} - \sum_{\forall j} X_{j\rightarrow k}}.$$

$X_{k\rightarrow j}$ and $X_{j\rightarrow k}$ represent the total number of cross-participating organizations from Groups k to j and j to k, respectively.

The utility density for Group k can then be expressed as:

$$\upsilon'_k = \frac{U'_k + \sum_{\forall j} X_{k\rightarrow j} \times u'_j}{N_k - \sum_{\forall j} X_{j\rightarrow k}}.$$

The derivations of utility densities u'_1 and u'_2 for a two-group consideration can be found in [13].

When the number of players N_1 and N_2 are finite, players are allowed to play a mixed strategy, with the game always having an equilibrium $X_{1\rightarrow2}$ and $X_{2\rightarrow1}$ values where:

$$\frac{\partial u'_1}{\partial X_{1\rightarrow2}} = 0 \quad \text{and} \quad \frac{\partial u'_2}{\partial X_{2\rightarrow1}} = 0.$$

One group's utility is proportional to the gain (or loss) of the other group's utility; hence, it looks like a zero-sum game. The strategy space of the players in a two-way game can be defined as S = {Attack, No attack}. The outcome of the game and dominant strategies for both group/players can be found in Table 7.1, with examples shown in Figure 7.4.

Table 7.1 Expected utility of each group.

	Group 2—Attack	**Group 2—No Attack**
Group 1—Attack	$u''_1 < u_1,\ u''_2 < u'_2$	$u''_1 > u_1,\ u''_2 < u'_2$
Group 2—No Attack	$u''_1 < u'_1, u''_2 > u'_2$	$u'_1,\ u'_2$

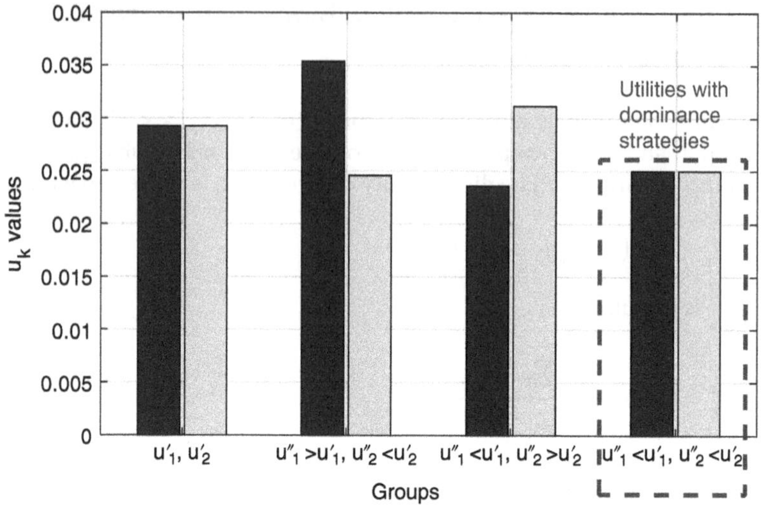

Figure 7.4 Example of expected group utilities.

7.7 Stackelberg Game for Cyberattack and Defense Analysis

Often attackers (known as outsiders) launch cyberattacks on BIS without participating in the information-sharing process. The security level of an organization, k, can then be considered as $0 \leq \ell_k \leq 1\ \forall k$ where the security level is directly proportional to a system hardening investment of the organization based on past attacks and successful recovery rate from the attacks. The average security level of an organization can be expressed as $\overline{\ell_k} = \frac{1}{N}\sum_{K=1}^{N} \ell_k$. The probability of cyberattacks for a given organization, k, can also be expressed as:

$$p_k = (1 - \ell_k)(1 - \bar{\ell}_k),\ \forall k.$$

The cyberattacks and defense actions can be modeled as a typical multi-agent game for security. The organizations' strategies are attacked by the malicious actions of attackers. Defense actions based on the attackers' strategies are also taken by defensive organizations and shared through BIS. This game can be formulated as a Stackelberg game with leader and follower subgames. It should be noted that government and industrial standard practices about hardening the network system on occurrence of cyberattacks and detection of vulnerabilities must be upheld by organizations. Thus, in the Stackelberg game, attackers are treated as leaders since they initiate attacks on the organizations' network system, while legitimate organizations are treated as followers since they only react to the cyberattacks or known vulnerability.

Defenders/follower subgame—This game is represented as an optimization problem with the goal for a given organization, k, being to minimize the impact of the attack. Based on the security state of an organization and motivation of attack, an attacker chooses a strategy a_k, $\forall k$ with a security impact level to the victim organization, k, as $i_{m,k}$. The optimization problem is presented as:

$$\begin{aligned}
&\underset{\Psi_k, p_k, \forall k}{\text{minimize}}\ O_{U_k} = p_k S_k \beta_k \log(1+\Psi_k)\\
&\qquad \text{subject to } \sum_{\forall m} i_{m,k}\Psi_k \le \overline{B_k};\\
&\qquad\qquad i_{m,k} \ge 0;\ \forall m,\ \forall k;\\
&\qquad\qquad\quad \Psi_k \ge \overline{\Psi_k};\ \forall k\\
&S_k \in \{1,0\},\ s_k > 0,\ \text{and } c_k > 0;\ \forall k,
\end{aligned}$$

where $\overline{B_k}$ is the maximum tolerable socioeconomic level of organization k due to cyberattacks, $i_{m,k}$ is the targeted impact level of cyberattack m to a given organization, k, using an attack strategy a_k, and $\Psi_k \ge \overline{\Psi_k}$ is the investment level constraint of each organization for cyber-defense. S_k is the binary strategy set with a value of 1 indicating "share". The information-sharing and participation cost is represented by $s_k > 0$ and $c_k > 0$, respectively. The utility scaling factor β_k is considered to be 1 for simplicity. The problem is then expressed as:

$$\begin{aligned}
&\underset{\Psi_k, p_k, \forall k}{\text{minimize}}\ O_{U_k} = p_k \log(1+\Psi_k)\\
&\quad \text{subject to } \sum_{\forall m} i_{m,k}\Psi_k \le \overline{B_k};\\
&\qquad\quad i_{m,k} \ge 0;\ \forall m,\ \forall k;\\
&\qquad\qquad \Psi_k \ge \overline{\Psi_k};\ \forall k.
\end{aligned}$$

The problem is then solved using the Lagrangian method to arrive at the best response for the follower subgame for the given attack strategies, expressed as:

$$\Psi_k = \frac{\sum_{\forall m} i_{m,k} + \overline{B_k}}{K i_{m,k}} - 1,\ \forall k.$$

Attacker/leader subgame—A possibility is for attackers to attack the organization through noncooperation with an aim to gain continued unauthorized access to information or other economic benefits. In this case, the noncooperative attacker game (AG) is then represented as $A_G = \langle \mathcal{K}, \{A_k\}_{k\in K}, \mathcal{U}_k(.)\rangle$. This game is composed of three components:

- The set of active attackers $\mathcal{K} = \{1, 2, \ldots, K\}$ whose victim can be one or more organizations.

- The set of attacking strategies used by the attackers $\{a_1, a_k, \dots, a_K\}$.
- The strategy space mapping to a positive real number representing the payoff, expressed as $\mathcal{U}_k(.) : \{\mathcal{A}_1 \times \dots \times \mathcal{A}_K\}$.

For an attacker with an attacking strategy a_k, the utility optimization problem is then expressed as:

$$\underset{a_k, \forall k}{\text{maximize}}\ A_{U_m}(a_k, a_{-k}) = \sum_{k=1}^{N} p_k(1 - i_{m,k}(a_k))(1 - \Psi_k)$$
$$\text{subject to } \{a_k\} \neq \emptyset,\ \forall k,$$
$$\bar{i}_{m,k} \geq i_{m,k} \geq 0,\ \forall m,\ \forall k$$
$$p_k > 0,\ \forall k.$$

To maximize the attacker's utility, at least one attack strategy, indicated by $\{a_k\} \neq \emptyset$, is required. Solving this maximization problem by the Lagrangian method and taking the first derivative equated to zero yields the impact level value. The expected impact level of a cyberattack, m, on a given organization, k, is then expressed as:

$$i_{m,k}(a_k) = \max\{\eta_{m,k} r_b(m, k) + \theta_{m,k} r_d(m, k) + \mu_{m,k} r_r(m, k) - \iota_k, \bar{i}_{m,k}\},$$

where $r_b = [0, 1]$ represents a denial-of-service attack, $r_d = [0, 1]$ indicates a delayed response to users' requests, and $r_r = [0, 1]$ represents the reduction in reputation of a given organization. The weighting factors for halting business operations, causing delay in users request response, and reduction in reputation levels are represented by $0 \leq \eta_{m,k} \leq 1$, $0 \leq \theta_{m,k} \leq 1$ and $0 \leq \mu_{m,k} \leq 1$, respectively, as an effect of a cyberattack, m, by taking an attack action a_k to a victim organization, k.

Performance evaluation—To evaluate the performance of the approach discussed so far in this section, a scenario of four organizations with varying security and investment levels is set up with four varying expected impact level attackers. An attacker with $\bar{B}_k = 0.1\ \forall k$ attacks all four organizations iteratively. Although the maximum effective attack-impact level could be 0 or 100%, simulations considered intermediate values such that $\bar{i}_{m,k} = \{0.27, 0.26, 0.25, 0.24\}$.

Plotting the utilities of the four different organizations against the number of attack iterations, as shown in Figure 7.5, a decrease in the expected utilities of the organizations is visible with increasing iterations due to the increasing attack-impact levels from the attacker. Figure 7.6 shows a decrease in the security/investment levels of organizations for given investment levels as the attacker's attack-impact level increases. A plot of the expected impact levels against the attack iterations (Figure 7.7) shows that the organization with the lowest expected attack impact from the attacker (in this case, organization 3)

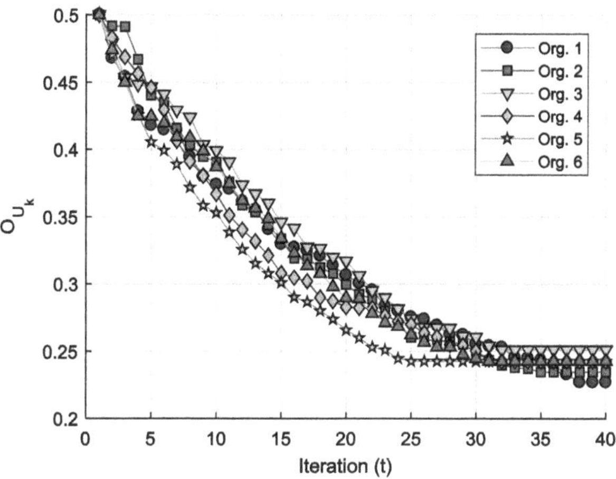

Figure 7.5 Expected utility of different organizations with different security/investment levels vs. iterations.

experiences the highest security level for a chosen organization investment (as shown in Figure 7.5). In a bid to show the relationship between the attacker's utilities for different expected attack-impact levels and attack iterations, Figure 7.8 highlights that the organization with the lowest (or highest) investment level (as shown in Figure 7.5) is subjected to the highest (or lowest) attacker utility. Furthermore, the simulation results shows the convergence of the game at a unique equilibrium point.

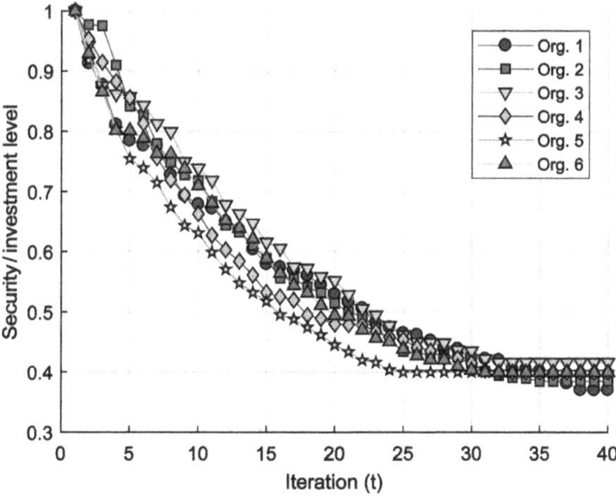

Figure 7.6 Expected security/investment levels caused by cyberattack impact vs. iterations.

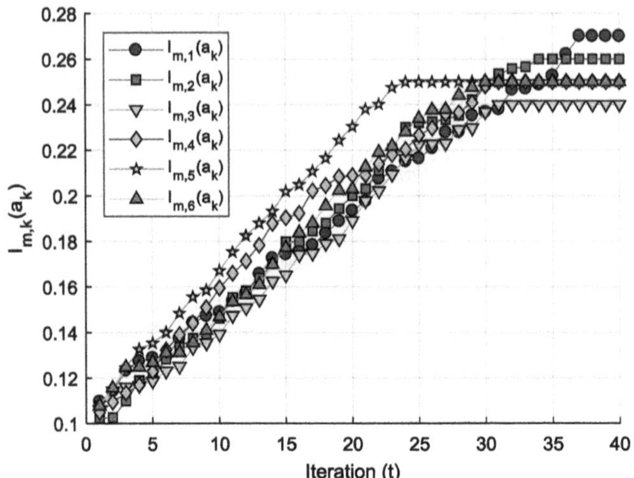

Figure 7.7 Variation of attack impact vs. iterations.

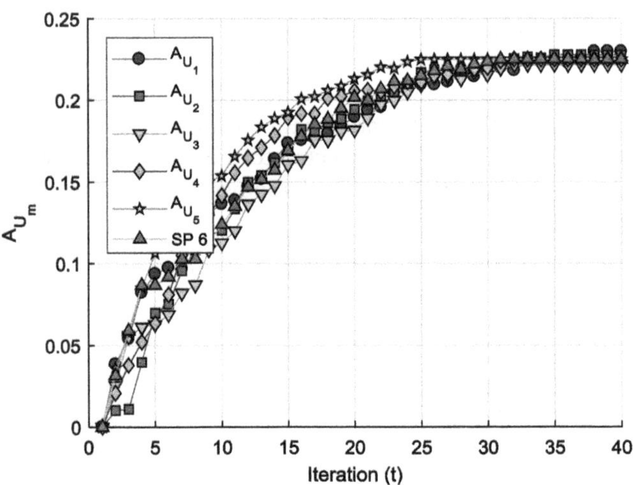

Figure 7.8 Variation of expected attacker utility vs. iterations.

7.8 Conclusion

The need for intelligence gathering as a tool for combating cyberattacks in the future cannot be overemphasized. Even though reservations are being experienced by organizations despite knowing the potential benefit of such collaborations, the approach employed by BIS as discussed in this chapter further increases the chance of adoption. BIS leverages on the concept of Blockchain, used in the popular Bitcoin system to enhance the integrity of shared information while maintaining privacy. Participating organizations in the Blockchain-based BIS framework maintain ownership and control of shared data without the need of a trusted third party usually responsible for control and security. A formal description of games with malicious participating organizations in a bid to jeopardize the cyber-defense mechanism or engage in cross participation was discussed. Furthermore, a description of a Stackelberg-game-based cyber-attack and a defense analysis involving attacks on participating organizations from outsiders was given.

References

1 R. Armstrong, J. Mayo, and F. Siebenlist, "Complexity science challenges in cybersecurity," Sandia National Laboratories SAND Report, 2009.
2 D. B. Rawat and C. Bajracharya, *Vehicular Cyber Physical Systems: Adaptive Connectivity and Security*. Springer, 2016.
3 D. B. Rawat and C. Bajracharya, "Detection of false data injection attacks in smart grid communication systems," *IEEE Signal Processing Letters*, vol. 22, no. 10, pp. 1652–1656, October 2015.
4 D. B. Rawat and S. Reddy, "Software defined networking architecture, security and energy efficiency: A survey," *IEEE Communications Surveys & Tutorials*, vol. 19, no. 1, pp. 325–346, 2017.
5 A. Rutkowski, Y. Kadobayashi, I. Furey, D. Rajnovic, R. Martin, T. Takahashi, C. Schultz, G. Reid, G. Schudel, and M. Hird, "CYBEX: The cybersecurity information exchange framework (x.1500)," *ACM SIGCOMM Computer Communication Review*, vol. 40, no. 5, pp. 59–64, 2010.
6 C. Clifton, M. Kantarciolu, A. Doan, G. Schadow, J. Vaidya, A. Elmagarmid, and D. Suciu, "Privacy-preserving data integration and sharing," in *Proceedings of the 9th ACM SIGMOD Workshop on Research Issues in Data Mining and Knowledge Discovery*, 2004.
7 T. Benson, *Principles of Health Interoperability HL7 and SNOMED*. Health Informatics, 2010.
8 Y. Lindell and B. Pinkas, "Secure multiparty computation for privacy-preserving data mining," *Journal of Privacy and Confidentiality*, vol. 1, no. 1, p. 5, 2009.
9 A. Dorri, S. Kanhere, and R. Jurdak, "Towards an optimized blockchain for IoT," in *Proceedings of the Second International Conference on Internet-of-Things Design and Implementation*, 2017.
10 X. Yue, H. Wang, D. Jin, M. Li, and W. Jiang, "Healthcare data gateways: Found healthcare intelligence on blockchain with novel privacy risk control," *Journal of Medical Systems*, vol. 40, no. 10, p. 218, 2016.
11 S. Nakamoto, "Bitcoin: A peer-to-peer electronic cash system." [Online]. 2008. Available: http://www.bitcoin.org/bitcoin.pdf. [Accessed May 21, 2017].

12 T. Simonite, "What Bitcoin is, and why it matters." [Online]. May 25, 2011. Available: https://goo.gl/Btqrfc. [Accessed June 1, 2017].
13 D. B. Rawat, L. Njilla, K. Kwiat, and C. Kamhoua, "iShare: Blockchain-based privacy-aware multi-agent information sharing games for cybersecurity," in *International Conference on Computing, Networking and Communications*, Maui, Hawaii, 2018.
14 G. Carl, G. Kesidis, R. Brooks, and S. Rai, "Denial-of-service attack-detection techniques," *IEEE Internet Computing*, vol. 10, no. 1, pp. 82–89, 2006.
15 F. Pasqualetti, F. Dorfler, and F. Bullo, "Attack detection and identification in cyber-physical systems," *IEEE Transactions on Automatic Control*, vol. 58, no. 11, pp. 2715–2729, 2013.

Part III

Blockchain Security Analysis

8

Blockcloud Security Analysis

Deepak Tosh,[1] Sachin S. Shetty,[2] Xueping Liang,[2] Laurent Njilla,[3] Charles A. Kamhoua,[4] and Kevin Kwiat[5]

[1] *University of Texas at El Paso, Department of Computer Science, El Paso, TX, USA*
[2] *Old Dominion University, Virginia Modeling, Analysis and Simulation Center, Norfolk, VA, USA*
[3] *US Air Force Research Lab, Cyber Assurance Branch, Rome, NY, USA*
[4] *US Army Research Lab, Network Security Branch, Adelphi, MD, USA*
[5] *Haloed Sun TEK, LLC, CAESAR Group, Sarasota, FL, USA*

8.1 Introduction

Blockchain technology has attracted tremendous interest from a wide range of stakeholders, including finance, healthcare, utilities, real estate, and government agencies. Blockchain networks utilize a shared, distributed, and fault tolerant ledger platform that every participant in the network can share but no entity can control. Blockchains assume the presence of adversaries in the network and nullify adversarial strategies by harnessing the computational capabilities of the honest nodes; the information exchanged is resilient to manipulation and destruction. Blockchain technology will be beneficial to cloud services that have a strong desire for assured data provenance and support cloud auditing. To enable data integrity over the public ledger in a blockchain cloud, cryptographically enforced blocks join in the blockchain after a consensus is reached in the decentralized network, where transactions in the blocks are authenticated by peers of the network. This shared ledger could potentially contain the history of every transaction related to any sort of asset irrespective of its type—financial, physical, or digital—that can be verified, monitored, and cleared without the involvement of the cloud administrator. The combination of cryptographic mechanism and a decentralized public ledger allows to build any kind of application on top of the blockchain without worrying about trust components of users and maliciousness in the blockchain-enabled cloud system.

Since blockchain update occurs in a peer-to-peer (P2P) network, the state of the blockchain must be kept intact among every peer. This necessitates the

Blockchain for Distributed Systems Security, First Edition. Edited by Sachin S. Shetty, Charles A. Kamhoua, and Laurent L. Njilla.

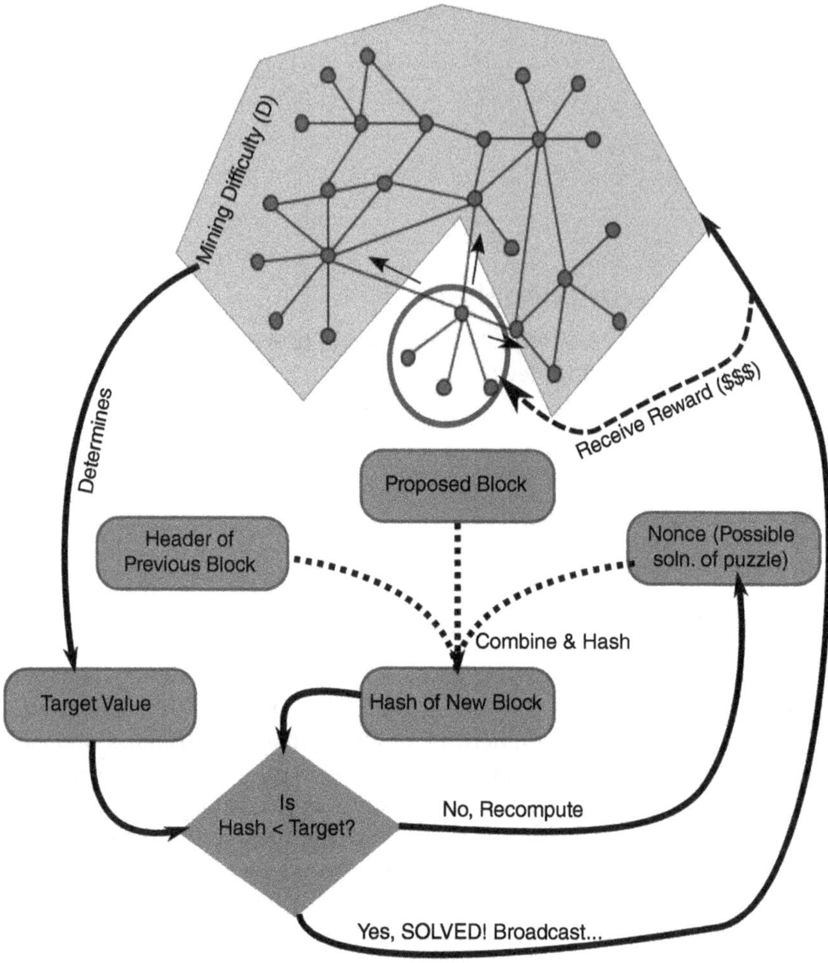

Figure 8.1 Overview of block mining process.

use of distributed consensus mechanisms so that block inclusion would not disturb the state of the blockchain. We discuss various consensus mechanisms suitable for blockchain in the next section, among which proof of work (PoW) consensus is a famous one, which is being used for Bitcoin's blockchain. In this scheme, for successfully adding a block in the blockchain, the miners need to solve a crypto puzzle that is computationally hard. The process is depicted in Figure 8.1. The solution is hard to find but easy to verify, and the difficulty is dynamically set by the network. Therefore, solving such crypto puzzles comes at a price in terms of hashing power, electricity, hardware, etc., but succeeding in the competition rewards well too. Since mining alone is costly and receiving reward is so infrequent, honest miners prefer to work in pools.

However, irrational malicious parties can come up with their own mining power to disrupt the other honest miners' operations. Block withholding attack [1] is one of the well-known schemes, which adversaries may adopt to make the pool lose the block-finding competition. In block withholding attacks, malicious pool members, who have joined for truthfully mining blocks, never actually publish the successfully mined blocks; they only submit their regular *shares* that are not solutions. Hence, the attacker decreases the expected revenue of the pool by withholding the valid blocks but increases its own reward by submitting as many *shares* as possible to the pool manager.

In order to realize a blockchain cloud, it is important to understand the vulnerabilities of the technology. In this chapter, we focus on investigating the need or blockchain in developing a secure cloud system and perform in-depth analysis on various possible vulnerabilities in the blockchain cloud. The vulnerabilities in a blockchain cloud will primarily arise due to the requirement of computational power to achieve PoW-based consensus. There exist other consensus mechanisms, such as Proof of Stake (PoS), Perfect Byzantine Fault Tolerance (PBFT), Proof of Activity (PoA), and Proof of Elapsed Time (PoEA), which do not necessarily require high computational abilities to mine blocks. However, current public blockchain implementations rely on PoW to achieve consensus. So, the miners need to be computationally efficient to produce valid blocks as quickly as possible to get rewarded. At the same time, rogue miners may stand against them to disrupt the block mining process by empowering their hash powers. Most importantly, we model a critical issue named block-withholding attack, which may occur in a blockchain cloud during pool mining, to identify the constraints on an attacker's hashing power in order to defeat the purpose of pool mining. The scenario is analyzed individually when the pool operator employs different rewarding schemes, such as proportional reward and Pay-per-Last-N-Shares (PPLNS) reward.

The chapter is organized as follows. Section 8.1 briefs various consensus mechanisms available for blockchain. In Section 8.2, we extensively discuss blockchain preliminaries and its importance in provisioning cloud security. We also discuss several critical vulnerabilities related to blockchain in this section. Section 8.3 presents the system model that we consider to analyze block withholding attack in pool mining. Section 8.4 expresses various mechanisms by which an attacker could increase its hashing limits. In Section 8.5, we model the block withholding attack by considering two different pools with distinct reward mechanisms. Simulation results are discussed in Section 8.6. Section 8.7 concludes the chapter.

8.2 Blockchain Consensus Mechanisms

Consensus mechanisms are important to maintain consistency of the blockchain or distributed ledger systems without any help from a centralized authority. In general, consensus models can be described as a common acceptance of laws, rules, and norms by a group of individuals that are homogeneous with respect to the consensus procedure. In the sense of distributed ledger technology, when the blocks from various peers are broadcast to others in the P2P network, the consensus mechanism enables every node to agree on a particular block so as to include it in the mainstream blockchain. In addition, consensus mechanisms allow the P2P network members to work as a group and consistently converge on a common value, even when some members fail or behave erroneously in the system. To provide a better understanding, we discuss and analyze some of the currently adopted consensus protocols in the following sections.

8.2.1 Proof-of-Work (PoW) Consensus

As described before, this mechanism leverages the computational power of the miners to solve an extremely difficult crypto puzzle. The one who solves the puzzle first becomes the leader of the consensus process and its proposed block gets included in the blockchain. As the participating miners' computational abilities are heterogeneous in general, the block generation happens to be asynchronous in most of the slots. However, the probability of finding more than one block is not completely nullified. In this situation, forking of the blockchain occurs and miners start working on the longest chain they have seen so far. Before the consensus, each miner creates its block by including all transactions that satisfy the following criteria: (1) the transaction originator must have assets in its account that are higher than those that are transferred; (2) the originator's acquired assets are recognized as valid; (3) the recipient of the transaction will be the new owner of the asset; and (4) the sender is not reclaiming the already transferred assets.

After verifying the transactions, only the valid ones are included in a block and their Merkle root is included in the block's header, as shown in Figure 8.2. The header also contains several other attributes, such as the hash of the previous block, timestamp information, difficulty of the puzzle in bits, and the solution of the puzzle or nonce, which are required to compose the cryptopuzzle of the PoW consensus. The puzzle is to find a value (nonce) such that the hash of the block header, calculated by the SHA-256 function, is less than a 256-bit target value that has "difficulty" number of zeros in the beginning. Mathematically, it tries to find the nonce (x) by trying different x, such that:

$$Hash(block\_header(x)) \leq \frac{M}{D}. \tag{8.1}$$

where M is the maximum possible value of the difficulty $(2^{256} - 1)$, and D is the current difficulty. It can be observed that as the value of D increases, more trials are needed to find a valid solution. The expected value of required trials needed to find a solution is exactly D.

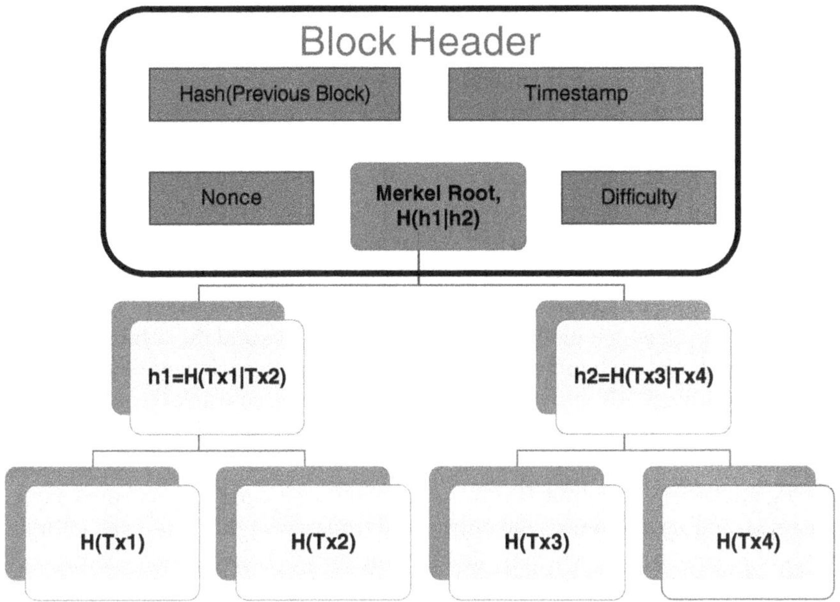

Figure 8.2 Layout of a block in Blockchain.

Although this mechanism provides a robust way to achieve consensus by utilizing the computational power of every participant, it has the following downsides too:

1. Reward out of this procedure clearly depends on the cost of electricity for solving such a hard puzzle. Therefore, the miner's location also comes into play because this cost varies geographically.
2. The puzzle's difficulty is not feasible for a user with limited computational resources to mine because it will take years to find a solution, whereas, pool mining allows to tract the problem in a limited time. Thus, it leads to some sort of centralization in the system, which is far away from the design goal of blockchain.
3. As the mining rewards fade away in the future, it will be less motivating for the miners to devote their computational power for such consensus. The incentive model of this mechanism also needs to be revisited to keep motivating the miners.

8.2.2 Proof-of-Stake (PoS) Consensus

The PoS consensus protocol provides block-inclusion decision making power to those entities who have stakes in the system irrespective of the blockchain's length or history of the public ledger. The principal motivation behind this scheme is to place the power of leader election in the blockchain update process in the hands of the stakeholders. This is done to ensure that the security of the system will be maintained while the member's stakes are at risk. Roughly speaking, this approach is similar to the PoW consensus, except the computational part. Hence, a stakeholder's chances to extend the blockchain by including its own block depends proportionately on the amount of stake it has in the system.

Since the PoW consensus turned out to be energy inefficient [2], researchers came up with alternative techniques to achieve consensus for the blockchain system. The first conceptual design of PoS consensus was described by King and Nadal in [3], which included the age of currencies and the total amount to define the stake of each miner in the system. To gain the privilege of generating a PoS-based block, the miner has to make a special coinstake transaction to himself so as to reset the coin age and prove that its stake is valid. According to their approach, a miner has a chance to extend the blockchain with his block having total unspent output $\mathcal{U}$, given the following condition is satisfied. Here, the unspent output refers to the output of a transaction that is not yet an input of another transaction, which means that the output has not been spent.

$$hash(hash(\mathbb{B}_{prev}), \mathcal{U}, t) \leq D \times balance(\mathcal{U}) \times age(\mathcal{U}). \tag{8.2}$$

where $\mathbb{B}_{prev}$ is the previous block on which the blockchain is to be extended, $balance(\mathcal{U})$ is the miner's stake amount, $age(\mathcal{U})$ is the aggregated age of the stake, and D is the mining difficulty, which is of higher value unlike the traditional PoW-based consensus. As seen in Eq. 8.2, the computed hash value on the left side of inequality depends on the miner's stake amount, so a large stakeholder can easily find a hash and hence has higher probability of adding its block in the blockchain.

This consensus mechanism also has several issues, which we describe below.

1. The first issue is that the rich miner gets even richer in this case. Since high-stake owners have better probability of including their blocks in the blockchain, the consensus is driven towards centralizing the block-inclusion process in proportion to the stake distribution.
2. The other issue is the "nothing at stake" problem. When forking happens in block mining, the rational PoS miners can mine on all branches simultaneously, which was not possible in PoW. Therefore, it is easier to perform double-spending attacks in this scenario.
3. Coin age can be exploited by accumulating coins for a longer period of time to reduce the difficulty of the puzzle that PoS miners solve.

A variant of PoS, namely Delegated Proof of Stake (DPoS), is also available, which allows a predefined set of users in the system to perform mining operations. These delegates control the blockchain update process and are rewarded for their truthful service, while they may be punished upon performing any malicious activity. The delegates are involved in building blocks of transactions and validating the generated blocks by digitally signing it. The validation usually requires signatures of a selected set of delegates or validators, which changes periodically depending on certain rules. The stakes of the users can be used for selecting the set of delegates and defining the voting power of the delegates in the system. In some cases, advance deposit is needed in order to participate in the consensus process, which may be forfeited upon any malicious activity. In addition, consensus in the blockchain-enabled cloud environment is an important issue to address since the original stake concept does not apply in the cloud domain. Considering the computing, networking, and storage resources at stake, a PoS model is proposed in [4] to achieve consensus in a federated cloud platform.

8.2.3 Proof-of-Activity (PoA) Consensus

This is a hybrid consensus protocol built on top of the proof-of-work model by including PoS as an extension. It has been developed to offer better security against possible future attacks on Bitcoin when the block mining reward will diminish and each miner will rely on the transaction fees only. This gives rise to a "tragedy of commons" situation where participants act in a selfish and dishonest manner at the cost of harming other peers. In this proof-of-activity (PoA) [5] protocol, initially the mining process starts with the PoW mechanism, where every miner uses their hashing power to generate an empty header w.r.t. the genesis block. This header does not refer to any transaction but contains the hash of the previous block, the public key of the miner, the height/length of the current block, and nonce. Similar to PoW, block generation only succeeds when the hash of the block header is smaller than the difficulty. From this point, the PoA consensus switches to PoS and the empty block is broadcast, which derives N pseudo random miners as validators for the PoS mechanism. Selection of these N users depends on their stakes in the system, i.e. the more the amount of coins a miner holds, the higher is the chance of getting selected as a validator. After all N stakeholders sign on the blank block, the Nth validator gets the permission to wrap transactions in that block and the reward received by the Nth validator is shared by all N miners. In case some of the validators out of N are not available during the process of signing the block, the current block is discarded and the next winning block is chosen with a new set of N validators. This process is continued until all correct signatures are gathered. The flow of the PoA consensus mechanism is depicted in Figure 8.3.

The natural constraints of this mechanism are derived from the PoW and PoS models, which are briefly discussed in the following points:

1. The PoA mechanism relies on the assumption that the majority of stakeholders must be honest in nature. However, in reality, there is no predefined way to control this assumption in a completely distributed network. The security

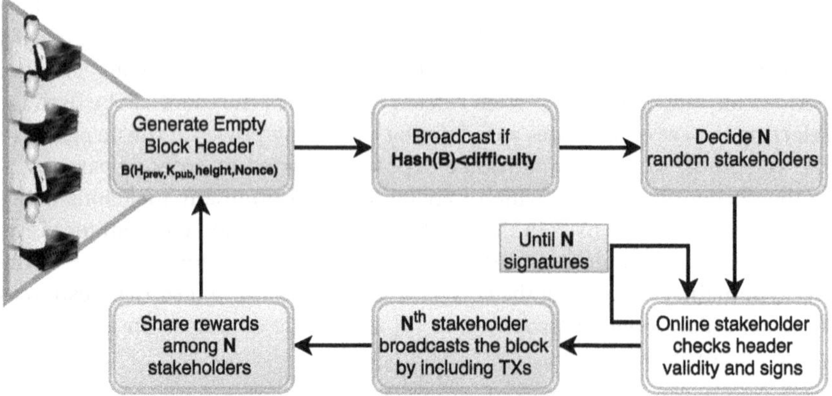

Figure 8.3 Proof of Activity (PoA) in flow.

of PoA can be compromised when a malicious entity can influence a set of validators to withhold their signatures. Especially when N is large, the possibility of a bribe attack becomes feasible.

2. Although this mechanism has higher security compared to the PoW-based consensus model, it consists of extra rounds of interaction among the N stakeholders for completion of the signing process, which may take longer depending on how many of the validators are online. Therefore, it is believed to have higher intervals between two consecutive blocks compared to PoW.

8.2.4 Practical Byzantine Fault Tolerance (PBFT) Consensus

Since blockchain operates in a distributed P2P network and malicious attacks along with uncertain software errors are common events, nodes in a P2P network can be faulty and show Byzantine behavior. Several BFT models [6][7] are studied in the distributed computing domain to enhance robustness and performance of distributed systems. Blockchain's append-only log is very much applicable to implement smart contracts, which is nothing but a state machine by itself. Furthermore, the underlying state machine of blockchain allows to keep track of all transactions and verify its content at the same time. BFT state machine replication protocols are particularly of interest because they help to achieve blockchain consensus in minimal network latency, while attaining high transaction throughput.

The PBFT mechanism can be roughly explained as follows: A set of N designated validator nodes are assigned to validate transactions from every participant, where $N = 3f + 1$ and there can be at max f faulty/malicious validators in the system. The blockchain participants propose their blocks of transactions to the validators who are involved in endorsing the blocks. Then, the validators check the transaction validity in the proposed block and vote their opinion to other members. When the system of validators receives at least $f + 1$ confirmations on a particular block, every node in the P2P network updates their blockchain with this new block. Then, the above process reiterates with the beginning of a new slot. The mechanism is proved to satisfy the safety and liveness property, which means that two nonfaulty nodes will always agree on the same proposed block and the consensus process will end within a finite period of time.

Although this consensus offers a better transaction rate with minimal network delay, it suffers from a scalability issue. Being invented from the perspective of distributed systems to offer high availability and redundancy, the performance of BFT protocols gets hampered as the number of nodes (N) grows. This is due to intensive communication among the validator nodes, which is roughly in order of $O(N^2)$ messages/block.

8.2.5 Proof-of-Elapsed-Time (PoET) Consensus

This mechanism applies a similar procedure as PBFT; however, the leader selection in this process is a bit different and unique. This model was proposed by Intel [8] and exploits the trusted execution environment (TEE) embedded in their processors using secure CPU instructions. With this, a guaranteed safety and random leader selection process is proposed that does not require any powerful or specialized hardware as compared to other consensus procedures. As the important part in consensus algorithms is to find a leader with no bias, Intel's Software Guard eXtension (SGX) platform leverages a close door execution environment using enclaves to perfectly randomize the leader selection process.

In PoET, leader election occurs in a very simplistic way. The validators in the system request for a wait time from the trusted environment and the one whose waiting timer ends first becomes the leader of that slot. Various application programming interface (API) calls can be made to the enclave for creating and checking timers. For e.g. the "CheckTimer" method is used to verify whether the timer has been expired; if so, an attestation is generated to verify that the validator waited until the allocated time before it became a leader. After the leader is selected, the rest of the process is similar to PBFT. Due to the above characteristics, PoEA satisfies the properties of a good lottery algorithm, which are (i) fairness–distribution of the leadership role fairly among the large population of nodes; (ii) investment—proportionate leader selection cost with respect to the value of the leader; and (iii) verification—easier to verify whether the selected leader is legitimate.

Although the mechanism provides an elegant and lightweight model to build consensus, it completely relies on Intel's TEE, which is a specialized piece of hardware embedded inside the processor. Therefore, the following dilemma needs to be resolved—whether it is worth opting for a consensus that requires an expensive CPU, but at a reduced electricity cost, or not.

8.2.6 Proof-of-Luck (PoL) Consensus

As in PoW consensus, blocks are generated in an interval of 10 minutes on an average and six succeeding blocks are needed to confirm a transaction; point of sales type applications are seemingly impractical. To address such issues, authors in [9] propose this new consensus model using modern TEEs. TEEs help in preventing the creation of Sybils and correct processing of critical applications. This consensus primitive is designed having the following objectives in mind: (i) low-latency transaction validation, (ii) deterministic confirmation time, (iii) minimal energy consumption, and (iv) uniformly distributed mining. The protocol involves two functions, namely POLROUND and POLMINE, which run inside the TEE. The purpose of the former function is to prepare the TEE for chain mining by parsing the latest block (*roundBlock*), while the POLMINE(*header, prevBlock*) function is invoked after waiting for a fixed time (*ROUND_TIME*). The argument *prevBlock* and *roundBlock* may not be the same block; however, they may have a common parent. This enables the participants to change their mining to the latest and luckier block during the mandatory waiting period as well, after which a new round starts. Furthermore, to define the winning block and compute the luck of a chain, a uniform random value $l \in [0, 1)$ is used. The communications in the protocol are optimized by introducing a monotonically decreasing function $f(l)$, which is used to delay the release of proof. That is, a luckier chain (with high l) would have smaller delay, while the unlucky chain waits longer.

At beginning of the PoL consensus, participants initialize their current chain and transaction set to empty, after which they listen for a new network message from peers. If the message is "transaction", they then include the transaction in their transactions list, if they were not added before, and broadcast them to their peers too. In case of a new "chain" message, participants verify whether the chain has valid blocks and compute its luck to decide whether to switch to this new chain or not. If the luck of this chain is higher than that of the current chain, then a new round with this chain is started and this information is broadcast to the peers. At the beginning of a new round, the function POLROUND is invoked and new callbacks are scheduled by clearing all prior ones. In the callbacks, pending transactions are appended in a new chain, and processed further to check the luck factor of this chain. Although this PoL consensus model uses a TEE similar to that of the PoET consensus, the novelty lies in defining the luck component of the chains, which is not well defined. It will also be interesting to compare this protocol with PoET for understanding their performance, because both mechanisms use a costly TEE, such as Intel SGX platform, for the consensus.

8.2.7 Proof-of-Space (PoSpace) Consensus

Proof of Space consensus mechanism [10] exploits the disk space of users in the decentralized network to achieve consensus. The assumption of the technique is that the users must posses a significant amount of unused disk space. The PoSpace mechanism does not require much energy or computational power compared to the PoW technique, which is the costliest consensus model so far. In the PoSpace consensus, two entities are involved, namely *prover* ($\mathcal{P}$) and *verifier* ($\mathcal{V}$), where the *prover* has to prove to the *verifier* that it has dedicated a required amount of disk space, while the *verifier* validates whether the *prover* is lying. The protocol runs in two phases: (i) initialization, and (ii) execution. In the initialization phase, $\mathcal{P}$ and $\mathcal{V}$ operate on a set of common parameters (prm), such as identifier (id) and storage bound $N \in \mathbb{N}$. The operation is denoted as $(\phi, S) \leftarrow \langle \mathcal{V}, \mathcal{P} \rangle(prm)$, where ϕ and S (of size N) are the output for the verifier and the prover, respectively, that are stored at each end for future verification. ϕ can be null when a malicious prover is detected. In the execution phase, the above stored values (ϕ at $\mathcal{V}$ and S at $\mathcal{P}$) are used to find out whether the prover has stored S or not by executing the protocol. The prover does not have any output while the verifier either accepts or rejects. This is denoted as $(\{accept, reject\}, null) \leftarrow \langle \mathcal{V}(\phi), \mathcal{P}(S) \rangle(prm)$. Using graph pebbling and random hashing function ($\mathcal{H} : \{0,1\}^* \rightarrow \{0,1\}^L, L \in \mathbb{N}$) that is commonly available to everyone, $\mathcal{P}$ generates a hashtree (S) that requires $o(N)L$ bits of storage, and the root (ϕ) of S is sent to the verifier.

Although it is proven that this mechanism enables an efficient and unique way of using the disk storage for bringing consensus in a distributed network, the provers have to store the entire hashtree in order to succeed in the execution phase. Therefore, a good amount of storage must be in hand to participate in this type of consensus, which may not be feasible for handheld system such as cellphones and tablets. This limits the usability of this protocol to only users with high storage and thus opens an attack surface for the organizations that offer cloud storage services to a large mass.

8.3 Blockchain Cloud and Associated Vulnerabilities

Among all the security issues that exist in the cloud environment, blockchain will be very effective in addressing the challenges involved in the implementation of assured data provenance [11]. We present the challenges associated with assured data provenance in the cloud and blockchain's capabilities to address them.

8.3.1 Blockchain and Cloud Security

Cloud computing allows users to remotely store their data in the cloud and provides on-demand applications and services from a shared pool of configurable computing resources. The security of the outsourced data in the cloud is dependent on the security of the cloud computing system and network. However, the cloud's key characteristics, on-demand services, uninterrupted network access, resource pooling, and rapid elasticity are susceptible to vulnerabilities. In addition, cloud computing's core technologies for virtualization, cryptography, and web services have vulnerabilities, which are results of insecure implementation. At the same time, security controls, such as key management, in the cloud computing environment have several challenges. For instance, implementation of an effective key management system in the cloud computing infrastructure requires management and storage of various kinds of keys. The difficulty in assigning standard key management stems from the fact that virtual machines usually have heterogeneous hardware/software, and cloud-based computing and storage are geographically distributed.

The protection of data exchanged within the cloud infrastructure currently relies on PKI-based signatures. Specifically, there is a need for stronger attribution to detect unauthorized changes to the data and identify the responsible entity. Data provenance provides information on all the changes performed on data exchanged between multiple entities. Researchers have proposed security solutions, such as PKI signatures, to ensure provenance. However, implementation of PKI signatures typically depends on a centralized authority, which is not effective in the cloud infrastructure.

Blockchain and keyless signatures have been proposed as an alternative to PKI signatures, where the blockchain technology facilitates secure transfer of information through a sequence of cryptographically-secure keys across a distributed system. There is no need for a central authority because it is executed by a system of distributed ledgers, which records all actions performed on the data and is shared among all the participating entities. The transactions in the public ledger are verified by a consensus of the majority of participating entities. The blockchain contains a verifiable record of every transaction that cannot be changed. Keyless signature addresses the issue of "PKI key compromise" by decoupling the processes for identifying signer and integrity protection from the processes that are responsible for maintaining the secrecy of the keys [12]. The processes for identifying signer and integrity protection are handled by cryptographic tools that are chosen from options such as asymmetric cryptography and keyless cryptography [12]. Examples of keyless cryptography include one-way collision-free hash functions. Keyless signature processes include hashing, aggregation, and publication. The realization of keyless signatures requires a Keyless Signature Infrastructure (KSI), which consists of a hierarchy of co-operative aggregation servers that generate global hash trees. Verification in KSI hinges on the security of hash functions and the availability of a public ledger (blockchain). The ledger is publicly available, and rules for updating, distributed consensus, and mode of operation are well defined [13].

Guardtime has proposed changes to traditional blockchain technology by integrating with KSI [13]. The KSI blockchain technology was developed to mitigate challenges associated with mainstream blockchain technologies. The challenges are lack of scalability, consensus time, and lack of formal security proof. The KSI blockchain technique scales at $O(t)$ complexity as compared to

$O(n)$ for traditional blockchain, where n refers to the number of transactions. In a blockchain cloud, it is likely that with the increasing granularity of measurements, blockchain complexity will be concerning. The linear growth with time would lead to better scalability as there will be no dependence on the number of sensor measurements. There is a need to achieve quick consensus and ensure synchronous availability of all updates to the distributed ledger. Finally, formal security proof will provide better assurance to the security of the blockchain. Recently, Ericsson and Guardtime integrated the KSI blockchain technology on a cloud computing platform to enable organizations to assure provenance of data with forensically provable and complete attribution capabilities [14]. The capability will make real-time governance of cloud operations and scalable data feasible.

Data provenance in the cloud—Assurance of data transfer within intracloud and intercloud environments is very crucial. Typical assurance of data focuses on ensuring the confidentiality, integrity, and availability of the data contents. However, assurance of the ancestry of the data (where the data came from) is a challenge in cloud environments. Data provenance addresses such issues based on the detailed derivation of data objects. If true data provenance existed in the cloud for all data stored on cloud storage, distributed data computations, data exchanges and transactions, detecting insider attacks, reproducing research results, and identifying the exact source of system/network intrusions would be achievable. Unfortunately, the state of the art in data provenance in cloud does not provide such assurances.

Data provenance will be very critical for cloud computing system administrators to debug break-ins to the system or network. Cloud computing environments are typically characterized by data transfers between diverse system and network components. These data exchanges could take place within a data center or across federated data centers. The data does not usually follow the same path due to multiples copies of the data and the diversity of paths taken to ensure resilience. This design adds a degree of difficulty for administrators to accurately identify the origin of the attack, what software and/or hardware components caused the attack, and the impact of the attack. Security violations need to be identified at a fine granularity and provenance can assist. Current provenance systems in the cloud support the above tasks through logging and auditing technologies. These technologies are not effective in cloud computing systems, which are complex in nature, due to several layers of inter operating software and hardware components spanning across geographical and organizational boundaries. To identify and resolve the malicious activities in cloud environment, it is required to analyze the forensics and logs from a diverse and disparate set of sources, which is an insurmountable task. Although cyber-threat information sharing [15][16] can be a viable option to achieve situational awareness about the cloud attack surface at a reduced investment [17], it faces the issue of information tampering. Maintaining provenance could track all the operations performed on every data object in the cloud, and blockchain technology will come in handy to ensure the content is unalterable.

Blockchain-based data provenance in cloud—Cloud computing systems are typically comprised of multiple nodes (physical machines), which host one or more virtual machines (VMs). Each VM has an owner and includes components such as software (application resources) and data. The execution of software in the VM and exchange of information with VM results in multiple artifacts, such as variables, intermediate data output, and final output artifacts. All of them are of interest and concern for the provenance. Blockchain technology provides such capability and resolves many needed functionalities as well as properties for effective provenance in cloud. In essence, blockchain is a P2P ledger system, where information that constitutes provenance for physical, virtual, and application resources can be stored publicly for transparent verifiability and audit. As such, both transparency and cost effectiveness are provided, while access control and privacy for individual users of the ledger are ensured through encryption techniques, where individuals can see only parts of the ledger that are related to them. Furthermore, blockchain technology provides much needed functionalities that happen to be part of the cloud, including asset transfer and provenance [18].

8.3.2 Blockchain Cloud Vulnerabilities

Blockchain cloud is realizable provided the majority of nodes in the network are honest and authentic. However, in the cloud environment, it is possible for rogue nodes to negatively impact the mining and/or consensus processes. In this section, we present the vulnerabilities associated with blockchain technology.

Double-spending attack—This vulnerability is particularly attributed in Bitcoin Technology, where adversaries look forward to using the same digital cryptocurrency for more than one transaction. Since reproduction of digital information is easy to achieve, the occurrence of double spending is possible in reality. To conduct such an event, the attackers must have strong hash power and must be able to generate a longer private chain compared to the public blockchain. The attack is carried out in the following steps:

1. Starting from block N, privately mine to extend the blockchain as much as possible but do not publicize.
2. Broadcast the transaction to the organization of interest.
3. Wait patiently until enough confirmations are received and the transaction successfully gets recorded in the blockchain, so that the merchant dispatches the product.
4. Secretly mine for extending the private branch until it is longer than the public branch. If succssful, publicize the secret branch that will be eventually be accepted as valid and the block containing the payment to merchant will be discarded.

From the hash-rate based analysis in [19], it is found that the probability of succeeding in a double spending attack (a_z) is governed by the following expression:

$$a_z = \min\left(\frac{q}{p}, 1\right)^{\max(z+1,0)} = \begin{cases} 1 & \text{if } z < 0, q > p \\ (q/p)^{z+1} & \text{if } z \geq 0, q \leq p. \end{cases}$$

where p, q are the hash rate proportion of the honest nodes pool and the attacker pool, respectively, and z is the number of blocks by which the honest network has an advantage over the attacker. If z becomes negative (< 0), the attacker pool can publicize their blocks and overtake the honest users, mined chain. Hence, the following remarks can be made on the success of such an attack:

- The success of double spending depends on the hash power of the attacker and the number of blocks (leading or lagging).
- If the attacker's hash power (q) is more than 50%, it always succeeds.
- If $q < p$, then success probability decreases exponentially.

The above analysis was conducted when the number of confirmations on a transaction did not affect the merchant's decision. However, when the requirement of n confirmations for validating a transaction is enforced, the expression of success probability is given in Eq. 8.3.

$$a_z = \begin{cases} 1 & \text{if } q \geq p \\ 1 - \sum_{m=0}^{n} \binom{m+n-1}{m} p^n q^m - p^m q^n & \text{if } q < p. \end{cases} \tag{8.3}$$

Thus, it is observed that a double-spending attack is successful for an attacker with any hash rate and the probability decreases exponentially as the number of confirmations increase. Hence, there is no relevance of the "6 confirmations requirement" (often cited) as this value was chosen based on the assumption that an attacker may not have more than 10% hash rate compared to the rest of the network.

Selfish mining attack [20, 21]—Since mining cryptocurrencies like Bitcoin is hard for a single miner due to the requirement of high computing power for solving the cryptopuzzle, a set of miners generally collude to form a pool with each other and share the received reward among themselves after successfully solving the puzzle. This also helps individual miners to generate a constant income instead of infrequent (random interval) payment, when they mine alone. It is argued that incentives to the pool of honest miners can be dominated if there exists a pool of selfish miners that intentionally aims to invalidate the work of honest miners by following a selfish mining strategy [20], and generate better revenue for themselves. Similar to double-spending attacks, in a selfish mining attack, the pool mines on their private chain and publishes it strategically depending on the state of the pool. The states are defined based on the parameter *lead* (the difference in lengths of the private chain and the public chain) and branching (honest and selfish pools are working on different parent blocks). In brief, the selfish mining strategy can be stated in the following way (assuming the honest pool always accepts the longest chain):

- If *lead* = 2 and the honest pool mines the next block, then publish the entire private chain.
- If *lead* = 0, part of the honest pool works on the selfish pool's mined block, and the selfish pool mines the next block, then publishes the entire private chain.
- If *lead* ≥ 0 and the selfish pool mines the next block, then keep the mined block secret.

With the possibility of different states, Eyal and Sirer calculated the following expected revenue (R_{pool}) of the selfish pool:

$$R_{pool} = \frac{\alpha(1-\alpha)^2(4\alpha+\gamma(1-2\alpha))-\alpha^3}{1-\alpha(1+(2-\alpha)\alpha)}. \quad (8.4)$$

where α is the hash power of the selfish pool and γ is the proportion of honest miners that choose to mine on the pool's block. Thus, the selfish pool's revenue is governed by their hashing power and propagation factor (γ). In general, $0 \geq \alpha \geq 0.5$ must be satisfied in order to avoid the 51% attack; however, [20] proposed that the pool of selfish miners can gain higher revenue if the following constraint on their hashing power (α) is satisfied:

$$\frac{1-\gamma}{3-2\gamma} < \alpha < 0.5. \quad (8.5)$$

It can also be observed that the revenue of each selfish miner will increase if the pool size increases beyond the threshold. As a consequence, most of the honest miners would prefer to join the pool for generating higher incentives, and eventually the pool becomes the major player that controls the blockchain. Thus, decentralization would not hold any more.

To resolve this issue, the authors suggest that it is necessary to raise the threshold so that no pool can benefit by executing selfish mining. Rather, miners must propagate all the blocks when they learn about competing branches of the same length in the blockchain and randomly choose one to mine. In that case, $\gamma = 0.5$, thus the threshold gets raised to 0.25. But raising the threshold to 0.25 still keeps the range open to a selfish mining attack, which may be successful if a pool can be formed with a hash power of at least 25% of the total network.

An extension to selfish mining strategy has been proposed in [22] that states that the revenue of a selfish miner can be even higher if it adopts their proposed stubborn strategies.

Eclipse attack [23]—This type of attack is performed to take advantage of the P2P network that is used to broadcast information among Bitcoin nodes.

In the Bitcoin network, the nodes randomly select eight other peers to maintain a long-lived outgoing connectivity for propagating and storing information about other peers. Additionally, nodes with public IP can accept up to 117 unsolicited incoming connections from any other IP. Thus, the openness and decentralization of the P2P network attracts adversaries to join and perform an eclipse attack, where "the attacker strategically takes control of all the incoming and outgoing communications of a victim node", thereby stopping all connections from other legitimate nodes. The attack is performed by rapidly and repeatedly making unsolicited connection requests to the victim node from the attacker-controlled nodes by sending irrelevant information until the victim restarts. With such effort, there is a high chance that the victim will have the eight outgoing connections to the attacker-controlled nodes.

In the core of Bitcoin's P2P network, network information is propagated through DNS seeders (servers that resolve DNS queries with respective IP addresses) and ADDR messages (that are used to obtain network information from the peers and contain up to 1000 IP addresses). Each node also locally maintains two tables (`tried` and `new`) to keep the public IPs. The `tried` table contains the addresses of the peers with whom the node has successfully established a connection along with timestamp information, whereas the `new` table contains addresses of peers with whom connection is not yet initiated. When a node restarts or a connection is dropped, the next peer selection follows a probabilistic approach, where an address for $(\omega + 1)^{th}$ connection is chosen from the `tried` table with the following probability:

$$P[\text{Select from } \texttt{tried}] = \frac{\sqrt{\rho}(9-\omega)}{(\omega+1)+\sqrt{\rho}(9-\omega)}. \tag{8.6}$$

where ρ = ratio of # of addresses in the `tried` and `new` tables.

The eclipse attack takes advantage of the above selection process for monopolizing all connections of a victim node.

1. Populate the `tried` table with attacker-controlled nodes' IP address by sending unsolicited messages.
2. Overwrite addresses of the `new` table with garbage addresses (not related to peers' IPs).
3. Once the node restarts, with high probability all the connections are monopolized

Block discarding attack and difficulty raising attack [24]—Block discarding attack is carried out by an attacker that has a good hold of network connections compared to a normal node. Since propagation of mined blocks is an important characteristic to add it into the mainstream blockchain, the attacker would preferably place multiple slave nodes to improve its network superiority. With this placement, the attacker could easily get informed of freshly mined blocks and instantly propagate the it's block faster than the rest of the network.

Thus, when any node publicizes a block, the attacker can immediately dispatch its own mined blocks, so as to discard others' blocks.

However, the difficulty raising attack takes advantage of the attacker's hashing power to manipulate the difficulty level of the cryptopuzzle. In this attack, it is claimed in [24] that the probability of discarding a block at depth n (i.e. $[n - 1]$ blocks have been mined after this) is p^n, where p is the ratio of the hash power of the attacker and the rest of the network. To succeed in doing so, the attacker must wait for enough time.

Block withholding attack [25]—In this type of attack, some pool members, who have joined to help mining blocks, would actually never publish any block, thus decreasing the expected revenue of the pool. These attacks are also known as "Sabotage" attacks, where the rogue miner never gains anything, and rather makes everyone lose. However, an analysis with practical instantiation in [1] claims that a rogue miner could also gain profit from such an attack.

Anonymity issues in blockchain cloud—It has been acknowledged that the underlying blockchain technology of the Bitcoin ecosystem is not completely anonymous in nature. The transactions are permanently recorded in the public ledger; hence, everybody can see the balance, and transactions related to any Bitcoin address. The real identity and privacy of a user will not get exposed until the user reveals any information during purchase or any special circumstances. Therefore, Bitcoin is pseudo-anonymous, i.e. Bitcoin addresses can be created by anyone but tracing back to the real person is not possible unless any information is found from another source. To maintain higher privacy and better anonymize transactions in the Bitcoin environment, users are encouraged to have multiple Bitcoin addresses. Since the convenience of the e-cash system and pseudo-anonymity attract darknet markets to make illegal transactions anonymously, it has been a topic of interest for government and security industries to track down such illicit activities from the publicly available blockchain.

The work presented in [26] focuses on deanonymizing the owner of Bitcoin transactions through mapping of the Bitcoin address with the IP address of the actual owner. By collecting all the network-level traffic data including IP information and performing offline processing, they found evidence of tracing back the IP address from the Bitcoin address. Besides pruning irrelevant transaction data, there are five crucial steps they follow to achieve the mapping: (i) hypothesize an owner IP for each TX, (ii) create granular pairings of Bitcoin address and IP, (iii) define statistical metrics for the pairings, (iv) identify potential pairings that signify actual ownership, and (v) remove unwanted pairing based on a threshold. Targeting the Bitcoin peers behind NAT or firewall, [27] proposed a generic method to build a correlation between pseudonyms of Bitcoin users and their public IPs. The method utilizes the connected user set or entry nodes for identifying the origin of transactions. The outcome is a list, $\mathbf{I} = \{(IP, Id, PK)\}$, where Id is used to distinguish the clients using the same IP, and PK is the pseudonames used in a transaction. Finding the entry nodes (at least three) and mapping the transactions to these nodes are two important steps, as mentioned in the chapter, to effectively deanonymize the clients.

After understanding important security vulnerabilities related to blockchain implementation, we undertake one important case called the block withholding attack and analyze the situation rigorously to understand the strategies of a powerful attacker that lead to bring anomaly in the mining pool. The attacker joins the pool with intentions to withhold the successful blocks and look for opportunities to specifically demotivate honest members from mining in the pool. We theoretically analyze the attacker's strategy by considering different types of pools whose rewarding schemes are different.

8.4 System Model

In this work, we consider a pool $\mathcal{P}$, where n miners work continuously trying to solve the cryptographic puzzle using their hashing power. The pool is assigned with a pool operator, who is responsible for collecting transactions from the network, creating a block, keeping track of puzzle difficulty, recording the number of *shares* submitted by pool members, dispatching the successfully mined block to the P2P network, and collecting and redistributing the reward among miners. The pool members are considered to be honest in nature, which means they report their solutions or *shares* to the pool operator immediately as they find them. Assuming the miner i has hashing power α_i of the total mining power ($\mathcal{M}$), where $0 \leq \alpha_i \leq 1$, the overall mining power of the pool is $\beta = \sum_{i=1}^{n} \alpha_i$. For simplicity, we assume that $\beta < 1$; thus, the pool is not the only computing entity but there exist other solo miners or pools whose computational power is fixed with respect to the pool $\mathcal{P}$. Additionally, the miners of pool $\mathcal{P}$ receive rewards based on their contributions in a round, where a round is defined as the interval between two valid blocks found. The contribution of the miners is calculated based on the number of *shares* reported, and each *share* could be a full solution with probability $1/D$, where D is the overall difficulty of the cryptopuzzle that is assumed to be fixed. Finding a *share* is inevitably easier than finding the valid solution because the *share* is only meant to prove that a miner has worked enough to find it. Thus, the difficulty of finding a *share* is determined by the pool operator, which is less than D. As a standard, a particular hash is a valid *share* with probability $\frac{1}{2^\kappa}$, where κ is specified by the private blockchain creator so that $0 \ll 2^\kappa < D$. The description of all the symbols used in the rest of the chapter is given in Table 8.1.

On the other hand, the attacker is considered to be a powerful miner who willingly participates in the pool $\mathcal{P}$ and aims to maximally damage the mining activity of the pool by withholding successfully mined blocks. The attacker joins the pool $\mathcal{P}$ with an initial hashing rate of $\alpha_{\mathcal{A}}$ but we assume that the attacker has the ability to augment its mining power by incorporating additional physical

Table 8.1 Symbol table.

Symbol	Meaning
α_i	Hash power of miner i
α_A	Hash power of attacker
D	Difficulty of PoW puzzle
R	Block reward
$\mathcal{M}$	Total mining power of the pool
δ	Percentage of reward for pool operator
κ	Difficulty required for a block to be a share
$h(.)$	Function determining number of shares produced by a miner
B	Average number of blocks found in last N shares
T	Mean amount of time required to find a block

Application-Specific Integrated Circuit (ASIC) resources or leasing computing power from cloud vendors. Although such efforts for increasing hashing power may be costly by themself, the attacker's irrationality makes it feasible by our assumption. In this chapter, we aim to understand how much of extra mining power a block-withholding attacker may need to completely sabotage a pool, thus leading to a situation where no single miner would prefer to honestly mine in the pool. This analysis would then help to perform a cost benefit analysis of leasing cloud/noncloud computational resources for a successful attack. By saying sabotaging a pool we mean that the attacker comes up with such strategies that dominate the reward distribution in the pool, therefore leading to a situation where other members' reward variance out of pool mining is more than the variance out of solo mining.

8.5 Augmenting with Extra Hash Power

For increasing the hashing ability of a miner, there are different possible options available to undertake. The first option is mining hardware. Mining has progressed from the era of CPU to GPU and finally to the ASIC era. Currently, miners opt for ASIC chips to mine blocks since these give a great amount of hashing power at minimal cost. ASIC chips are designed purposely for block mining, and hence cannot be used for any other task. The ASIC mining hardware offers 50× to 100× increase in hashing power while reducing power usage by 7× compared to previous technologies. The company, Avalon [28], manufactures ASIC mining chips for the Bitcoin miners' market where each server can process 3.65 TH/s at a power efficiency of 0.29 W/GH.

The second option is renting mining services from cloud providers, which is called cloud mining or cloud hashing. There are three kinds of possibilities to perform remote mining: (i) hosted mining, (ii) virtual hosted mining, and (iii) leased hashing power. In case of hosted mining, the user leases a machine that is capable of mining and is hosted by the provider on cloud. In virtual hosted mining, the user creates a mining environment from scratch on the virtual private server. In case of the leased hashing power technique, which is mostly used in the current scenario, the user leases the required amount of hashing power from the provider without any hassle of managing the infrastructure. This allows users to purchase hashing capacity from the cloud provider's mining hardware that is already installed in their data centers. This enables another viable way to get rid of the issues related to installing mining hardware, managing electricity consumption, or network connectivity and bandwidth requirements. Such services exist in practice and providers, such as Hashflare [29], Genesis Mining [30], Hashnest [31], and Eobot [32], for offer competitive prices in exchange for hashing capabilities.

8.6 Disruptive Attack Strategy Analysis

Considering the attacker is going to withhold the valid blocks only; it may publish the *shares* that are not exactly solutions of the cryptopuzzle. Thus, the only way an attacker can do damage to the pool is to take away as much reward as it can by submitting a sufficient number of *shares*. Since mining pools are characterized by the schemes they adopt to reward the participating miners, the attacker's disruption strategy may vary accordingly, which we discuss in the following sections.

8.6.1 Proportional Reward

This is a very naive scheme [25], where the total reward is divided proportionately according to the number of *shares* each miner contributed in that round of competition. The round in this context means the interval between finding two successfully mined valid blocks. As a pool operator receives a challenge from the blockchain network, the competition round starts, where it assigns the task to participating miners in the pool. The members utilize their hashing ability to solve the cryptopuzzle. Upon finding a valid block, the honest members usually forward it to the pool operator, which then broadcasts in the blockchain network. The pool operator receives a fixed reward R if the network of miners reaches consensus on its mined block, and from this point the next round starts. The pool operator may keep a fixed percentage of the reward, and the remaining is then distributed among the members in proportion to the number of *shares* each miner has contributed with respect to the total number of *shares* received in that round.

Assuming that δ portion of reward is reserved for the pool operator, the pool members share the total reward of $(1-\delta)R$. Now, to estimate the expected number of *shares* in a particular round of competition, we assume that the time taken to find a *share* by miner i is exponentially distributed with parameter α_i. Thus, the expected time of finding a *share* is $\frac{1}{\alpha_i}$, which can be a full solution with probability $\frac{1}{D}$. Considering the round lasts for T units of time, the miner i could produce $\alpha_i \mathcal{M} T$ number of hashes on average in that round. However, the total number of *shares* the miner produces is modeled as the function, $h(\alpha_i \mathcal{M} T)$, where $h(.)$ is monotonically increasing function with respect to i's mining power, i.e. $\frac{\partial h}{\partial \alpha_i} > 0$. Thus, the total number of *shares* submitted to the pool operator can be represented as:

$$H = \sum_{i \in \mathcal{P}} h(\alpha_i \mathcal{M} T). \tag{8.7}$$

So, the expected reward received by miner i out of the pool that adopts the proportional reward scheme is:

$$\mathcal{U}_i = \frac{(1-\delta)Rh(\alpha_i \mathcal{M} T)}{H}. \tag{8.8}$$

Block withholding attack in the proportional reward pool—When a malicious miner with hashing power $\alpha_{\mathcal{A}}$ joins the pool, the inherent power of the pool increases to $\sum_{i=1}^{n} \alpha_i + \alpha_{\mathcal{A}}$. Thus, the number of *shares* submitted in a round increases from H to H', where $H' = \sum_{i \in \mathcal{P}} h(\alpha_i \mathcal{M} T) + h(\alpha_{\mathcal{A}} \mathcal{M} T)$. As the hashing power of the attacker increases, its *share* contribution in the pool also increases proportionately. Since the attacker never submits valid blocks (solutions) and rather withholds them, the length of the round does not depend on its mining power. The goal of the attacker is to impose maximum disruption on the pool members so that pool mining is no longer profitable for them, and eventually forces them to leave the pool. There are two different ways an attacker can affect the block mining of pool members: (i) eclipsing the blockchain network, where the attacker can control the network connections and hence manipulate the victim's mining activity directly, and (ii) increasing hashing power, which could produce more number of *shares*; hence, the overall reward received may dominate over rewards to all other members. We have chosen to analyze the second scenario, where the attacker could get extra mining power to dominate in the pool and increase the reward variance of pool members.

To start absorbing rewards, the attacker needs to know the amount of extra hashing power it requires on top of $\alpha_{\mathcal{A}} \mathcal{M}$ to generate x more *shares* because the only way to decrease the payout of pool members is to submit more *shares* to the pool operator. Now, if the attacker generates extra x *shares*, the rewards to the pool member i can be represented as:

$$U_i = \frac{(1-\delta)Rh(\alpha_i \mathcal{M}T)}{H' + h(x)}. \tag{8.9}$$

This means that the payoff of miner i is inversely proportional to the mining power of the attacker and therefore its net reward goes down if the attacker generates more *shares*. However, it is not possible to make the utility of honest miners very close to zero because it will need an enormous amount of *shares* to be generated. Pursuing that would equivalently require large computing ability, which may not be possible for an attacker. Instead, we plan to find the lower bound on x that will still paralyze the miners to be better off with solo mining. Thus, the attacker's optimization function can be characterized as:

$$x^* = \underset{x}{\text{minimize}} \left[\sum_{i=1}^{n} \frac{(1-\delta)Rh(\alpha_i \mathcal{M}T)}{H' + h(x)} \right] \tag{8.10}$$

Subject to,

$$prop\_var(U_i) \geq var\left(U^i_{solo}\right) + \epsilon, \forall i \in [1, \cdots, n].$$

where $0 < \epsilon \ll 1$ is a very small amount that signifies the point at which the payout variance out of pool mining crosses the variance of solo mining. $prop\_var(U_i)$ is the payout variance of miner i per each *share* while mining in the pool and $var(U^i_{solo})$ is the payout variance per *share* while mining solo. The constraint signifies that if $prop\_var(U_i)$ is higher than that of solo mining, then the attacker successfully demotivates them to not participate in the pool. If the variance is high, then the reward will not be consistent, which is what the attacker wants to achieve.

Now, we find the variance of payout for miner i when mining solo with a constant hash rate of α_i. In case of solo mining, the reward is given if it finds an actual block. Thus, the expected reward out of solo mining is $Pr(\text{finding a block})R = \frac{\alpha_i R}{2^\kappa D}$. Block finding as a solo miner can be characterized as a Poisson process with rate parameter $\lambda = \frac{\alpha_i}{2^\kappa D}$. Hence, the total expected reward that solo miner i can receive by mining for T amount of time is the following:

$$U^i_{solo} = \frac{\alpha_i TR}{2^\kappa D}. \tag{8.11}$$

From the property of Poisson distribution, we know that variance (σ^2) is the same as the rate parameter (λ). Hence, the variance of payout from solo mining can be:

$$var\left(U^i_{solo}\right) = \frac{\alpha_i TR^2}{2^\kappa D}. \tag{8.12}$$

To model the payout variance per *share* in pool mining, we first need to consider an appropriate distribution for the total number of *shares* produced in the pool. Now, considering $N = H' + h(x)$ as the random variable representing the total number of *shares* reported in the pool during a round, $Pr(N)$ represents the corresponding probability distribution function (PDF). The average value of reward per *share* to miner i in the round can be:

$$\mathbb{E}[U_i] = \sum_{N=1}^{\infty} \frac{(1-\delta)R}{N} Pr(H' + h(x) = N). \tag{8.13}$$

where $\frac{(1-\delta)R}{N}$ is the per *share* reward as we found earlier. Now, the expected squared payout can be defined as:

$$\mathbb{E}\left[U_i^2\right] = \sum_{N=1}^{\infty} \frac{(1-\delta)^2 R^2}{N^2} Pr(H' + h(x) = N). \tag{8.14}$$

Hence, the payout variance can be expressed as:

$$prop\_var(U_i) = (1-\delta)^2 R^2 \sum_{N=1}^{\infty} \frac{\left[Pr(N) - (Pr(N))^2\right]}{N^2}.$$

Now, to find the concrete value of the payout variance, we can model the total number of *shares* using different standard probability distribution functions such as geometric and negative binomial. These PDFs provide a near natural model to estimate the total number of *shares* in a round [25].

8.6.2 Pay-per-last *N*-shares (PPLNS) Reward

Since the proportional reward scheme is very naive in nature, it suffers from pool-hopping attack, where malicious miners can strategically choose different pools to mine in a round to obtain maximum reward. Therefore, several advanced schemes are proposed to avoid such a scenario and is PPLNS reward scheme is one of them that supposedly resists the pool-hopping nature of greedy miners. Unlike the proportional reward scheme, which is round based, PPLNS considers temporal *share* submission activities to reward pool members irrespective of rounds in the mining process. In this scheme, the reward is distributed among the miners who recently submitted their *shares* no matter how many actual blocks are found in the considered interval.

A simple variant of PPLNS is to set a threshold for total recent *shares* to N and the total reward is distributed among the miners based on the last N *shares* submitted. Now, taking the same notations into account and considering total

B blocks are found during the last N *shares*, the payout per *share* (U_{pplns}) can be represented as:

$$U_{pplns} = \frac{(1-\delta)RB}{N}. \tag{8.15}$$

where B follows the Poisson distribution with mean $\frac{N}{2^{\kappa}D}$. In this variant, it is assumed that the difficulty D and reward R are kept constant. Altogether, RB defines the total expected reward received by the pool operator during the last N *shares*.

The pool employing the PPLNS reward function typically works in the following manner: The operator keeps track of the history of at least the last N submitted *shares* irrespective of the round in which they have been reported. Therefore, the rounds in this case are interdependent on each other. The ordering of *shares* is maintained using a sliding window of length N, which is later used to divide the total reward proportionately among the contributors. Considering the sliding window at k^{th} *share* as $\mathbf{s_k} = \{s_{k-N}, s_{s-N+1}, \cdots, s_k\}$, the reward for miner i can be expressed as:

$$U^{i}_{pplns} = (1-\delta) \times \frac{\#\{s_j : s_j \in \mathbf{s} \text{ and } s_j = i\}}{N} \times RB. \tag{8.16}$$

In the above expression, the total reward received in the window the of last N *shares* is divided proportionately among each pool member $i \in \mathcal{P}$, who submitted their *shares* in the considered window.

Block withholding attack on the PPLNS reward pool—Similar to the previous reward scheme, one malicious miner is introduced in the PPLNS pool who aims to disrupt the normal operation of pool mining via accumulating as much reward for itself. Unlike the strategy adopted in the proportional reward pool, the attacker would have to opt for a different strategy in the PPLNS pool because submitting as many *shares* may not be the optimal case anymore due to the fact that only the last N *shares* will be considered for reward distribution irrespective of the rounds in which they are submitted. If we consider that there are N slots to place N *shares*, the attacker can opt for the following strategies to disturb the fairness of the pool reward system: First, the attacker with mining power $\alpha_{\mathcal{A}}$ must mine at a faster rate compared to other pool members, where successfully mined blocks are withheld. Next, the *shares* are published in such a way that they reside in the window of the last N *shares*, so that the majority of the reward is returned to the attacker instead of the pool members.

The attacker's reward can equivalently be defined as per Eq. 8.16, where the number of *shares* it contributes in the last N slots is dependent on its hashing power.

$$U^{\mathcal{A}}_{pplns} = (1-\delta)RB\left[\frac{\Phi(N,\alpha_{\mathcal{A}})}{N}\right]. \tag{8.17}$$

where $\Phi(.)$ is a function that models the average number of *shares* the attacker can contribute in the window of N slots. The function Φ depends on the hashing power of the attacker and follows a Poisson distribution with a mean parameter of $\lambda = \frac{\alpha_A \mathcal{M} N}{2^\kappa}$. At the same time, the random variable B also follows a Poisson distribution with mean $\frac{\mathcal{M}N}{2^\kappa D}$. However, due to the fact that the attacker withholds the successfully mined blocks, the mean value of B will exclude the hashing capability of the attacker. So, the mean of Poisson-distributed random variable B will be $\frac{(1-\alpha_A)\mathcal{M}N}{2^\kappa D}$. Hence, the expected reward for the attacker can be represented as:

$$\mathbb{E}\left[U^{A}_{pplns}\right] = (1-\delta)R\frac{\alpha_A(1-\alpha_A)\mathcal{M}^2 N}{2^{2\kappa} D}. \tag{8.18}$$

Understanding the overall utility of the attacker, its goal would be to maximize this quantity with the help of additional hashing power from external sources. Compared to the optimization goal defined in the proportional reward pool, where the goal was to minimize the other pool members' reward by finding an optimal amount of computational power, the objective here is to maximize its own reward in the window of N slots by submitting as many *shares* so that other members' net reward will automatically decline. Now, considering the attacker comes up with additional $y\mathcal{M}$ amount of computational power into the pool, the net objective function of the attacker can be defined as follows:

$$y^* = \underset{y}{\text{maximize}}\left[(1-\delta)R\frac{(\alpha_A + y)(1-\alpha_A)\mathcal{M}^2 N}{2^{2\kappa} D}\right]. \tag{8.19}$$

Subject to,

$$pplns\_var(U_i) \geq var(U^i_{solo}) + \epsilon, \text{ for an } i \in \{1, \cdots, n\}.$$

The constraint posed in the above optimization problem is similar to the proportional pool, but here we are looking for one such miner whose reward variance from pool mining is more than that from solo mining. In that case, miner i would prefer to leave the pool and mine alone. Therefore, this process can be iterated to eliminate miners one by one, thereby harming the pool mining process. Now, to define the variance of a miner i from the PPLNS pool when the attacker has incorporated extra $y\mathcal{M}$ amount of hashing power, the expected reward for miner i needs to be formulated, which is $\frac{(1-\delta)R\alpha_i\mathcal{M}'N}{2^\kappa DN} = \frac{(1-\delta)R\alpha_i\mathcal{M}'}{2^\kappa D}$. Due to the presence of the block-withholding attacker, the total mining power of the pool is modified to $\mathcal{M}'$, which is defined as $(1-\alpha_A - y)\mathcal{M}$. Hence, the corresponding reward variance can be presented as:

$$pplns\_var(U_i) = \frac{(1-\delta)^2 R^2 \alpha_i (1-\alpha_A - y)\mathcal{M}}{2^\kappa DN}. \tag{8.20}$$

The reward variance out of solo mining will be the same as that defined in the previous subsection, where the period T will be replaced with N.

8.7 Simulation Results and Discussion

In this section, we evaluate the block-withholding attack instance by considering a private proof-of-work based blockchain that may be operable in small-scale enterprises. It is assumed that all nodes mine on a single pool, and one of them is malicious in nature and looks forward to disrupt the honest mining performed by the rest of the nodes. We consider the initial total mining power of the pool ($\mathcal{M}$) to be 100 GH/s and the difficulty of the cryptopuzzle (D) to be 2096, which is kept fixed throughout. Considering a homogeneous environment, where all the miners have equal computational power, we have experimented by provisioning extra hashing to the attacker and observing the average reward variation. All the miners, including the attacker, are assumed to have 20% of the hashing power in the beginning. For computing the number of *shares* in a round, we assume the value of κ to be 10, which is typically half the number of bits than the actual difficulty (D). The total *shares* submitted by a miner with power α_i, denoted by $h(\alpha_i)$, is sampled from a Poisson distribution of mean $\frac{\alpha_i}{2^\kappa}$.

Since the attacker has possible means of increasing its hashing capability, we first analyze the impact of such an action on the overall reward of the attacker as well as the honest miners. Considering a maximum reward (R) of 10 for successfully mining a block, we can observe from Figure 8.4 that increasing the hash power of an attacker in pool mining has an adverse effect on the honest miner group. Therefore, the honest miners' reward decreases gradually, as depicted by the red dotted line. Although the attacker could potentially increase its hashing ability to a higher amount, such a costly attempt is not necessary for demotivating honest miners to leave the pool. Rather, the attacker would prefer to have a threshold amount of computational power so that the total reward of honest miners goes just below the attacker's reward, which happens to occur at $x = 0.6$ in our considered case. When the submitted *shares* are considered with respect to increasing the hashing power of the attacker, we can observe from Figure 8.5 that the total number of *share* submissions from the attacker increases exponentially, whereas the honest pool's submissions are fixed on an average. This situation is created due to the fact that the attacker has growing computational power, while the honest miners' hashing limits are fixed.

In Figure 8.6, the reward variation with respect to the attacker's increasing hashing ability is depicted, when the pool employs the PPLNS reward mechanism. Here, we observe that the overall reward a pool can obtain, is higher than the proportional pool. This is because of the fact that more than one successful block could be found during the submission of the last N *shares*. However, when the attacker gathers extra computational power, it can take away the honest miners' incentives for mining in a pool. We could observe that with additional power of $y = 0.6 + \epsilon, \epsilon > 0$, the attacker dominates over the honest pool members. Another interesting observation can be made from Figure 8.7 that by increasing the window size in multiples of difficulty (D), the total reward to the attacker does not increase at a growing rate, whereas the honest miners are

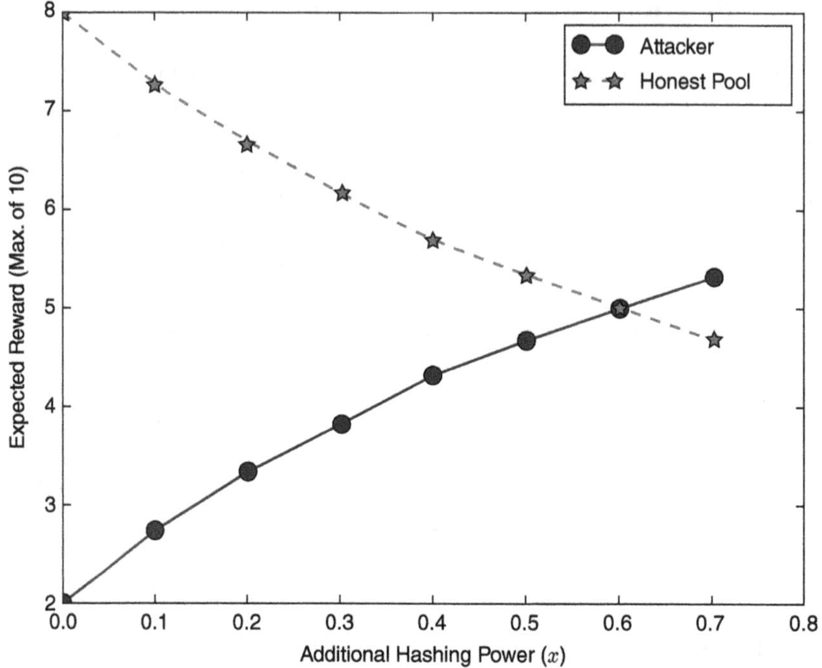

Figure 8.4 Effect on average reward in proportional pool.

rewarded higher than the attacker. This happens due to the fact that more number of *shares* come from the honest pool while the attacker, with a constant hash rate, can not make profit unless extra computational power is added. This gives an idea about how the window size (N) can be chosen to build a barrier for a block-withholding attacker that aims to take away the honest miners' rewards.

8.8 Conclusions and Future Directions

Since blockchain technology is one of the next generation technologies that employs cryptographically enforced distributed ledger system, its security evaluation is necessary to assure its usefulness in the cloud computing domain. Therefore, we investigate the applicability and security implications of blockchain in realizing blockchain cloud. A number of security vulnerabilities are discussed that may have a harmful impact while integrating blockchain with the cloud system. We then particularly model the issue of block-withholding attack that is prevalent in PoW-based mining pools to understand the attacker's strategy toward taking over the pool members' rewards. Simulation results demonstrate that the attacker's access to extra computational power could disrupt the honest mining operation in blockchain cloud. The attacker's strategy

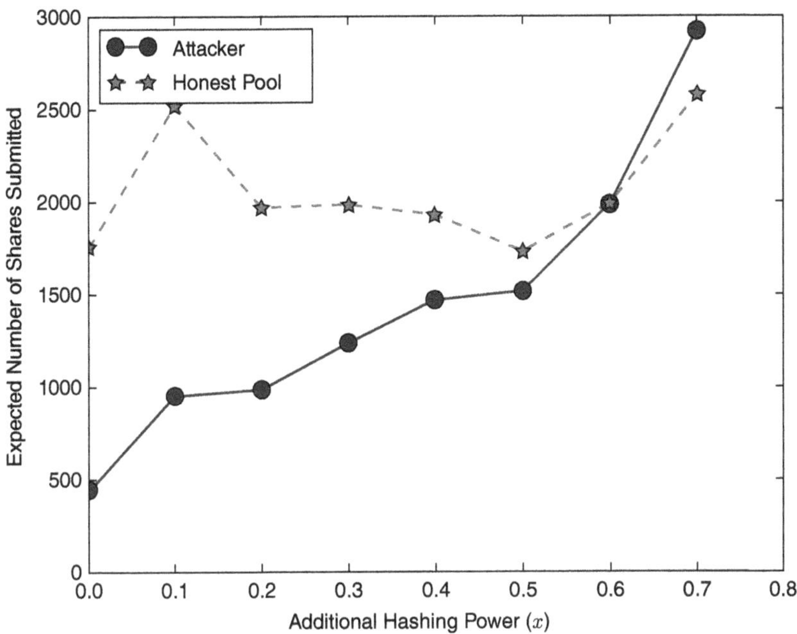

Figure 8.5 Effect on average number of *Shares* in proportional pool.

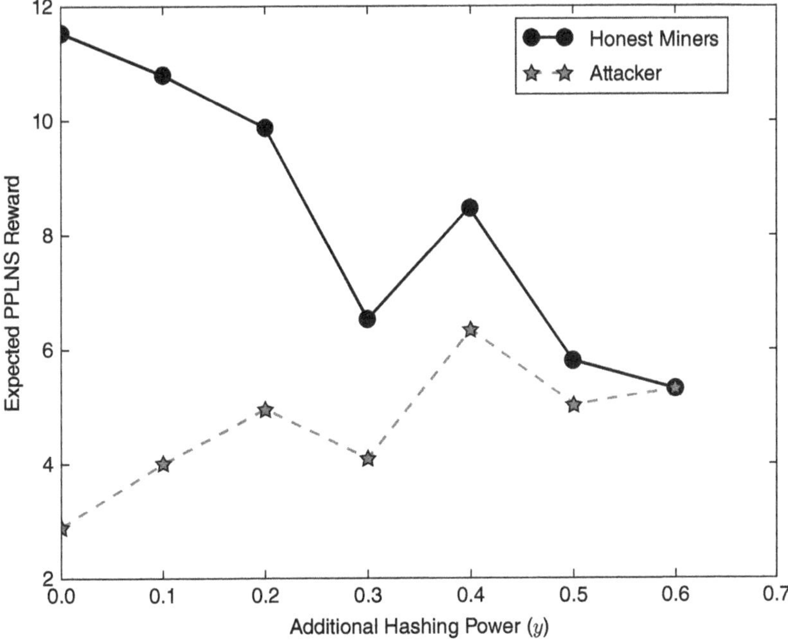

Figure 8.6 Effect on average reward in PPLNS pool.

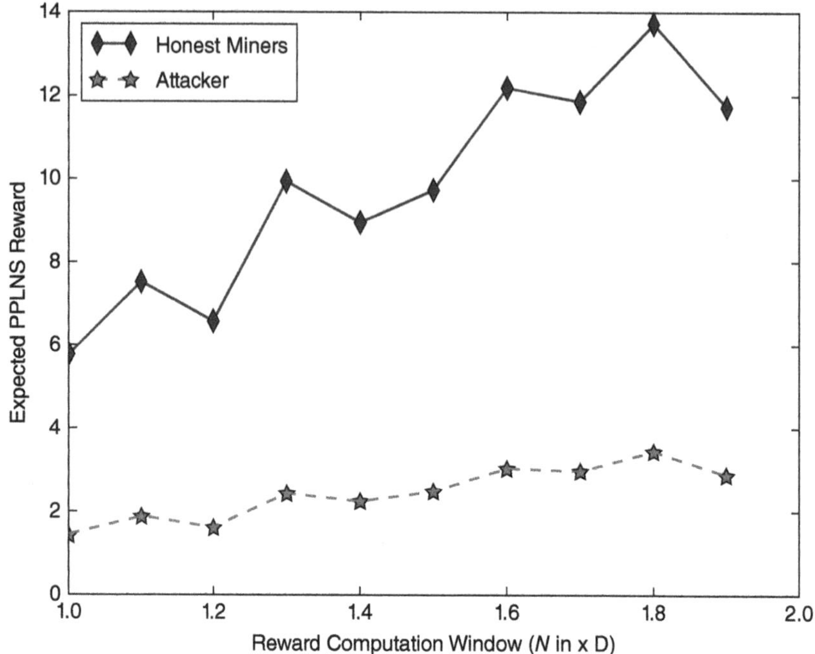

Figure 8.7 PPLNS reward variation vs. window length (*N*).

is analyzed based on two different pools, where reward schemes are different. We found that the pay-per-last N-shares (PPLNS) scheme could be useful in keeping the attacker's impact lesser than the proportional reward scheme. In the future, we aim to extend our analysis on proof-of-stake based blockchain cloud and test instances on real-time private blockchain platform.

Acknowledgment

This work was supported by the Office of the Assistant Secretary of Defense for Research and Engineering (OASD [R&E]) agreement FA8750-15-2-0120 and the Air Force Material Command award FA8750-16-0301.

References

1 N. T. Courtois and L. Bahack, "On subversive miner strategies and block withholding attack in Bitcoin digital currency." arXiv preprint arXiv:1402.1718. 2014.

2 K. J. O'Dwyer and D. Malone, "Bitcoin mining and its energy footprint," in *25th IET Irish Signals & Systems Conference 2014 and 2014 China-Ireland*

International Conference on Information and Communities Technologies (ISSC 2014/CIICT 2014), Limerick, 2014.

3 S. King and S. Nadal, "PPCoin: Peer-to-peer crypto-currency with proof-of-stake," [Online]. Self-published Paper, August 19, 2012. Available: https://pdfs.semanticscholar.org/0db3/8d32069f3341d34c35085dc009a85ba13c13.pdf.

4 D. K. Tosh, S. Shetty, P. Foytik, C. Kamhoua, and L. Njilla, "CloudPoS: A proof-of-stake consensus design for blockchain integrated cloud," in *IEEE International Conference on Cloud Computing (CLOUD)* San Francisco, 2018.

5 I. Bentov, C. Lee, A. Mizrahi, and M. Rosenfeld, "Proof of activity: Extending Bitcoin's proof of work via proof of stake," *ACM SIGMETRICS Performance Evaluation Review*, vol. 42, no. 3, pp. 34–37, 2014.

6 M. Castro and B. Liskov, "Practical Byzantine fault tolerance and proactive recovery," *ACM Transactions on Computer Systems (TOCS)*, vol. 20, no. 4, pp. 398–461, 2002.

7 A. Clement, E. L. Wong, L. Alvisi, M. Dahlin, and M. Marchetti, "Making Byzantine fault tolerant systems tolerate Byzantine faults." in *NSDI '09 Proceedings of the 6th USENIX Symposium on Networked Systems Design and Implementation*, 2009, pp. 153–168.

8 Intel Corporation, "Sawtooth lake." [Online]. 2017. Available: https://intelledger.github.io/introduction.html.

9 M. Milutinovic, W. He, H. Wu, and M. Kanwal, "Proof of luck: an efficient blockchain consensus protocol," in *Proceedings of the 1st Workshop on System Software for Trusted Execution*, ACM, 2016, p. 2.

10 S. Dziembowski, S. Faust, V. Kolmogorov, and K. Pietrzak, "Proofs of space," in *Advances in Cryptology—CRYPTO 2015: 35th Annual Cryptology Conference, Santa Barbara, CA, USA, August 16-20, 2015, Proceedings, Part II*. Springer, 2015, pp. 585–605.

11 X. Liang, S. Shetty, D. Tosh, C. Kamhoua, K. Kwiat, and L. Njilla, "Provchain: A blockchain-based data provenance architecture in cloud environment with enhanced privacy and availability," in *International Symposium on Cluster, Cloud and Grid Computing*, IEEE/ACM, Madrid, 2017.

12 A. Buldas, A. Kroonmaa, and R. Laanoja, "Keyless signatures infrastructure: How to build global distributed hash-trees," in *Nordic Conference on Secure IT Systems*. Springer, 2013, pp. 313–320.

13 Guardtime, "KSI Technology Stack". [Online]. 2018. Available: https://guardtime.com/technology/ksi-technology.

14 Ericsson, "Ericsson and Guardtime create secure cloud and big data." [Online]. 2014. Available: https://www.ericsson.com/news/1853499.

15 D. Tosh, S. Sengupta, C. A. Kamhoua, and K. A. Kwiat, "Establishing evolutionary game models for CYBer security information EXchange (CYBEX)," *Elsevier Journal of Computer and System Sciences*, 2016. [Online]. Available: http://dx.doi.org/10.1016/j.jcss.2016.08.005.

16 C. Kamhoua, A. Martin, D. K. Tosh, K. Kwiat, C. Heitzenrater, and S. Sengupta, "Cyber-threats information sharing in cloud computing: A game

theoretic approach," in *IEEE 2nd International Conference on Cyber Security and Cloud Computing (CSCloud)*, 2015, pp. 382–389.

17 D. K. Tosh, M. Molloy, S. Sengupta, C. A. Kamhoua, and K. A. Kwiat, "Cyber-investment and cyber-information exchange decision modeling," in *IEEE 7th International Symposium on Cyberspace Safety and Security*, 2015, pp. 1219–1224.

18 D. K. Tosh, S. Shetty, X. Liang, C. Kamhoua, and L. Njilla, "Consensus protocols for blockchain-based data provenance: Challenges and opportunities," in 2017 IEEE 8th Annual *Ubiquitous Computing, Electronics and Mobile Communication Conference (UEMCON)*, IEEE, 2017, pp. 469–474.

19 M. Rosenfeld, "Analysis of hashrate-based double spending." arXiv preprint arXiv:1402.2009. 2014.

20 I. Eyal and E. G. Sirer, "Majority is not enough: Bitcoin mining is vulnerable," in *Financial Cryptography and Data Security*. Springer, 2014, pp. 436–454.

21 A. Sapirshtein, Y. Sompolinsky, and A. Zohar, "Optimal selfish mining strategies in bitcoin." arXiv preprint arXiv:1507.06183. 2015.

22 K. Nayak, S. Kumar, A. Miller, and E. Shi, "Stubborn mining: Generalizing selfish mining and combining with an eclipse attack," in *2016 IEEE European Symposium on Security and Privacy (EuroS&P)*, IEEE, 2016, pp. 305–320.

23 E. Heilman, A. Kendler, A. Zohar, and S. Goldberg, "Eclipse attacks on Bitcoin's peer-to-peer network," in *24th USENIX Security Symposium (USENIX Security 15)*, 2015, pp. 129–144.

24 L. Bahack, "Theoretical Bitcoin attacks with less than half of the computational power (draft)." arXiv preprint arXiv:1312.7013. 2013.

25 M. Rosenfeld, "Analysis of bitcoin pooled mining reward systems," arXiv preprint: http://arxiv.org/abs/1112.4980, 2011.

26 P. Koshy, D. Koshy, and P. McDaniel, "An analysis of anonymity in Bitcoin using P2P network traffic," in *Financial Cryptography and Data Security*. Springer, 2014, pp. 469–485.

27 A. Biryukov, D. Khovratovich, and I. Pustogarov, "Deanonymisation of clients in Bitcoin P2P network," in *Proceedings of the 2014 ACM SIGSAC Conference on Computer and Communications Security*, ACM, 2014, pp. 15–29.

28 https://bitcoinmagazine.com/articles/avalon-releases-new-asic-miner-begins-shipping-worldwide-through-blockc-partnership 1447268188.

29 Hashflare, "Bitcoin cloud mining." [Online]. Last Accessed: Dec. 4, 2018, Available: https://hashflare.io.

30 "Genesis mining." [Online]. Last Accessed: Dec. 4, 2018, Available: https://www.genesis-mining.com.

31 "Hashnest cloud mining." [Online]. Last Accessed: Dec. 4, 2018, Available: https://www.hashnest.com.

32 Eobot, "Bitcoin cloud mining and the best way to mine cryptocurrency." [Online]. Last Accessed: Dec. 4, 2018, Available: https://www.eobot.com.

9

Permissioned and Permissionless Blockchains

Andrew Miller

University of Illinois Urbana-Champaign, Department of Electrical and Computer Engineering, Urbana-Champaign, Illinois, USA

9.1 Introduction

Most analyses of blockchain protocols that we have seen so far, ranging from traditional consensus protocols like Paxos and Practical Byzantine Fault Tolerance (PBFT) to Nakamoto consensus, all rely on the "majority honest" assumption, where we assume a majority of the parties follow the protocol correctly.

But why should we be willing to assume that *any* of the peers will be honest and run *exactly* the protocol P? "Honest" here is really jargon, and means in a strict sense for a peer to follow exactly the specified protocol P, regardless of their moral nature. The peers may be honest but self-interested, and a variation of the protocol P' might give them an individual benefit (see for instance selfish mining). It may also be more computationally expensive to run P than P', for example if P' is some approximation. The peers may even be affected by external influences; what if someone offers a reward for running P' instead?

To justify the honest majority assumption, blockchains typically provide some mechanism for selecting the participants in a way that hopefully attracts "good" participants. Blockchains can be roughly divided into two categories, "permissioned" and "permissionless," which differ in how participants are selected. In permissionless blockchains, participants self-select, but must expend resources (either money, in the case of proof of stake, or computational resources in the case of proof of work) to participate. This arrangement justifies the honest majority assumption through *incentive alignment* as long as participants cannot benefit much by running P' instead of P. Permissioned blockchains, in contrast, rely on inputs of some external selection process. The identities of selected participants may be hardcoded into the software, or dynamically updated. In either case, the authority to choose typically resides with an institutional or organizational process, such as an industry consortium.

Blockchain for Distributed Systems Security, First Edition. Edited by Sachin S. Shetty, Charles A. Kamhoua, and Laurent L. Njilla.

In this chapter, we discuss two security design approaches and apply them to both permissioned and permissionless models. The first design approach is committee election, by which a large population of participants are winnowed down into a small, fairly sampled subset, where the attacker does not have much presence in the committee. This approach applies equally well in both permissionless and permissioned blockchains, since it can improve performance versus having the entire population active.

The second design approach we discuss is privacy enhancement. Blockchain applications often need to provide privacy guarantees for users, for example if they involve sensitive information about financial transactions or about the realtime location of Internet of Things devices. Here, cryptography can be employed. If we have a high degree of trust in the peers, as in a permissioned setting, secret sharing is a natural approach, since we assume a majority of peers will not be breached. On the other hand, in a context with less trust, zero-knowledge proofs allow clients to prevent *any* of the peers from seeing protected data.

9.2 On Choosing Your Peers Wisely

In a permissionless blockchain, peers are self-selected according to some automated mechanism, which does not rely explicitly on administrators. Ideally, the self-selection process should promote aligned incentives. That is, the self-selected participants should have "skin in the game," meaning they have a financial interest in seeing the blockchain succeed.

The most successful public cryptocurrencies to date have used proof of work as the basis for their underlying consensus system. Mining requires continuous expenditure of computational effort. This requires electric power, as well as cooling and maintenance of mining equipment (racks of Graphics Processing Unit (GPUs), Field Programmable Gate Array (FPGAs), or specialized Application-Specific Integrated Circuit (ASIC) equipment). The incentive argument goes as follows: miners that participate must believe in the future value of the currency, at least for the short term, since they will at some point need to sell off some of the coins they mine to pay their ongoing utility bills. In addition to the ongoing costs, proof-of-work mining further requires an initial capital investment in the mining equipment itself. Some resources like GPUs can be reconfigured easily to mine on different proof-of-work puzzles. Many ASIC-resistant proofs of work, such as Equihash and Ethash, are designed to be mined using GPUs, with diminishing returns for specialized equipment. This is thought to encourage decentralization, since GPUs are widely available on mass markets. For equipment that is specialized to a particular cryptocurrency, miners may have to sell their equipment at a loss. This adds further support to the argument that miners have an interest in the success of the blockchain.

Proof-of-work schemes can vary widely according to what computational resources they require. We describe just a few examples:

- *Proof of work*—based on the rate of computing hash functions; specialized ASICs exist.
  Examples: Bitcoin, Litecoin
- *Memory-hard proof of work*—based on access to random access memory, which is (hopefully) more difficult for designing custom ASICs with significant performance improvement versus commodity components.
  Examples: Ethash, Equihash
- *Proof of storage*—required to contribute storage capacity. Storage is also resistant to specialized equipment and requires less ongoing energy expenditure.
  Examples: Filecoin, Spacemint

Proof of stake—as an alternative to consuming computational resources, some cryptocurrencies require participants to spend *money* to participate. Naturally, if the blockchain is used to support a virtual currency application, then the virtual currency itself could be collected from participants. Blockchains are called "proof of stake" if they use their own tokens or currency as rewards for participating in their underlying permissionless consensus protocol.

Proof-of-stake blockchains differ widely according to how their virtual currency is used to select participants. In some cases, like Peercoin, just holding the currency qualifies you to participate in mining. In other protocols, like Decred, Casper, and Tezos, participants must explicitly deposit their coins ahead of time in order to participate. In these schemes, coins that are "staked" by their owners are locked up for some time period, during which they cannot be withdrawn. In either case, the incentive alignment argument goes similarly to that of proof-of-work mining. Stakers forego their ability to spend their coins today, for the promise of a larger number of coins later. This is only rational if they expect the future value of the currency will be maintained.

Permissioned blockchains—since permissionless blockchains are designed to run without an administrator, they are especially appropriate for settings where it is desired to avoid reliance on trust in external institutions. However, many blockchain applications enjoy a less adversarial environment, where it may be helpful and acceptable to rely on trusted external institutions.

A permissioned blockchain is one in which some institution or organizational process chooses which servers participate in the protocol. In the simplest case, a fixed group can be determined from the start, with a hardcoded list of public keys or addresses included in the initial software release. More complicated systems with dynamic group updates are possible too. For example, Hyperledger Fabric is a permissioned blockchain software that uses "control transactions" to modify the list of active participants.

In a permissioned blockchain, the process of choosing the parties is outside the scope of the underlying consensus protocol design and implementation. However, the degree to which the blockchain is decentralized and/or trustworthy likely does depend on the quality and transparency of the selection process. For example, Hyperledger is a blockchain-oriented industry consortium with publicly documented policies for group decision making among its members. It currently has a 21-seat governing board composed of representatives of its full members.[1] As such, this institutional process is decentralized (across multiple independent stakeholders), and can be dynamic since a two-thirds majority vote among the board can install new members. There are many other related examples of blockchain industry consortia, such as Ethereum Enterprise Alliance and R3. Permissioned blockchains can be decentralized if they have an effective institutional process for choosing participants.

Summary—permissioned and permissionless blockchains differ in how their participants are selected. Incentives may play a role in both, although incentive mechanisms tend to be more explicit in permissionless cryptocurrencies. It remains to be seen whether proof-of-work or proof-of-stake cryptocurrencies will continue to exhibit long-term incentive alignment, or whether their underlying assumptions will turn out to be unjustified. Proof-of-stake cryptocurrencies are somewhat newer and less battle tested than the largest proof-of-work cryptocurrencies. For example, the earliest proof-of-stake cryptocurrency, Peercoin, has until recently featured a centralized checkpointing mechanism. Other proof-of-stake cryptocurrencies are newer, and many of the most anticipated projects (such as Tezos and Casper) are still undergoing development. Given the important role played by incentives in permissionless blockchains, it is unclear how a permissionless blockchain can be launched without also launching a cryptocurrency. The high energy cost of proof-of-work cryptocurrencies means that they too are difficult to successfully launch. Permissioned blockchains on the other hand can make use of external trusted institutions, which inherit the decentralized qualities of their governance structure.

9.3 Committee Election Mechanisms

The previous section looked at how peer populations are chosen in permissioned and permissionless blockchain networks. In both cases, the blockchain approach is to avoid single points of failure by distributing control among multiple disparate participants. However, many consensus protocols, such as PBFT, run slower and slower depending on how many parties participate, since additional bandwidth is required to replicate transactions to all of the peers. Latency is especially critical for real-time applications such as micropayments among Internet of Things devices. Even if 10,000 parties (approximately the number of reachable peers on the Bitcoin network) are mostly honest, we wouldn't actually

---

1 Captured April 1, 2018. https://web.archive.org/web/20180401182711/https://www.hyperledger.org/about/charter

want to run an instance of a PBFT consensus protocol directly among them. Nakamoto consensus scales gracefully to a large number of users, although recall that it is high latency to commit a transaction (since it takes many blocks worth of confirmations to gain confidence that the transaction is actually committed).

A useful, broadly-applicable approach for running an expensive protocol like PBFT among a large scale of participants is "committee election," where a small subset of parties are randomly selected from among a large membership. In terms of security guarantees, committee elections essentially translate an assumption of the form:

> *At least 80% of a population of at least 10,000 members can be counted on to correctly follow the protocol.*

into a guarantee of the form

> *Among a 100-person committee sampled from the population, at least $\frac{2}{3}$ of the committee follow the protocol.*

In other words, committee elections can be used to amplify the starting assumptions while sampling fairly.

Committee election can be applied to either proof-of-work or proof-of-stake permissionless blockchains. For example, the SCP protocol [1] involves using proof of work to assign identities to a potentially large set of participants, from which a small subset is selected to improve performance. In proof-of-stake cryptocurrencies, the population can be defined a large set of eligible account holders, where the committee sample can be weighted by the account balance.

Leaving aside the choice of how the population is formed, committee election protocols differ widely in the mechanism they use to select a committee. Algorand [2] uses a cryptography "sortition" mechanism, which ensures privacy around the committee election. Essentially, the committee election is kept secret, and each member of the population learns privately whether or not they are a member of the next committee.

Analyzing committee size with Chernoff bounds—when selecting a committee, the main security goal is to ensure that an attacker does not have too much representation in the committee. We assume, as a starting point, that the attacker does not have too much representation in the population overall. The challenge is to choose a large enough committee so that we get a representative sample from the population.

To work through an example, consider a population of 1000 peers. Suppose we assume that 85% are uncorrupted while the remaining 15% may be compromised by an attacker. Suppose we take a random sample of 100 out of the peers (choosing with replacement, such that peers may end up holding multiple seats). What is the probability that at least 67 of the committee seats are assigned to uncompromised peers? This can be computed using binomial distribution. Letting X be a random variable corresponding to the number of corrupt committee members, we can look the probability up in a table, or compute it with standard packages:

$$\Pr[X \leq 33] \geq 0.999998. \tag{9.1}$$

More generally, consider a committee of k peers that are randomly sampled from a large population such that some constant $\alpha < \frac{1}{3}$ of the population is corrupted (e.g. $\alpha = 0.15$ in the running example). We want the maximum number of corrupted parties in the committee to be γ, where $\alpha < \gamma$ (typically $\alpha < \gamma < \frac{1}{3}$, since this is the typical maximum fault tolerance for a consensus protocol executed by this committee. As a function of the committee size k (ignoring α and γ as constants), the probability that $\frac{1}{3}$ or more of the committee is corrupted is $O(\exp[-k])$. This is a negligible function of k, meaning that we can can increase the sample size to effectively reduce the probability of attack success.

To give a more explicit bound, we can use the Chernoff bounds technique [3] to approximate this probability as a function of γ, α, and k. We first describe the expected number of corrupted peers in the sample, $\mu = \alpha k$. Notice that we assume that $\alpha < \gamma$ so that the expected number of corrupt peers is smaller than the desired bound, $\mu < \gamma k$. We want to bound the probability that more than $(1 + \delta)\mu$ corrupt parties are chosen, where we define $\delta > 1$ in terms of α, γ as follows:

$$\delta = \min\left(\left(\frac{\gamma}{\alpha} - 1\right), \left(\frac{\gamma}{\alpha} - 1\right)^2\right).$$

Applying the standard Chernoff bound technique then gives us the following (probabilistic) upper bound for the number of compromised peers in the committee, X:

$$\Pr[X \geq \gamma k] \leq \exp\left(-\frac{\delta\alpha k}{3}\right). \tag{9.2}$$

When we plug in the example values from earlier, i.e. $\alpha = 0.15$, $\gamma = \frac{1}{3}$, and $k = 100$, we get $\delta = \frac{\gamma}{\alpha} - 1 = \frac{11}{9}$, and $\Pr[X > 33] < 0.00222$. Note that the Chernoff bound agrees with the directly-computed lower bound (9.2), but is looser by some factor. The Chernoff bound is useful mainly for establishing asymptotic guarantees.

Committees for sharding and scalability—committee election enables a blockchain protocol to "scale" in the sense that additional peers can join the network without harming performance. However, true scalability means that adding more peers to the network should *increase* the attainable throughput. A promising approach to achieve this goal is "sharding," which involves partitioning the application into distinct shards, such that one committee is responsible for each shard. Omniledger, Scalable Consensus Protocol, RSCoin, Aspen, and Chainspace are all examples of blockchain protocols that make use of this approach. The key challenge is ensuring consistency for transactions that involve multiple shards. Transactions that only involve application data within a shard can be processed locally to a committee. However, a transaction from one shard to another requires communication between the committees and therefore appropriate coordination and locking mechanisms. Race conditions and coordination hazards abound, underscoring the need for rigorous analysis.

9.4 Privacy in Permissioned and Permissionless Blockchains

There is a fundamental tension between privacy and fault tolerance when designing a blockchain-based system. On one hand, blockchains get their fault tolerance benefits by widely replicating data across many peers. However, this poses privacy hazards, especially since data can be sensitive. For example, in Bitcoin, the Bitcoin transaction graph is known to leak plenty of information, linking financial activities across different pseudonyms or addresses.

The protocol may specify that peers have a duty to delete secrets once no longer needed (i.e. securely erasing log entries). Under the assumption that all the peers follow the protocol, this may be effective. However, unlike in the case with equivocation, it does not appear possible in general to directly detect whether an individual peer has suffered a data breach or leaked data. The usual argument based on reputations does not work as well if the perpetrator of the leak is concealed.

Tradeoff between privacy and availability—in a permissioned blockchain, we may be be more inclined to expect the peers to be trusted with keeping client records confidential, and only revealing information on a need-to-know basis (e.g. clients can only query their own account balance but not that of others). Regardless, this introduces a tradeoff between availability (preferring more replicas) and privacy (preferring fewer replicas). Some permissioned blockchain implementations, such as Hyperledger Fabric and Quorum, provide support for applications to tune their operating points along this tradeoff. Hyperledger Fabric's "private channels" abstraction allows for some application functionality to be restricted to processing by only a designated subset of the participating peers. This reduces the attack surface for a privacy loss or data breach. However, the availability of the system now depends on the liveness of this designated subset.

Zero-knowledge proofs—cryptography can come to the aid here, sidestepping the tradeoff by allowing users to conceal their private information while still storing it encrypted in the blockchain, *hidden in plain sight.* Zero-knowledge proofs are especially useful in this context, since they enable a user to prove that a piece of encrypted data satisfies some property, even without revealing the data itself.

Consider the following design for a blockchain-based virtual currency with private account balances: The public blockchain stores the balance of each user P_i as a cryptographic commitment $C = \mathsf{Com}(r, \$\mathsf{bal})$, where the user knows his real balance $\mathsf{bal}, as well as the randomness r used by the commitment. Now suppose the virtual currency needs to support a feature whereby a user withdraws some amount $\$X$ of "publicly visible" money from their account, without revealing any information about the remaining balance. In other words, the user must accomplish the following without revealing anything about $bal:

1. Prove that $\$X$ is smaller than the secret balance committed to by C.
2. Post an updated account balance C' and show that it is $\$X$ smaller than that of C.

A zero-knowledge proof for this application is described precisely below, using a versatile notation called the Camenisch-Stadler notation. This is used to specify the public information (the statement) known to the prover and verifier, the private information (the witness) known only to the prover, and the required relationship between them (the predicate, or language).

$$\textsc{zk}\{(r, r', \$\mathsf{bal}) : C = \mathsf{Com}_r(\$\mathsf{bal}) \wedge C' = \mathsf{Com}_{r_1}(\$\mathsf{bal} - \$X)\}.$$

To summarize, this notation says that the prover must convince a verifier that he/she knows how to open the two commitments C and C' to the values $bal and $(\mathsf{bal} - \$X)$, respectively, and that $\$\mathsf{bal} \geq \$X$ so no overflow occurs.

Applications expressed in this notation can be systematically compiled to zero-knowledge proof schemes [4], with varying performance tradeoffs. The example above most closely resembles the confidential transactions [5] cryptocurrency design. Many other variations are possible. Ring signatures can be combined with confidential transactions to obscure the identity of the sender [6]. The Zcash security layer, based on Zcash [7], hides the amounts, sender, and receiver.

Applications based on zero-knowledge proofs are especially appealing for permissionless blockchains, since they avoid revealing information to any of the peers. However, a downside is that if the client loses their keys, the private data is lost with them.

Secret sharing and secure multiparty computation—suppose we can trust a majority of the blockchain peers to keep a secret. For example, suppose among N available servers, we believe no more than t of them will suffer a data breach in the next year. Secret sharing is a technique for this setting that lets a client store sensitive data s as a shared secret $[\![s]\!]$, distributed among the N servers, such that learning any information about s requires the interaction of $t + 1$ or more servers.

Shamir's secret sharing scheme works as follows: Consider a secret field element $s \in \mathbb{F}_p$ where p is a large prime number. We can represent the secret element s by a random degree-t polynomial $f(\cdot)$ over $\mathbb{F}_p$ where the secret is the evaluation at 0, $s = f(0)$. The idea is that then each peer in the network is responsible for storing one point on the polynomial, i.e. party P_i stores $[\![s]\!]^{(i)} = f(i)$. Since the polynomial is of degree-bound t, then any $t + 1$ parties can interact with each other to recover $f(\cdot)$ (and hence s) through polynomial interpolation. However, if up to t peers suffer a data breach, the attacker learns nothing about the secrets.

Instead of simply reconstructing the secret value, we can use Secure Multiparty Computation (SMC) to perform computations over the secret-shared values. In theory, this approach is completely general, and we can support arbitrary computations over secret-shared data by representing the program as an arithmetic circuit [8, 9]. In practice, this compilation can be expensive. For example, while linear operations on secret-shared values can be computed locally, multiplications require a round of interaction (using the BGW protocol [9], or Beaver triples [10]). Providing efficient and general instantiations of the computing-on-shared-data approach remains an active area of ongoing research.

Secret sharing introduces a tradeoff between privacy and availability. Many SMC protocols tolerate a maximum threshold parameter of $t < \frac{N}{3}$. Notice that for a given setting of N, the parameter t determines the privacy guarantee, since up to t peers may be compromised without endangering the secret. However, since at least $t + 1$ peers must interact to perform any computations on the secret, if $N - t$ crash then the secret could be lost. Some recent SMC protocols, such as SPDZ [11], provide privacy in the "dishonest majority" setting, where up to $t \leq N - 1$ parties can be compromised without revealing information about the secret. However, in this setting, if even one server crashes, then the secret is lost.

9.5 Conclusion

Blockchains can distribute trust but not eliminate it entirely. All of the desired security and properties rely on a majority of the participating parties to behave appropriately. Whether these parties are appointed, chosen randomly, or offered incentives, the overall goal is the same—get many different folks to participate and to take their role seriously.

A wide range of approaches to achieve this have been proposed, and many practical deployments are underway. Permissioned and permissionless designs represent two ends of a spectrum based on the degree of influence that a trusted authority has in the process. Blockchains featuring a digital currency typically reward participants with units of this currency. There seems to be an inherent tension between having "more" participants and "better" participants.

Requiring participants to expend energy or make a financial deposit are attempts at raising the barrier to entry so only dedicated individuals participate. It is difficult to keep a secret among a large group, although cryptographic mechanisms can be used to provide privacy to users. Although, in general, more participants means more cost, sampling a small committee can be an effective mitigation strategy.

Future blockchain designs will surely experiment with more approaches as well. We do not yet have a comprehensive model to comparatively evaluate such designs. How participants respond to incentives can depend on factors outside the scope of system design, such as fluctuations in the market price of the virtual currency denominating their rewards. We would prefer to evaluate system designs in isolation, for simplicity. However, the blockchain ecosystem is already quite complex, and miners and other blockchain participants must choose among many competing networks where to direct their efforts and attention. We envision that a successful model may combine ideas from distributed systems and behavioral economics, perhaps inspired by empirical insights obtained from ongoing blockchain deployments.

References

1 L. Luu, V. Narayanan, K. Baweja, C. Zheng, S. Gilbert, and P. Saxena, "SCP: A computationally-scalable Byzantine consensus protocol for blockchains," *IACR Cryptology ePrint Archive*, vol. 2015, p. 1168, 2015.

2 Y. Gilad, R. Hemo, S. Micali, G. Vlachos, and N. Zeldovich, "Algorand: Scaling Byzantine agreements for cryptocurrencies," in *Proceedings of the 26th Symposium on Operating Systems Principles*, ACM, Shanghai, 2017, pp. 51–68.

3 M. Mitzenmacher and E. Upfal, *Probability and Computing: Randomized Algorithms and Probabilistic Analysis*. Cambridge University Press, 2005.

4 B. Parno, J. Howell, C. Gentry, and M. Raykova, "Pinocchio: Nearly practical verifiable computation," in *2013 IEEE Symposium on Security and Privacy (SP)*, IEEE, Berkeley, 2013, pp. 238–252.

5 G. Maxwell, "Confidential transactions." [Online]. 2015. Available: https://github.com/ElementsProject/elementsproject.github.io/blob/master/confidential_values.md.

6 S.-F. Sun, M. H. Au, J. K. Liu, and T. H. Yuen, "RingCT 2.0: A compact accumulator-based (linkable ring signature) protocol for blockchain cryptocurrency Monero," in *European Symposium on Research in Computer Security*, Springer, 2017, pp. 456–474.

7 E. B. Sasson, A. Chiesa, C. Garman, M. Green, I. Miers, E. Tromer, and M. Virza, "Zerocash: Decentralized anonymous payments from Bitcoin," in *2014 IEEE Symposium on Security and Privacy (SP)*, IEEE, San Jose, 2014, pp. 459–474.

8 A. Ben-David, N. Nisan, and B. Pinkas, "FairplayMP: A system for secure multi-party computation," in *Proceedings of the 15th ACM Conference on Computer and Communications Security*, ACM, 2008, pp. 257–266.

9 G. Asharov and Y. Lindell, "A full proof of the BGW protocol for perfectly secure multiparty computation," *Journal of Cryptology*, vol. 30, no. 1, pp. 58–151, 2017.

10 I. Damgård, M. Geisler, M. Krøigaard, and J. B. Nielsen, "Asynchronous multiparty computation: Theory and implementation," in *International Workshop on Public Key Cryptography*, Springer, Irvine, 2009, pp. 160–179.

11 I. Damgård, M. Keller, E. Larraia, V. Pastro, P. Scholl, and N. P. Smart, "Practical covertly secure mpc for dishonest majority–or: breaking the spdz limits," in *European Symposium on Research in Computer Security*, Springer, Egham, 2013, pp. 1–18.

10

Shocking Blockchain's Memory with Unconfirmed Transactions: New DDoS Attacks and Countermeasures

Muhammad Saad,[1] Laurent Njilla,[2] Charles A. Kamhoua,[3] Kevin Kwiat,[4] and Aziz Mohaisen[1]

[1] *University of Central Florida, Department of Computer Science, Orlando, Florida, USA*
[2] *US Air Force Research Lab, Cyber Assurance Branch, Rome, NY, USA*
[3] *US Army Research Laboratory, Network Security Branch, Adelphi, MD, USA*
[4] *Haloed Sun TEK, LLC and CAESAR Group, Sarasota, Florida, USA*

10.1 Introduction

Blockchain technology has redefined the way people view trust mechanisms in distributed systems. Blockchain serves as a tamper-proof and transparent public ledger that is easily verifiable but difficult to corrupt. Blockchains use an append-only model backed by proof of work, for example, that offers the capability of augmenting trust in decentralized peer-to-peer settings. Due to such features, Blockchain is being used in applications such as smart contracts, insurance, decentralized-data storage, cloud, Internet of Things (IoT), and anti-counterfeit solutions [1–4].

Although Blockchains are publicly verifiable and tamper proof, they appear to be vulnerable to a number of attacks [5], with a high incentive for attackers to attack them. The application space of Blockchain systems has experienced a massive growth in the last two years [6], while the number of attacks on those applications has also increased [7]. Some of the well-known attacks on Blockchains include the 51% attack, selfish mining, double spending, block withholding, block forks, and distributed denial-of-service (DDoS) attacks [8–11]. Vasek et al. [12] state that denial of service is the most prevalent form of attack that afflicts Bitcoin users.

In the general Blockchain systems, DDoS attack is launched against miners, users, and third parties (e.g. exchanges) [13]. In peer-to-peer settings, a DDoS attack may take various forms. Upon bootstrapping, users or miners can be rerouted towards a counterfeit network, denying them access to the real

Blockchain for Distributed Systems Security, First Edition. Edited by Sachin S. Shetty, Charles A. Kamhoua, and Laurent L. Njilla.

network. Maria Apostolaki et al. [14] estimated that an attacker can isolate more than 50% of the network's hashing power in widely deployed Blockchain systems today, by hijacking a few (< 100) BGP prefixes. Another form of DDoS attack exploits the block-size limit and network throughput to prevent legitimate users from getting their transactions verified in the network. For example, in typical Blockchain systems, the block size is limited to a certain size, e.g. 1 MB, and the average time of block mining is 10 minutes in PoW systems. The size of individual transaction varies from 200 bytes to 1k bytes. Under these constraints, such Blockchains can only verify 3–7 transactions per second [15, 16]. The low transaction throughput creates a competitive environment where only selected transactions get accepted into a block. It also makes such Blockchain systems vulnerable to flood attacks [17], where malicious users exploit the block size limit (e.g. 1 MB) to overwhelm the Blockchain with spam transactions. This further causes delay in verification of legitimate transactions. To prevent such attacks that exploit block size limit, miners apply priority checks on incoming transactions. Priority is given to the transactions that offer a higher mining fee.

In Blockchain, the memory pool (mempool) acts as a repository where all the transactions waiting to be confirmed are logged. Once a user generates a transaction, it is broadcast to the entire network. The transaction is then stored into the mempool where it waits for confirmation. If the rate of the incoming transactions at the mempool is less than the throughput of the network (3–7 transactions/sec), there is no queue of unconfirmed transactions. Once the rate increases beyond the throughput, a transaction backlog starts at the mempool. Transactions that remain unconfirmed for a long time eventually get rejected. Such an attack is not theoretical and can be applied to existing Blockchain applications in general, including those that are widely deployed. For example, on November 11, 2017, the mempool size exceeded 115k unconfirmed transactions, resulting in 700 million USD worth of stall transaction [18]. As the mempool size grows, users pay more mining fee per transaction to prioritize their transactions.

In this chapter, we identify mempool flooding as an attack that causes DoS for legitimate users in Blockchain systems. We establish a relationship between the mempool size and transaction fees and demonstrate how attackers can use it to make legitimate users pay a higher than normal fee. Mempool flooding creates a state of uncertainty among users and they pay a higher fee to prevent their transactions from getting stuck or rejected in the network [19]. To the best of our knowledge, there is no effective mechanism to prevent spam transactions from flooding the mempool and creating panic among legitimate users.

Contributions—In summary, we make the following contributions:

1. First, we identify the effect of mempool flooding on legitimate users in Blockchain systems and the way it shapes into a denial-of-service attack.

2. We present the threat model, the attack procedure of this attack, and the way the attacker can exploit the current protocols of the system to achieve his/her goals.
3. We propose effective countermeasures including fee-based and age-based designs for transaction filtering that optimize mempool size, limit the attacker's capabilities, prevent mempool flooding, and favor legitimate users.
4. We test the performance of our proposed countermeasures through discrete-event simulations and evaluate their performance under varying attack conditions.

Organization—In Section 10.2, we review the related work. In Section 10.3, we outline the preliminaries of this work, including the operations of cryptocurrencies, DDoS attack on mempools, and data collection for this study. In Sections 10.4 and 10.5, we describe the threat model attack procedure that leads to mempool flooding and rise in the mining fee. We propose countermeasures in Section 10.6. Experimental results are reported in Section 10.7. Concluding remarks are made in Section 10.8.

10.2 Related Work

As described earlier, well-known attacks on Blockchains include selfish mining, the 51% attack, the block-withholding attack, double-spending attack, Blockchain forks, and denial-of-service attacks. In this section, we review notable work covering those attacks, and security aspects of Blockchains. Selfish mining is a form of attack where miners choose not to publish their block after computation, hoping to mine subsequent blocks and get more reward. The problem of selfish mining has been addressed by Eyal and Sirer [20], Sapirshtein et al. [11], Solat and Potop-Butucaru [21], and Heilman [22]. Eyal and Sirer [20] proposed defense strategies to deter selfish mining attacks on Blockchains. Block Withholding Attack (BWH), introduced in [23], is an attack in which miners in a pool choose to submit partial proof of work, instead of the full proof. As a result, they get rewarded for participating in the pool although the pool suffers a loss due to partial solutions. Kwon et al. [24] studied a new form of attack on Blockchains called Fork After Withholding (FAW) attack, an attack in which the rewards are always greater than the rewards of block withholding attacks.

The 51% attack can be launched if a mining pool in the network gains more than 50% of the network's hashing power. With more than half the hashing power of the network, the attacker can prevent transactions from getting verified and other miners from computing a block. To address the attack, the Two-Phase Proof of Work (2P-PoW) was proposed by Eyal and Sirer [25] and was analyzed by Bastiaan [26]. Double spending or equivocation happens when a user generates two transactions from the same inputs and sends them to two recipients [10,27]. The problem of double spending has been addressed using one-time signatures in Blockchains [28].

Distributed denial-of-service (DDoS) attacks have been quite prevalent [12,29]. DDoS attacks are repeatedly launched against mining pools and legitimate users. Johnson et al. [30] performed a game-theoretic analysis of DDoS attacks against Blockchain mining pools. Vasek et al. [12] illustrated empirically denial-of-service attacks on a Blockchain system. Prior to their release, certain Blockchains suffered a massive DDoS attack [18,31]. Exchanges, a central entity in public Blockchains, have also been frequently targeted by attacks, as reported in various studies [32–34], and no clear or specific mitigation procedures for those attacks have been proposed. Another form of DDoS attack on Blockchain includes spamming the network with low valued dust transactions. This attack is also called the *penny-flooding* attack. Baqer et al. [17] performed Blockchain stress testing to analyze the limitations of the Blockchain network and how attackers exploit them. Similar to their work, in this chapter we analyze the effect of flooding attacks on users when a spam attack is carried out on the mempool of the Blockchain and complement this analysis with countermeasures through *memory pool optimization*. To the best of our knowledge, this is the first study conducted to analyze the effect of spam attacks on mempool and explore their countermeasures.

10.3 An Overview of Blockchain and Lifecycle

Transaction lifecycle—In public Blockchain systems that use fee structures as an incentive (see the next paragraph), a user generates a transaction by using the current value of the transaction (spendable balance; e.g. credit and quota in information sharing system, etc.) [35]. The spendable balance is comprised of "Unspent Transaction Outputs" (UTXOs) [36] that a user previously received from other transactions. UTXOs are confirmed transactions that are part of the Blockchain. To generate a new transaction, UTXOs are used as inputs and the transaction is broadcast to the entire network. When users receive a broadcast transaction, they store it into their *mempool* and forward it to other users. Finally, miners pick the transaction from the mempool, validate the authenticity of the UTXOs, and mine them into a block. In Figure 10.1, we show a transaction lifecycle.

Relay fee and mining fee—Relay fee in Blockchains is an incentive mechanism for participation in public Blockchains and is defined as the minimum fee paid for a transaction to be included in a mempool. If a transaction does not include the relay fee, peers in the Blockchain system do not forward the transaction to other peers [37]. Mining fee, or transaction fee, is the fee paid to a miner as an incentive to include the transaction into a block [38].

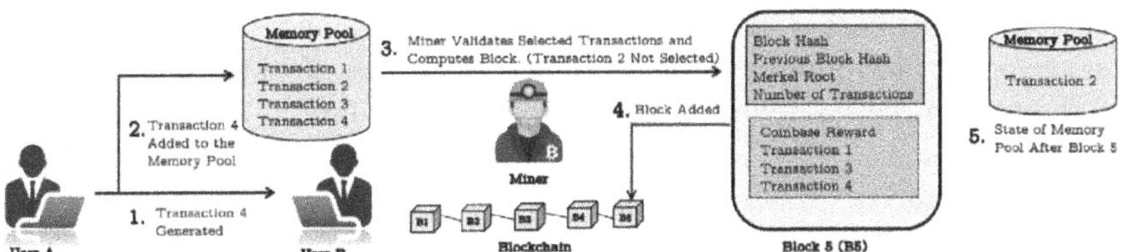

Figure 10.1 Transaction life cycle in a Blockchain-based cryptocurrency.

Confirmation—Confirmation of a transaction means that a transaction has been successfully mined into a block [39]. A confirmation score of a transaction, also known as the age of a transaction, is the difference between the block number in which it was mined and the most current block computed by the network. A confirmation score of 0 means that the transaction has been broadcast to the network but not mined in any block. Such a transaction is also called an "unconfirmed transaction." Blockchain developers discourage users from trusting unconfirmed transactions for the risk associated with them [40, 41].

Memory pool—In Blockchains, a memory pool (*mempool*) can be viewed as a cache that stores all unconfirmed transactions. A transaction that pays a minimum relay fee gets relayed between nodes in the network. Furthermore, every full client in the Blockchain network has a mempool that caches the incoming transactions [42]. Once a transaction is mined, it is removed from the mempool and included in the Blockchain. If a transaction does not get mined into a block for a long time, mempools discard it.

Dust transactions—In the initial Blockchain design and deployment [43], it is anticipated that the minimum transaction input is set to a smaller value to encourage adoption. Later, when the number of users and transactions increase, the threshold for the minimum number of transactions is raised, to control growth [44]. Transactions with small input values are known as "dust transactions" [45]. Dust transactions contribute very little to the volume of Blockchain transactions but consume as much space in the block as a high valued transaction [17]. In generic Blockchain systems used for provenance, for example, the value herein can be associated with a class (type) of digital asset, to ensure provenance in the Blockchain system.

Throughput—The block size in Blockchains is restricted to cope with decentralization and the need to disseminate those blocks on a large network (e.g. 1 MB). Furthermore, the average block computation time is often multiple minutes in typical PoW systems to control the behavior of peers and force a one-node one-vote structure indirectly (e.g. it takes about 10 minutes to compute a block in typical PoW Blockchains). Furthermore, many Blockchain systems adjust their difficulty parameter, a parameter used to control how quickly a block is computed, every certain number of blocks (2016 in Bitcoin, an example of such a PoW-based Blockchain system, which corresponds to 2 weeks). The difficulty adjustment is based on the aggregate hashing power of the network; on average, in 10 minutes, a total transaction volume of 1 MB can be verified by the system. This amounts to a network throughput of 3–7 transactions per second [16].

Mining priority—Blockchain systems deal with the problem of spam transactions by giving miners full control over the transaction policy [46]. As such, miners prefer to mine transactions offering more fee per size (incentive).

10.3.1 DDoS Attack on Mempools

There are two types of DDoS attacks on Blockchain-based systems. In the classical attack, the attacker exploits the size limitation of the block (e.g. 1 MB) and the throughput of the network (3–7 transactions per second) and generates dust transactions to occupy the space in the block and prevent other transactions from mining. This type of DDoS attack has been addressed by the research community [17] and there are countermeasures adopted by miners to prevent it. The miners prioritize the transactions based on fee and select the ones that pay a higher mining fee as an incentive. As such, this prevents dust transactions from occupying space in the block and preventing legitimate transaction from mining. The other form of DDoS attack is the attack on the mempools of the Blockchain system. In this attack, the attacker floods the mempool by generating a series of unconfirmed dust transactions. Although these transactions may be rejected by the miners eventually, their presence in the mempool creates another major problem. In Blockchain systems in general, the size of the mining pool determines the fee paid to the miners. If the mempool size is big, miners have a limited choice for mining the transactions and as a result, the users try to prioritize their transactions by paying a higher mining fee. One such attack on mempool was carried out recently on a popular public Blockchain system, when the mempool was flooded with over 115k unconfirmed transactions, resulting in a substantial rise in the mining fee and transaction confirmation time [18].

10.3.2 Data Collection for Evaluation

To observe the relationship between the size of the mempool and the fee paid by the users, we used a public dataset provided by a company called "Blockchain" [47, 48], which is a leading software platform that keeps a record of digital assets and Blockchain systems measurements. For our study, we gathered the dataset of mempool size and fee over approximately a year of one such popular and widely deployed Blockchain systems. In Figure 10.2, we plot the results obtained from the dataset and we use the min.–max. normalization to scale our dataset in the range (0, 1). The min.–max. scaling is conducted as:

$$z = \frac{x_i - \min(x)}{\max(x) - \min(x)}$$

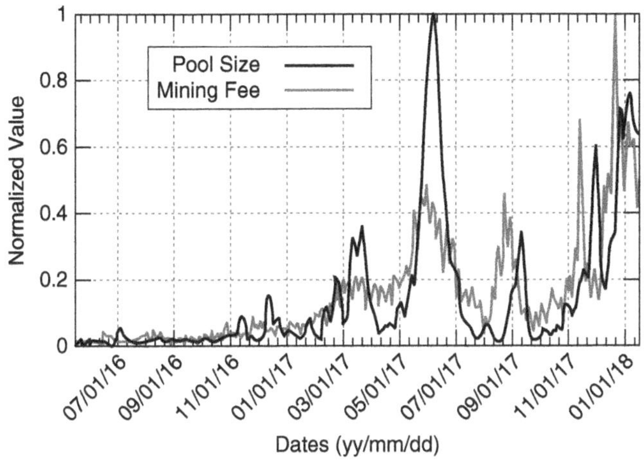

Figure 10.2 Temporal study of mempool size and mining fee paid by the users in a popular Blockchain system.

10.4 Threat Model

In this work, we assume that the attacker is a client with a complete Blockchain and a memory pool at his/her machine. The attacker has spendable transactions denoted by "UTXOs"; those transactions have previously been mined into the Blockchain. In many Blockchain systems, transactions can be split into various small transactions [43]. We assume that a balance in the attacker's possession is large enough that it can be split into fractions of dust transactions; each of those transactions is at least capable of providing the mining fee as an incentive to miners. We also assume that the attacker controls a group of Sybil accounts, each with multiple public addresses. These public addresses could be used to exchange transactions during an attack. The attacker and the Sybil accounts have a priori knowledge of each other's public addresses. Furthermore, the attacker and Sybil have client-side software and scripts [49, 50], which enables them to initiate a flood of "raw transactions" [51] in a short time span. We assume that Sybils (collectively) have a capacity of exchanging transactions at a much higher rate than the network's throughput [16]. Although being a full client in the network, we also assume that the attacker does not have the capability of mining transactions. This means that the attacker does not possess enough computational power to mine a block in a PoW-based setting, discard a transaction, reverse a transaction, or delay other transactions from being mined. Moreover, the attacker does not have control over other legitimate users in the network and, as such, cannot prevent them from broadcasting their transactions and accessing the mempool or other resources in the network. The attacker is also constrained by a "budget"; since every transaction requires a minimum fee to be relayed to the network, the fee limits the number of transactions that an attacker can generate.

Attacker's goal—The end goal of the attacker is to flood mempools in the network with *unconfirmed transactions*. The attacker will broadcast dust transactions at a higher rate than the throughput of the network. At mempools, the arrival rate corresponds to the flow of incoming transactions and the departure rate corresponds to the rate of transaction mining (posting on the Blockchain system). The departure rate is fixed, because the average block computation time and the size of the block are currently fixed. When the arrival rate increases due to a flood of dust transactions, it results in transactions backlog. As the queue size grows, the mempool size increases accordingly. Overwhelming the mempool size alarms the legitimate users, who naturally start paying higher mining fee to prioritize their transactions.

After flooding the mempools, the secondary objective of the attacker will be to reduce the cost of attack by getting his/her transactions rejected. For the attacker, mining transactions will result in losing the mining fee to the miners. However, if the transactions get rejected, the attacker will have yet another chance to carry out the same attack. In prior related work, the target of attack is either a mining pool [30] or the Blockchain itself [17, 52]. In our threat model, the targets of attack are the mempools in the system, as outlined in Figure 10.1. The victims in every attack are the benign users in the network who are denied normal service. Another distinguishing feature of this threat model is that the attacker does not want his/her transactions to be mined. In the analysis performed by Baqer et al. [17], the intent of the spam attack was to flood blocks in the Blockchain by exploiting the block size limit; such an attack requires transaction mining in the Blockchain. While there is a limit on the block size in Blockchain systems, there is no limit on the size of mempools and flooding them does not require transaction mining. Furthermore, the attack exploiting block size can be effectively countered by miners while the attack on mempools cannot be countered in the same way. As transaction mining involves a mining fee while the attack objective is only mempool flooding, for this attack, transaction acceptance in a block remains undesirable for the attacker. According to the taxonomy of DDoS attack [53], mempool flooding attack can be characterized as a "semantic attack of variable rate."

10.5 Attack Procedure

As mentioned earlier, when the rate of incoming transactions exceeds the network's throughput, a backlog of unconfirmed transactions builds up at the mempool. As backlog grows, competition for transaction mining also increases. Users try to prioritize their transactions by offering more fee to the miners. As a result, the fee per transaction paid to the miners increases. To facilitate usage, public Blockchain systems are anticipated to provide online services to estimate the mempool size and the average fee paid [54]. Based on that, a fee is recommended for users who want to get their transactions confirmed within a desired time.

The mempool size affects the way users pay the mining fee, which creates an attack possibility for an adversary to exploit the mempool size and create panic among legitimate users. When a legitimate user sees the mempool size growing, the user, as a rational agent, will try to prioritize his/her transactions by adding more mining fees to them. Dust transactions of an attacker will eventually be rejected by the miners, to protect Blockchain from spam. Although it protects the system from spam, the policy in itself also works in favor of the attacker, since the attacker loses no fees as an outcome. On the other hand, legitimate users end up paying more than the required fee to get their transactions confirmed. Upon rejection of transactions, the attacker can re-launch the attack multiple times to flood the mempools.

As shown in Figure 10.2, there is a high correlation between the mempool size and the transaction fee paid to the miners. During 2017, it was reported that a spam attack of unconfirmed transactions that led to higher mining fee was launched on a popular Blockchain [18,55]. From Figure 10.2, it can be observed that during this timeframe of the attack, the mempool size was much larger than the average size. As a result, the mining fee pattern also followed a growing trend that was similar to that of the mempool size. In December 2017, the problem of mempool flooding was highlighted by crypto analysts [56,57] suggesting that it was an attempt to increase the mining fee and drive the users away from adoption and participation in the Blockchain system. To further establish a relationship between the mining fee and the mempool size, we computed Pearson correlation [58] on our dataset. The Pearson correlation coefficient is defined as:

$$\rho(X, Y) = \frac{\mathrm{Cov}(X, Y)}{\sqrt{\mathrm{Var}(X)\mathrm{Var}(Y)}}.$$

We observed a high correlation of 0.69 between the mempool size and the mining fee. As a result, we conclude that overwhelming the mempool size can also lead to other problems in the Blockchain. Delay in transaction verification can create multiple problems, including possibilities of *equivocation* and *double spending* [28].

To sum up, and as described in the threat model, the objective of the attacker is to maximize the size of the mempool and minimize the cost of the attack. The cost of the attack is the fee paid to the miner if a transaction gets mined in a block. The fee consists of the relay fee and the mining fee. Higher fee increases the priority of the transaction and the chances of a transaction mining [59]. To avoid that, the attacker will design his/her transactions in a way that they are less likely to be prioritized by miners. At the same time, the attacker wants his/her transactions to stay in the mempools for as long as possible. To this end, we envision that this attack can be carried out in two phases—the *distribution phase* and the *attack phase.*

10.5.1 The Distribution Phase

In the distribution phase, the attacker estimates the minimum relay fee of the network, divides his/her spendable transactions ("UTXOs") into various transactions and sends them to the Sybil accounts. This can be done in two ways—(i) The attacker may generate a dust transaction from a previous UTXO, send it to a Sybil account, and get in return a new transaction (unspent). The attacker uses the new transaction as new input and repeats the procedure multiple times for all Sybil addresses. (ii) An alternative way is to use the spendable transactions and generate a series of outputs to all the addresses of the Sybil nodes. Unlike the previous method, this will result in only one transaction to all the Sybil outputs. Transactions of this nature are known as "send many" transactions [60] because the user is sending transactions to various addresses within one transaction. Since the aim of the attacker is to generate as many transactions as possible, he/she will not opt for the "send many" option. All transactions to the Sybil addresses will be generated *independently.* The transactions made in the distribution phase will have input "UTXOs", which will have been previously mined in the Blockchain. Hence, these transactions will have greater-than-zero age and will be capable of paying the minimum mining fee.

10.5.2 The Attack Phase

Once the distribution phase is completed, all Sybil accounts will have sizable balance. In the attack phase, all Sybils will carry out "raw transactions" [51] from the balance received in the distribution phase. Sybils will generate dust transactions and exchange them with each other. To maximize the severity of the attack, they will prefer to have one recipient per transaction. The rate of transactions will be much higher than the throughput of the network. As a result, the arrival rate of the transactions at the mempools will be higher than the departure rate of mined transactions. This will increase the transaction backlog and the size of the mempools over the duration of the attack. The attack will be carried out until all the spam transactions get into the mempools. The transactions made in the attack phase will have the transactions of the distribution phase as input "UTXOs". These inputs will still be awaiting confirmation in the Blockchain. Due to that, their confirmation factor or age score will be zero.

10.5.3 Attack Cost

As mentioned earlier, one of the objectives of the attacker is to minimize the *attack cost.* To be able to achieve that, the attacker requires transactions to be part of the mempool but not part of the Blockchain system. This can be achieved by adding the minimum relay fee R_f to each transaction but not the minimum mining fee. The relay fee is necessary for a transaction to be broadcast to all peers in the network and be accepted by the mempool. If the attacker adds the mining fee, his/her transactions will attain priority from a miner and might get mined. To avoid that, the Sybil only pays the relay fee. If a transaction has i inputs, where each input contributes a size of k bytes, and o outputs, where each output contributes a size of l bytes, then the total size of the transaction and its associated cost are determined by Eq. 10.1 and 10.2, respectively:

$$S(\text{bytes}) = (i \times k) + (o \times l) + i. \tag{10.1}$$

$$C(\text{cost unit}) = R_f \times \frac{S}{1024} = R_f \times \frac{[(i \times k) + (o \times l) + i]}{1024}. \tag{10.2}$$

Assuming that the attacker is limited by a budget B and a minimum value set by the network as T_{min}, then, using Eq. 10.2, the total number of transactions T_a that the attacker can generate can be computed in Eq. 10.3.

$$T_a = \frac{B \times 1024}{R_f \times T_{\min} \times [(i \times k) + (o \times l) + i]}. \tag{10.3}$$

Now we look at the system from the standpoint of a legitimate user. A legitimate user who intends to get his/her transaction mined into the Blockchain pays a relay fee for transaction broadcast and a mining fee as an incentive to the miner [44]. For such a user, contributing T transactions, the cost incurred per transaction and the total cost of all transactions can be derived using Eq. 10.4 and 10.5.

$$C(\text{cost unit}) = [R_f + M_f] \times \frac{[(i \times k) + (o \times l) + i]}{1024}. \tag{10.4}$$

$$T_l(\text{cost unit}) = \mathrm{T} \times [R_f + M_f] \times \frac{[(i \times k) + (o \times l) + i]}{1024}. \tag{10.5}$$

As mentioned in the threat model (Section 10.4), the aim of the attacker is to increase the cost per transaction paid by the legitimate user (equation 10.4). A legitimate user will aim to have his/her transactions mined; therefore, he/she will pay the relay fee and a high mining fee. The attacker will only aim to get his/her transactions into the mempool and eventually not get mined, so he/she will only pay the relay fee. In these settings, the attacker will incur maximum loss if all of his/her transactions get mined. The cost in such a case will be equal to the product of the total number of transactions and the relay fee. The attacker can relaunch the same attack with a new balance of $B - (T_a \times R_f)$.

10.6 Countering the Mempool Attack

To counter DDoS on Blockchain's mempool, we propose two countermeasures that leverage the nature of incoming transactions and prevent spam on the system. One of the effective countermeasures against spam attack in Blockchain is to prevent the transmission of dust transactions in the network. We envision that if mempools can discard spam transactions and stop relaying them to other mempools (nodes in the Blockchain), the pool size can be effectively controlled, and spam can be countered. The existing countermeasures require increasing the block size or reducing the confirmation time to increase the throughput. We argue this is not a useful strategy; if the block size is increased to accommodate more transactions, attackers can increase the number of dust transactions to occupy even more space in the block. A better solution would be to filter spam transactions, which we explore in the rest of this chapter.

10.6.1 Fee-based Mempool Design

Any design that aims to optimize the size of the mempool would require filtering of spam transactions upon arrival to nodes. As the threat model states, an attacker only intends to relay spam transactions between the mempools and does not want them to be mined. To achieve this goal, the attacker only pays the minimum relay fee in transactions so that mempools accept and relay them. To prevent the transactions from being mined, the attacker does not pay the mining fee. We use this insight to construct a *"fee-based mempool design"*, as shown in Algorithm 1.

For this design, we assume that the mempool is initially empty when transactions begin to arrive at the node. We also assume that each incoming transaction has its associated relay fee and mining fee. We also fix a threshold beyond which the mempool starts spam filtering. Initially, when transactions arrive in the pool, and for each transaction, the mempool checks whether the transaction pays a minimum relay fee. If the transaction pays the minimum relay fee, it is accepted and the mempool size is updated. As the transactions get added into the mempool, the size of the mempool grows. When the size reaches a threshold, the mempool starts applying the fee-based policy. Now, if the incoming transaction pays both the minimum relay fee and the minimum mining fee, only then it is accepted in the mempool. The key idea behind this scheme is that only those transactions should be accepted that eventually get mined into the Blockchain. As a result, this technique puts a cap on the incoming transactions and filters spam transactions, thereby reducing effectively the mempool size. If the new size is less than the baseline size threshold, then the mempool can proceed with its operation of relay fee check. Otherwise, it will continue with the fee-based design.

Analysis of fee-based mempool design—In the following, we will analyze the workings of the fee-based design and its utility in light of our threat model. We will limit the number of transactions an attacker can generate within his/her budget by increasing the mining fee threshold. We also observe how this design affects other legitimate users within the same network.

Algorithm 1: Fee-based Mempool Design

```
Inputs: incoming transactions;
        minimum relay fee;
        minimum mining fee;
        Threshold Size;
Output: Mempool Size
State: Mempool Empty
foreach transaction ∈ incoming transactions do
    while (Mempool Size < Threshold Size) do
        if (transaction relay fee > minimum relay fee) then
            Mempool ← transaction
            UPDATE(mempool); /* update mempool size
             after accepting transaction */
        else
            (transaction relay fee < minimum relay fee)
             transaction rejected;
    State: Mempool Size Exceeds Threshold Size
    while (Mempool Size > Threshold Size) do
        while (transaction relay fee > minimum relay fee) do
            if (transaction mining fee > minimum mining fee)
             then
                Mempool ← transaction;
                UPDATE(mempool);
            else
            (transaction mining fee < minimum mining fee)
            transaction rejected ;          /* transaction pays
            relay fee but does not pay mining fee */
    return Mempool Size
Result: Spam Transactions Rejected
```

In the current settings of Blockchains, where an attacker only pays a relay fee to broadcast his/her transactions, if the mempools employ the fee-based design, all spam transactions will be rejected. As such, the mempool will only accept transactions that pay both the relay fee and the mining fee. Legitimate users, on the other hand, will benefit by this design, since they will always pay the relay and the mining fee, so their transactions will be accepted. Once the attacker becomes aware of the fee-based design, the only way it can carry out the attack is by adapting to the new settings and masquerading as a legitimate user. The attacker can do that by adding the mining fee to each transaction. Given a budget B, adding the mining fee to each transaction will reduce the total number of transactions T_a the attacker could generate in Eq. 10.3, which will now become

$$T_a = \frac{1024 \times B}{[(i \times k) + (o \times l) + i] \times [R_f + M_f] \times T_{\min}}. \tag{10.6}$$

From Eq. 10.6, we now observe that the number of transactions the attacker can generate has an inverse relationship with the total fee paid per transaction,

Table 10.1 Confusion matrix.

		Actual Transaction	
		Legitimate	**Malicious**
Mempool	Legitimate	TP	FP
Transaction	Malicious	FN	TN

as naturally expected. Using that relationship, we can adjust the fee parameter and investigate how it limits the attacker's capabilities. To do that, we simulate the effect of increasing the mining fee on the volume of transactions that the mempool accepts. We allocate a fixed budget to the attacker and select thresholds of minimum mining fee and maximum mining fee. Using Eq. 10.3, we select a suitable budget for the attacker that results in 1000 transactions with a minimum mining fee. Then, we generate 1000 legitimate transactions, each with a mining fee normally distributed over the range of the minimum and maximum mining fees. Using a custom-built discrete-event time simulation, we increase the mining fee and monitor its effects on the attacker and the legitimate users.

Evaluation parameters—We use the confusion matrix as our evaluation metric, defined as follows (and highlighted in Table 10.1). We use the following parameters to test the effectiveness of the results obtained from our simulations.

1. **Precision**—Precision is the measure of relevant information obtained from an experiment with respect to total information. Mathematically, it is defined as the ratio of true positive and the sum of true positive and false positive $\frac{TP}{TP+FP}$.
2. **Recall**—Recall is the measure of relevant information obtained from an experiment with respect to total relevant information. Mathematically, it is defined as the ratio of true positive and the sum of true positive and false negative, $\frac{TP}{TP+FN}$.
3. **F1 score**—F1 score uses both precision and recall and provides their harmonic average. F1 score can be computed as $\frac{2 \times precision \times recall}{precision+recall}$.
4. **Accuracy**—In machine learning, accuracy measures the strength of a classifier in determining the nature of experimental outcomes. Accuracy can be computed as $\frac{TP+TN}{TP+TN+FP+FN}$.
5. **Negative rate**—Negative rate or specificity is the measure of truly identified negatives in the complete set of negative values. Negative rate can be computed as $\frac{TN}{TN+FN}$.

We will use this evaluation criteria for all the experiments described in the rest of the paper.

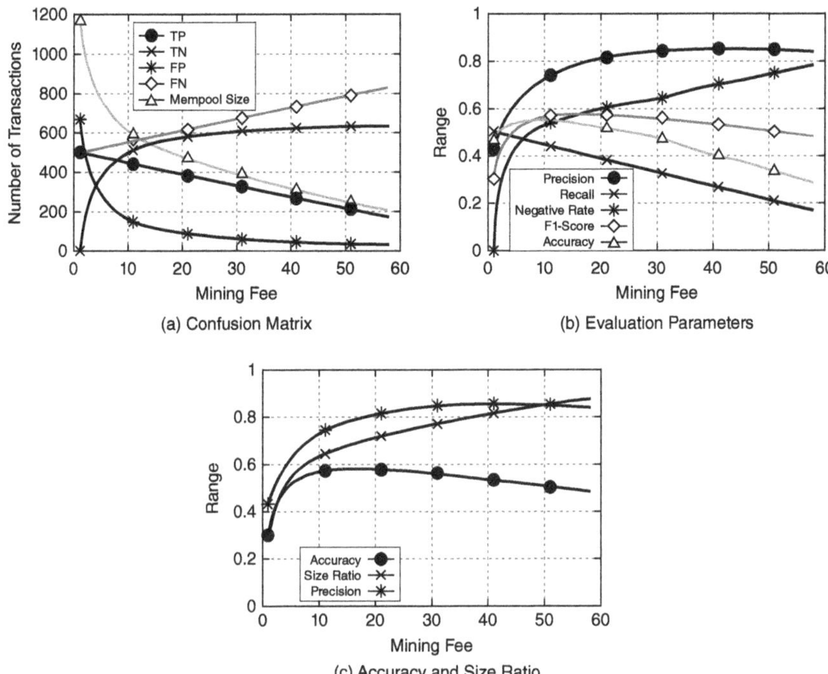

(a) Confusion Matrix

(b) Evaluation Parameters

(c) Accuracy and Size Ratio

Figure 10.3 Analysis of fee-based design. Notice that as the mining fee increases, the mempool size reduces. However, increasing the mining fee also affects legitimate transactions, which is why the accuracy of detection decreases with increasing mining fee.

Evaluation results—We plot the results in Figure 10.3 using the confusion matrix in Table 10.1 to evaluate the effect of the fee-based design on the mempool. We classify the true positives and false positives as legitimate and malicious transactions accepted by the mempool, respectively. We classify the false negatives and true negatives as legitimate and malicious transactions rejected by the mempool. We plot the results of the confusion matrix in Figure 10.3(a). The results show that with the increase in the mining fee threshold, the mempool size (TP + FP), malicious transactions (FP), and legitimate transactions (TP) decrease. With a fixed budget, increasing the mining fee decreases the total number of transactions. Accordingly, the size of the mempool also decreases due to fewer spam transactions (FP). However, increasing the mining fee also limits the fee-paying legitimate users. This, in turn, explains the trend of decreasing (TP).

Using the results from Figure 10.3(a) and the evaluation criteria defined above, we measure the precision and accuracy of our design. From the plots in Figure 10.3(b), we observed that accuracy increased with the mining fee to a maximum value, and then decreased. Using that, we found a *minimum fee cut-off* corresponding to the *maximum accuracy*.

In Figure 10.3(c), we plot accuracy and size ratio; the size ratio is the fraction of mempool transactions out of the total number of incoming transactions, where a lower size ratio indicates higher size optimization. The results in Figure 10.3(c) show that at a fee threshold of 13, we achieve 60% accuracy, 70% size optimization, and 78% precision. Increasing the fee parameter further increases size optimization but decreases the accuracy. Therefore, the fee-based design presents a trade-off between size efficiency and the accurate detection of malicious transactions used for launching a DDoS attack on the mempool.

Limitations of fee-based mempool design—In the following paragraphs, we highlight the limitations of the fee-based design and motivation for our second design.

To understand the limitations of the "fee-based mempool design," we highlight the nature of some transactions in Blockchain. Suppose Alice sends a transaction to Bob (herein, such a transaction could be virtual, meaning that a digital resource, such as a threat indicator in Blockchain-based information sharing is transferred between stakeholders). That transaction is yet to be verified and mined, but Bob spends them by sending 5 BTC to Charlie. For Bob's transaction to be successfully mined, its parent transaction by Alice needs to be mined first. This sequence of transactions is known as a parent–child transaction [61,62]. For a child transaction to become legitimate, its parent transaction needs to be mined first. Oftentimes, however, when the priority factor of a parent transaction is low, the child transaction increases the mining fee to increase the overall priority factor. This process is called "Child Pays for Parent" (CPFP) [61].

For legitimate users, this situation might be undesirable, since more child transactions can lead to transactions getting stuck in the mempool. However, the same situation can be viewed as an opportunity by the attacker to circumvent the fee-based design and carry out the same attack at an even lower cost. For transactions made in the attack phase, their parent transactions in the distribution phase need to be verified and mined. The attacker can minimize the probability of transaction acceptance in the first phase by reducing their priority factor, e.g. by paying a minimum relay fee and no mining fee. Once the parent transactions have lower probability of acceptance in the first phase, the child transactions can increase their priority factor by adding higher relay fee and mining fee. In such a situation, and when the mempools apply fee-based countermeasures, spam transactions of the attack phase will get into the mempool. After the size of the mempool reaches the size threshold, the mempool will check for incoming transactions that pay the minimum relay and mining fees. Since the transactions of all Sybil accounts will pay both the relay and the mining fees, they will be accepted by the mempool and the attacker will be successful, demonstrating a limitation of the fee-based design.

Countermeasure—One way to address this problem is to prioritize incoming transactions on the basis of the mining fee. The mempool can sort the incoming transactions for the fee value and accept the ones that have higher fees. As we increase the mining fee, the capability of the attacker to produce transactions decreases (equation 10.6). The attacker is constrained by the budget and increasing the mining fee reduces the number of transactions he/she can produce. We can observe this trend in Figure 10.3(a). Although this reduces the number of spam transactions in the mempool and optimizes its size, it also reduces the accuracy and the number of legitimate transactions that get accepted. As the fee parameter is increased, the capability of all of the legitimate users to pay higher fees also decreases. To this end, the fee-based countermeasures do limit the attacker from flooding the mempool, but they also limit the number of legitimate transactions that successfully pass the fee threshold. To address these limitations, we propose *age-based countermeasures.*

10.6.2 Age-based Countermeasures

Age-based mempool design—To limit the attacker's chances of success, we propose the "Age-based Mempool Design", which addresses the limitations of our previous model. For this design, we leverage the confirmation factor or "age" of a transaction to distinguish between legitimate and malicious transactions. In Blockchain systems, the age of a transaction is generally used to determine how many block confirmations it has achieved over time.

For this design in Algorithm 2, we assume that the baseline size threshold of the mempool has been reached, and the mempool is only accepting transactions that are paying the relay fee as well as the mining fee. Now, for each incoming transaction, as highlighted above, we count the number of inputs or parent transactions. We initialize a variable "average age" and set its value to 0. Next, we calculate the average age of the transaction by adding the age of each parent transaction and dividing by the total number of parent transactions. This gives an estimate of the confirmation score of the incoming transaction. Then, we apply a "minimum age limit" filter on the mempool. The minimum age limit can take any arbitrary value greater than 0 [63]. If the transaction's mean age value fulfills the criteria of age limit, then the mempool accepts the transaction. Otherwise, the mempool discards this transaction.

A transaction in Blockchain systems can have an input pointer pointing to the spendable transaction that it has previously received. For spam transactions, these inputs are not spendable and therefore less likely to be mined. This serves the objectives of the attacker who intends to broadcast spam transactions, which eventually get rejected. Although the age factor is taken into account for transactions, it is not considered while broadcasting those transactions. As such, attackers may exploit this feature of the system by broadcasting spam transactions and flooding the mempools without losing fees. In this design, we apply the check on the age of the incoming transactions. In the attack phase, the spam transactions will have input pointers of a parent transaction that will not be confirmed in any block. The age of all those parent transactions, made in the distribution phase, will be 0.

Using this knowledge about the nature of spam transactions, we compute the average age of all the input pointers (parent transactions); a minimum age value of 1 means that all transactions coming into the pool are confirmed in at least the most recent block of the Blockchain. In particular, once the transaction is mined into a Blockchain, its parent transaction is removed from the "UTXO" set and cannot be spent again (double-spending avoidance measure). The transaction itself becomes the new spendable "UTXO." With these advantages, the age-based design can safeguard the Blockchain system from spam transactions and double spending.

Once this design is implemented, if a user tries to spend his/her transactions, he/she needs to have at least one valid confirmation backing up his/her transaction. This gives an advantage to legitimate users who can make a normal transaction with a confirmed parent transaction of significant age. On the other hand, most of the spam transactions of the attacker will be rejected due to a low confirmation factor despite paying high mining fee.

Algorithm 2: Age-based mempool design

Inputs: incoming transactions;
minimum relay fee;
minimum mining fee;
minimum age limit;
age of each input of transaction;
Threshold Size;
Output: Mempool Size
State: Mempool Size Exceeds Threshold Size

for each *transaction* ∈ *incoming transactions* **do**
  initialize;
  average age = 0;
  N ← number of parent transactions of current transaction;
  while *(transaction relay fee > minimum relay fee)* **do**
    while *(transaction mining fee > minimum mining fee)* **do**
      average age = $\frac{(\Sigma_{i=1}^{N} parent_i)}{N}$; /* apply age filter */
      if *(average age > minimum age limit)* **then**
        Mempool ← *transaction*;
        UPDATE(mempool); /* update mempool size after accepting transaction */
      else
        (*average age* < minimum age limit) *transaction rejected* ; /* Reject transaction if its age factor is below the threshold */
  return *Mempool Size*;
Result: Spam Transactions Rejected

Analysis of age-based mempool design—We analyze the working of "Age-based Mempool Design" and how it counters a DDoS attack. For this design, we have established that the attacker has the capability of circumventing the "fee-based design" and is willing to pay the relay and the mining fees in all transactions. Also, the attacker knows that his/her transactions will not be verified, so it pays comparatively higher relay and mining fee than the fee paid by the legitimate users.

We carried out our second experiment to analyze the working of the age-based countermeasures. We set a minimum age limit and a maximum age limit as thresholds for the incoming transactions. For the attacker, the only set of transactions with age value greater than 1 are generated in the distribution phase. Child transactions made in the attack phase were assigned 0 age value due to unconfirmed parent transactions. To capture that, we normally distribute the average age value of all malicious transactions from 0 to the minimum age limit. The average age value of all legitimate transactions was set from 0 to the maximum age limit. A total of 2000 transactions were generated with half of them being malicious and half being legitimate. Then, we applied the age-based design on all the incoming transactions at the mempool. We increased the age requirement for the incoming transactions and evaluated the accuracy of detection and the state of mempool for each transaction.

Evaluation results—Using the same confusion matrix parameters as those in Table 10.1, the results in Figure 10.4 show that upon increasing the average age the malicious transactions (FP) decrease sharply. The mempool size decreases to a point where there are only legitimate transactions left in the mempool. Due to low FP and higher TP, the precision reaches close to 1 in Figure 10.4(b). In Figure 10.4(c), it can be observed that at an average age value of 100 we achieve accuracy, size optimization, and precision. As we increase the age parameter to 200, the accuracy does not decrease as in the fee-based design, while the size ratio increases up to 90% and precision increases up to 98%. This shows that this policy prevents a majority of malicious transactions from entering the mempool and helps the legitimate users in getting their transactions accepted.

In these settings, if the attacker intends to spam the network, he/she needs to have a majority of his/her transactions confirmed in the Blockchain. However, in our attack model, we have described that confirmation is undesirable for the attacker since it results in losing mining and relay fee, creating asymmetry in the attack cost. In PoW-based Blockchains, as highlighted earlier, we recall that the average block mining time is 10 minutes. As a result, for a single confirmation of all of the transactions, the attacker has to wait, on average, for 10 minutes. Using the results from Figure 10.4(c), the attacker will have to wait a minimum of 100 blocks to relaunch the attack. With the average block computation time of 10 minutes, 100 blocks lead to 16 hours of delay, which can be further controlled by adjusting the Blockchain operation parameters.

Even if the attacker still plans to carry out the attack after waiting and paying all the fees, he/she will not be able to flood the mempool. The best the attacker

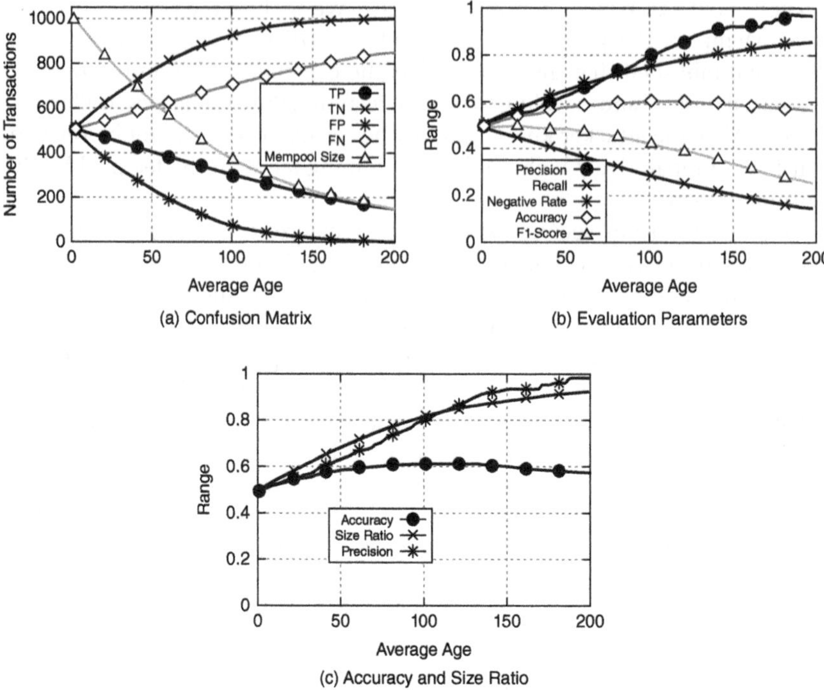

Figure 10.4 Analysis of age-based design. Notice that with age-based design, the accuracy, precision, and size ratio are comparatively higher than the fee-based design.

might achieve will be occasional network stressing with a series of transactions; higher attack cost and low incentive will discourage the attacker. Therefore, the age-based design offers more security against DDoS attacks while ensuring regular service provision for the legitimate users.

Limitations of age-based countermeasures—Although the age-based countermeasures provide an effective defense against DDoS attacks on Blockchains, there are some limitations in this design. Primarily, it requires all the incoming transactions to have a confirmed parent transaction. Depending on the bottleneck and size of the mempool, transaction verification can take even longer time. In low-latency, high-throughput Blockchains, fast transactions are unavoidable, where users cannot wait for verification [27, 28], and their transactions will be rejected by the mempool [64]. However, we do not see Blockchains evolving into such applications any time soon, so we do not consider it a significant problem.

10.7 Experiment and Results

In this section, we describe the experiments we performed to compare our designs when the mempool is under attack. We present a scenario similar to

[18], where a group of attackers flooded Blockchain mempools with dust transactions.

For our simulations, we generate a series of legitimate and spam transactions. Each transaction has an age, relay fee, and mining fee features. For both types of transactions, we normally distribute the relay fee and mining fee over a selected range of fee values. As per our attack procedure, we generate the spam transactions with low age factor, though we observed in the distribution phase that an attacker may possess some transactions that can have some age value. To capture that, we normally distribute the age of spam transactions from 0 to a lower age limit threshold. For legitimate transactions, we normally distribute the age factor from 0 to an upper age limit.

For our experiment, we fixed the size of legitimate transactions and sequentially increased the number of malicious transactions from 0 to 90% of the total transactions. We found TN and FP from the confusion matrix as suitable measures to determine the efficiency of fee- and age-based models in detecting spam. In Figure 10.5(a) and Figure 10.5(b), we plot TN and FP for mempools under no policy, fee-based design and age-based design. It can be observed that both designs are efficient in detecting and discarding malicious transactions when the attack grows. Although both designs effectively reduce FP, the age-based design achieves better efficiency. As malicious transactions increase, the age-based design discards all the unconfirmed transactions and the fee-based design caps the fee-paying capacity of the attacker.

In Figure 10.5(c) and Figure 10.5(d), we plot the negative rate and accuracy. The figure shows that the accuracy of the age-based design increases as malicious transactions increase. The accuracy of the fee-based design is low at the beginning, but it grows as the percentage of malicious transactions grows. The reason for the low accuracy at the start is the low detection rate TP. Although the age-based design appears to be the best choice for detecting malicious transactions, we see in Figure 10.5(e) that the fee-based model achieves better size efficiency.

The mempool size is determined by the true positive and false positive values TP + FP. For both designs, we plot the mempool size in Figure 10.5(e). The figures show that just below the number of malicious transactions, the fee-based design has lower mempool size. After that, the age-based design becomes more size-efficient due to the low FP. To understand the mempool size optimization ratio, we use the model in Eq. 10.7.

$$size\ ratio = 1 - \frac{mempool_{size_{under_{design}}}}{mempool_{size_{no_{design}}}}. \tag{10.7}$$

This equation gives a ratio of size difference of the mempool when countermeasures are applied. The results in Figure 10.5(f) show that the fee-based design achieves consistent size optimization irrespective of malicious transactions percentage. The size ratio for the age-based design increases with the

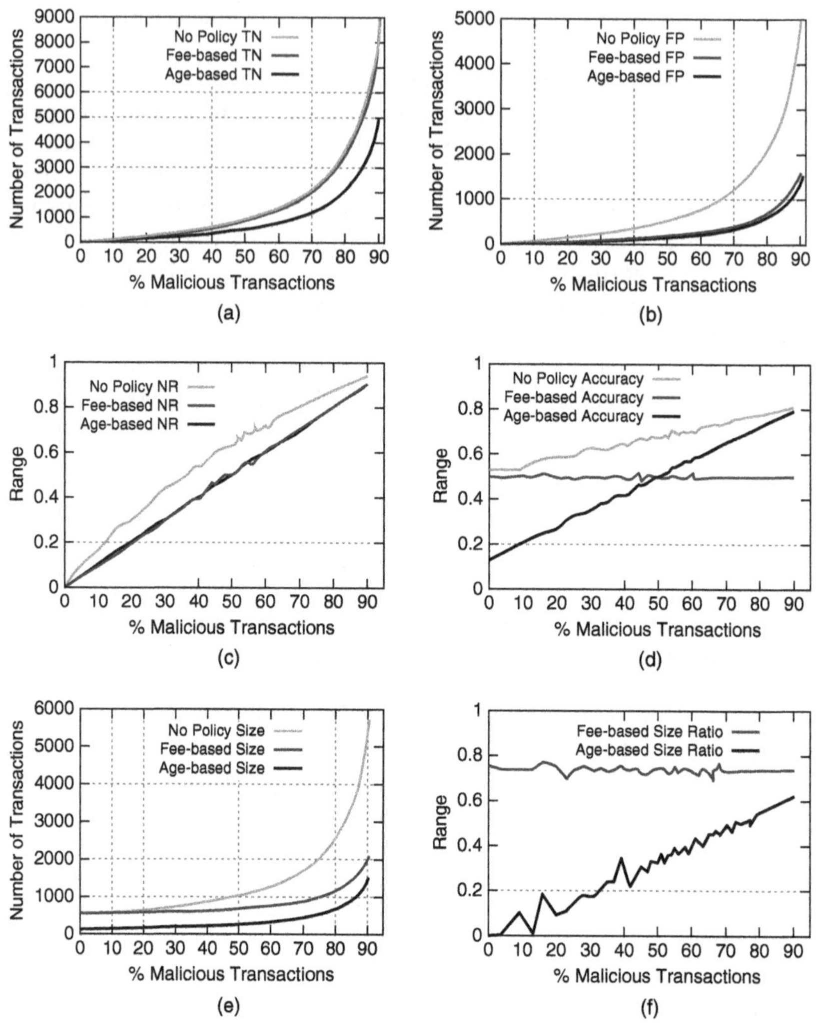

Figure 10.5 Performance of fee-based and age-based designs under mempool DDoS attack. Notice that when the percentage of malicious transactions is low, indicating less severe attack, the fee-based policy is effective in terms of accuracy and size optimization. However, as the attack rate increases, the age-based policy also becomes effective with better negative rate.

percentage increase in malicious transactions. With 88% of transactions being malicious, the age-based design achieves a size ratio of 60%. From Figure 10.5, it can be inferred that there is a trade-off between detection accuracy and size optimization.

We can use the size and accuracy trade-off to select appropriate countermeasures during a DDoS attack. If the attack is less severe but the pending transaction backlog is high, the fee-based design will limit the incoming malicious transactions and optimize the mempool size until the backlog is cleared. If the attack is severe [18] and majority of incoming transactions are unconfirmed then age-based design will be more useful in detecting malicious transactions, reducing the FP and optimizing mempool size.

10.8 Conclusion

In this chapter, we identify a DDoS attack on Blockchain mempools that trap users into paying a higher mining fee. Attacks on Blockchain mempools have not been addressed previously, and we propose two countermeasures to the problem—fee-based and age-based designs. From our analysis and simulation results, we conclude that when the attack is not severe, the fee-based design is more effective in mempool size optimization. However, it does so by affecting both the attacker and the legitimate users. In contrast, when the attack is severe, the age-based design is more useful in helping legitimate users while discarding maximum spam transactions. Although the size optimization achieved by the age-based design is less compared to that achieved by the age-based design, its accuracy of spam detection is higher. Extending our analysis and design towards a hybrid model that leverages the benefits of both designs and achieves maximum spam detection and size optimization is an area for further study.

References

1 M. Crosby, P. Pattanayak, S. Verma, and V. Kalyanaraman, "Blockchain technology: Beyond Bitcoin," *Applied Innovation*, vol. 2, pp. 6–10, 2016.
2 G. Danezis and S. Meiklejohn, "Centrally banked cryptocurrencies." arXiv Preprint arXiv:1505.06895. 2015.
3 A. Extance, "The future of cryptocurrencies: Bitcoin and beyond," *Nature*, vol. 526, no. 7571, pp. 21–23, 2015.
4 X. Xu, C. Pautasso, L. Zhu, V. Gramoli, A. Ponomarev, A. B. Tran, and S. Chen, "The blockchain as a software connector," in *2016 13th Working IEEE/IFIP Conference on Software Architecture (WICSA)*, 2016, pp. 182–191.
5 R. Kaushal, "Bitcoin: Vulnerabilities and attacks," *Imperial Journal of Interdisciplinary Research*, vol. 2, no. 7, pp. 944–946, 2016.
6 W. Richter, "3 charts show the crazy gains of cryptocurrencies." [Online]. Business Insider, 2017. Available: https://goo.gl/nBY7dL.
7 Superadmin, "DDoS attacks on cryptocurrency exchanges intensify as Bitcoin price surges." [Online]. Coinfox, 2017. Available: https://goo.gl/GgN8GA.
8 Learn Cryptography, "51% Attack." [Online]. 2017. Available: https://learncryptography.com/cryptocurrency/51-attack.

9 M. Rosenfeld, "Analysis of hashrate-based double spending." *arXiv Preprint arXiv:1402.2009*. 2014.

10 I. D. Rubasinghe and T. N. K. De Zoysa, "Transaction verification model over double spending for peer-to-peer digital currency transactions based on blockchain architecture," *International Journal of Computer Applications*, vol. 163, no. 5, pp. 24–31, 2017.

11 A. Sapirshtein, Y. Sompolinsky, and A. Zohar, "Optimal selfish mining strategies in Bitcoin," in *Financial Cryptography and Data Security—20th International Conference, FC 2016*, Revised Selected Papers, Christ Church, Barbados, February 22–26, 2016, pp. 515–32. https://doi.org/10.1007/978-3-662-54970-4_30.

12 M. Vasek, M. Thornton, and T. Moore, "Empirical analysis of denial-of-service attacks in the Bitcoin ecosystem," in *Financial Cryptography and Data Security*. Springer, 2014, pp. 57–71.

13 P. Muncaster, "World's largest Bitcoin exchange Bitfinex crippled by DDoS." [Online]. 2017. Available: http://bit.ly/2kqo6HU.

14 M. Apostolaki, A. Zohar, and L. Vanbever, "Hijacking Bitcoin: Routing attacks on cryptocurrencies," in *2017 IEEE Symposium on Security and Privacy (SP)*, IEEE, 2017.

15 S. Bano, M. Al-Bassam, and G. Danezis, "The road to scalable blockchain designs," *USENIX Security*, 2017.

16 K. Croman, C. Decker, I. Eyal, A. E. Gencer, A. Juels, A. Kosba, A. Miller, P. Saxena, E. Shi, E. G. Sirer, D. Song, and R. Wattenhofer, "On scaling decentralized blockchains," in *International Conference on Financial Cryptography and Data Security*. Springer, 2016, pp. 106–125.

17 K. Baqer, D. Y. Huang, D. McCoy, and N. Weaver, "Stressing out: Bitcoin 'stress testing'," in *International Conference on Financial Cryptography and Data Security*. Springer, 2016, pp. 3–18.

18 F. Memoria, "700 million stuck in 115,000 unconfirmed transactions." [Online]. CryptoCoinsNews, 2017. Available: https://goo.gl/mYX14V.

19 W. Woo, "Charts: Determining the ideal block size for Bitcoin." [Online]. 2017. Available: https://goo.gl/CPmWCW.

20 I. Eyal and E. G. Sirer, "Majority is not enough: Bitcoin mining is vulnerable," in *Financial Cryptography and Data Security*. Springer, 2014, pp. 436–454.

21 S. Solat and M. Potop-Butucaru, "ZeroBlock: Preventing selfish mining in Bitcoin." *arXiv Preprint arXiv:1605.02435*. 2016.

22 E. Heilman, "One weird trick to stop selfish miners: Fresh Bitcoins, a solution for the honest miner," in *Financial Cryptography and Data Security*. Springer, 2014, pp. 161–162.

23 M. Rosenfeld, "Analysis of Bitcoin pooled mining reward systems." arXiv Preprint arXiv:1112.4980. 2011.

24 Y. Kwon, D. Kim, Y. Son, E. Vasserman, and Y. Kim, "Be selfish and avoid dilemmas: Fork after withholding (FAW) attacks on Bitcoin," in *CCS '17*

Proceeding of the 2017 ACM SIGSAC Conference on Computer and Communications Security, 2017, pp. 195–209.
25 I. Eyal and E. G. Sirer, "How to disincentivize large Bitcoin mining pools." [Online]. 2014. Available: http://bit.ly/1srPhPs.
26 M. Bastiaan, "Preventing the 51%-Attack: A stochastic analysis of two phase proof of work in Bitcoin." [Online]. 2015. Available: https://goo.gl/cNACCq.
27 G. O. Karame, E. Androulaki, and S. Capkun, "Double-spending fast payments in Bitcoin," in *Proceedings of the 2012 ACM Conference on Computer and Communications Security—CCS 12*, 2012.
28 M. Saad and A. Mohaisen, "Towards characterizing blockchain-based cryptocurrencies for highly-accurate predictions," in *International Workshop on Hot Topics in Pervasive Mobile and Online Social Networking, HotPOST 2018*, 2018.
29 M. Saad, M. T. Thai, and A. Mohaisen, "Deterring DDoS attacks on blockchain-based systems through mempool optimization," in *13th ACM ASIA Conference on Information, Computer and Communications Security, ASIACCS 2018*, 2018.
30 B. Johnson, A. Laszka, J. Grossklags, M. Vasek, and T. Moore, "Game-theoretic analysis of DDoS attacks against Bitcoin mining pools," in *Financial Cryptography and Data Security: FC 2014 Workshops, Bitcoin and Wahc 2014, Christ Church, Barbados, March 7, 2014, Revised Selected Papers*, R. Böhme, M. Brenner, T. Moore, and M. Smith, Ed. Berlin, Heidelberg: Springer Berlin Heidelberg, 2014, pp. 72–86. https://doi.org/10.1007/978-3-662-44774-1_6.
31 F. Memoria, "Massive DDoS attack takes down Bitcoin Gold's website." [Online]. CryptoCoinsNews, 2017. Available: https://goo.gl/7rzDz1.
32 C. Baldwin, "72 million stolen from Bitfinex exchange in Hong Kong." [Online]. Thomson Reuters, 2016. Available: http://reut.rs/2gc7iQ9.
33 Bitcoi16bg, "Ethereum exchange Poloniex down DDoS attack again!" [Online]. 2016. Available: https://goo.gl/YnhDKH.
34 D. Siegel, "Understanding the DAO attack." [Online]. 2016. Available: https://www.coindesk.com/understanding-dao-hack-journalists/.
35 X. Xu, I. Weber, M. Staples, L. Zhu, J. Bosch, L. Bass, C. Pautasso, and P. Rimba, "A taxonomy of blockchain-based systems for architecture design," in *2017 IEEE International Conference on Software Architecture (ICSA)*, 2017, pp. 243–252.
36 Blockchain Community, "Developer guide: UTXO." [Online]. Developer Guide, 2017. Available: https://goo.gl/6qTyMK.
37 Blockchain Community, "Transaction fee and miner fee." [Online]. 2018. Available: https://blockchain.info/charts.
38 Blockchain Community, "Total transaction fees in USD." [Online]. 2017. Available: https://blockchain.info/charts/transaction-fees-usd.
39 Blockchain Community, "Spam transactions." [Online]. 2018. Available: https://goo.gl/31SpQy.

40 Blockchain Community, "Developer guide: Verifying payments." [Online]. Developer Guide, 2017. Available: https://goo.gl/A5dTm5.

41 Y. Sompolinsky and A. Zohar, "Secure high-rate transaction processing in Bitcoin," in *International Conference on Financial Cryptography and Data Security*. Springer, 2015, pp. 507–527.

42 O. Beigel, "What is the mempool?" [Online]. 2017. Available: https://goo.gl/fnAfQC.

43 S. Nakamoto, "Bitcoin: A peer-to-peer electronic cash system." [Online]. 2008. Available: https://bitcoin.org/bitcoin.pdf.

44 Murch, "What's the minimum transaction with Bitcoin?" [Online]. Stack Exchange, 2017. Available: https://goo.gl/wCqDWa.

45 J. A. Kroll, I. C. Davey, and E. W. Felten, "The economics of Bitcoin mining," in *Proceedings of The Twelfth Workshop on the Economics of Information Security (WEIS 2013)*, Washington, DC, 2013.

46 Blockchain Community, "Mempool size." [Online]. 2017. Available: https://goo.gl/DP2Qpr.

47 Blockchain Community, "Confirmation score, confirmed transaction." [Online]. 2018. Available: https://goo.gl/ZY6Prg.

48 Blockchain Community, "Minimum relay fee." [Online]. 2018. Available: https://goo.gl/rAvtMu.

49 Blockchain Community, "Developer guide: Peer discovery." [Online]. Making Transactions, 2017. Available: https://goo.gl/famYFA.

50 D. Cousens, "BitcoinJS: The clean, readable, proven library for Bitcoin JavaScript development." [Online]. BitcoinJS, 2018. Available: https://goo.gl/2E7Yfi.

51 Bitcoin Wiki, "Raw Transactions." [Online]. 2018. Available: https://goo.gl/gP1Z4Y.

52 C. Wueest, "The continued rise of DDoS attacks," Security Response, Symantec Corporation White Paper, 2014.

53 J. Mirkovic and P. Reiher, "A taxonomy of DDoS attack and DDoS defense mechanisms," ACM SIGCOMM Computer Communication Review, vol. 34, no. 2, 2004.

54 Blockchain Community, "Fee estimation." [Online]. Recommended Optimal Fees, 2017. Available: https://estimatefee.com/.

55 Guysir, "Someone is spamming the mempool with extremely low-fee transactions." [Online]. Reddit, 2017. Available: https://goo.gl/AadTcu.

56 J. P. Buntinx, "Transaction fees continue to cripple the Bitcoin network." [Online]. Blockchain Network, News, Charts, Guides & Analysis, 2017. Available: https://goo.gl/4NKhb9.

57 J. Young, "Analyst: Suspicious Bitcoin mempool activity, transaction fees spike to $16." [Online]. Cointelegraph, 2018. Available: https://goo.gl/hKU8X7.

58 N. J. D. Nagelkerke, "A note on a general definition of the coefficient of determination," *Biometrika*, vol. 78, no. 3, pp. 691–692, 1991.

59 M. Möser and R. Böhme, "Trends, tips, tolls: A longitudinal study of Bitcoin transaction fees," in *International Conference on Financial Cryptography and Data Security*. Springer, 2015, pp. 19–33.

60 Chain Query, "The sendmany RPC creates and broadcasts a transaction which sends outputs to multiple addresses." [Online]. 2018. Available: https://goo.gl/Auj5ZC.

61 J. P. Buntinx, "What is child pays for parent?" [Online]. The Merkle, 2017. Available: https://goo.gl/AhN8j2.

62 Data Dive, "Solving unconfirmed Bitcoin transactions in Electrum." [Online]. 2017. Available: https://goo.gl/C5jCxh.

63 Blockchain Community, "Bitcoin is an innovative payment network and a new kind of money." [Online]. Blockchain Transactions, 2017. Available: https://goo.gl/taHqbJ.

64 T. Bamert, C. Decker, L. Elsen, R. Wattenhofer, and S. Welten, "Have a snack, pay with Bitcoins," in *2013 IEEE Thirteenth International Conference on Peer-to-Peer Computing (P2P)*, IEEE, 2013, pp. 1–5.

11

Preventing Digital Currency Miners from Launching Attacks Against Mining Pools Using a Reputation-based Paradigm

Mehrdad Nojoumian,[1] *Arash Golchubian,*[1] *Laurent Njilla,*[2] *Kevin Kwiat,*[3] *and Charles A. Kamhoua*[4]

[1] *Department of Computer & Electrical Engineering and Computer Science, Florida Atlantic University, Boca Raton, FL, USA*
[2] *US Air Force Research Lab, Cyber Assurance Branch, Rome, NY, USA*
[3] *Haloed Sun TEK, LLC and CAESAR Group, Sarasota, FL, USA*
[4] *US Army Research Laboratory, Network Security Branch, Adelphi, MD, USA*

11.1 Introduction

Security games are mainly designed and used to model interaction between attackers and defenders [1, 2]. In these models, two-player games—extendable to any number of players—are proposed in which both attackers and defenders try to maximize the utility that each can gain. For instance, the defenders will be able to provide value to the system and, as a result, gain utility by enabling features, shifting the attack surface, and reducing the attack surface measurement. Likewise, the attackers will be able to gain utility if features are disabled or the attack surface measurement is increased.

In the majority of existing security games, attackers and defenders play the game by choosing various actions from the action profiles based on their strategies in each round of the game. For instance, the defenders can modify the setting of the targeted system to shift the attack surface, whereas the attackers can manipulate the system to disable some features. After each round of the game, the game moves to a new state and the players receive their rewards based on some utility functions.

One of the fascinating research areas where the security games can be used is the verification of transactions in the context of digital currencies, e.g. Bitcoin [3], or similar paradigms. The mining operation is very resource intensive. As

Blockchain for Distributed Systems Security, First Edition. Edited by Sachin S. Shetty, Charles A. Kamhoua, and Laurent L. Njilla.

The conference version without proofs appeared in the Proceedings of the Computing Conference, Springer AISC 857, pp. 1118–1134, 2018.

a result, players form different coalitions to verify each block of transactions in return for a reward. This leads to intense competition among competitors since only the first coalition that accomplishes the mining process will be rewarded.

To address what issues this competition may cause, different strategies are analyzed in the literature. Rosenfeld [4] introduced the *block-withholding attack*, where a dishonest player only reveals a partial solution of the verification problem whenever he/she has the complete solution to act in favor of another competing coalition. As a result, the dishonest miner shares the revenue obtained by the entire coalition without any contribution. Eyal and Sirer [5] introduced *selfish mining*, where the players of a coalition keep their discovered blocks private and continue to verify more blocks privately until they get a subchain whose length is threatened. As a result, selfish players receive the reward. Johnson et al. [6] look at the malicious activity of the players from another perspective. The authors compare an honest approach with a dishonest strategy, i.e. players of a coalition can invest to acquire additional computing resources, or launch *distributed denial-of-service* attacks against competing coalitions. The authors provide game-theoretical analyses by exploring the trade-off between these two strategies when two groups of varying sizes are involved. More attacks were introduced recently—for example, *eclipse attack* [7], which makes a node invisible in the network, or *stubborn mining* as a generalization of selfish mining [8].

We therefore propose a new reputation-based framework in which miners are not only incentivized to conduct honest mining, but also disincentivized to commit any malicious activities against other mining pools, such as a block-withholding attack, selfish mining, eclipse attack, and stubborn mining, to name a few. We first illustrate the architecture of our reputation-based paradigm, explain how miners are rewarded or penalized in our model, and, subsequently, provide game-theoretical analyses to show how this new framework encourages the miners to avoid dishonest mining strategies.

The rest of this chapter is organized as follows: Section 11.2 provides preliminary materials on digital currencies and game theory. Section 11.3 reviews the existing digital currency literature where game theory is used. Section 11.4 illustrates our model. Section 11.5 explains how our reputation-based scheme works. Section 11.6 explains the main results and proofs. Finally, Section 11.7 concludes with final remarks.

11.2 Preliminaries

11.2.1 Digital Currencies: Terminologies and Mechanics

In digital currency frameworks, specifically Bitcoin, transactions are grouped in blocks to be verified by a subset of nodes in the network, known as *miners*. The mining process, named *proof of work*, is computationally intensive with a specific difficulty factor that is increased over time as the computational power of hardware systems grows. Therefore, nodes form *mining pools* under the supervision of *pool managers* to accomplish the mining task. In some technical articles, the mining process of Bitcoin (or even other digital currencies) is referred to as the miners' *mathematical puzzle.*

The first mining pool that accomplishes the proof of work is rewarded a certain amount of freshly mined Bitcoins as an incentive for miners' works. That is why this process is also known as *mining.* As soon as a block is verified, it is attached to the list of existing verified blocks, known as *Blockchain.* Immediately after that, all miners stop the mining process of the already verified block and start working on the next block.

Each block consists of a block number, a nonce value, a list of transactions, the hash value of the previous block (address of the previous block), and the hash value of the next block (address of the next block). During the mining process, the miners try to generate a valid hash value of a block that is less than a threshold, i.e. it starts with a certain number of zeros. They will conduct this process by trying different nonce values. It is clear that generating a hash value that starts with, say five zeros, is harder than a generating a hash value that begins with four zeros; this is what we call the *difficulty factor* of mining.

The hashing rate, h_r, also known as *mining power,* is the total number of hashes that a miner can calculate during a specific time interval. Therefore, the average time to find a valid hash value, also known as *full* proof of work, correlates to a miner's hashing rate. In fact, the pool manager sends different templates of the current block to his/her miners so that they can find a valid hash value by changing the nonce value. If a miner accomplishes the full proof of work, he/she will then send it to his/her pool manager. Consequently, the pool manager publishes the legitimate block on behalf of the entire pool. He/she will then distribute the revenue among miners based on their mining powers. Note that new coins are put explicitly in the block by the miner(s) who created it.

To estimate each miner's power, the pool manager determines a *partial target* for each miner, which is much easier than the actual target of the system. For instance, instead of calculating a hash value that starts with, say five zeros, a hash value with a single zero is sufficient. Note that this is just a simple example for the sake of clarification. Therefore, each miner is instructed to send a valid hash value according to the partial target. This partial target is defined in such a way that a partial solution can be calculated frequently enough so that the manager can fairly estimate the miners' powers because, as we stated earlier, the revenue is distributed based on the miners' powers.

11.2.2 Game Theory: Basic Notions and Definitions

A *game* consists of a set of *players,* a set of *actions* and *strategies* (strategy is the way that each player selects actions), and finally, a *utility function* that is used by each player to compute how much benefit he/she obtains by choosing a certain action. In *cooperative games,* the players collaborate and split the aggregated utility among themselves, that is, cooperation is incentivized by agreement. However, in *noncooperative games*, the players cannot form any agreement to coordinate their behaviors. In other words, any cooperation among the players must be self-enforcing. We briefly review some well-known game-theoretic concepts [9] for our further analyses and discussions.

Definition 1: Let A $\stackrel{\text{def}}{=} A_1 \times A_2 \times \ldots \times A_n$ be an action profile for n players, where A_i denotes the set of possible actions of player P_i. A *game* $\Gamma = (A_i, u_i)$ for $1 \leq i \leq n$, consists of A_i and a utility function $u_i : A \rightarrow R$ for each player P_i. We refer to a vector of actions $\vec{a} = (a_1, \ldots, a_n) \in A$ as an *outcome of the game.*

Definition 2: *Utility function* u_i illustrates the preferences of player P_i over different outcomes. We say P_i *prefers* outcome $\vec{a}$ to $\vec{a}'$ if $u_i(\vec{a}) > u_i(\vec{a}')$, and he/she *weakly prefers* outcome $\vec{a}$ to $\vec{a}'$ if $u_i(\vec{a}) \geq u_i(\vec{a}')$.

To allow the players to follow randomized strategies, we define σ_i as a probability distribution over A_i for a player P_i. This means he/she samples $a_i \in A_i$ according to σ_i. A strategy is said to be a *pure strategy* if each σ_i assigns probability 1 to a certain action; otherwise, it is said to be a *mixed strategy*. Let $\vec{\sigma} = (\sigma_1, \ldots, \sigma_n)$ be the vector of players' strategies, and let $(\sigma'_i, \vec{\sigma}_{-i}) = (\sigma_i, \ldots, \sigma_{i-1}, \sigma'_i, \sigma_{i+1}, \ldots, \sigma_n)$, where P_i replaces σ_i by σ'_i and all the other players' strategies remain unchanged. Therefore, $u_i(\vec{\sigma})$ denotes the expected utility of P_i under the strategy vector $\vec{\sigma}$. A player's goal is to maximize $u_i(\vec{\sigma})$. In the following definitions, one can substitute action $a_i \in A_i$ with its probability distribution $\sigma_i \in S_i$, or vice versa.

Definition 3: A vector of strategies $\vec{\sigma}$ is in *Nash equilibrium* if, for all i and any $\sigma'_i \neq \sigma_i$, it holds that $u_i(\sigma'_i, \vec{\sigma}_{-i} \leq u_i(\vec{\sigma})$. This means no one gains any advantage by deviating from the protocol as long as the others follow the protocol.

Definition 4: Let $S_{-i} \stackrel{\text{def}}{=} S_1 \times \ldots \times S_{i-1} \times S_{i+1} \times \ldots \times S_n$. A strategy $\sigma_i \in S_i$ (or an action) is *weakly dominated* by $\sigma'_i \in S_i$ (or another action) with respect to S_{-i} if for all $\vec{\sigma}_{-i} \epsilon S_{-i}$, it holds that $u_i(\sigma_i, \vec{\sigma}_{-i}) \leq u_i(\sigma'_i, \vec{\sigma}_{-i})$. There is a $\vec{\sigma}_{-i} \epsilon S_{-i}$ such that $u_i(\sigma_i, \vec{\sigma}_{-i}) < u_i(\sigma'_i, \vec{\sigma}_{-i})$. This means player P_i can never improve its utility by playing σ_i, and he/she can sometimes improve it by not playing σ_i. A strategy $\sigma_i \in S_i$ is *strictly dominated* if player P_i can always improve its utility by not playing σ_i.

11.3 Literature Review

Even though the concept of Blockchain is relatively new, introduced by an unknown author or authors in 2008, it has gained considerable attention from the computer science and economics communities because of its unique approach in decentralizing verification of transactions related to a digital currency, and its inherent security because of this decentralized nature. However, the body of work that is focused on the study of Blockchain through the use of game-theoretic methods is limited. In this section, research works related to game theory and Blockchain are reviewed.

The authors Johnson et al. [6] study the incentives for a mining pool to carry out a distributed denial-of-service (DDoS) attack against another mining pool. The authors scrutinize this problem from an economic point of view where the incentive for an attack is to increase one's own probability of successfully verifying the next block of transactions, and hence, earning the Bitcoin rewards from this mining operation. They conclude that there is a greater incentive to attack a large mining pool rather than a small pool. The authors point out that this finding is consistent with statistics reported in [10] that shows 17.1% of small mining pools have suffered from DDoS attacks, whereas 62.5% of large pools have been affected by such attacks. The authors make two other interesting observations as well. First of all, the ability to mitigate the DDoS attacks will increase the market threshold for the size at which a pool becomes vulnerable to the DDoS attack. This makes intuitive sense since the ability to mitigate such attacks will decrease the attacker's utility. Second, the cost of these attacks will keep small pools out of the DDoS market since the incentive for attacking such pools is relatively low.

Babaioff et al. [11] look at a different problem that is present in the Bitcoin protocol. In fact, this problem will intensify once the mining reward is ended in the Bitcoin network. In the current design, the nodes that authorize a transaction are rewarded through two separate methods. The first is through the generation of new Bitcoins for every new block that is added to the Blockchain, and the second method is through a transaction fee. The maximum number of Bitcoins is limited to about 21 million [12] and the creation of new Bitcoins becomes exponentially smaller until the maximum limit is reached. The transaction fee will be the only resource to incentivize the miners when the maximum threshold is reached. At that point, miners are incentivized to keep the information of a possible transaction secret as there will be no new Bitcoins to be mined from the efforts of mining, that is, there is only the transaction fee that is given to the verifier of transactions. This incentive to keep information secret can potentially cripple the Bitcoin system as the time for confirming a transaction will be long when there is only one node attempting to verify the transaction.

Kroll et al. [13] study Bitcoin as a consensus game and consider the economics of Bitcoin from the mining perspective to determine whether any incentive exists for rational players to deviate from the mining protocol. The authors show that there is a Nash equilibrium outcome for which all players cooperate with the Bitcoin reference implementation. However, there are infinitely many equilibria where the players can behave otherwise. The authors show that a motivated adversary may be capable of crashing the currency; as a result, governance structures will be necessary.

Even though Barber et al. [14] don't refer to any game-theoretic models, they detail several possible vulnerabilities within the Blockchain protocol that are great candidates for game-theoretic study, such as deflationary spiral, the history revision attack, and delayed transaction confirmation. Carlsten et al. [15] study the issues of Bitcoin and Blockchain when the last block reward is collected. The authors show that once the mining reward is removed from the protocol, leaving only the transaction fees, the incentive for defection increases.

Luu et al. [16] scrutinize the block-withholding attack on mining pools, introduced by Rosenfeld [4]. They show that the attack always has incentive when looking at a long-term operation, but it may not be profitable for a short-term operation. Eyal [17] studies the same subject and concludes that when two pools attack each other, it results in a version of the prisoner's dilemma, named the *Miner's Dilemma*. Lewenberg et al. [18] introduce a modification to the Blockchain protocol to allow for inclusion of forked blocks with the aim of increasing the rate of operation. They then provide a game-theoretic model of the competition for fees between the nodes under the new protocol.

11.4 Reputation-based Mining Model and Setting

As illustrated in Figure 11.1, our model consists of a set of pool managers $M_{(i,p_i)}$ who form coalitions for the proof-of-work computations, for $1 \leq i \leq I$, where

i	1	2	3	...	I − 1	I
p_i	250B	125B	0B	...	200B	75B

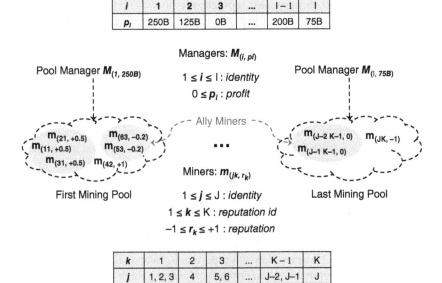

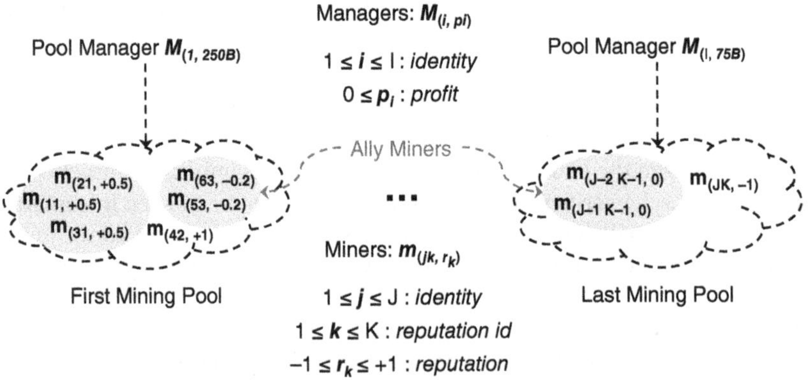

Managers: $M_{(i,\,pi)}$

$1 \leq i \leq$ I : *identity*

$0 \leq p_i$: *profit*

Pool Manager $M_{(1,\,250B)}$

Pool Manager $M_{(I,\,75B)}$

$m_{(21,\,+0.5)}$ $m_{(63,\,-0.2)}$ $m_{(11,\,+0.5)}$ $m_{(53,\,-0.2)}$ $m_{(31,\,+0.5)}$ $m_{(42,\,+1)}$

First Mining Pool

Ally Miners

...

$m_{(J-2\ K-1,\,0)}$ $m_{(JK,\,-1)}$ $m_{(J-1\ K-1,\,0)}$

Last Mining Pool

Miners: $m_{(jk,\,r_k)}$

$1 \leq j \leq$ J : *identity*

$1 \leq k \leq$ K : *reputation id*

$-1 \leq r_k \leq +1$: *reputation*

k	1	2	3	...	K − 1	K
j	1, 2, 3	4	5, 6	...	J–2, J–1	J
r_k	+0.5	+1	–0.2	...	0	–1

Figure 11.1 Reputation-based mining model.

$0 \leq p_i$ denotes profits that pool managers have so far accumulated; a set of miners/ally miners $m_{(jk,r_k)}$ who perform proof of works, for $1 \leq j \leq J$ and $1 \leq k \leq K$, where $-1 \leq r_k \leq +1$ denote the reputation value of a miner/ally miners. In our model, miners/ally minors may commit malicious activities through direct attacks (e.g. a DDoS attack) or collusion attacks (e.g. block withholding) to disrupt the proof-of-work computations of certain mining pools. As such, two actions are considered in the miners' action profile, that is, commit malicious activity to disrupt computations of mining pools, denoted by D: *dishonest mining*, or conduct the proof of work honestly, denoted by H: *honest mining*.

Note that in the current setting of digital currencies, each miner is defined by a unique identity, j. However, in our proposed framework, each miner is also assigned a public reputation value, r_k, where k is the index of this value. In fact, the reputation value reflects how well the miner has so far performed in the system in terms of mining performance as well as honest or malicious activities (i.e. a history of behavior). This public reputation value r_k is updated after a specific period of time, based on different criteria, e.g. the ratio of full proof of work over partial proof of work, detection of any malicious activity such as collusion with other miners, selfish mining, or contribution to a DDoS attack. Moreover, each pool manager i is also assigned a parameter p_i that defines the profit that he/she has so far accumulated through his/her pool. As p_i reflects how well a manager is performing, it can be interpreted as his/her reputation.

In our setting, a subset of miners who highly trust each other (due to partnerships, personal relationships, common nationality, or even geographical proximity) can form an alliance, named *ally miners*, and request a single reputation value r_k even though they each have a separate identity j. This means that while members of a coalition can build a reputation all together through r_k by collaborations over time, they are all responsible for malicious activities triggered by even a single member of their coalition. This leads to the notion of *neighborhood watch*, meaning that each member of an alliance is incentivized to monitor his/her allies. For instance, members can agree to execute a randomized algorithm to monitor each other through various methods, that is, cybersecurity detection techniques or transparency policies, to make sure no one has ever received any bribe from other mining pools due to any sort of collusion attacks. As a result, the pool manager does not need to have any concern for every single member of his/her mining pool. Furthermore, if a member decides to launch an attack, he/she may need to convince all his/her coalition members or act solo, which might be caught by his/her allies through randomized monitoring before it can even affect the mining procedure.

Occasionally, the pool managers rearrange their groups to form new coalitions for the proof of work. They send invitations (i.e. an invitation-based approach) to miners/ally miners based on a nonuniform probability distribution that is defined by the reputation values, r_k. In other words, the miners/ally miners who are more reputable have a higher chance to be invited to the mining pools and those who are not trustworthy have a lower chance to receive invitations. The miners/ally miners can also choose whom they would like to join if they receive multiple invitations, that is, a mutual *merit-based* setting for both miners and managers.

Since this public reputation system is sustained over time, it will be in the best interests of the miners/ally miners to become reputable (or sustain their high reputation) to maximize their long-term utility. This will incentivize the miners/ally miners to avoid any dishonest behavior even if it has a short-term utility. Note that the underlying reputation system must be immune against re-entry attack (that is, cheat and come back to the scheme with a new identity j). We use the proposed idea of *rational trust modeling* [19] to make sure our proposed mining paradigm is not vulnerable to these sorts of attacks against reputation systems.

Furthermore, in our proposed model, while ally miners are incentivized to form larger coalitions to sustain a high reputation value and consequently gain more revenue, they are not incentivized to admit any new miner to their alliance unless they fully trust the newcomer. This is due to the fact that a single miner can harm the entire coalition. Moreover, it is worth mentioning that though ally miners only have a single reputation identity r_k, a miner cannot commit malicious activities in a set and then simply join another alliance because each miner still has a unique identifier j.

Our proposed model can be seen as a *global* community where each mining pool represents a *federal* authority and each alliance represent a *state* authority. Therefore, each alliance is responsible to detect malicious activities inside the coalition on a smaller scale. In addition, each alliance can be changed in size and moved to a new mining pool when the rearrangement occurs. This approach not only leads to less managerial overheads for the pool managers, but it also creates a framework where practical implementations of preventive and detective protocols become possible.

11.5 Mining in a Reputation-based Model

Since our approach is designed using a reputation-based paradigm, it is necessary to use a reputation/trust model that is resistant to the well-known *re-entry attack*, that is, corrupted players return to the scheme using new identities. Otherwise our approach cannot be utilized properly. We will discuss this in the next section.

11.5.1 Prevention of the Re-entry Attack

To deal with the re-entry attack in our reputation-based scheme, we use the proposed approach of *rational trust modeling* [19]. We provide a high-level description of how this modeling technique works. Suppose there exist two trust functions as follows: The first function $f_1(\mathcal{T}_i^{p-1}, \alpha_i)$ has two inputs, that is, trust value $\mathcal{T}_i^{p-1}$ of player P_i in period $p - 1$ and action α_i (cooperation or defection) selected by player P_i in period $p - 1$. This function computes the updated trust value $\mathcal{T}_i^p$ of player P_i for the next round p based on these two inputs. However, the second function $f_2(\mathcal{T}_i^{p-1}, \alpha_i, \ell_i)$ has an extra input value that defines the player's lifetime, denoted by ℓ_i. This extra input determines how long a player with a reasonable number of interactions exists in a reputation-based scheme, for instance, in our proposed reputation-based mining framework.

Using the second function, the reputation-based scheme should then be designed in a way that a player with a longer lifetime can be rewarded (or penalized) more (or less) than a player with a shorter lifetime, assuming that the other two inputs (i.e. the current trust value and the action) are the same. In this setting, "reward" means gaining a higher trust value/becoming more trustworthy, and consequently, receiving a higher utility, and "penalty" means otherwise. In other words, if two players P_i and P_j both cooperate $\alpha_i = \alpha_j = \mathrm{C}$ and their current trust values are equal $\mathcal{T}_i^{p-1} = \mathcal{T}_j^{p-1}$ but their lifetime parameters are different, say $\ell_i > \ell_j$, the player with a higher lifetime parameter gains a higher trust value for the next round, i.e. $\mathcal{T}_i^p > \mathcal{T}_j^p$. This helps player P_i to accumulate more utility/revenue in the targeted reputation-based framework.

To exemplify, consider a situation in which sellers, in a reputation-based e-commerce setting, have options to sell the "defective" versions of an item with more revenue or the "nondefective" versions of the same item with less revenue. If the first sample function f_1 is used in the scheme, it might be tempting for a seller to sell the defective items with more revenue and then return to the e-commerce framework with a new identity (i.e. re-entry attack). However, if the second sample trust function f_2 is used, it is no longer in a seller's best interest to sell the defective items because if he/she returns to the community with a new identity, his/her lifetime indicator becomes zero and he/she loses all the credits that he/she accumulated over time. Consequently, he/she loses huge potential revenue that he/she could gain because of his/her lifetime parameter, i.e. buyers always prefer a seller with a longer lifetime (longer existence with a reasonable number of transactions) over a seller who is a newcomer.

We emphasize that this is just an example of rational trust modeling. In fact, the second sample function uses the lifetime parameter ℓ_i to enforce trustworthiness and prevent the re-entry attack. It is worth mentioning that different parameters can be incorporated into trust functions/reputation systems based on the context (e-commerce, mining in Blockchains, etc.), and consequently, different attacks can be prevented.

11.5.2 Technical Discussion on Detection Mechanisms

Detection mechanisms are required to reward or penalize miners in our reputation-based setting. In this section, we provide technical discussions and mechanisms by which noncooperative actions by miners (e.g. block withholding, selfish mining, DDoS attack, eclipse attack, stubborn mining, or upcoming attacks that are unknown) can be detected.

A mining pool can detect whether it is under a block-withholding attack with a relatively high accuracy. In fact, calculation of the partial proof of work is much easier than calculation of the full proof of work. Therefore, a mining pool can simply estimate its expected mining power in addition to its actual mining power. As a result, any difference between the expected and actual mining powers, which is above a certain threshold, can be an indication of a block-withholding attack.

To determine which registered miner is the perpetrator, there are two possibilities. First, if the mining power of a miner/ally miner is high enough, the ratio of the full proof of work over the partial proof of work can indicate whether the miner/alliance is committing to the block-withholding attack. Second, if the mining power is not high, the frequency of success to find the full proof of work is very low, and statistically, we may not be able to define whether a miner is really committing to the block-withholding attack. However, the latter case has a negligible (close to zero) impact on the mining process and can simply be ignored, i.e. block-withholding attack by a single miner or miners with a low mining power cannot negatively affect the fair mining process.

As suggested by Eyal and Sirer [5], an increase in the number of orphaned blocks can be an indication of selfish mining in the Blockchain. Furthermore, the amount of time taken to release consecutive blocks in the Blockchain can potentially provide evidence of selfish mining. Several researchers have investigated this issue through experimental analysis. In other words, two blocks in close succession should be a very rare incident when miners are honest, and this is more common when a miner/a group of miners quickly releases selfishly mined blocks to overcome the honest miners. As a result, it is not hard to detect which miners are committing to the selfish mining.

As stated by Heilman et al. [7], the eclipse attack has several signatures and properties that make it detectable, e.g. a flurry of short-lived incoming TCP (Transmission Control Protocol) connections from diverse IP addresses. Moreover, an attacker that suddenly connects a large number of nodes to the Bitcoin network could also be detected. Therefore, anomaly detection software systems that look for similar behaviors can be helpful to detect the attacker. Likewise, there are many other techniques in the security literature that can be used to detect the DDoS attack, stubborn mining, and so on.

Other methods might be used to detect bribes and illegal money exchanges among registered miners in the transparent network of Bitcoin (unless they exchange bribes outside of the Bitcoin network). This is how government agencies usually detect money laundering/illegal money exchanges in the traditional banking system. In other words, detection of these bribes might be an indication of collusion—why miners from two competing pools should frequently exchange money with a certain amount.

11.5.3 Colluding Miner's Dilemma

In this section, we consider a scenario in which two miners (independent or from two different alliances) have to decide whether to collude with an attacker to disrupt another mining pool's effort or not. Two collusion scenarios can be considered, i.e. a single miner colludes with the attacker, or multiple miners form a coalition with the attacker. We consider the latter case as it is the general case of the first scenario. It is worth mentioning that game-theoretical paradigms are usually used to analyze interaction between honest parties and attackers. However, we intend to model collusion between miners and an attacker in the context of Blockchain's proof of work. In our setting, we initially consider a two-miner game, named *colluding miner's dilemma*, which may or may not collude with the attacker to disrupt the mining efforts of a targeted mining pool. We further extend this scenario to an n-miner game that is played repeatedly among all the miners of the Blockchain network for an unknown number of rounds.

In the two-miner setting, shown in Table 11.1, if both miners collude with the attacker, they each gain a half unit of utility. In other words, the attacker's budget will be equally shared between both miners. However, if one miner colludes with the attacker but the other one acts honestly, the colluding miner will receive one unit of utility from the attacker. As a result of this dilemma, collusion is in Nash equilibrium, meaning that miners always collude because it is in their best interest to gain a higher utility. This is a realistic assumption where an attacker with a limited budget tries to disrupt the proof-of-work computation of a mining pool in favor of another alliance. Note that the budget is limited because mining reward is fixed in the Blockchain network.

We approach the colluding miner's dilemma by setting a sociorational model [20, 21], i.e. a repeated game among rational foresighted players with public reputation values where these values directly affect players' utilities over time, in which:

1. Each pool manager sends invitations to miners to form his/her mining pool for the proof-of-work computation. He/she not only tries to maximize his/her pool's revenue, but also intends to protect his/her pool against any malicious activity. These invitations are defined based on miners' trust values using a nonuniform probability distribution.

Table 11.1 Payoff in colluding miner's dilemma.

$m(j\,k, r_k)$ \ $m(j'\,k', r'_k)$	H: Honest Mining	D: Dishonest Mining
H: Honest mining	(0, 0)	(0, Ω)
D: Dishonest mining	(Ω, 0)	$(\frac{\Omega}{2}, \frac{\Omega}{2})$

2. On the other hand, the attacker uses his/her limited budget to collude with the miners and consequently compromises the proof-of-work computation of a targeted pool.

In this setting, if a miner colludes with the attacker, he/she may gain some utility in the current round of the game; however, the pool managers will select that miner with a lower probability in the future if his/her malicious activity is detected. This is due to the reduction of his/her reputation value. See [22,23] for a trust/reputation management system. Therefore, it will be in the best interest of the miners not to collude with the attacker because a malicious miner will lose his/her public reputation and thus lose many future mining opportunities with much larger gains.

11.5.4 Repeated Mining Game

We use a trust model that is resistant to the re-entry attack in a repeated game setting. The miners try to maximize their utilities through the proof-of work computation as well as collusion with the attacker or any dishonest mining strategies. We show that by using our proposed model, cooperation (not colluding with the attacker or committing any malicious activity) is always in Nash equilibrium because of a *long-term utility* function that we consider in our model in addition to a *short-term utility* function. Our model not only rewards honest miners but also penalizes colluding/dishonest miners. For the sake of simplicity and without loss of generality, two classes of actions are defined in our setting, i.e. *dishonest/collude* as a noncooperative action and *honest/not collude* as a cooperative action, similar to [24].

The mining game is repeatedly played for an unknown number of rounds. Each miner $m_{(jk,r_k)}$ has a public reputation value r_k, where the initial value is zero, and it is bounded as follows: $-1 \leq r_k \leq +1$. In addition, each miner's action $\alpha_j \in \{\mathbf{H},\ \mathbf{D},\ \perp\}$, where $\mathbf{H}$ and $\mathbf{D}$ denote *honest mining* and *dishonest mining*, respectively, and $\perp$ indicates miner $m_{(jk,r_k)}$has not been selected by any pool manager $M_{(i,p_i)}$ in the current round. Finally, each miner calculates two utility functions to select his/her action, that is, a long-term utility function u_j and an actual utility function u'_j. Note that each round of the game consists of a sequence of block verification, for instance, after verifying a constant number of blocks or after a certain amount of time.

1. Suppose we have a nonuniform probability distribution over types of miners, i.e. honest, dishonest, and new miners. Each pool manager $M_{(i,p_i)}$ sends invitations to a subset of miners based on this probability distribution in each round of the game.
2. Each miner $m_{(jk,r_k)}$ computes his/her long-term utility u_j, and then selects a new action from the action profile, i.e. employ honest or dishonest mining strategies.

3. Each $m_{(jk,r_k)}$receives his/her short-term utility u'_j, i.e. the actual reward that each miner gains, at the end of each round of the game based on the proof of works' outcomes.
4. The reputation values r_k of the selected miners/ally miners are publicly updated based on each miner's/alliance's behavior, using a reputation system.

11.5.5 Colluding Miners' Preferences

Let $u_j(\vec{a})$ denote $m_{(jk,r_k)}$'s long-term utility in outcome $\vec{a}$ by taking into account the current and future games, and let $u'_j(\vec{a})$ denote $m_{(jk,r_k)}$'s short-term utility in outcome $\vec{a}$ of the current game. Also, let $d_j(\vec{a}) \in \{0, 1\}$ denote whether the miner $m_{(jk,r_k)}$ has employed dishonest mining strategies in the current game, and define $\Delta(\vec{a}) = \sum_i d_j(\vec{a})$, that is, the total number of miners who have used dishonest mining strategies. Let $r_k^{\vec{a}}(p)$ denote the reputation of $m_{(jk,r_k)}$ after outcome $\vec{a}$ in period p; note that $\vec{a}$ and $\vec{a}'$ are two different outcomes of our repeated game.

The miners' preferences are as follows: $d_i(\vec{a}) = d_i(\vec{a}')$ & $r_k^{\vec{a}}(p) > r_k^{\vec{a}'}(p) \Rightarrow u_j(\vec{a}) > u_j(\vec{a}')$, that is, each miner $m_{(jk,r_k)}$ prefers to sustain a high reputation value over time despite employing honest or dishonest mining strategies as he/she can potentially gain a higher long-term utility; $d_i(\vec{a}) > d_i(\vec{a}') \Rightarrow u'_j(\vec{a}) > u'_j(\vec{a}')$, that is, if a miner $m_{(jk,r_k)}$ uses a dishonest mining strategy, he/she gains a short-term utility from the attacker; and finally, $d_i(\vec{a}) > d_i(\vec{a}')$ & $\Delta(\vec{a}) < \Delta(\vec{a}') \Rightarrow u'_j(\vec{a}) > u'_j(\vec{a}')$, that is, if $m_{(jk,r_k)}$ employs dishonest mining strategies and the total number of dishonest miners in $\vec{a}$ is less than the total number of dishonest miners in $\vec{a}'$, the miner gains a higher short-term utility in $\vec{a}$.

11.5.6 Colluding Miners' Utilities

In our setting, the long-term utility function u_i is computed based on the utility that each miner $m_{(jk,r_k)}$ potentially gains or loses by considering both current and future games, i.e. taking into account all stated utility preferences. However, the short-term utility function u'_i is only calculated based on the current gain or loss in a given time interval, i.e. taking into account the last two utility preferences, as mentioned previously.

Let φ_j be the reward factor that is determined by each pool manager $M_{(i,p_i)}$ based on the r_k of each miner $m_{(jk,r_k)}$, and let $\delta_j(\vec{a}) = r_k^{\vec{a}}(p) - r_k^{\vec{a}}(p-1)$ be the difference of two consecutive reputation values. Note that $\tau_j = |\delta_j(\vec{a})|/\delta_j(\vec{a})$ is positive if the selected action in period p is **H:** *honest mining*, and it is negative if it is **D:** *dishonest mining*. Also, let $\Omega > 0$ be a unit of utility, for instance, \$50. To satisfy the miners' preferences, we compute the long-term utility $u_j(\vec{a})$ through the following linear combination:

$$u_j(\vec{a}) = \Omega\left(\tau_j\varphi_j + d_j(\vec{a}) + \frac{d_j(\vec{a})}{\Delta(\vec{a}) + 1}\right). \tag{11.1}$$

Note that the actual utility $u'_j(\vec{a})$ only consists of the second and third terms, that is, $u'_j(\vec{a}) = \Omega(d_j\vec{a}) + d_j(\vec{a})/(\Delta(\vec{a}) + 1))$. The first term of the utility function denotes miner $m_{(jk,r_k)}$ gains or loses φ_i units of utility in future games due to his/her behavior as reflected in r_k. This is due to τ_j, which depends on the miner's reputation value r_k. The second term illustrates miner $m_{(jk,r_k)}$ gains one unit of utility if he/she employs dishonest mining strategies or colludes with the attacker in the current game, and he/she loses this opportunity otherwise. Finally, the last term results in almost one unit of utility being shared among all dishonest miners.

11.6 Evaluation of Our Model Using Game-theoretical Analyses

In this section, we evaluate our proposed reputation-based mining paradigm using game-theoretical analyses. We first consider a (2, 2)-game that is played between two miners to show honest mining always dominates dishonest mining in our setting. We further extend this analysis to an (n, n)-game that is played among n miners.

Theorem 1: In a (2, 2)-game between two miners, honest mining **H** strictly dominates dishonest mining **D** when we use utility function $u_j(\vec{a})$, as defined in Eq. 11.1.

Proof: We compute u_j of each outcome for $m_{(jk,r_k)}$. Let $m_{(j'k',r_k')}$ be the other miner.

1. If both miners employ honest mining strategies, δ_j is positive, $d_j = 0$, and $\Delta = 0$:

$$(\delta_j > 0, d_j = 0, \Delta = 0) \Rightarrow u_j^{(\mathbf{H},\,\mathbf{H})} = \Omega\varphi_j.$$

2. If only $m_{(jk,r_k)}$ uses honest mining strategies, δ_j is positive, $d_j = 0$ since $m_{(jk,r_k)}$ has not colluded, and $\Delta = 1$ since $m_{(j'k',r_k')}$ has used dishonest mining strategies:

$$(\delta_j > 0, d_j = 0, \Delta = 1) \Rightarrow u_j^{(\mathbf{H},\,\mathbf{D})} = \Omega\varphi_j.$$

3. If only $m_{(j'k',r_k')}$ uses honest mining strategies, δ_j is negative, $d_j = 1$ since miner $m_{(jk,r_k)}$ has employed dishonest mining strategies, and $\Delta = 1$:

$$(\delta_j < 0, d_j = 1,\ \Delta = 1) \Rightarrow u_j^{(\mathbf{D},\,\mathbf{H})} = \Omega(-\varphi_j + 1.50).$$

4. If both miners employ dishonest mining strategies, δ_j is negative, $d_j = 1$, and $\Delta = 2$ because both miners have colluded:

$$(\delta_j < 0, d_j = 1, \Delta = 2) \Rightarrow u_j^{(\mathbf{D},\,\mathbf{D})} = \Omega(-\varphi_j + 1.33).$$

If reward factor $\varphi_i \geq 1.5$, which is defined by each pool manager $M_{(i,p_i)}$, we will have the following payoff inequalities that prove our theorem:

$$\overbrace{u_j^{(\mathbf{H},\,\mathbf{H})}(\vec{a}) = u_j^{(\mathbf{H},\,\mathbf{D})}(\vec{a})}^{m_{(jk,r_k)}:\ \text{honest mining}} > \overbrace{u_j^{(\mathbf{D},\,\mathbf{H})}(\vec{a}) > u_j^{(\mathbf{D},\,\mathbf{D}\,)}(\vec{a})}^{m_{(jk,r_k)}:\ \text{dishonest mining}}.$$

Likewise, if we assume φ_i is at least 1.5 (note that the minimum value is defined based on the model's parameters), the payoff matrix is as follows in Table 11.2:

Table 11.2 (2, 2)-Game between two miners.

$m(j\,k, r_k)$ \ $m(j'\,k', r_k')$	**H: Honest Mining**	**D: Dishonest Mining**
H: Honest mining	(1.5, 1.5)	(1.5, 0)
D: Dishonest mining	(0, 1.5)	(− 0.17, − 0.17)

As shown, honest mining is always in Nash equilibrium in our reputation-based mining paradigm. To expand our proof to a case with n miners, let $\mathbf{H}_j$ (or $\mathbf{D}_j$) denote miner $m_{(jk,r_k)}$ employs honest mining strategies (or dishonest mining strategies), and let $\mathbf{H}_{-j}$ (or $\mathbf{D}_{-j}$) denote, excluding miner $m_{(jk,r_k)}$, all other miners use honest mining strategies (or dishonest mining strategies), and finally, let $\mathcal{M}_{-j}$ denote, excluding $m_{(jk,r_k)}$, some miners employ honest mining strategies and some of them use dishonest mining strategies.

Theorem 2: In an (n,n)-game among n miners, honest mining **H** strictly dominates dishonest mining **D** when we use the utility function $u_j(\vec{a})$, as defined in Eq. 11.1.

Proof: We compute the utility of each outcome in different scenarios. Let $n > k \geq 2$.

1. If all miners employ honest mining strategies, or $m_{(jk,r_k)}$ and $k-1$ miners employ honest mining strategies, or only $m_{(jk,r_k)}$ conduct honest mining, and as a result, δ_j is positive, $d_j = 0$, and $\Delta \in s = \{0, n-k, n-1\}$:

$$(\delta_j > 0, d_j = 0, \Delta \in s) \Rightarrow u_j^{(\mathbf{H}_j, \mathbf{H}_{-j})} = u_j^{(\mathbf{H}_j, \mathcal{M}_{-j})} = u_j^{(\mathbf{H}_j, \mathbf{D}_{-j})} = \Omega\varphi_j.$$

2. If only $m_{(jk,r_k)}$ uses dishonest mining strategies, δ_j is negative, $d_j = 1$, and $\Delta = 1$:

$$(\delta_j < 0, d_j = 1, \Delta = 1) \Rightarrow u_j^{(\mathbf{D}_j, \mathbf{H}_{-j})} = \Omega(-\varphi_j + 1.5).$$

3. If $m_{(jk,r_k)}$ as well as $k-1$ miners employ dishonest mining strategies, and the rest of them use honest mining strategies:

$$(\delta_j < 0, d_j = 1, \Delta = k) \Rightarrow u_j^{(\mathbf{D}_j, \mathcal{M}_{-j})} = \Omega\left(-\varphi_j + \frac{k+2}{k+1}\right).$$

4. If all miners use dishonest mining strategies, δ_j is negative, $d_j = 1$, and $\delta = n$ because no one has conducted honest mining:

$$(\delta_j < 0,\ d_j = 1,\ \Delta = n) \Rightarrow u_j^{(\mathbf{D}_j, \mathbf{D}_{-j})} = \Omega\left(-\varphi_j + \frac{n+2}{n+1}\right).$$

Our analysis will be as follows: Let $*_{-j}$ be $\mathbf{H}_{-j}$, $\mathcal{M}_{-j}$, or $\mathbf{D}_{-j}$. It is easy to show that:

$$1.5 > \frac{k+2}{k+1} > \frac{n+2}{n+1} \text{ when } n > k \geq 2.$$

Likewise, if we assume φ_i is at least 1.5, honest mining or not colluding with the attacker is always in Nash equilibrium. As a result, it is always in $m_{(jk,r_k)}$'s best interests to use honest mining strategies no matter what other miners do:

$$u_j^{(\mathbf{H}_{j,*-j})}(\vec{a}) > u_j^{(\mathbf{D}_{j,*-j})}(\vec{a}).$$

11.7 Concluding Remarks

In this chapter, we proposed a new reputation-based mining paradigm for the proof-of-work computation in Blockchain. We first illustrated the problem of dishonest mining, demonstrated our proposed model, and, subsequently, provided a candidate solution concept to the aforementioned problem. Note that by dishonest mining we refer to any malicious activity against other mining pools or competitors, such as block-withholding attack, selfish mining, eclipse attack, and stubborn mining, to name a few.

Our proposed mining game is repeatedly played among a set of pool managers and miners where the reputation value of each miner or mining ally is continuously measured by a trust management scheme that is resistant to the re-entry attack. For each round of the game, pool managers send invitations only to a subset of miners based on a nonuniform probability distribution defined by the miners' reputations. It is worth mentioning that each round of the game consists of a sequence of block verification, for instance, after verifying a constant number of blocks or after a certain amount of time.

We showed that by using our proposed solution concept, honest mining attains Nash equilibrium in our setting. In other words, it will not be in the best interests of the miners to disrupt the proof-of-work computation or commit to dishonest mining even by gaining a short-term utility. This is due to the consideration of a long-term utility function in our model and its impact on the miners' utilities over time. For our future work, we are interested in implementing our proposed game through a simulation-based approach using real data from the Bitcoin network.

Acknowledgment

Research was sponsored by the Army Research Office and was accomplished under Grant Number W911NF-18-1-0483. The views and conclusions contained in this document are those of the authors and should not be interpreted as representing the official policies, either expressed or implied, of the Army Research Office or the U.S. Government. The U.S. Government is authorized to reproduce and distribute reprints for Government purposes notwithstanding any copyright notation herein.

References

1 S. Roy, C. Ellis, S. Shiva, D. Dasgupta, V. Shandilya, and Q. Wu, "A survey of game theory as applied to network security," in *Proceedings of the 43rd IEEE Hawaii International Conference on System Sciences (HICSS)*, 2010, pp. 1–10.

2 X. Liang and Y. Xiao, "Game theory for network security," in *Proceedings of the IEEE Communications Surveys and Tutorials*, vol. 15, no. 1, pp. 472–486, 2013.

3 S. Nakamoto, "Bitcoin: A peer-to-peer electronic cash system." [Online]. 2008. Available: https://bitcoin.org/bitcoin.pdf.

4 M. Rosenfeld, "Analysis of Bitcoin pooled mining reward systems." *arXiv preprint arXiv:1112.4980*. 2011.

5 I. Eyal and E. G. Sirer, "Majority is not enough: Bitcoin mining is vulnerable," in *Proceedings of the International Conference on Financial Cryptography and Data Security*. Springer, 2014, pp. 436–454.

6 B. Johnson, A. Laszka, J. Grossklags, M. Vasek, and T. Moore, "Game theoretic analysis of DDoS attacks against Bitcoin mining pools," in *Proceedings of the International Conference on Financial Cryptography and Data Security*. Springer, 2014, pp. 72–86.

7 E. Heilman, A. Kendler, A. Zohar, and S. Goldberg, "Eclipse attacks on Bitcoin's peer-to-peer network," in *Proceedings of the USENIX Security Symposium*, 2015, pp. 129–144.

8 K. Nayak, S. Kumar, A. Miller, and E. Shi, "Stubborn mining: Generalizing selfish mining and combining with an eclipse attack," in *Proceedings of the 1st IEEE European Symposium on Security and Privacy (Euro S&P)*, 2016, pp. 305–320.

9 M. J. Osborne and A. Rubinstein, *A Course in Game Theory*. MIT press, 1994.

10 M. Vasek, M. Thornton, and T. Moore, "Empirical analysis of denial-of-service attacks in the Bitcoin ecosystem," in *Proceedings of the International Conference on Financial Cryptography and Data Security*. Springer, 2014, pp. 57–71.

11 M. Babaioff, S. Dobzinski, S. Oren, and A. Zohar, "On Bitcoin and red balloons," in *Proceedings of the 13th ACM Conference on Electronic Commerce*, 2012, pp. 56–73.

12 A. M. Antonopoulos, *Mastering Bitcoin: Unlocking Digital Cryptocurrencies*. O'Reilly Media, 2014.

13 J. A. Kroll, I. C. Davey, and E. W. Felten, "The economics of Bitcoin mining, or Bitcoin in the presence of adversaries," in *The Twelfth Workshop on the Economics of Information Security (WEIS 2013)*, Washington, DC, 2013.

14 S. Barber, X. Boyen, E. Shi, and E. Uzun, "Bitter to better—How to make Bitcoin a better currency," in *Proceedings of the International Conference on Financial Cryptography and Data Security*. Springer, 2012, pp. 399–414.

15 M. Carlsten, H. Kalodner, S. M. Weinberg, and A. Narayanan, "On the instability of Bitcoin without the block reward," in *Proceedings of the ACM SIGSAC Conference on Computer and Communications Security*, 2016, pp. 154–167.

16 L. Luu, R. Saha, I. Parameshwaran, P. Saxena, and A. Hobor, "On power splitting games in distributed computation: The case of Bitcoin pooled mining," in *Proceedings of the 28th IEEE Computer Security Foundations Symposium (CSF)*, 2015, pp. 397–411.

17 I. Eyal, "The miner's dilemma," in *Proceedings of the 2015 IEEE Symposium on Security and Privacy (SP)*, 2015, pp. 89–103.

18 Y. Lewenberg, Y. Sompolinsky, and A. Zohar, "Inclusive block chain protocols," in *Proceedings of the International Conference on Financial Cryptography and Data Security*. Springer, 2015, pp. 528–547.

19 M. Nojoumian, "Rational trust modeling," in Proceedings of the 9th International Conference on Decision and Game Theory for Security. Springer LNCS 11199, 2018, pp. 418–431.

20 M. Nojoumian and D. R. Stinson, "Socio-rational secret sharing as a new direction in rational cryptography," in *Proceedings of the 3rd International Conference on Decision and Game Theory for Security*. Springer LNCS 7638, 2012, pp. 18–37.
21 M. Nojoumian, "Generalization of socio-rational secret sharing with a new utility function," in *Proceedings of the 12th IEEE International Conference on Privacy, Security and Trust*, 2014, pp. 338–341.
22 M. Nojoumian and T. C. Lethbridge, "A new approach for the trust calculation in social networks," in *E-business and Telecommunication Networks (E-BTN): Selected Papers of ICETE 06*, vol. 9. Springer CCIS, 2008, pp. 64–77.
23 M. Nojoumian, "Novel secret sharing and commitment schemes for cryptographic applications," PhD thesis, Department of Computer Science, University of Waterloo, Canada, 2012.
24 M. Nojoumian, A. Golchubian, N. Saputro, and K. Akkaya, "Preventing collusion between SDN defenders and attackers using a game theoretical approach," in *Proceedings of the IEEE INFOCOM: Advances in Software Defined & Context Aware Cognitive Radio Networks*, 2017, pp. 802–807.

Part IV

Blockchain Implementation

12

Private Blockchain Configurations for Improved IoT Security

Adriaan Larmuseau[1] and Devu Manikantan Shila[2]

[1] *United Technologies Research Center China, Software and Intelligent Systems, Shanghai, China*
[2] *United Technologies Research Center, Software Systems Group, East-Hartford, USA*

12.1 Introduction

As the Internet of Things (IoT) continues to expand, bad security practices, flawed protocols, and slow patch updates have made the cyber security of IoT devices and networks an increasing concern. Consequently, IoT deployments stand to benefit from the tamper proof, decentralized, distributed, and secure chain of transactions provided by blockchain technology [1]. This secure chain of transactions can be leveraged to provide IoT device networks with, for example, micropayments [2], trustworthy identity management [3], and verifiable digital artifacts [4].

In addition to this secure chain of transactions, recent blockchain frameworks provide support for smart contracts [5]. A smart contract is a piece of code stored within the blockchain, that executes transactions that are verified by some or all of the members of the blockchain network. Once verified, these transactions are also stored on the blockchain. In our vision, blockchain technology combining the secure chain with smart contracts has the ability to radically reshape the way IoT device deployments are developed, managed, and trusted.

However, a major challenge when deploying blockchain as an IoT protocol is finding the right way to configure the blockchain for your IoT device network. The first major point of contention is whether to go with a *public* or *private* blockchain. A *public* blockchain is accessible to every user on the internet, creating strong network effects for those public blockchain networks that gain widespread adoption. These network effects boost the fundamental security property of a blockchain—its immutable chain of transactions—by increasing the number of replications of this chain of transactions, increasing the length

Blockchain for Distributed Systems Security, First Edition. Edited by Sachin S. Shetty, Charles A. Kamhoua, and Laurent L. Njilla.

of the chain and thus increasing the amount of hash power needed to alter it, as well as increasing the amount of computational power available to secure the blockchain's consensus model. In practice, however, most popular public blockchains have had to trade this boosted security for poor performance, particularly when it comes to scaling the overall throughput of the blockchain.

Ethereum [6], the most popular public blockchain that features advanced smart contract capabilities manages to, for example, scale to around 15 transactions per second. While this rate of 15 transactions/sec is impressive for a public blockchain of Ethereum's size, in particular when compared to Bitcoin's 7 transactions/sec [7], large scale deployments of IoT devices require much higher throughputs. Uber provided an average of 126 rides per second in 2017 [8], and the Visa payment system, whose network of millions of connected payment terminals forms arguably one of the largest IoT deployments in the world, is capable of handling up to 56000 transactions/sec [9]. While certain newer blockchain technologies such as IOTA [10] and Nano [11] are attempting to create blockchains capable of handling comparable levels of transaction throughput, none of these high-throughput blockchains have so far managed to combine top-level performance with a robust smart contract platform.

As such, this chapter explores the intricacies of configuring private blockchains for IoT deployments. Much is made of the different kinds of consensus algorithms that blockchain frameworks employ to determine which transactions will be the next to be added to the blockchain. Traditional blockchain frameworks such as Bitcoin employ a proof-of-work (PoW) consensus protocol where an energy-consuming cryptographic puzzle must be solved to *mine* new blocks [12], while newer blockchain frameworks are exploring alternative consensus protocols such as Proof of Authority (PoA) [13], Delegated Proof of Stake (DPoS), and Practical Byzantine Fault Tolerance (PBFT) [14].

In this chapter, we present one blockchain IoT deployment that employs the PoW consensus method and one that employs the PBFT consensus method. The performance differences between these two consensus protocols are, however, of less interest to us than the roles that the IoT devices play within the blockchain deployment and the security guarantees that the blockchain can provide the IoT device in that role. Blockchain frameworks tend to differentiate between two device roles—*full nodes* and *light clients*. *Full nodes* are the backbone of a blockchain network; they download incoming blocks of transactions and check them against the blockchain consensus rules and store full or compressed copies of the blockchain in question. In blockchain frameworks that enforce network-wide smart contracts, full nodes are also responsible for executing and verifying calls to the smart contracts stored on the blockchain. *Light clients*, in contrast, do not help to support a blockchain network. Instead, they participate in blockchain networks by submitting new transactions to the blockchain as well as by observing those transactions that are of interest to them.

In this chapter, we consider the differences in system functionality and cyber security guarantees between systems where IoT devices are configured as either private blockchain light clients or blockchain unaware devices and systems where IoT devices serve as full nodes on a private blockchain. We denote these two different IoT blockchain deployment strategies as *Blockchain-enabled Gateway* and *Blockchain-enabled Smart End Devices.*

In what follows, we discuss these two different deployment strategies (Sections 12.2 and 12.3), illustrating the advantages and limitations of each by means of example implementations. Next, this chapter lists related work (Section 12.4) and then concludes (Section 12.5).

12.2 Blockchain-enabled Gateway

The Blockchain-enabled Gateway IoT deployment strategy is centered around a gateway device that centrally processes the transactions between the IoT network and a cloud/gateway-based private blockchain (Figure 12.1). The IoT devices contributing these transactions are not full blockchain nodes; they are instead configured as either blockchain light clients or as devices completely unaware of the blockchain. In this setup, the IoT devices thus do not work to power the private blockchain; instead, they rely on the gateway to serve as a full node on the blockchain to which they can send their transactions and from which they can receive updates.

12.2.1 Advantages

The advantages of configuring an IoT deployment by means of the Blockchain-enabled Gateway strategy in comparison to a more traditional database and centralized command server approach are, in our opinion, fourfold.

- **Fault-tolerance**—by employing a distributed database such as blockchain, which in the Blockchain-enabled Gateway strategy is distributed between

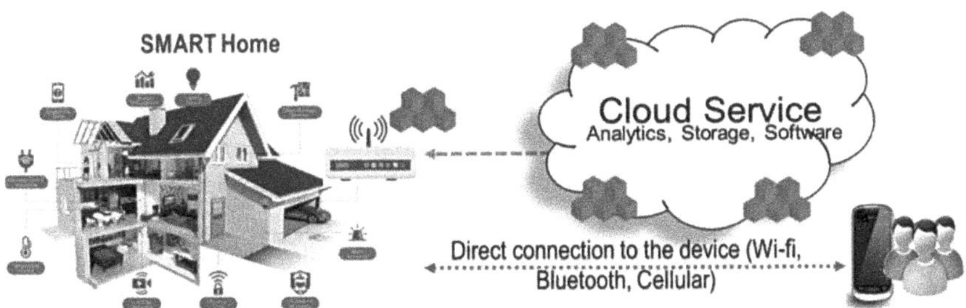

Figure 12.1 The blockchain-enabled gateway strategy implemented for a smart home.

the gateways and servers that power the private blockchain network, the resilience of the system is improved as there is no longer a single point of failure.

- **Secure, trustworthy log**—a blockchain is an immutable chain of transactions. The transactions collected onto this immutable chain can thus be considered a trustworthy log of network-wide events that have taken place within the IoT network.
- **Secure device registration**—combining the immutability provided by blockchain with the built-in authentication mechanism (generally implemented by means of public key cryptography) enables the creation of a secure registry of authenticated IoT devices with minimal effort.
- **Trustworthy business logic**—by implementing business logic rules as smart contracts that are stored on the blockchain, this logic becomes fixed and transparent. In addition, the execution of this logic can be verified by some/all of the computing power of the blockchain network. Modifying or derailing the execution of this logic can only be achieved by a resource-intensive majority attack against the blockchain network [15].

12.2.2 Limitations

All of the four previously cited advantages are, to a certain extent, limited due to our focus on a private blockchain, whose network size is constrained by the resources of the private company or consortium that funds it. In contrast, a public blockchain with cryptocurrency-driven rewards may grow as exponentially fast as the increase in the value of its cryptocurrency. The Ethereum public blockchain network, for example, grew to 25,000 nodes (light clients and full nodes) in less than 2 years [16]. Such a large public blockchain will, of course, provide better *fault tolerance.* The chain of blockchain transactions is also more immutable on such a large public blockchain, as the network contains more replications of the chain and the chain is longer, requiring more hashing power to alter the chain. This increased immutability means that a public blockchain implementation can provide a more *trustworthy log* and more *secure device registration.* Lastly, a large public blockchain will also assign more computing power to verifying smart contract computations, thus increasing the trustworthiness of the results of the implemented *business logic.* All these public blockchain security and reliability benefits do, as discussed in the introduction, come at a substantial performance cost, particularly in the area of transaction processing speed. As such, until public blockchains overcome their transaction processing limitations, the optimal solution will remain to deploy a large-scale private or consortium-based blockchain.

An additional limitation is that while applying the Blockchain-enabled Gateway strategy may provide an IoT system with a *trustworthy log* of all the transactions that happened within the IoT network, where the built-in authentication ensures that those transactions are only coming from the devices that have been *securely registered*, this blockchain configuration strategy cannot guarantee that the message content of those transactions is accurate. In an IoT system where, for example, the Blockchain-enabled Gateway strategy is applied to record sensor values, there are no guarantees about the *correctness* of those sensor values. The strategy only guarantees that those sensor values come from trusted devices, were not modified in transit, and were not modified while stored within the chain.

In what follows, we present a deployment of the Blockchain-enabled Gateway strategy for a private blockchain implementing an access control system. Particular attention will be paid to the advantages and limitations of the Blockchain-enabled Gateway strategy for such a use case.

12.2.3 Private Ethereum Gateways for Access Control

To illustrate the pros and cons of the Blockchain-enabled Gateway strategy, we discuss its application in a blockchain prototype of a building access control system—a security system where users use a smartphone to unlock door locks. These locks, implemented using Raspberry Pi 3B IoT devices, communicate with the smartphones over an application layer Bluetooth Low Energy (BLE) protocol using application level 128-bit AES-CCM encryption to achieve authenticated encryption between the lock and the phone. The locks function as BLE peripherals, advertising their presence to the smartphones, which operate as BLE centrals. Once authenticated, the smartphones transmit a 16 byte user identifier to the lock, and the lock uses this user identifier as its input to the access control system running on the blockchain. Once the lock receives its response from the blockchain access control system, it sends a notify packet to the smartphone to inform it whether the door shall remain open/closed.

The locks, as per the Blockchain-enabled Gateway strategy, are setup as Ethereum light clients that communicate with a company's private Ethereum blockchain network by means of Ethereum gateways (Figure 12.2). These gateways are computers that run one or more Ethereum PoW miners that bundle the transactions submitted from the locks into blocks onto the private blockchain. These gateways should ideally be sourced from the different stake holders in the building, such as, for example, the building owner, the tenants, and the security service provider; as such, a multistakeholder private blockchain is the most trustworthy kind of private blockchain. In this prototype implementation, the private network, however, consists of four gateways sourced by the authors.

To enable high transaction throughput, the Ethereum PoW mechanism was modified to start from a trivial difficulty (blocks can be mined in less 200 milliseconds by the network of four gateways) and to never increase in difficulty. This is in contrast to the PoW of the public Ethereum blockchain, which continuously updates the PoW difficulty to create a new block every 14.7 seconds. Note that our fast block mining times do not, in any way, present a solution

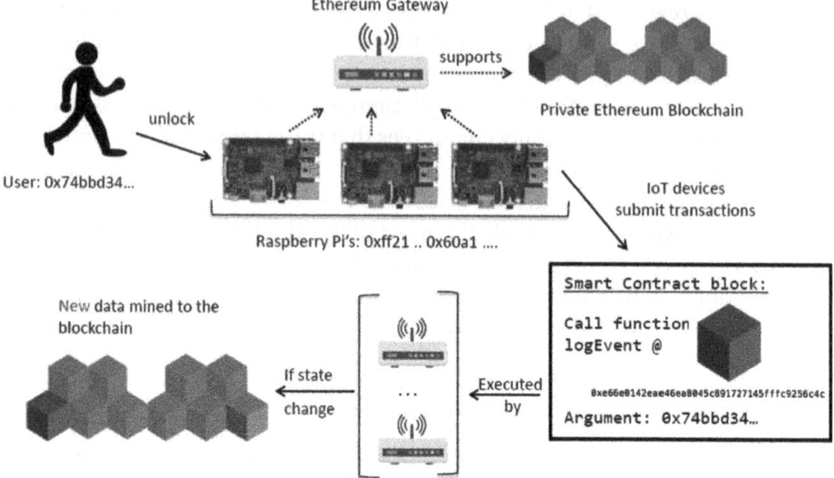

Figure 12.2 Our Ethereum gateway prototype implements a local access control solution. In this system, the locks and gateways are identified by Ethereum addresses (0xab...). The access control rules are implemented through smart contracts mined onto the blockchain at the initiation stage of the system (smart contract blocks are darker).

to blockchain scaling. Because this prototype is a private blockchain network, we are able to make our own trade-offs between PoW difficulty and the related risk of a network takeover by one of the gateways we trusted to join the network and the transaction throughput of the system. In this prototype, we configured the system for 200 milliseconds to ensure that the BLE protocol between the lock and the smartphone was not too delayed by the blockchain transaction processing.

The private Ethereum blockchain implements the building access control system by means of a smart contract deployed on the blockchain. This smart contract is mined onto the blockchain in the setup phase of the prototype, before the locks join the network. When the locks join the network, they are informed of the blockchain address of this smart contract so that they may transact with it by means of Ethereum's Web3 interface. The gateway miners receive these transactions, process them by executing the smart contract code, and compete to mine the results of the code onto the blockchain. A snippet of the smart contract used in this prototype is listed in Figure 12.3.

Our smart contract, written in Solidity, inherits `Ownable`, a standard ownership contract by OpenZeppelin[1] that assigns ownership of the smart contract and hence ownership of the building access control system to the Ethereum

1 github.com/OpenZeppelin/openzeppelin-solidity/blob/master/contracts/ownership/Ownable.sol

```
contract BuildingControl is Ownable {

 mapping(address => bool) private lockRegistry;
 mapping(address => mapping(uint128 => bool)) private
     lockPermissions;
 mapping(address => mapping(uint128 => uint)) private Successes;
 mapping(address => mapping(uint128 => uint)) private Failures;

 function registerLock(address _lock,bool _registered) public
     onlyOwner {
  lockRegistry[_lock] = _registered;
 }

 function logEvent(uint128 _user) public returns (bool) {
  if(lockRegistry[msg.sender] == true &&
   lockPermissions[msg.sender][_user] == true) {
   Successes[msg.sender][_user] = block.timestamp;
   return true;
  }
  Failures[msg.sender][_user] = block.timestamp;
  return false;
 }
}
```

Figure 12.3 An edited snippet of the Solidity smart contract used to manage the building access control. The mappings are defined to create blockchain registries of devices, permissions, and events. The public functions enforce the access control rules.

account that deploys the contract on the blockchain. The contract defines four mappings, whose contents are stored onto the blockchain. The first mapping, `lockRegistry`, creates a blockchain registry of all the locks permitted to submit events to the access control smart contract. The registry identifies the locks by their Ethereum address which is the last 20 bytes of a Keccak-256 hash of the public key of the asymmetric encryption key pair used by the lock to identify itself to the Ethereum blockchain. A lock can thus not participate within the building access control system until an owner of the smart contract has explicitly, by means of the lock's Ethereum address, added it to this registry. Through this `lockRegistry` mapping we thus leverage the *secure authentication* provided by Ethereum to build a trustworthy register of permitted devices. The second mapping `lockPermissions` creates a blockchain registry of all locks and the users, identified by 128-bit numbers, that are allowed to unlock them. The third and fourth mappings `Successes` and `Failures` create a blockchain registry of the most recent time that a user either successfully or unsuccessfully interacted with a lock. Note that the registry only stores the most recent time as the historical times can be obtained by browsing the blockchain.

The listed contract snippet denotes one example public function—`logEvent`. The blockchain connected locks submit transactions that call this function every time they receive a user identifier from a smartphone over BLE.

The `logEvent` function checks that the device submitting the transaction is a registered device and that the submitted user is a user with permission to access the lock and updates the blockchain with the result of that check. In addition, the boolean result of the function is received by the lock to inform it whether or not to open the lock.

12.2.4 Evaluation

In this prototype implementation of a building access control system, we leverage the four key advantages of the Blockchain-enabled Gateway strategy as follows:

- **Fault-tolerance**—unlike existing building access control systems where locks are controlled by centralized command servers, the presented system will maintain a queryable record of the access control even after numerous gateway failures. Note that the full availability of the system under gateway failure depends on whether or not the locks have network access to more than one gateway.
- **Secure, trustworthy log**—every time a user either succeeds or fails to open a door this event is logged onto the immutable blockchain. Such a log of unalterable of access control events may be of particular interest to various kinds of high-security facilities.
- **Secure device registration**—all IoT devices are registered on the blockchain by means of their Ethereum addresses, which derive from the device's public key, enabling simple and secure authentication.
- **Trustworthy business logic**—by implementing the access control rules as smart contracts, those rules are fixed, transparent, and continuously verified by the computing power of the private blockchain network.

Note that the trustworthiness of the log and the access control rules as well as the overall fault-tolerance is limited in this prototype deployment, as our deployment features only four gateways running an easy PoW consensus mechanism. The more that stakeholders provide gateways to help power this private blockchain network, the more the overall trustworthiness and fault tolerance will improve, though it will never, as mentioned earlier, achieve the same kind of trust and dependability provided by a public blockchain.

In addition, this prototype only guarantees that the locks that submitted the access control request are locks that we explicitly authorized and that the log of these requests is immutable. The accuracy of the data within those requests is not guaranteed as the Blockchain-enabled Gateway strategy only provides the advantages of blockchain to those transactions that IoT submits to the blockchain network. In this use case, attackers capable of hijacking a lock may falsify the records stored within the blockchain by preventing or delaying the lock from sending a transaction or by modifying the user identifiers contained within a transaction. In this way, attackers may frame an unknowing individual for access control violations that the individual did not perpetrate.

12.3 Blockchain-enabled Smart End Devices

The Blockchain-enabled Smart End Devices strategy is implemented by configuring the contributing IoT devices as full blockchain nodes that download and validate all incoming blocks of transactions and execute calls to the smart contracts stored on the blockchain (Figure 12.4). This kind of blockchain deployment can thus consist solely of IoT devices without any added gateways or back-end cloud services. However, gateways and cloud back-ends can be added to extend the network and increase security.

12.3.1 Advantages

Like the Blockchain-enabled Gateway strategy of Section 12.2, the Blockchain-enabled Smart End Devices strategy can leverage blockchain technology to obtain a **secure, trustworthy log** of events, enforce proper authentication by means of **secure device registration** and enjoy transparent **trustworthy business logic**. The Blockchain-enabled Smart End Devices strategy also provides two concrete improvements over the Blockchain-enabled Gateway strategy:

- **Fault-tolerance**—by deploying a blockchain framework over more of the devices that submit blockchain transactions, the blockchain is replicated more often and is thus more fault tolerant. In addition, as more of the data and behavior of the IoT device is stored and implemented on the blockchain itself, dealing with IoT device failures becomes easier as getting an IoT device configured and running becomes as simple as starting the blockchain client on the device.

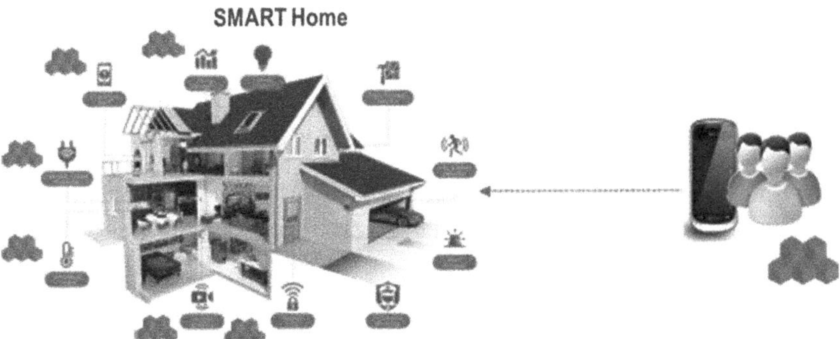

Figure 12.4 The Blockchain-enabled End Devices strategy implemented for a smart home. This deployment strategy allows for IoT/user devices to be full blockchain nodes. Gateways and back-end cloud services are optional.

- **Trusted IoT device behavior**—the biggest improvement that the Blockchain-enabled Smart End Devices strategy provides to an IoT system, is the ability to leverage the smart contract mechanism of the blockchain framework as a way to run a trusted code on IoT devices. Note that this is not the same as the previously discussed **trustworthy business logic**. While that blockchain-enabled security and trust improvement leverages the entire blockchain network to verify high-level business logic, this trusted IoT device behavior need not be high-level code nor verified by the entire network. This trusted IoT device behavior may be the reading of a sensor device, establishing network connections, installing software updates, and so on. To achieve trust in such operations, the blockchain framework is utilized as a way of verifying that the code that is executing a behavior of the IoT device has not been modified (by checking against an exact copy of the code stored on the blockchain). In addition, the blockchain framework can be utilized as a way of verifying that the outcome of the behavioral code is replicable, by forcing a small number of equivalent IoT devices to replicate the behavior.

12.3.2 Limitations

As for the previously discussed Blockchain-enabled Gateway strategy, all security and fault-tolerance advantages are limited within a private blockchain as the network size is constrained. In addition, the Blockchain-enabled Smart End Devices strategy is only suitable for IoT devices with a sizeable amount of memory and processing power as most fully featured blockchain node clients in existence at the time of writing are highly resource intensive. The technical execution of *trusted device behavior* is also hard to achieve in most current blockchain frameworks as it requires a smart contract programming model that is flexible enough support the low-level operations of IoT devices such as sensor reading or patch application.

Lastly, while utilising the blockchain framework to control the behavior of IoT devices improves our confidence in the submitted data, as it increases our control over the creation of the data that is submitted onto the blockchain, this approach is still not entirely trustworthy. Behavior-defining smart contracts still rely on the correct execution of the underlying blockchain execution environment, device operating system, and hardware. All these components of the underlying stack may still be exploited by a resourceful attacker to successfully tamper with the data being submitted to the blockchain.

12.3.3 Private Hyperledger Blockchain-enabled Smart Sensor Devices

To illustrate the pros and cons of the Blockchain-enabled Smart End Device strategy, we discuss its application in a blockchain prototype of a supply chain temperature monitoring solution. The supply chain is a key area for blockchain-based innovation, as blockchain, by means of its immutable, multistakeholder database, provides an ideal platform for building systems that track products from manufacturers to warehouses to end users. Food and pharmaceutical supply chains, in particular, are undergoing various blockchain experiments. In these experiments, IoT devices play a critical role as they provide the data to be added to the blockchain. However, there are various points along the supply chain, such as for example during transport, where a blockchain-powered gateway such as the one detailed previously in Section 12.2.1 may not be desired due to, for example, connectivity constraints or concerns about the validity of the data submitted to the gateway. As such, we investigated a prototype network of temperature-sensing IoT devices, again implemented as Raspberry Pi devices, within a truck shipping fresh foods. This prototype applies the Blockchain-enabled Smart End Device strategy by directly hosting the blockchain between the sensor devices, with each device a fully-enabled Hyperledger Fabric node.

Hyperledger Fabric [17] is an open-source blockchain framework that is primarily used for the deployment of trusted databases between multiple organizations. Unlike Ethereum, the Hyperledger Fabric blockchain does not employ PoW as a consensus protocol, but instead provides support for consensus protocols such as Practical Byzantine Fault Tolerance [14] that do not require resource-intensive mining computations. While it is by design a cloud framework, implementing the blockchain as a series of micro services hosted in various docker containers, we chose to port it down to our light-weight IoT devices (the resulting custom containers for Raspberry Pi are available online[2]) due to it being the only widely tested and well-documented blockchain framework that provides a flexible and capable programming model for smart contracts.

Traditional smart contracts such as the one we used in our Ethereum-based prototype of Section 12.2.1, are limited to a certain set of computations and features to (i) make it possible for all full nodes of the blockchain to execute and verify a smart contract regardless of their underlying hardware and (ii) simplify the determination of how much the computation of the smart contract on a public blockchain should cost, by assigning a price to each operation. The latter also ensures that smart contracts cannot sabotage the blockchain network by running indefinitely as those that wish to have the smart contract executed can only commit a limited amount of financial resources to it.

Hyperledger Fabric smart contracts (known as chaincode), in contrast, are isolated docker containers that support full-featured programming languages such as Java and Golang. This allows developers to utilize the same libraries and frameworks that they use in nonblockchain code as long as they can get it to run

2 Containers named hyperledger-* @https://hub.docker.com/r/sylvarantinc/

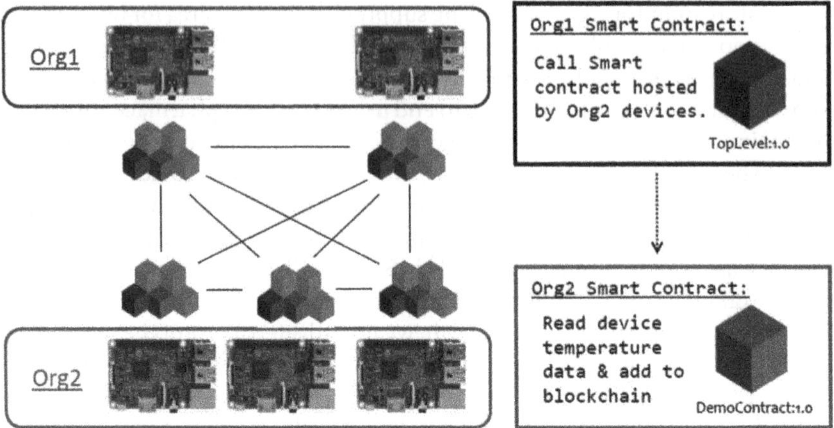

Figure 12.5 Our Hyperledger-fabric enabled temperature sensors host a blockchain between them, where sensor data is added to the blockchain by means of a smart contract that specifies how the devices of `Org2` should interact with the temperature sensor.

within the environment of the container. In addition, Hyperledger Fabric smart contracts are limited only in the maximum amount of time that an invocation of the smart contract may take. This is a blockchain-wide set constraint that in our prototype was set to 2 minutes, which is more than enough time for our IoT devices to read from their temperature sensors. A final advantage of the Hyperledger Fabric smart contract model is that it allows blockchain administrators to constrain the execution of certain smart contracts to only a select subset of the nodes (referred to as organizations) within the blockchain network.

Our prototype, as illustrated in Figure 12.5, utilizes Hyperledger Fabric's *membership service* to create two organizations, `Org1` and `Org2`, where each organization is defined by a set of self-signed certificates that constitute the root of trust for authenticating the IoT devices that make up the respective organizations. The organization `Org1` models an authoritative organization within the supply chain, such as, for example, a super market under taking delivery of food, whereas `Org2` models a low-ranked organization aiding with the monitoring of the temperature within the supply chain.

The devices in each organization run an organization-specific smart contract. We enforced this segregation by utilizing a Hyperledger feature called *endorsement policies* that restricts the validity of smart contract transactions to those transactions that are approved by the respective organization. This approval is verified by the nodes running the Hyperledger Fabric framework by inspecting the digital signatures that are used to sign smart contract transactions.

The devices in `Org2`, which are Raspberry Pi devices connected to a temperature sensor, run a smart contract (written in Golang) called

```
func (t *Demo) putSensor(stub shim.
   ChaincodeStubInterface, args []string) pb.Response{
 ...
 pin,e := rpi.OpenPin(7,rpi.IN)
 if e != nil { panic(e) }
 pinVal,e1 := pin.Read()
 if e1 != nil { panic(e1) }
 ...
 e2 := stub.PutState(sender,[]byte(tempVal))
 if er2 != nil { return shim.Error(err.Error()) }
 ...
 return shim.Success([]byte(tempVal))
```

Figure 12.6 A Hyperledger smart contract storing sensor values.

`DemoContract` that provides a callable function, `putSensor`. A snippet of that function is listed in Figure 12.6. This `putSensor` smart contract function serves as a blockchain-integrated device driver for the attached temperature sensor. It starts by opening the Raspberry Pi GPIO pins to which our temperature sensors are connected, reads from them and then writes the resulting temperature value to the blockchain using the Hyperledger Fabric blockchain storage function `stub.putState`. The Hyperledger Fabric blockchain model is that of a key value database; in the listed example, we thus store an association between the sender of the transaction calling the smart contract with the value read from the sensor onto the blockchain. If that write to the blockchain is successful, the `putSensor` function terminates by returning the blockchain-written sensor value as a message to the device that initiated the smart contract transaction.

Note that the Hyperledger Fabric blockchain framework does not, by design, provide support for this kind of hardware-integrated smart contract functionality. Hyperledger Fabric smart contracts are designed to be containers that are as device-agnostic as possible, enabling developers to easily replicate them across all kinds of cloud machines. To enable this new kind of hardware integrated smart contract, we extended Hyperledger Fabric with custom smart contract containers that have read and write access to the Raspberry Pi GPIO pins (Figure 12.7). This was achieved by mounting as volumes to the container the Linux sysfs [18] virtual file interface to the GPIO pins. In addition, extra Golang packages are incorporated into the container to enable easy high-level interaction with the GPIO pins. As of right now, these hardware interfacing containers work only on Hyperledger Fabric nodes that run Hyperledger Fabric's more permissible development mode.

In contrast to the IoT devices of `Org2`, the devices of `Org1` run a smart contract called `TopLevel` that calls the `putSensor` function of the contract run

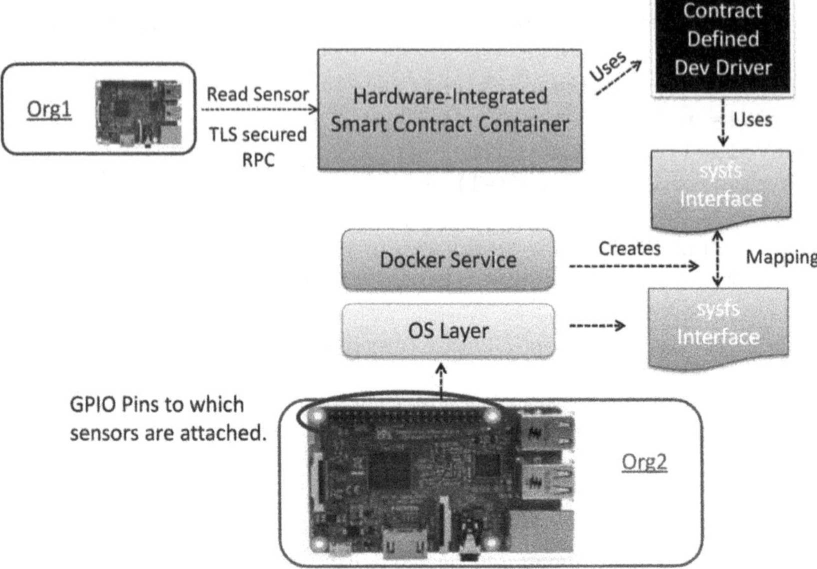

Figure 12.7 Our hardware-integrated smart contract architecture allows for device drivers inside smart contracts by pushing hardware interfaces up to the contract containers.

on by the devices of `Org2` and then compares the resulting temperature sensor value to the value it expected, as listed in Figure 12.8. A third party, such as, for example, an auditor of the supermarket modeled by `Org1` may thus audit the food safety of the shipment by invoking the `TopLevel` smart contract on the `Org1` devices by means of a blockchain transaction; this transaction then spawns a transaction from the `TopLevel` contract to the temperature sensor reading smart contract running on the devices of `Org2`. The devices of `Org1` thus do not contribute directly to the collecting of sensor data but instead use the Hyperledger blockchain framework to enforce their authority over the devices in `Org2`.

```
invokeArgs := ToChaincodeArgs("putSensor")
resp := stub.InvokeChaincode("DemoContract",
   invokeArgs,"")
if resp.Status == shim.OK {
 tempValue, err = strconv.Atoi(string(resp.Payload))
 if(tempValue < ExpectedValue)
 ...
```

Figure 12.8 The contract of `Org1` invokes the sensor reading function `putSensor` of the smart contract running on the devices of `Org2`, and inspects the result.

12.3.4 Evaluation

Like the access control solution of Section 12.2.1, this multi-organization temperature-sensing prototype leverages the blockchain framework to obtain a **secure, trustworthy log** of all events (in this case temperature reads), **secure device registration** of the IoT devices (by utilising from Hyperledger Fabric's membership service), and **trustworthy business logic** for some of the logic of the supply chain. In addition, this prototype leverages the unique advantages of Blockchain-enabled Smart End Devices as follows:

- **Fault-tolerance**—In this supply chain prototype, the sensor data is replicated across all devices of `Org1` and `Org2`. The prototype can easily handle the loss of multiple IoT devices as data is never lost and device behavior is set at the blockchain level, allowing one to configure a device by simply connecting it to the private blockchain network.
- **Trusted IoT device behavior**—the biggest improvement that the Blockchain-enabled Smart End Devices strategy provides to an IoT system is the ability to leverage the smart contract mechanism of the blockchain framework as a way to run trusted behavior-enforcing code on the IoT devices. In this prototype, we ensure that we have a trusted way of reading values from the temperature sensors by means of the `DemoContract` smart contract that specifies the exact code for how the sensor value should be read from the sensor before it is stored on the blockchain. Because an exact copy of that code is stored on the blockchain, any attempts at modifying or faking the container running the sensor-reading code will fail to produce transactions that the blockchain system accepts.

Note that even in this prototype, the temperature values stored on the blockchain are not entirely trustworthy. Obtaining the correct temperature sensor values within the `DemoContract` smart contract running on the devices of `Org2` relies on an untampered Linux operating system and its sysfs interface as well as an untampered mapping between the virtual files of sysfs and the containers running the smart contract. The temperature sensors and IoT devices are also still susceptible to various forms of hardware-based tampering. In our setup, we can limit the security challenges that arise from either hardware or operating system level tampering by leveraging the core blockchain feature of verifying computations through replication. In particular, we may want to configure that all calls to the `putSensor` function of the `DemoContract` be validated by all devices in `Org2` (as they reside in the same truck container). In such a setup, a new sensor value is only written to the blockchain if all devices read the same temperature value for the sensor. While Hyperledger does provide features that enable this kind of behavior, our experiments found that in the version of Hyperledger that we utilized to build this prototype (1.0), this functionality was still unreliable and unfinished[3].

3 goo.gl/xTUWTB

Finally, an important limitation of the Blockchain-enabled End Devices strategy is that configuring an IoT device as a fully featured blockchain node requires lots of memory and computational resources from that IoT device. As noted previously, this prototype ran a port of Hyperledger Fabric's container-based architecture on our Raspberry Pi devices. While running this container architecture on an IoT device is indeed memory and computation intensive, the limitations we encountered were quite reasonable. With maximum memory per smart contract configured to be capped at 100MB, we maxed out the CPU performance of our Raspberry device at six containers, where one container is the Hyperledger Fabric full blockchain node microservice and the other five containers are smart contracts. In our experiments, this five simultaneous smart contracts constraint has not been limiting.

12.4 Related Work

The majority of research on blockchain has so far focused on revealing and improving the privacy and security limitations of blockchain [19]. Related to our efforts in this chapter to investigate blockchain as a framework for IoT deployments is the ADEPT project by IBM that leverages blockchain as a network of IoT devices [20]. ADEPT, however, only considers the Ethereum blockchain framework and does not explore the application of IoT end devices as fully capable blockchain peers, opting instead to segregate blockchain peers based on IoT device capabilities. Publications on the project are also lacking in concrete details on the security benefits of such a scheme. Likewise, Zhang et al. design blockchain IoT architectures for scenarios such as authenticating carbon emission rights, securing physical systems, trading power resources and coordinating between multi-energy systems [21]. They do not, however, implement any of these scenarios. Blockchain is also increasingly considered as a means of implementing IoT back-end services. Daza et al., for example, propose blockchain as a better way to discover devices within IoT networks [22]. In a closely related work, Samaniego and Deters explore network latency related issues regarding the delivery of blockchain services from the IBM Bluemix cloud platform compared to a blockchain hosted locally on Arduino Iot devices [23].

In a work similar to our Ethereum gateway prototype of Section 12.2.1, Huh et al. have explored employing Ethereum on a network of Raspberry Pi devices as a means of managing the cryptography keys used by those devices [24]; they provide examples of smart contracts but do not explore the limitations of their scheme. In another effort similar to our exploration of blockchain-based gateways in Section 12.2.1, Dorri et al. explore blockchain as a network for smart home devices with a central miner that enables the processing of incoming and outgoing transactions [25]. Their experimental evaluation, however, is based on results obtained through simulation in contrast to the functional prototypes presented in this work.

Several start-ups are exploring multi-organizational blockchain supply chain solutions like our supply chain temperature monitoring prototype of Section 12.3.1. The most prominent are VeChain and Waltonchain. VeChain is a public blockchain that aims to integrate its identifiers (VIDs) into numerous IoT tags such as QR codes, NFC, and RFID [26]. This enables a simpler blockchain-based tracking of supply chain products. To resolve the public blockchain throughput challenges detailed in the introduction, VeChain is experimenting with the use of Proof of Authority as a consensus mechanism. Similarly, Waltonchain is a public blockchain aimed at tracking products throughout the supply chain; their key differentation is a custom RFID-integrated circuit that is directly integrated with the blockchain [27].

12.5 Conclusion

In this chapter, we described, implemented, and compared two different configuration strategies for deploying a private blockchain on a network of IoT devices. The Blockchain-enabled Gateway strategy provides blockchain features to IoT devices without the IoT devices themself being fully featured blockchain clients; instead a gateway is introduced to enable the IoT devices to interface with a blockchain. This connection between IoT devices and a blockchain enables developers to securely register IoT devices, to store data in a trustworthy log, and to execute high-level business logic in a way that is transparent and network verified. The Blockchain-enabled Smart End Devices strategy, in contrast, configures IoT devices as fully capable blockchain nodes, providing the blockchain network improved fault tolerance and enabling important security features such as the trustworthy collection of sensor data directly within a smart contract. Both strategies were illustrated by means of prototype implementations of a blockchain based access control system and a blockchain-improved supply-chain temperature monitoring system, respectively.

References

1 S. Nakamoto, "Bitcoin: A peer-to-peer electronic cash system." [Online]. 2008. Available: http://bitcoin.org/bitcoin.pdf [Accessed: September 18, 2017].

2 T. Lundqvist, A. de Blanche, and H. R. H. Andersson, "Thing-to-thing electricity micro payments using blockchain technology," in *2017 Global Internet of Things Summit (GIoTS)*, June 2017, pp. 1–6.

3 S. Raju, S. Boddepalli, S. Gampa, Q. Yan, and J. S. Deogun, "Identity management using blockchain for cognitive cellular networks," in *2017 IEEE International Conference on Communications (ICC)*, May 2017, pp. 1–6.

4 B. Gipp, C. Breitinger, N. Meuschke, and J. Beel, "Cryptsubmit: Introducing securely timestamped manuscript submission and peer review feedback using

the blockchain," in *2017 ACM/IEEE Joint Conference on Digital Libraries, JCDL 2017*, Toronto, ON, Canada, June 19–23, 2017, pp. 273–276.

5 N. Szabo, "The idea of smart contracts." [Online]. 1997. Available: http://bit.ly/2HVLXXW.

6 V. Buterin, "Ethereum: A next-generation smart contract and decentralized application platform." [Online]. 2014. Available: https://github.com/ethereum/wiki/wiki/White-Paper [Accessed: September 18, 2017].

7 K. Croman, C. Decker, I. Eyal, A. E. Gencer, A. Juels, A. E. Kosba, A. Miller, P. Saxena, E. Shi, E. G. Sirer, D. Song, and R. Wattenhofer, "On scaling decentralized blockchains (a position paper)," in *Financial Cryptography and Data Security—FC 2016 International Workshops, BITCOIN, VOTING, and WAHC*, Revised Selected Papers, Christ Church, Barbados, February 26, 2016, pp. 106–125.

8 J. Bhuiyan, "Uber powered four billion rides." [Online]. January 2018. Available: http://bit.ly/2IlFlou.

9 Visa Incorporated, "Visa Inc. at a glance." [Online]. 2015. Available: https://vi.sa/2wmbO95.

10 S. Popov, "The Tangle." [Online]. 2017. Available: https://assets.ctfassets.net/r1dr6vzfxhev/2t4uxvsIqk0EUau6g2sw0g/45eae33637ca92f85dd9f4a3a218e1ec/iota1_4_3.pdf.

11 C. LeMahieu, "Nano: A feeless distributed cryptocurrency network." [Online]. 2017. Available: https://nano.org/en/whitepaper.

12 M. Jakobsson and A. Juels, "Proofs of work and bread pudding protocols," in *Secure Information Networks*. Springer, 1999, pp. 258–272.

13 P. Szilagyi, "Clique poa protocol." [Online]. 2017. Available: https://github.com/ethereum/EIPs/issues/225 [Accessed: March 18, 2018].

14 M. Castro and B. Liskov, "Practical Byzantine fault tolerance," in *Proceedings of the Third Symposium on Operating Systems Design and Implementation*, 1999, pp. 173–186.

15 M. Conti, S. K. E, C. Lal, and S. Ruj, "A survey on security and privacy issues of Bitcoin," *IEEE Communications Surveys & Tutorials*, 2017. https://doi.org/10.1109/COMST.2018.2842460.

16 Trustnodes, "Ethereum now has three times more nodes than Bitcoin." [Online]. May, 2017. Available: http://bit.ly/2Kf6WVJ.

17 C. Cachin, "Architecture of the Hyperledger blockchain fabric." [Online]. 2016. Available: https://ibm.co/2FaSlaI [Accessed: August 10, 2016].

18 P. Mochel, "The sysfs filesystem," in *Linux Symposium*, 2005, pp. 313–326.

19 J. Yli-Huumo, D. Ko, S. Choi, S. Park, and K. Smolander, "Where is current research on blockchain technology? A systematic review," *PLOS ONE*, vol. 11, no. 10, pp. 1–27, October 2016.

20 IBM, "ADEPT: An IoT Practitioner Perspective," 2015. Available: http://static1.squarespace.com/static/55f73743e4b051cfcc0b02cf/55f73e5ee4b09b2bff5b2eca/55f73e72e4b09b2bff5b3267/1442266738638/IBM-ADEPT-Practictioner-Perspective-Pre-Publication-Draft-7-Jan-2015.pdf

13

Blockchain Evaluation Platform

Peter Foytik and Sachin S. Shetty

Old Dominion University, Virginia, USA

13.1 Introduction

In this chapter, we will focus on the development of the testing platform to evaluate the approaches presented in prior chapters. This chapter will assume the reader has some knowledge of programming or scripting and object-oriented design, and will be most beneficial to readers who are familiar with open source software. Software code will be available to the reader via an online repository and can be downloaded and run on any system that is capable to meet the open sourced software requirements. One example available to the reader is a custom-built, simplistic blockchain simulation application built in C#. This application will require a freely available Microsoft .NET framework. Another example that will be used is a Hyperledger Fabric example. Hyperledger Fabric [1, 2] is an open sourced blockchain application and toolset managed by the Linux Foundation. It will require the user to run the open sourced framework docker, which will allow prebuilt applications containers to be hosted, and a few open sourced software/scripting languages such as GoLang and JavaScript.

The two examples offer opportunity to evaluate algorithms and protocols proposed in previous chapters in a couple of different environments. The simple implementation in C# is a way to simulate some of the theories in an iterative way. Simulating some of the protocols with blockchain is very beneficial in that it allows researchers to evaluate algorithms or protocols without the need to know the operational aspects of the entire system. The Hyperledger Fabric example is a fully capable blockchain platform that can be modified to work in a practical environment. Both examples can be scaled to evaluate the performance of algorithms and protocols.

The source code, materials, and additional documentation needed to run the examples can be found on GitHub at https://github.com/odu-vmasc/Blockchain_BookChapter.

Blockchain for Distributed Systems Security, First Edition. Edited by Sachin S. Shetty, Charles A. Kamhoua, and Laurent L. Njilla.

13.1.1 Architecture

Ledgers have been used to record state changes in software and physical systems throughout the existence of humans and documentation. Simply, put the ledger is a key value pair where the key and the value can be any number of representations. Every change in the state of this key value pair is associated or represented with a hash value that is computed with a combination of the prior hash value and the data representing the key value pair including the change in state. The key piece of implementation that needs to be planned and discussed is how the representation of key aspects will be implemented. These key aspects are:

1. Distributed ledger
2. Participating nodes
3. Consensus nodes or integration to the peer nodes
4. Messaging methods between participating nodes

13.1.2 Distributed Ledger

From the perspective of software implementation, which this chapter focuses on, ledgers exist natively in many programming languages but are referred to by more common forms such as linked list, array, dictionary, or map. Any of these forms of data structures can be used as a ledger though limited to the functionality of the specific nature of those data types.

The most commonly used data structure to represent the blockchain ledger is the linked list. Linked lists provide a dynamic structure that can grow without having to specify an initial size. The linked list can be described as a chain of nodes where each node can be a data structure. The structure of the node (block) can be customized based on the type of data that needs to be stored in the list. At a minimum, for it to function as a blockchain, it will need to contain a link or a pointer that links the node to the prior node. The current node's hash value needs to be based on the prior node's state and hash value. Each node needs to be able to link to the next node in the same manner that it linked to the prior node.

In addition to the aforementioned aspects, a developer has a great deal of leeway in determining the information represented in the node. This should mostly focus on the representation of states for the system the blockchain is supporting. A great deal of research is being done to determine limits on the amount of data that is beneficial to store in blockchains. The consensus is that for large data systems, the blockchain will only manage the states of the system and the data to be stored in more traditional database systems. The traditional data and state for blockchains is typically a key and value pair. The key would be an ID that represents the object in which a state is being observed, and the value would be a representation of the state for that object. For more flexible implementations, the key and the value would be represented using a string, which would provide a more robust representation. However, there is no reason that other data types could be used for the key and the value such as integers or Boolean values. Strategically choosing the data type could potentially reduce the size of the data allowing for better performing blockchains.

The hash function that is used should be determined based on the latest standards as well as the size of the data that is to be included in the hash. The developer should be mindful of the vulnerabilities of the hash function chosen as well as the performance of the hash function regarding the size of the data that will be hashed. The data that should be hashed is the value of the hash from the prior block and some aspect of the key value pair data associated with the current block. Producing a value from the hash function will then represent a uniquely identified value for the current state block within the blockchain. This hash value will then not only represent a clear value that provides integrity of the data, but also a clear value that provides integrity of the location in the blockchain of that data. Many of the hash functions that exist openly (SHA-2, SHA-3, BLAKE2) are very good and have been tested by the community, and the performance of these functions is greatly documented. Implementations of these hash functions exist as libraries in C# and within the Hyperledger Fabric tool kit that can be utilized by the developer for ease of use.

13.1.3 Participating Nodes

Since the blockchain is decentralized in nature, the components that are to be decentralized need to be handled as participating nodes within the system. These nodes ideally would be decentralized on many machines. Depending on the implementation of the blockchain a number of nodes can be defined to do the decentralized tasks. The types of nodes required for the decentralized blockchain system will vary based on the implementation strategies used. At a minimum, peer nodes need to be defined that can communicate with each other in a peer to peer network. These peer nodes would need to be able to read and write to a local ledger to maintain and keep the state of the blockchain. In most cases, the peers need to be able to communicate with each other, but in some instances a manager node can be used. Clearly, adding manager nodes makes the system more centralized and strays away from the decentralized purpose and goal of blockchain systems.

Decentralized in nature, the nodes need to be modular and developed as objects that can be scaled in numbers. This can be done using independent computers that run the node application, from virtual machines running the node application, containerized instances of the node application, or using programmed objects within the software code of a simulation. The last example is a way to test blockchain protocols from a centralized environment.

13.1.4 Communication

Protocols of communication from the participating nodes can vary based on the nature and strategy of the implementation. At a minimum, the nodes need to be able to communicate with each other in a one-to-one manner. All participating nodes might have the ability to communicate with each other in a peer-to-peer manner or at least be able to communicate with a managing node that can relay or communicate with all of the other nodes. In many cases, a method of broadcast is desired to ensure the most efficient message transfer to all participating nodes. The broadcast method sends a message to all nodes or a portion of nodes on the participating network simultaneously.

Another strategy is gossip network protocol where information propagates throughout the entire network through neighboring peers. This strategy utilizes properties of the spreading behavior of diseases and epidemics to propagate information through a network of connected nodes. Knowledge of neighboring nodes is needed for this method to work, as well as a highly connected network. If there are large portions of the network that are only connected through one link, this can greatly degrade the performance of the information spread.

Implementation of the communication can be done using standard protocols based on the design of the blockchain system. Individual machines can be the participating nodes connected to the internet using HTTP to communicate, in a private setting through a local area network, or even from a virtual network on a single machine. Each one of these setups can be designed with the same communication protocols to allow for future scaling and duplication of work from various settings.

In a simulated environment, the communication method becomes very simple as a message can be as simple as a function call to the peer object. The challenge in this case becomes the accurate representation of the asynchronous nature of the real system in the simulated environment. This can be achieved in a couple of ways. By using threading and parallel processing of the individual participating nodes at times when there are simultaneous processes, a slight delay that can occur in the process for each thread or forked process will offer more variation in the system. Additionally, delays can be applied to those message function calls that are simulating the communication of peer objects. The delay value can be a static pause, or a looped process based on a static iterator value. To make things even more asynchronous, it could be more beneficial to utilize a randomly selected value for the pause or looped iterator.

13.1.5 Consensus

A core issue in any asynchronous decentralized systems is consensus of the order of messages to the system. Good consensus methods on the decentralized system ensure that there is trust in the order of messages that happen on the system. If two messages enter the system at two different ends of the network at nearly the same time, how does the decentralized system determine which message occurred first? Naturally, the local participating node to each message will perceive the nearest message as entering before the farther message. Ensuring that the message that reached the network first is processed in that order is the main challenge in blockchain systems consensus algorithms.

This chapter will briefly describe three consensus algorithms that can be implemented by the reader. The focus in this chapter regarding the consensus algorithms is on how these algorithms affect the blockchain system's ability to perform. In many cases, the biggest bottleneck of blockchain systems is the consensus algorithm. This is because finding consensus among a large network of nodes is very difficult and time consuming. Consider the speed of a network hop, then consider it having to go through nodes to get to others until all of the nodes or at least a majority of the nodes have received the message. Very quickly, one can start to see that depending on the method used to find consensus, the more decentralized the system becomes the worse the performance might get. When it comes to performance, there tends to be a trade-off in blockchain systems, where more performance comes with more centralization. The challenge is to strive for good performance and good decentralization that is appropriate for the use case the blockchain is being designed or implemented for.

13.2 Hyperledger Fabric

Hyperledger Fabric is an open sourced toolkit that is managed and maintained by the Hyperledger product of the Linux Foundation [1]. It allows developers to build a permissioned blockchain system. Permissioned blockchain, as it is with Hyperledger Fabric, distributes a ledger amongst participating nodes that are granted permission using cryptographic certifications assigned either beforehand or through a certificate authority. By doing this, the ledger is not publicly distributed in large numbers but privately distributed to a much smaller number of nodes; it is designed that only those nodes have access to the information in and of the ledger.

Since nodes require access, Hyperledger Fabric is considered a permissioned blockchain. This type of system has pros and cons. The benefit of permissioned systems is that the content and system remains inaccessible to the public. Permission and access control requires a protocol for distributing and enforcing access such as certificate authority nodes. The cost of having the data private is that the immutable properties are limited to a subnetwork of limited machines. The public networks, though open to all connected devices, offer a bigger opportunity to distribute the blockchain ensuring a larger network and a much smaller probability that a large portion of the network would be controlled in order gain majority.

13.2.1 Node Types

- Client—a node that is given permission or allowed to communicate with the chaincode installed on peer nodes.

- Peer—a node that participates on the network as a validating node, host to a local copy of the ledger, and host of the chaincode.
- Orderer—a node that provides organization of the participating peer nodes; since Hyperledger Fabric v1 the orderer node determines the consensus method used and can handle much of the message broadcasts to all participating nodes.
- Certificate Authority—a node that provides cryptographic files with permissions to communicate and operate with other Hyperledger Fabric nodes.
- Kafka and Zookeeper—special nodes that allow for the operation of Kafka consensus with Hyperledger Fabric.

13.2.2 Docker

Docker is a framework to build containerized images of aspects of a computer system to provide a means to rapidly start, scale, and run varying types of systems and applications on any environment. The idea is built on the premise that no matter what your system setup is (OS, parameters, software), one could host the docker platform that allows the user to launch docker containers. Once the docker container is launched, the container can interact with other containers as well as the physical machine the developer is on through the network interfaces that the docker platform sets up. The developer can also port forward internet traffic to that machine to specific docker containers to interface a container with the network.

A docker container can run on any machine that is hosting the docker platform, regardless of the operating system. The docker containers represent and function as a complete system that is running an application or service. The container is not a virtualized machine and only utilizes enough resources to perform the tasks required for the application or service. By doing this, a more efficient deployment of the applications and services is provided. This type of system also allows for an easy way to scale up systems where instead of having to create new machines and adding them to the network, one could just start up more docker containers of a type.

Starting docker containers firstly requires the development machine to have the docker platform installed. The developer then can install toolsets that help manage the docker containers, such as docker compose. The docker platform and the docker-compose toolset can both be installed on Windows, Linux, and Apple environments. For the most part, starting, stopping, and general management of the docker containers is done from the command line interface or terminal of the developer machine. Containers are represented as image files that are stored locally on the machine that is hosting the docker platform. These image files can be generated by the developers by building or modifying existing base images, or by creating completely new images from their own development environment. Docker provides a hub service where they host publicly many types of docker containers that developers can use or build from.

13.2.3 Hyperledger Fabric Example Exercise

In this section, we will demonstrate the operations required to conduct development on Hyperledger Fabric. For more details on the operations, the reader can refer to the Hyperledger Fabric documentation site [2]. Using docker compose, the Hyperledger Fabric network can be started from a single command using a docker-compose *.yaml file. The yaml file contains the information needed to define which images to start, what information to copy to the images on startup, what ports to communicate with the images on, what scripts or applications to start up on image boot, and what environment variables should be established and set. Assuming the docker and docker-compose environment has been set up and tested on the development machine, the user should be able to follow the instructions in this section. The graphics and examples will be shown using an Ubuntu Linux terminal for reference.

Using a terminal/command line interface, navigate to the directory with the scenario example files. This will be referred to as the directory *bookchapter*. Inside bookchapter you will notice a few other directories and several files. All filetypes of *.yaml are configure files that are used by docker compose to either start up or assist in starting up several docker containers. The directory contains yaml files for various Hyperledger Fabric setups. The directory *e2e_cli* contains files and directories needed for the fabric client, the participating node that will allow us to interact with the Hyperledger Fabric system. The directory *Kafka* contains the files and directories needed to start up a Hyperledger Fabric system that uses the Kafka consensus algorithm. The directory titled *fabric-samples* contains several samples provided by the Hyperledger Fabric community. One of the directories inside the directory *fabric-samples* is the directory titled *basic-network*, which contains the necessary files to start up Hyperledger Fabric's basic test network. The directory titled *scripts* contains bash script files that will be loaded into the fabric client docker container. The developer can modify these script files before starting up the fabric client using the text editor of their choice to provide an easier development platform.

13.2.4 Running the First Network

The basic network is built to run on a computer that is capable of executing bash script files. This chapter describes the execution of the first network in a Linux environment. Once the developer has installed the docker environment and the docker compose tool, and has run a test (for example, the docker whale hello world test), the developer will be ready to build a basic Hyperledger Fabric system. The most basic example is the Hyperledger Fabric's first network. Located in the directory *basic-network there*, there are a few script files (file type *.sh), a few config files (file types *.yaml or *.yml), and two directories—*config* and *crypto-config*—containing the needed cryptographic security files and initial states for the blockchain setup.

```
pfoytik@vmasc-001780:/usr/local/go/src/github.com/hyperledger/fabric-samples/basic-network$ ./generate.sh
org1.example.com
2018-03-23 15:42:27.833 EDT [common/configtx/tool] main -> INFO 001 Loading configuration
2018-03-23 15:42:27.849 EDT [common/configtx/tool] doOutputBlock -> INFO 002 Generating genesis block
2018-03-23 15:42:27.850 EDT [common/configtx/tool] doOutputBlock -> INFO 003 Writing genesis block
2018-03-23 15:42:27.857 EDT [common/configtx/tool] main -> INFO 001 Loading configuration
2018-03-23 15:42:27.859 EDT [common/configtx/tool] doOutputChannelCreateTx -> INFO 002 Generating new channel configtx
2018-03-23 15:42:27.859 EDT [common/configtx/tool] doOutputChannelCreateTx -> INFO 003 Writing new channel tx
2018-03-23 15:42:27.867 EDT [common/configtx/tool] main -> INFO 001 Loading configuration
2018-03-23 15:42:27.868 EDT [common/configtx/tool] doOutputAnchorPeersUpdate -> INFO 002 Generating anchor peer update
2018-03-23 15:42:27.868 EDT [common/configtx/tool] doOutputAnchorPeersUpdate -> INFO 003 Writing anchor peer update
```

Figure 13.1 Screenshot of artifact generation script output.

To start up the first network, the developer needs to navigate to the directory *basic-network.* Once inside the directory, the developer will need to run the script file generate.sh. This file will generate the blockchain initial state files such as the genesis block. After the script has run successfully, the user will see an output similar to Figure 13.1.

The generate.sh script uses precompiled applications such as configtxgen and cryptogen. The application configtxgen generates initial blocks for the Hyperledger Fabric and cryptogen generates the cryptographic cert files for the different peers and participating nodes of the Hyperledger Fabric system.

Once these files have been generated, the developer can now start the basic network by running the script file start.sh. Using a Linux environment from the terminal, simply run:

```
./start.sh
```

This script file starts up the Hyperledger Fabric basic network, as defined in the config file docker-compose.yml. It then establishes a blockchain channel on a single peer. If the script file has run correctly, the developer should see results like Figure 13.2.

The start.sh script uses docker compose and the config file docker-compose.yml to start up the basic network. The docker-compose toolset reads the config file to determine what container images need to start, what data will be added to the image, how the image will communicate with the network, and what commands the container should run on startup. The docker-compose toolset, when used, will then check the local container repository stored on the machine and check to see whether the container image exists locally; if not, it will download it from either a specified location or by default will reach out to the public docker hub. If necessary, the toolset will download the container image, then proceed to start it up based on the information specified in the .yml config file. The main command used to start up the network that start.sh uses is:

```
docker-compose -f docker-compose.yml up
```

The docker-compose command uses the –f flag, indicating that a file name will be specified for the config file. In this case, the config file used is docker-compose.yml. Finally, the command "up" is used, indicating that the

```
Creating network "net_basic" with the default driver
Creating orderer.example.com
Creating couchdb
Creating ca.example.com
Creating peer0.org1.example.com

# wait for Hyperledger Fabric to start
# incase of errors when running later commands, issue export FABRIC_START_TIMEOUT=<larger number>
export FABRIC_START_TIMEOUT=10
#echo ${FABRIC_START_TIMEOUT}
sleep ${FABRIC_START_TIMEOUT}

# Create the channel
docker exec -e "CORE_PEER_LOCALMSPID=Org1MSP" -e "CORE_PEER_MSPCONFIGPATH=/etc/hyperledger/msp/users/Admin@org1.example.com/msp" peer0.org1.example.com peer channel create -o orderer.exam
ple.com:7050 -c mychannel -f /etc/hyperledger/configtx/channel.tx
2018-03-23 20:07:44.238 UTC [msp] GetLocalMSP -> DEBU 001 Returning existing local MSP
2018-03-23 20:07:44.238 UTC [msp] GetDefaultSigningIdentity -> DEBU 002 Obtaining default signing identity
2018-03-23 20:07:44.239 UTC [channelCmd] InitCmdFactory -> INFO 003 Endorser and orderer connections initialized
2018-03-23 20:07:44.239 UTC [msp] GetLocalMSP -> DEBU 004 Returning existing local MSP
2018-03-23 20:07:44.239 UTC [msp] GetDefaultSigningIdentity -> DEBU 005 Obtaining default signing identity
2018-03-23 20:07:44.239 UTC [msp] GetLocalMSP -> DEBU 006 Returning existing local MSP
2018-03-23 20:07:44.239 UTC [msp] GetDefaultSigningIdentity -> DEBU 007 Obtaining default signing identity
2018-03-23 20:07:44.239 UTC [msp/identity] Sign -> DEBU 008 Sign: plaintext: 0A8C060A074F726731405330128006 2D...53610D706C65436F6E736F7274697560D
2018-03-23 20:07:44.239 UTC [msp/identity] Sign -> DEBU 009 Sign: digest: CA34B5110EF84BE4FE1FAE2E6E344335A82C4054DF33168EDEEE9FDD6209D02D
2018-03-23 20:07:44.239 UTC [msp] GetLocalMSP -> DEBU 00a Returning existing local MSP
2018-03-23 20:07:44.239 UTC [msp] GetDefaultSigningIdentity -> DEBU 00b Obtaining default signing identity
2018-03-23 20:07:44.239 UTC [msp] GetLocalMSP -> DEBU 00c Returning existing local MSP
2018-03-23 20:07:44.239 UTC [msp] GetDefaultSigningIdentity -> DEBU 00d Obtaining default signing identity
2018-03-23 20:07:44.239 UTC [msp/identity] Sign -> DEBU 00e Sign: plaintext: 0AC3060A1508021A0608908DD5D50522...793B75BF0E23C1488272A79636E092F4
2018-03-23 20:07:44.239 UTC [msp/identity] Sign -> DEBU 00f Sign: digest: EA55000C950BFF1B185DBA174B47A07B8455975A28284442FF12CA68C343B3AF
2018-03-23 20:07:44.261 UTC [msp] GetLocalMSP -> DEBU 010 Returning existing local MSP
2018-03-23 20:07:44.261 UTC [msp] GetDefaultSigningIdentity -> DEBU 011 Obtaining default signing identity
2018-03-23 20:07:44.261 UTC [msp] GetLocalMSP -> DEBU 012 Returning existing local MSP
2018-03-23 20:07:44.261 UTC [msp] GetDefaultSigningIdentity -> DEBU 013 Obtaining default signing identity
2018-03-23 20:07:44.261 UTC [msp/identity] Sign -> DEBU 014 Sign: plaintext: 0AC3060A1508021A0608908DD5D50522...74C2D1738C5412080A021A0012021A00
2018-03-23 20:07:44.261 UTC [msp/identity] Sign -> DEBU 015 Sign: digest: 6968B0852861EDCFFD18501FD5E55A037AB613A253454083FCCA6278E67A3321
2018-03-23 20:07:44.262 UTC [channelCmd] readBlock -> DEBU 016 Got status:*orderer.DeliverResponse_Status
2018-03-23 20:07:44.262 UTC [msp] GetLocalMSP -> DEBU 017 Returning existing local MSP
2018-03-23 20:07:44.262 UTC [msp] GetDefaultSigningIdentity -> DEBU 018 Obtaining default signing identity
2018-03-23 20:07:44.262 UTC [channelCmd] InitCmdFactory -> INFO 019 Endorser and orderer connections initialized
2018-03-23 20:07:44.462 UTC [msp] GetLocalMSP -> DEBU 01a Returning existing local MSP
2018-03-23 20:07:44.462 UTC [msp] GetDefaultSigningIdentity -> DEBU 01b Obtaining default signing identity
2018-03-23 20:07:44.463 UTC [msp] GetLocalMSP -> DEBU 01c Returning existing local MSP
2018-03-23 20:07:44.463 UTC [msp] GetDefaultSigningIdentity -> DEBU 01d Obtaining default signing identity
2018-03-23 20:07:44.463 UTC [msp/identity] Sign -> DEBU 01e Sign: plaintext: 0AC3060A1508021A0608908DD5D50522...A6DD4DCA6D5712080A021A0012021A00
2018-03-23 20:07:44.463 UTC [msp/identity] Sign -> DEBU 01f Sign: digest: 5F460463F4DABCD04719A0C5AB66CD9BAE509CF32ED52AA5020ABE5B30181D97
2018-03-23 20:07:44.468 UTC [channelCmd] readBlock -> DEBU 020 Received block:0
2018-03-23 20:07:44.469 UTC [main] main -> INFO 021 Exiting.....
# Join peer0.org1.example.com to the channel.
docker exec -e "CORE_PEER_LOCALMSPID=Org1MSP" -e "CORE_PEER_MSPCONFIGPATH=/etc/hyperledger/msp/users/Admin@org1.example.com/msp" peer0.org1.example.com peer channel join -b mychannel.bloc
k
2018-03-23 20:07:44.568 UTC [msp] GetLocalMSP -> DEBU 001 Returning existing local MSP
2018-03-23 20:07:44.568 UTC [msp] GetDefaultSigningIdentity -> DEBU 002 Obtaining default signing identity
2018-03-23 20:07:44.569 UTC [channelCmd] InitCmdFactory -> INFO 003 Endorser and orderer connections initialized
2018-03-23 20:07:44.569 UTC [msp/identity] Sign -> DEBU 004 Sign: plaintext: 0A8A070A5C08011A0C08908DD5D50510...426120DDB0991A000A000A000A000A00
2018-03-23 20:07:44.569 UTC [msp/identity] Sign -> DEBU 005 Sign: digest: F93E30C369A4167630C204EB42280121C5776E2347EA635F71AC5507C9E000B0
2018-03-23 20:07:44.925 UTC [channelCmd] executeJoin -> INFO 006 Peer joined the channel!
2018-03-23 20:07:44.925 UTC [main] main -> INFO 007 Exiting.....
```

Figure 13.2 Screenshot of console outputs from the start script for the basic-network example.

network should be started up. This command uses the docker compose tool to read in a config file and start up the services or containers that are described in the yml file using the settings and attributes defined in the config file.

Looking at the docker-compose.yml file in a text editor, the developer will see the details shown in Figure 13.3. The config yml and yaml files split up sections based on the service or container. The snapshot of Figure 13.3 shows the service

```
version: '2'

networks:
  basic:

services:
  ca.example.com:
    image: hyperledger/fabric-ca:x86_64-1.0.0
    environment:
      - FABRIC_CA_HOME=/etc/hyperledger/fabric-ca-server
      - FABRIC_CA_SERVER_CA_NAME=ca.example.com
    ports:
      - "7054:7054"
    command: sh -c 'fabric-ca-server start --ca.certfile /etc/hyperledger/fabric-ca-server-config/org1.example.com-cert.pem
--ca.keyfile /etc/hyperledger/fabric-ca-server-config/a22daf356b2aab5792ea53e35f66fccef1d7f1aa2b3a2b92dbfbf96a448ea26a_sk -bb
 admin:adminpw -d'
    volumes:
      - ./crypto-config/peerOrganizations/org1.example.com/ca/:/etc/hyperledger/fabric-ca-server-config
    container_name: ca.example.com
    networks:
      - basic

  orderer.example.com:
    container_name: orderer.example.com
    image: hyperledger/fabric-orderer:x86_64-1.0.0
    environment:
      - ORDERER_GENERAL_LOGLEVEL=debug
      - ORDERER_GENERAL_LISTENADDRESS=0.0.0.0
      - ORDERER_GENERAL_GENESISMETHOD=file
      - ORDERER_GENERAL_GENESISFILE=/etc/hyperledger/configtx/genesis.block
      - ORDERER_GENERAL_LOCALMSPID=OrdererMSP
      - ORDERER_GENERAL_LOCALMSPDIR=/etc/hyperledger/msp/orderer/msp
    working_dir: /opt/gopath/src/github.com/hyperledger/fabric/orderer
    command: orderer
    ports:
      - 7050:7050
    volumes:
      - ./config/:/etc/hyperledger/configtx
      - ./crypto-config/ordererOrganizations/example.com/orderers/orderer.example.com/:/etc/hyperledger/msp/orderer
      - ./crypto-config/peerOrganizations/org1.example.com/peers/peer0.org1.example.com/:/etc/hyperledger/msp/peerOrg1
    networks:
      - basic
```

Figure 13.3 Example view of a docker-compose yml configuration file.

of the Hyperledger Fabric certificate authority (CA). In this config file, the label associated with this container is ca.example.com. After the label, the image is defined for the container to use; in this file, the image is hyperledger/fabric-ca:x86_64-1.0.0. The characters after the colon indicate the tag or version to use. If there is not a colon and version, the docker compose uses the latest tag or version. This can be problematic as some containers do not have the latest version specified and this can result in an error. For simplistic purposes, the config files included with this book all have the x86_64-1.0.0 tag or version applied. More information on the other sections of detail can be found in the online docker documentation.

Looking at the docker-compose.yml file, the developer will notice that there are several services. Each of these services should start up as its own docker container. To see the containers that have started and are running, use the docker "ps" command to view the list of running containers. This can be done from a new terminal window if the prior terminal is displaying logs from the start script. To view the running containers, use the command:

```
docker ps
```

Running this command will produce a result like Figure 13.4

This report provides useful information of the ID of the containers, the image used for that container, the name, and the status, to list a few. At this point, the system is running and the developer can build applications that either interact with that system, or execute commands on the containers that are currently running. At any point, a developer can view any console output or logging done by the different containers by using the docker command:

```
docker logs <id or name>
```

For example:

```
docker logs orderer.example.com
```

The above example will provide an output of all logged outputs that the peer has produced from the start to the current time, and is shown in Figure 13.5.

In this example, the orderer logs are displayed where timestamps are provided with debug outputs associated with the actions of the orderer at that time.

```
CONTAINER ID        IMAGE                                      COMMAND                  CREATED             STATUS
 PORTS                                            NAMES
6ce400ce0abd        hyperledger/fabric-peer:x86_64-1.0.0       "peer node start"        25 minutes ago      Up 25 minutes
 0.0.0.0:7051->7051/tcp, 0.0.0.0:7053->7053/tcp   peer0.org1.example.com
bbe61328047f        hyperledger/fabric-couchdb:x86_64-1.0.6    "tini -- /docker-e..."   25 minutes ago      Up 25 minutes
 4369/tcp, 9100/tcp, 0.0.0.0:5984->5984/tcp       couchdb
7d362b698b48        hyperledger/fabric-orderer:x86_64-1.0.0    "orderer"                25 minutes ago      Up 25 minutes
 0.0.0.0:7050->7050/tcp                           orderer.example.com
beffb4ce1f11        hyperledger/fabric-ca:x86_64-1.0.0         "sh -c 'fabric-ca-..."   25 minutes ago      Up 25 minutes
 0.0.0.0:7054->7054/tcp                           ca.example.com
```

Figure 13.4 Example terminal results for the docker ps command of the basic network.

```
2018-03-26 13:37:04.171 UTC [orderer/main] func1 -> DEBU 6a3 Closing Deliver stream
2018-03-26 13:37:04.613 UTC [orderer/main] Deliver -> DEBU 6a4 Starting new Deliver handler
2018-03-26 13:37:04.613 UTC [orderer/common/deliver] Handle -> DEBU 6a5 Starting new deliver loop
2018-03-26 13:37:04.614 UTC [orderer/common/deliver] Handle -> DEBU 6a6 Attempting to read seek info message
2018-03-26 13:37:04.614 UTC [policies] GetPolicy -> DEBU 6a7 Returning policy Readers for evaluation
2018-03-26 13:37:04.614 UTC [cauthdsl] func1 -> DEBU 6a8 0xc420122010 gate 1522071424614100888 evaluation starts
2018-03-26 13:37:04.614 UTC [cauthdsl] func2 -> DEBU 6a9 0xc420122010 signed by 0 principal evaluation starts (used [false])
2018-03-26 13:37:04.614 UTC [cauthdsl] func2 -> DEBU 6aa 0xc420122010 processing identity 0 with bytes of 0a074f7267314d535012
fc052d2d2d2d2d424547494e202d2d2d2d2d0a4d4949434744434341622b67417749424167495156672466b6a587531366f4d764d766f7a54575148456a414b
42676771686b6a4f50515144416a427a4d5173770a43515944565151474574a56557a45544d42454741315554543424d4b5132467361575a76636d35705954
45574d425147413155454278 4d4e5532467549455a790a5957356a61584e6a627a455a4d426347413155454368 4d5162334a6e4d53356c654746746347786c
4c6d4e766254456344d426f4741315545417 84d54593245750a62334a6e4d53356c654746746347786c4c6d4e7662544165467730784f44417a4d6a4d794d44
41334d6a4661467730794f44417a4d6a41794d4441334d6a46610a4d467378437a414a42674e5642415954416c56544d524d774551594456515149457770 44
595778705a6d3979626d6c684d52597746415944565151484577315 40a59573467526e4a68626d4e7063324e764d5238774851594456515144457 85a775a57
56794d433576636d63784c6d5634595731776247555755 93239744d466b770a457759484b6f5a497a6a3043415159494b6f5a497a6a30444151634451674145
6d62467268626b326e45785748736d2b71346e2f395a594141302f44666461560a39707856395 02b434e6344664d426b6d63693771767949703262744 57253
3552685972356c577761734 14a6f694d68774930495175364e4e4d457377446759440a5652305041514 82f42415144416765414d417747413155644577 4542
2f7751434d4141774b7759445652306a42435177496f4167393971474b37356b424770560a703651766f4c476d324268643055683 6786e496d41655868494c
786337717777436759494b6f5a497a6a304541774944527741775241496763 7a4e5a61422b5a0a4f5967435950 5a6b7045682b3547654c4a4579445a594950
36336e564e6573334846454349484970487 65a703748677a445679726e7972556f714534566d33340a7831326a2b4b3568734c796e5a7852490a2d2d2d2d2d
454e44202d2d2d2d2d0a
2018-03-26 13:37:04.614 UTC [msp/identity] newIdentity -> DEBU 6ab Creating identity instance for ID &{Org1MSP 9fa8fd6e3594209
402fdcf1a13866e5393cf431727 84e1039ff793ffcfc1e212}
2018-03-26 13:37:04.614 UTC [cauthdsl] func2 -> DEBU 6ac 0xc420122010 identity 0 does not satisfy principal: The identity is a
 member of a different MSP (expected OrdererMSP, got Org1MSP)
2018-03-26 13:37:04.614 UTC [cauthdsl] func2 -> DEBU 6ad 0xc420122010 principal evaluation fails
2018-03-26 13:37:04.614 UTC [cauthdsl] func1 -> DEBU 6ae 0xc420122010 gate 1522071424614100888 evaluation fails
2018-03-26 13:37:04.614 UTC [cauthdsl] func1 -> DEBU 6af 0xc420122010 gate 1522071424614605886 evaluation starts
2018-03-26 13:37:04.614 UTC [cauthdsl] func2 -> DEBU 6b0 0xc420122010 signed by 0 principal evaluation starts (used [false])
2018-03-26 13:37:04.614 UTC [cauthdsl] func2 -> DEBU 6b1 0xc420122010 processing identity 0 with bytes of 0a074f7267314d535012
fc052d2d2d2d2d424547494e202d2d2d2d2d0a4d4949434744434341622b67417749424167495156672466b6a587531366f4d764d766f7a54575148456a414b
42676771686b6a4f50515144416a427a4d5173770a43515944565151474574a56557a45544d42454741315554543424d4b5132467361575a76636d35705954
45574d425147413155454278 4d4e5532467549455a790a5957356a61584e6a627a455a4d426347413155454368 4d5162334a6e4d53356c654746746347786c
4c6d4e766254456344d426f4741315545417 84d54593245750a62334a6e4d53356c654746746347786c4c6d4e7662544165467730784f44417a4d6a4d794d44
41334d6a4661467730794f44417a4d6a41794d4441334d6a46610a4d467378437a414a42674e5642415954416c56544d524d774551594456515149457770 44
595778705a6d3979626d6c684d52597746415944565151484577315 40a59573467526e4a68626d4e7063324e764d5238774851594456515144457 85a775a57
56794d433576636d63784c6d5634595731776247555755 93239744d466b770a457759484b6f5a497a6a3043415159494b6f5a497a6a30444151634451674145
6d62467268626b326e45785748736d2b71346e2f395a594141302f44666461560a39707856395 02b434e6344664d426b6d63693771767949703262744 57253
3552685972356c577761734 14a6f694d68774930495175364e4e4d457377446759440a5652305041514 82f42415144416765414d417747413155644577 4542
2f7751434d4141774b7759445652306a42435177496f4167393971474b37356b424770560a703651766f4c476d324268643055683 6786e496d41655868494c
786337717777436759494b6f5a497a6a304541774944527741775241496763 7a4e5a61422b5a0a4f5967435950 5a6b7045682b3547654c4a4579445a594950
36336e564e6573334846454349484970487 65a703748677a445679726e7972556f714534566d33340a7831326a2b4b3568734c796e5a7852490a2d2d2d2d2d
454e44202d2d2d2d2d0a
2018-03-26 13:37:04.614 UTC [msp/identity] newIdentity -> DEBU 6b2 Creating identity instance for ID &{Org1MSP 9fa8fd6e3594209
402fdcf1a13866e5393cf431727 84e1039ff793ffcfc1e212}
2018-03-26 13:37:04.614 UTC [msp] SatisfiesPrincipal -> DEBU 6b3 Checking if identity satisfies MEMBER role for Org1MSP
2018-03-26 13:37:04.614 UTC [msp] Validate -> DEBU 6b4 MSP Org1MSP validating identity
2018-03-26 13:37:04.615 UTC [cauthdsl] func2 -> DEBU 6b5 0xc420122010 principal matched by identity 0
2018-03-26 13:37:04.615 UTC [msp/identity] Verify -> DEBU 6b6 Verify: digest = 00000000  3d 16 07 d3 a4 cd a4 e6  9f 77 0f 44
cd 3c 54 8f  |=.......w.D.<T.|
00000010  25 a4 06 3b 47 4a fe 16  6e a1 00 0d b3 85 05 4c  |%..;GJ..n......L|
2018-03-26 13:37:04.615 UTC [msp/identity] Verify -> DEBU 6b7 Verify: sig = 00000000  30 45 02 21 00 90 36 b8  1e 0b 44 fc 1f
50 45 f2  |0E.!..6...D..PE.|
00000010  99 ee af 4c ed a1 3b a1  2a 76 c4 5b 09 d2 dc b0  |...L..;.*v.[....|
00000020  02 53 8f 6b 72 02 20 1c  7f f5 dd e3 d4 84 f3 15  |.S.kr. .........|
00000030  a8 ae ab b5 12 70 26 10  8b 34 17 ad 40 e8 e5 c8  |.....p&..4..@...|
00000040  27 cb cb 4b 32 29 28                             |'..K2)(|
2018-03-26 13:37:04.615 UTC [cauthdsl] func2 -> DEBU 6b8 0xc420122010 principal evaluation succeeds for identity 0
2018-03-26 13:37:04.615 UTC [cauthdsl] func1 -> DEBU 6b9 0xc420122010 gate 1522071424614605886 evaluation succeeds
2018-03-26 13:37:04.616 UTC [orderer/common/sigfilter] Apply -> DEBU 6ba Forwarding validly signed message for policy &{%!s(*c
ommon.ImplicitMetaPolicy=&{Readers 0}) %!s(int=1) [%!s(*policies.implicitMetaPolicy=&{0xc4202cfe40 1 [0xc420195008]}) %!s(*pol
icies.implicitMetaPolicy=&{0xc4202cf540 1 [0xc420194f68]})]}
2018-03-26 13:37:04.616 UTC [orderer/common/deliver] Handle -> DEBU 6bb [channel: mychannel] Received seekInfo (0xc420bfe3e0)
start:<specified:<number:1 > > stop:<specified:<number:18446744073709551615 > >
```

Figure 13.5 Terminal view of the output logs produced by the orderer node.

For situations where the developer wants to display a real-time feed of the logs, the developer can include the —follow command; for example:

```
docker logs -follow orderer.example.com
```

This command will occupy your terminal indefinitely until the docker container is stopped. If the developer intends to do this, make sure that it is done in a spare opened terminal dedicated to the real-time log feed of that docker container.

Congratulations, at this point a basic Hyperledger Fabric network has been started up and observed. To take the network down, the developer can use the stop script file. The stop file can be executed in a Linux terminal using the following command:

```
./stop.sh
```

The main command that is used is the following:

```
docker-compose -f docker-compose.yml stop
```

This command will stop the containers but save their current settings in the docker environment for later use. To stop and kill the containers in order to use the name or other unique settings with other containers the developer could use the teardown.sh by executing the following command in a Linux terminal:

```
./teardown.sh
```

The main command that is used is the following:

```
docker-compose -f docker-compose.yml down
```

This command essentially does the opposite of the up command; the up command initializes and starts up the containers, the down stops the containers and then removes their content from the docker environment. In general, the docker environment will keep a cache of previously used container images in its local library to speed up the startup process in case the developer decides to use those images later.

13.2.5 Running the Kafka Network

In the prior section, the basic network was started. The basic network used a simple solo consensus mechanism where all transactions in the system are verified with one of the peers only. This type of system is great for starting up very simplistic prototype networks. It is beneficial because the basic communication structure between a single peer, orderer, and client can be tested. Once this is confirmed, the user can run a more complex system where a more distributed decentralized consensus is required. In these types of systems, more peer nodes are required to run certain consensus algorithms. In the case of the next example, the Kafka consensus will require a minimum of one orderer node, a peer node per channel or organization, four Kafka nodes, and three zookeeper nodes. In addition, a client node will be started to interact with the Kafka network.

To start this network, navigate to the directory titled "Kafka". In this directory, there are a few config yaml files, a directory with generated system files such as the genesis block and channel information, and a directory with the cryptographic credentials for each node to use. In the basic-network example, a script was used to start up the network; in this example, we will use the docker-compose command to start up the orderer-Kafka.yaml network. The command to do this is:

```
docker-compose -f orderer-Kafka.yaml up
```

Figure 13.6 Terminal output for the Kafka example.

After running this, the developer should see outputs from each of the peer nodes, the Kafka nodes, the zookeeper nodes, and the orderer. These log outputs let you, the developer, know each container is up and running. If all of the containers start up but an error is presented, this is not catastrophic and the system can still perform as expected. Figure 13.6 shows an image of the orderer-Kafka start up and a minor http error:

To ensure that everything is running correctly, a docker ps command is given. The developer should see something like Figure 13.7, where there is a client node, four peer nodes (two for each organization), an orderer, four Kafka nodes, and three zookeeper nodes.

```
docker ps
```

In this example, the client node will communicate with a peer node that will communicate with the orderer node, and the orderer node will trust the Kafka nodes to verify the order of the message based on a consensus amongst the nodes utilizing the zookeepers. To execute commands with the client node, the

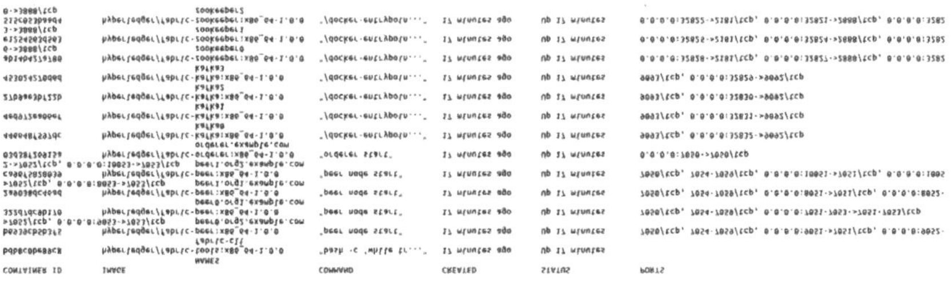

Figure 13.7 Terminal results for the docker ps command while running the Kafka system.

developer could ssh into that container using the exec command with the –it flag and the containers name. For example, to ssh into the client we would use the command:

```
docker exec -it fabric-cli bash
```

This will bring up a terminal of the fabric-cli container with the user as root. The developer can now execute commands on the client node. Displaying the contents of the default directory of the container (opt/gopath/src/github.com/hyperledger/fabric/peer), the developer will see three directories, with the one of most importance to the developer being the scripts directory. The scripts directory is a copy from the development machine. Located in the bookchapter directory, as described at the beginning of this section under project files, the directory scripts is the folder that is copied to the client node. If the developer wishes to make changes to the script files in this directory, it is best to do so before starting up the docker network as the files are copied at the startup of the containers. The scripts folder contains script files (.sh) that can be used to handle large and tedious commands to interact with the blockchain network. The script to run is the initialize_all.sh file by running the command from the default folder:

```
bash./scripts/initialize_all.sh
```

Executing this command will do several things that will take a minute or so; it is important to wait until the script prints all good and shows a large END sign like in Figure 13.8.

Once the script has finished running, the developer can scroll up to see everything that has run. The script has initialized a channel to operate the business-channel, established peer roles for the multiple organizations, then installed the example chaincode on two of the peers, one for each organization. Once the chaincode is started, a new docker container is started up on the machine that is hosting the docker containers. A chaincode container will start for each peer node to use. After the chaincode is installed, it is instantiated with an initial transaction. To ensure that the chaincode was installed for each peer, check the docker ps command one more time. The developer should see something similar to Figure 13.9.

The images with the name that starts dev- are the chaincode. Just as was done with other containers, the developer can always check the logs of the chaincode containers to receive any logs established in the chaincode source code.

To take down the Hyperledger Fabric Kafka network, first exit the fabric client by simply using the exit command:

```
exit
```

```
2018-03-26 20:42:37.924 UTC [chaincodeCmd] install -> DEBU 00f Installed remotely response:<status:200 payload:"OK" >
2018-03-26 20:42:37.924 UTC [main] main -> INFO 010 Exiting.....
===================== Chaincode is installed on remote peer PEER3 =====================

Instantiating chaincode on all 2 channels (once for each channel)...
CORE_PEER_TLS_ROOTCERT_FILE=/opt/gopath/src/github.com/hyperledger/fabric/peer/crypto/peerOrganizations/org1.example.com
/peers/peer0.org1.example.com/tls/ca.crt
CORE_PEER_TLS_KEY_FILE=/opt/gopath/src/github.com/hyperledger/fabric/peer/crypto/peerOrganizations/org1.example.com/peer
s/peer0.org1.example.com/tls/server.key
CORE_PEER_LOCALMSPID=Org1MSP
CORE_PEER_TLS_CERT_FILE=/opt/gopath/src/github.com/hyperledger/fabric/peer/crypto/peerOrganizations/org1.example.com/pee
rs/peer0.org1.example.com/tls/server.crt
CORE_PEER_TLS_ENABLED=true
CORE_PEER_MSPCONFIGPATH=/opt/gopath/src/github.com/hyperledger/fabric/peer/crypto/peerOrganizations/org1.example.com/use
rs/Admin@org1.example.com/msp
CORE_PEER_ID=fabric-cli
CORE_LOGGING_LEVEL=DEBUG
CORE_PEER_ADDRESS=peer0.org1.example.com:7051
cat: 'log.txtm[A]': No such file or directory
===================== Chaincode Instantiation on PEER0 on channel 'businesschannel' is successful =====================

CORE_PEER_TLS_ROOTCERT_FILE=/opt/gopath/src/github.com/hyperledger/fabric/peer/crypto/peerOrganizations/org2.example.com
/peers/peer0.org2.example.com/tls/ca.crt
CORE_PEER_TLS_KEY_FILE=/opt/gopath/src/github.com/hyperledger/fabric/peer/crypto/peerOrganizations/org1.example.com/peer
s/peer0.org1.example.com/tls/server.key
CORE_PEER_LOCALMSPID=Org2MSP
CORE_PEER_TLS_CERT_FILE=/opt/gopath/src/github.com/hyperledger/fabric/peer/crypto/peerOrganizations/org1.example.com/pee
rs/peer0.org1.example.com/tls/server.crt
CORE_PEER_TLS_ENABLED=true
CORE_PEER_MSPCONFIGPATH=/opt/gopath/src/github.com/hyperledger/fabric/peer/crypto/peerOrganizations/org2.example.com/use
rs/Admin@org2.example.com/msp
CORE_PEER_ID=fabric-cli
CORE_LOGGING_LEVEL=DEBUG
CORE_PEER_ADDRESS=peer0.org2.example.com:7051
cat: 'log.txtm[A]': No such file or directory
===================== Chaincode Instantiation on PEER2 on channel 'businesschannel' is successful =====================


===================== All GOOD, initialization completed =====================


 _____   _   _   ____
| ____| | \ | | |  _ \
|  _|   |  \| | | | | |
| |___  | |\  | | |_| |
|_____| |_| \_| |____/

root@fabric-cli:/opt/gopath/src/github.com/hyperledger/fabric/peer# |
```

Figure 13.8 Terminal output from the initialize_all script that runs and tests the Kafka blockchain.

```
CONTAINER ID        IMAGE                                       COMMAND                  CREATED             STATUS
         PORTS                                                                                                  NAMES
f2e4d99a9978        dev-peer0.org2.example.com-mycc9-1.0        "chaincode -peer.a..."   2 hours ago         Up 2 hours
                                                                                                                dev-peer0.
org2.example.com-mycc9-1.0
16fb35bd76d8        dev-peer0.org1.example.com-mycc9-1.0        "chaincode -peer.a..."   2 hours ago         Up 2 hours
                                                                                                                dev-peer0.
org1.example.com-mycc9-1.0
bdb8c0be89c8        hyperledger/fabric-tools:x86_64-1.0.0       "bash -c 'while tr..."   2 hours ago         Up 2 hours
                                                                                                                fabric-cli
b6939cb5b3f5        hyperledger/fabric-peer:x86_64-1.0.0        "peer node start"        2 hours ago         Up 2 hours
         7050/tcp, 7054-7059/tcp, 0.0.0.0:9051->7051/tcp, 0.0.0.0:9052->7052/tcp, 0.0.0.0:9053->7053/tcp        peer0.org2
.example.com
322d7dc9b170        hyperledger/fabric-peer:x86_64-1.0.0        "peer node start"        2 hours ago         Up 2 hours
         7050/tcp, 7054-7059/tcp, 0.0.0.0:7051-7053->7051-7053/tcp                                              peer0.org1
.example.com
2a9038dc46ad        hyperledger/fabric-peer:x86_64-1.0.0        "peer node start"        2 hours ago         Up 2 hours
         7050/tcp, 7054-7059/tcp, 0.0.0.0:8051->7051/tcp, 0.0.0.0:8052->7052/tcp, 0.0.0.0:8053->7053/tcp        peer1.org1
.example.com
ca96f5828039        hyperledger/fabric-peer:x86_64-1.0.0        "peer node start"        2 hours ago         Up 2 hours
         7050/tcp, 7054-7059/tcp, 0.0.0.0:10051->7051/tcp, 0.0.0.0:10052->7052/tcp, 0.0.0.0:10053->7053/tcp     peer1.org2
.example.com
03d38f26915a        hyperledger/fabric-orderer:x86_64-1.0.0     "orderer start"          2 hours ago         Up 2 hours
         0.0.0.0:7050->7050/tcp                                                                                 orderer.ex
ample.com
446648f597dc        hyperledger/fabric-kafka:x86_64-1.0.0       "/docker-entrypoin..."   2 hours ago         Up 2 hours
         9093/tcp, 0.0.0.0:32832->9092/tcp                                                                      kafka0
4ed972ea06ef        hyperledger/fabric-kafka:x86_64-1.0.0       "/docker-entrypoin..."   2 hours ago         Up 2 hours
         9093/tcp, 0.0.0.0:32831->9092/tcp                                                                      kafka1
27b9ae3bf22b        hyperledger/fabric-kafka:x86_64-1.0.0       "/docker-entrypoin..."   2 hours ago         Up 2 hours
         9093/tcp, 0.0.0.0:32830->9092/tcp                                                                      kafka2
453024270d6d        hyperledger/fabric-kafka:x86_64-1.0.0       "/docker-entrypoin..."   2 hours ago         Up 2 hours
         9093/tcp, 0.0.0.0:32829->9092/tcp                                                                      kafka3
ab14b427a780        hyperledger/fabric-zookeeper:x86_64-1.0.0   "/docker-entrypoin..."   2 hours ago         Up 2 hours
         0.0.0.0:32828->2181/tcp, 0.0.0.0:32827->2888/tcp, 0.0.0.0:32826->3888/tcp                              zookeeper0
e1254563d563        hyperledger/fabric-zookeeper:x86_64-1.0.0   "/docker-entrypoin..."   2 hours ago         Up 2 hours
         0.0.0.0:32825->2181/tcp, 0.0.0.0:32824->2888/tcp, 0.0.0.0:32823->3888/tcp                              zookeeper1
515c053baad4        hyperledger/fabric-zookeeper:x86_64-1.0.0   "/docker-entrypoin..."   2 hours ago         Up 2 hours
         0.0.0.0:32822->2181/tcp, 0.0.0.0:32821->2888/tcp, 0.0.0.0:32820->3888/tcp                              zookeeper2
```

Figure 13.9 Terminal output from the docker ps command; notice the chaincode containers that have been started.

Once back in the development machine, use the docker-compose tool to bring down the network with the command:

```
docker-compose -f orderer-Kafka.yaml down
```

This will stop all the containers and clear out the necessary content to allow the system to be restarted with a different network setup. This process will take a few seconds to a minute and will produce an output like Figure 13.10 when it is finished.

The developer can confirm that the containers have been taken down by running a docker ps command to ensure there aren't any containers running from the given examples.

```
Stopping fabric-cli ... done
Stopping peer0.org2.example.com ... done
Stopping peer0.org1.example.com ... done
Stopping peer1.org1.example.com ... done
Stopping peer1.org2.example.com ... done
Stopping orderer.example.com ... done
Stopping kafka0 ... done
Stopping kafka1 ... done
Stopping kafka2 ... done
Stopping kafka3 ... done
Stopping zookeeper0 ... done
Stopping zookeeper1 ... done
Stopping zookeeper2 ... done
Removing fabric-cli ... done
Removing peer0.org2.example.com ... done
Removing peer0.org1.example.com ... done
Removing peer1.org1.example.com ... done
Removing peer1.org2.example.com ... done
Removing orderer.example.com ... done
Removing kafka0 ... done
Removing kafka1 ... done
Removing kafka2 ... done
Removing kafka3 ... done
Removing zookeeper0 ... done
Removing zookeeper1 ... done
Removing zookeeper2 ... done
Removing network kafka_default
```

Figure 13.10 Terminal output after stopping the network.

13.3 Measures of Performance

When it comes to blockchain performance, there are several quantitative measures that are important. The performance measures can be improved but often come at a cost to security from increasing the centralization of the blockchain system. It is recognized that centralized systems have a better ability to function at a higher performance. This is mostly because consensus is not needed, leaving the performance metrics to how quickly the single machine can receive the message and process the request. The decentralized blockchain systems require a latency-dependent message and a process of consensus among the verifying nodes. When it comes to the performance of blockchain systems, it is very common to refer to the best performance metric as the measure of transactions per second (TPS).

Transactions per second can be defined in a couple of ways. As a basic measure, transactions per second is the rate at which the system can process a transaction. This can be measured in several ways—the time it takes one of the verifying nodes to completely write a transaction to the local ledger, the time it takes a majority of nodes to completely write the transaction to their individual ledgers, or the total number of transactions per time segment (often utilizing some method to batch), or the time it takes to process multiple transactions concurrently. The first described transaction can be referred to as the single transaction per second measure, and the second type of measure is total system transactions. In this case, the system might not have the fastest single transaction per second measure but can process many transactions a little slower, resulting in a larger number of transactions per time segment. In most real-world scenarios, the developers are mostly concerned with the maximum number of transactions the system can process within a second and tend to not be as concerned with the metric of a single transaction. However, the single transaction metric can be an important metric when comparing system performance from the developer's perspective, especially when there are opportunities to improve systems by adding methods of batching or parallel processing. The single transaction can offer a common ground measurement that allows for an apple to apples comparison.

Figure 13.11 shows the process of measuring a single TPS for a blockchain system. The simplest way to measure TPS is to record the start time a transaction was sent, then immediately start querying the blockchain system when the transaction that was sent finally shows up in the query record at the finish time. Take the difference of the finish time and the start time. This is the time to process a single transaction. In decentralized systems, there is often noise that can cause delays in the transaction such as networking issues or processing load on the verifying nodes, so it is a better idea to repeat this for a number of transactions. The number of transactions should depend on the variance that is observed from initial tests; the more variance the

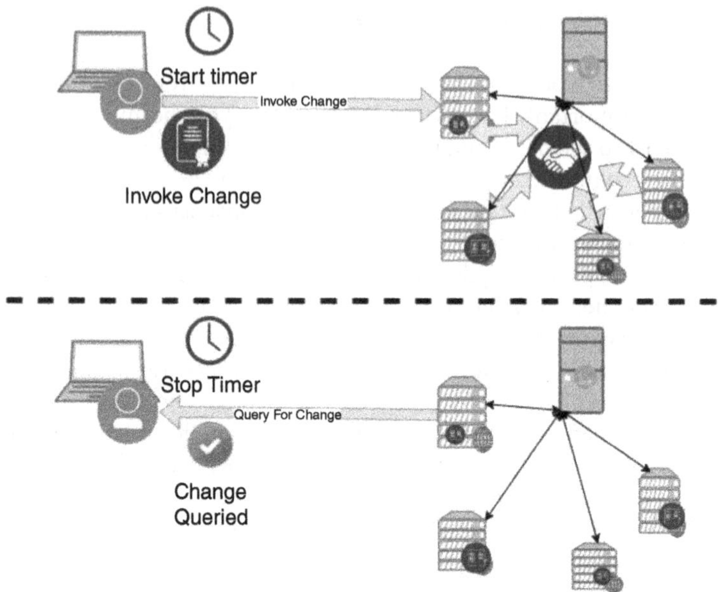

Figure 13.11 Illustration of the process to measure a single transaction per second.

developer sees in the measures of transactions per second, the more measures or samples that should be recorded in order to produce a good representation of the system. The transactions per second can then be described with simple descriptive statistics such as maximum, minimum, mean, mode, and standard deviation.

Figure 13.12 shows the process of measuring the total system TPS for a blockchain system. This becomes a little more challenging because transactions would likely be coming from many sources all at the same time. To measure total system TPS, the developer will often need to create a recording mechanism on one or many of the validating nodes. The measuring tool can now internally measure the time at which a transaction is reported on the system, and the time at which the peer node is authorized or recognizes that consensus is found to write the transaction to the ledger. There is a lot of detail that is not recorded in this method as the network time of when the transaction is initiated is not recorded. This method also provides the total system time as perceived from one of the verifying nodes. If this method is used, it is probably best to use the same method on multiple verifying nodes, then compare the results of many transactions. This will provide a sample that best represents the total system TPS and descriptive statistics can then be used to show the performance such as maximum, minimum, mean, median, mode, and standard deviation.

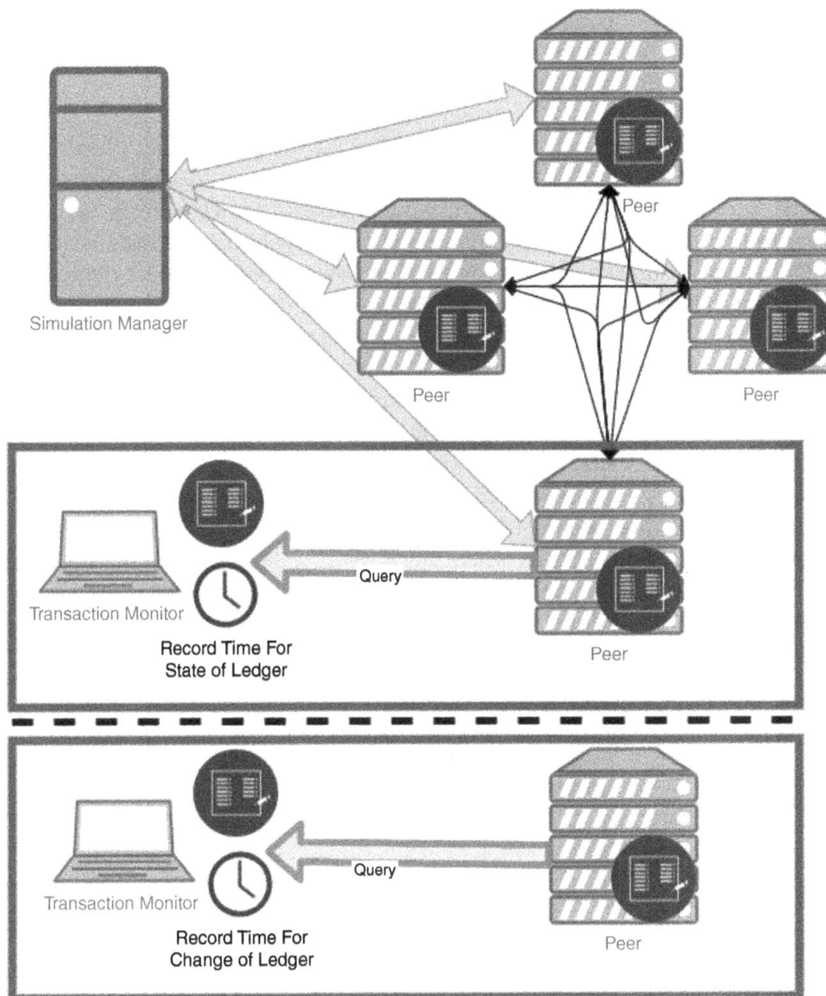

Figure 13.12 Illustration of measuring total system transactions per second.

13.3.1 Performance Metrics With the Proof-of-Stake Simulation

In this section, we provide the performance metrics for a proof-of-stake protocol [3]. Performance metrics are set up in the described simulation and include:

- Average stake claimed per validator.
- Average and total times each validator was the leader.
- Total number of times a leader was selected as validator but did not have the highest stake amount.

- Average, max./min. iterations to find a leader.
- Average, max./min. time in milliseconds to make progress and extend the blockchain with a new block.

These performance metrics were recorded for various number of validator nodes and various number of transactions for 30 different tests to allow for a good representation of the results since the simulation uses stochastic variables for selection of stake and delay. Initially, best-case scenarios are tested without delay to get a ground truth understanding of how the proof of stake application is working. The number of validators has a very large effect on the performance of this algorithm mostly because of the round robin nature of all the validators when selecting a leader. Figure 13.13 illustrates the performance of a PoS-enabled blockchain given an ideal scenario of negligible network delay and stake allocation delay. In this case, the latency of the consensus process is majorly dependent on the leader selection procedure. This latency variation over 30 experiments gives us an estimated ideal time of extending the blockchain with a new block. In other words, the duration of an ideal epoch is going be in the range of 0.4–0.8 milliseconds when there are 10 validators, and 0.1 milliseconds when five validators are present. As the number of validators increase, it is obvious that the leader election process takes more time to definitively find a leader, which is why average latency is increased.

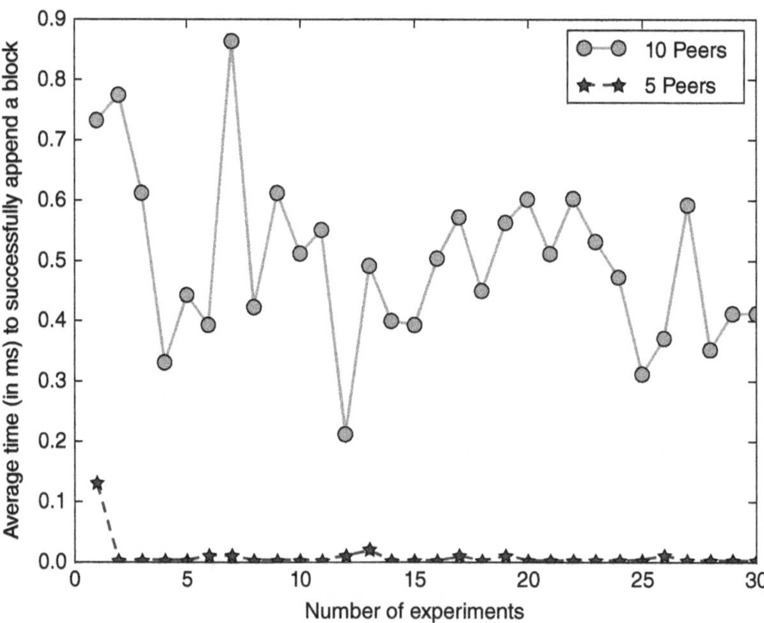

Figure 13.13 Example output of performance in simulated proof-of-stake blockchain system.

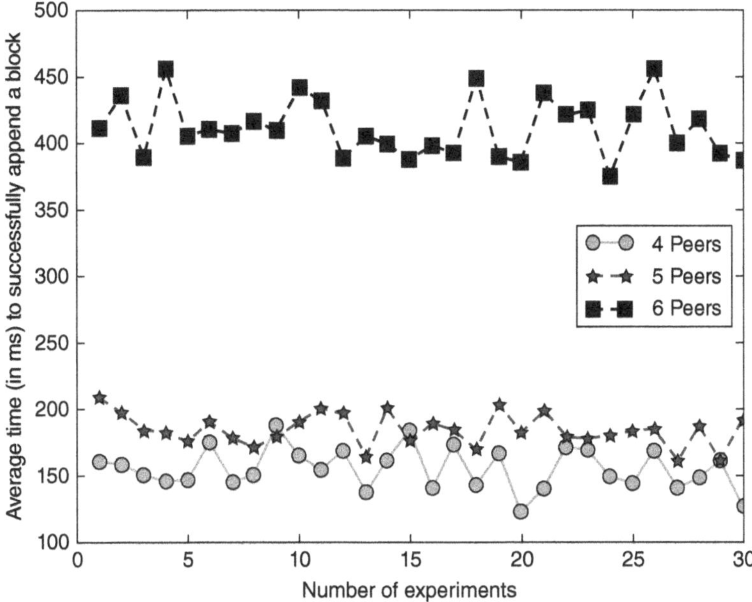

Figure 13.14 Example output of performance in simulated proof-of-stake blockchain system with communication delay added.

In Figure 13.14, a similar experiment is conducted but with the introduction of random communication delay. The delay component is sampled from a normal distribution in the range of 1–5 milliseconds. The 30 experimental rounds show that even with the presence of network delay, our PoS consensus eventually extends the blockchain and hence satisfies safety and liveness properties.

Experiments were and can be run to see whether the majority of stakeholders are always taking the opportunity to become a leader, or the minority group of validators have a chance to include their block in the blockchain. For this, tests were simulated with the prototype for 100 blocks and it was checked how many times a leader is selected in an epoch that does not have the highest stake in the system. The variation depicted in Figure 13.15 shows that a validator from the minority group of stakeholders is selected more than 50% of the time on average, which means that the highest stake holding validator does not get elected as leader all the time. It is interesting to notice that as the number of validators increase, the selected leader is most likely to fall in the minority category because the stake values will be closely distributed and hence the election timeouts will also be similarly distributed. Thus, it is preferred to have more validators in the system to make it fairer in terms of the leader selection process.

Optimization goals—Current implementation considers that stake allocation and verification occur at the beginning of every epoch, which can be a major bottleneck in the protocol. Since stake allocation requires adjustment of the

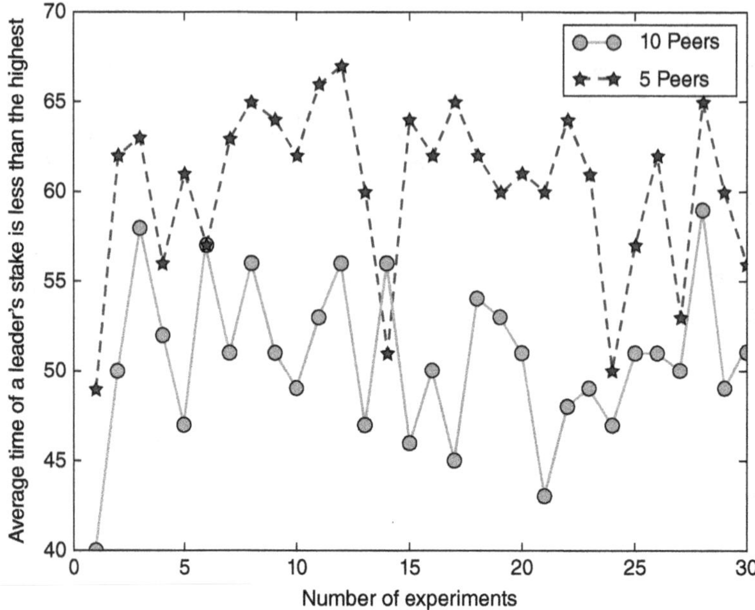

Figure 13.15 Example output reporting the average number of times the highest staked holder did not get elected as validation leader in the proof-of-stake process.

actual resource utilization dynamically, it could result in extra delay before any validator can verify the staked resource. In order to bypass this issue, we can enforce the staking of resources by validators for a fixed amount of time that is more than a typical epoch duration. A smart contract can be used for this purpose to prohibit the release of stakes before the agreed staking time, which can be a regulatory condition for becoming a validator in the distributed computing system.

13.3.2 Performance Measures With the Hyperledger Fabric Example

The Hyperledger Fabric blockchain system has the ability to plug in various consensus methods. Throughout the development of Hyperledger Fabric there have been several versions and consensus methods that have been tried and provided. Each consensus algorithm can provide a means for the decentralized peer-to-peer system to agree on the order and validity of asynchronous transactions. Each algorithm does it with a different strategy. The provided consensus methods within Hyperledger Fabric that have been provided are solo consensus, practical Byzantine fault tolerant consensus, and Kafka consensus.

The basic consensus method, which is more centralized, is referred to as solo consensus shown in Figure 13.16 and is a good method to test systems.

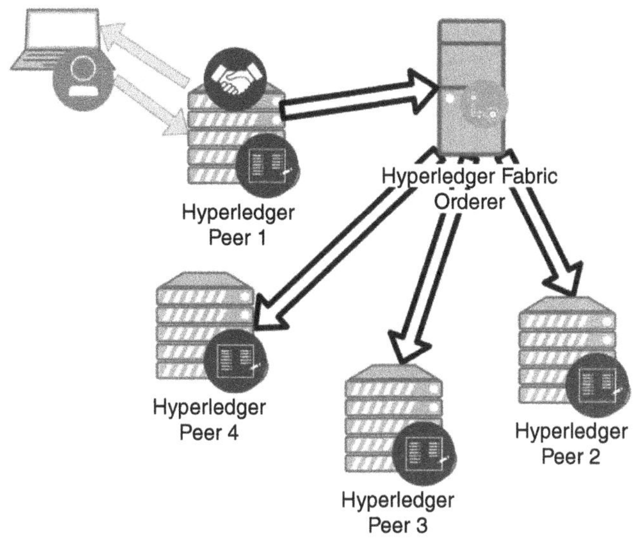

Figure 13.16 Illustration of a basic configuration of Hyperledger Fabric.

It is the method where a single node controls consensus for the transactions in the system. This is not recommended for a final production system as it is essentially a centralized blockchain system. In this case, a transaction is sent to an assigned peer, and the peer verifies the order of the transaction and writes the transaction to its ledger; if there are other nodes on the network, it broadcasts the transaction to the other nodes requesting that their ledgers also be updated. This system is not the best as there is a single point of failure to compromise the order of the transactions.

Practical Byzantine Fault Tolerant (PBFT) algorithm is based on the algorithm specified in [4]. This algorithm focuses on a strategy of many broadcasted messages. This consensus relies heavily on networked communication between all participating peer nodes. Figure 13.17 shows the process of the consensus, where a client starts with the message requesting an update to the blockchain. It is important to remember the scale of the situation; in an actual scenario, there are likely many clients sending requests to multiple peer nodes. The peer nodes need to utilize the PBFT algorithm to agree on the order of the messages received.

As a peer receives the message, it promptly broadcasts the message to all participating nodes. Each node receives the messages for a short period of time, and then responds to all nodes with a broadcast declaring what it believes is the order of the messages received to all participating nodes. Each node then observes the perspective of every other node's order of transactions. Each node then checks all the responses and if a consensus among all participating nodes

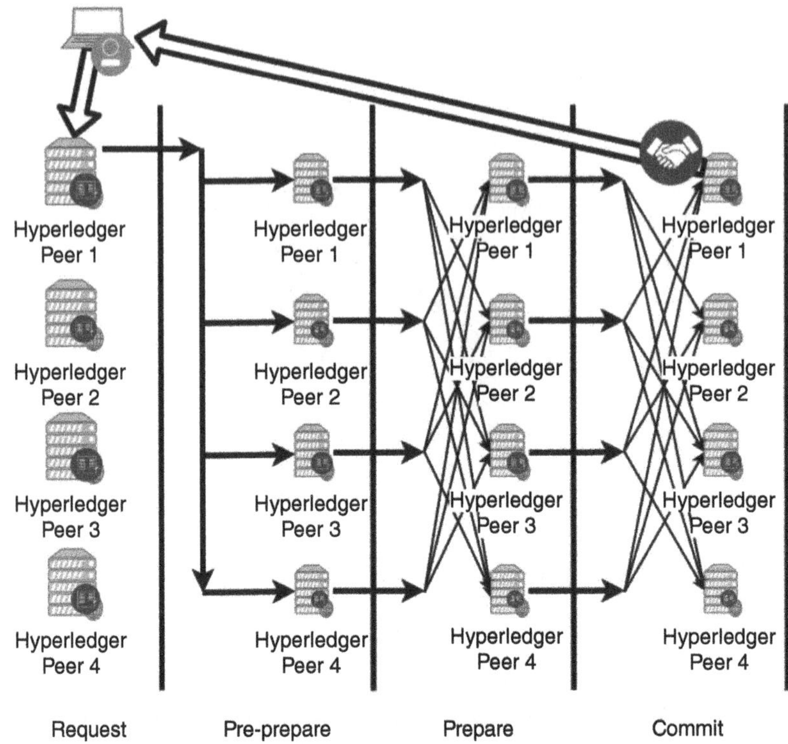

Figure 13.17 Illustration of a practical Byzantine fault tolerant consensus process.

is found, the peer nodes will write the request to the blockchain, and finally a response is sent to the client.

Comparisons for TPS were done for PBFT with Hyperledger Fabric 0.6, and Kafka with Hyperledger Fabric 1.0. The measure of TPS performed is the single transaction TPS. A client was run using a Python script that sends a transaction to the peer network, starts a timer, then repeatedly queries the blockchain until the expected result is produced; finally, the transaction timer is stopped and recorded. This occurs 1000 times to observe any fluctuations in the data. Example plots of the data produced by these tests are shown in Figure 13.18 for the PBFT results and in Figure 13.19 for the Kafka results.

The figures show how the TPS results can fluctuate and offer a quick glance at what amount of time it takes to process the single transaction. These results were generated with a simple network consisting of four peer nodes and one client, all on a local machine with virtual network using docker containers. The data can further be processed to populate a comparison table with descriptive statistics. Table 13.1 provides the results of descriptive statistics for both consensus algorithms.

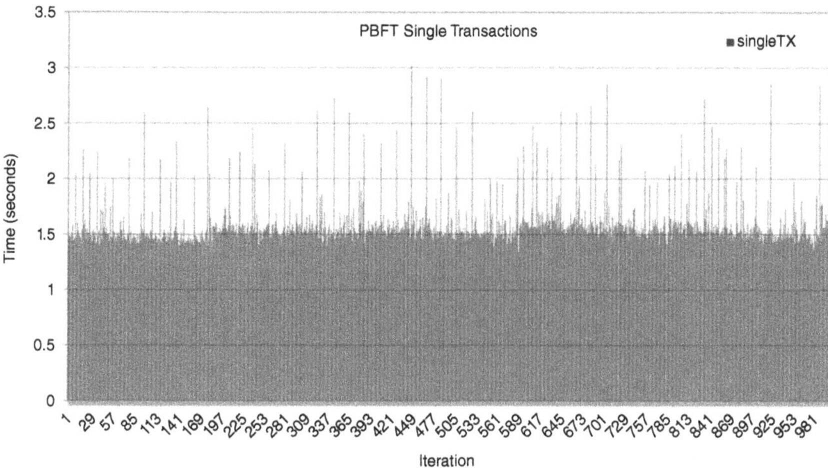

Figure 13.18 Performance in transactions per second to process a single transaction with PBFT consensus (Hyperledger Fabric 0.6).

The results can vary based on different scenarios, but in this simple test, PBFT was able to perform slightly better than Kafka. On average, the Kafka test took almost 1 second more to do a single transaction. The single transaction is a good benchmark to get an understanding but systems should also be observed in the total system TPS. Similar tests should be done with system TPS to give a representation of the system rather than just a single.

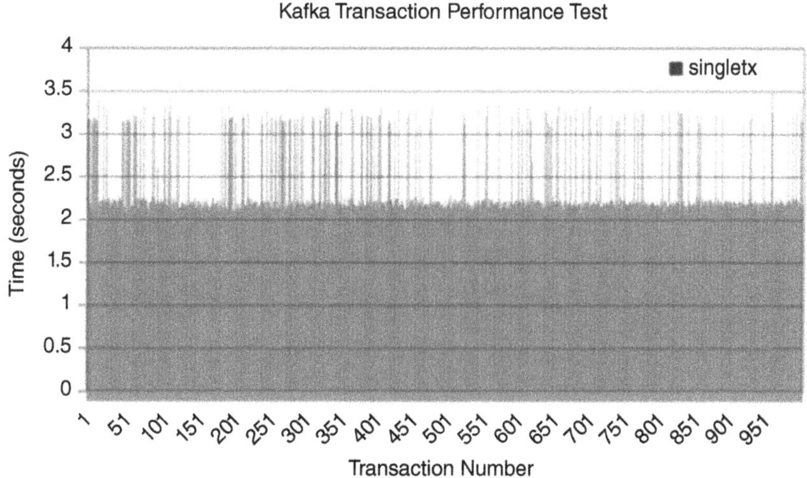

Figure 13.19 Performance in transactions per second to process a single transaction with Kafka consensus (Hyperledger Fabric 1.1).

Table 13.1 Sample results of performance metrics of single transaction per second for the PBFT and KAFKA consensus.

Consensus	PBFT (Hyperledger Fabric 0.6)	Kafka (Hyperledger Fabric 1.0)
Average (TPS)	1.59	2.37
Max. (TPS)	3.02	3.48
Min. (TPS)	1.34	2.09
Mode (TPS)	1.52	2.2

13.4 Simple Blockchain Simulation

A way to test different blockchain protocols is within a modeling and simulation environment. The benefit of using modeling and simulation is that the entire environment can be controlled. This can be important when specific components need to be tested. In actual implementations within a physical system, a lot of unknown variance can occur in the results from the additional components involved in the decentralized system. These additional variances are important to note and be aware of but can distort the analysis of components such as the consensus method. A simulation environment was developed to be able to test consensus methods and is described in this chapter. Information on how the simulation was developed, how other simulations can be developed for blockchain systems, and how to use the simulation described in this chapter is provided.

The implementation of the blockchain system is built within a custom C# application and simulation. The implementation uses a simple list data structure that represents the distributed ledger as shown in Figure 13.20. By implementing the application within a simulated environment first, a full spectrum of tests can be performed on the various algorithms. This allows for testing extreme scenarios or provides a better control of the environment. With this capability, a good understanding of the best case and worst case can be gained, and lessons can be learned from these exercises. This also offers a unique opportunity to verify that the algorithm is working as expected and provides a good way to document its effectiveness before a live or production version is implemented.

The simulation is developed as a test application where several validator nodes, a simulation controller, and associated blockchain infrastructure are spun up when started as shown in Figure 13.21. The blockchain architecture is a simple data structure based on a linked list where each block on the list is an object consisting of a hash value, key value, and message. The hash and message are represented by a byte array and the key value is represented as an integer. Adding a new block utilizes the hash value of the prior block and the

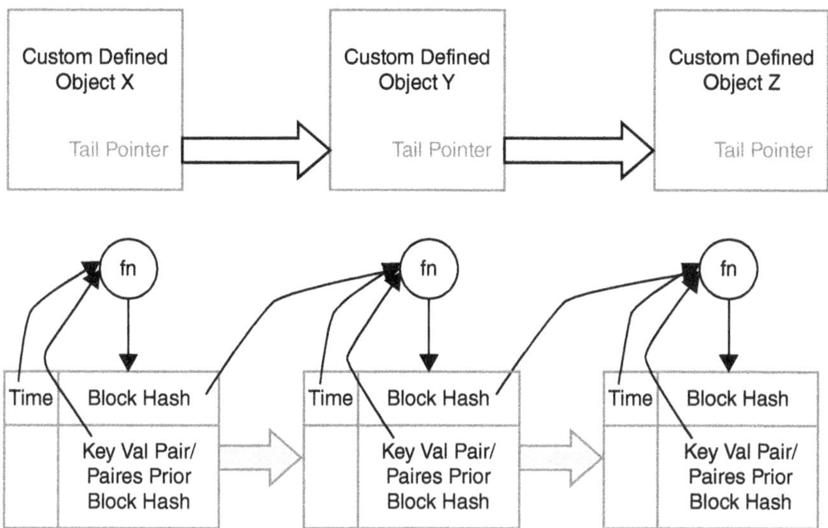

Figure 13.20 Illustration of linked list similarities to blockchain data structures.

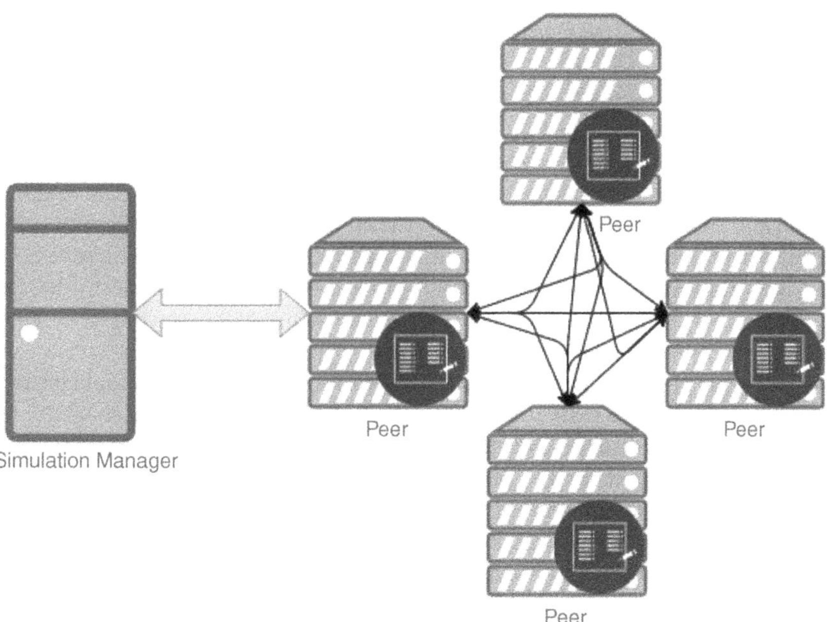

Figure 13.21 Illustration of a simulated blockchain system.

message of the new block to compute the new hash value. The hash algorithm used is SHA 256 from the C# system cryptography library. Different hash algorithms can be used instead if it is desired to test other hashing algorithms.

The original consensus algorithm that is tested with the simulated environment is a proof-of-stake algorithm. Each validator object in the simulation has a copy of the ledger that it hosts and uses to compare to the latest state of other validators and to append future data to when consensus has been derived. The validator object can choose a desired stake based on a random distribution or a set value for testing. The desired stake value is used as the mean value in a normal distribution that is used to select its current stake. Each validator's stake value is designed as a value between 0 and 100, which would be the amount of resources the validator is putting on hold for the proof-of-stake system. A delay is introduced in the simulation to the process where the validator selects its stake, representing the time it would take to occupy the resources. A delay can also be introduced in the process where validator nodes communicate with each other to represent some network delay.

The simulation controller runs the simulation, directing the flow of communication, and keeps track of statistical measures for analysis. The algorithm described above is implemented in the simulation controller and the validator object. The user tells the simulation controller how many validators are to be used and the number of transactions to be processed. With this information, the controller initializes everything and creates the gen block on the ledger that all validators receive.

Once the validators have their ledger, they are the sole controller of what can be written to their ledger. The controller then directs all validator objects to select their stake for the upcoming transaction. The controller compiles all validator nodes' claimed stake along with a weighted list based on each validator's stake and shares that information with the all nodes on the network. Next, the leader selection process is started. At this point, a timer is started based on a set loop iteration and each validator will have the ability to request a leader a set number of times before the leader selection process is started over. That selected number of times is based on their chosen stake. Of course, if consensus is met in this process with all validator nodes as to who the leader should be, the simulation controller exits the loop, proceeds to allowing the chosen leader to validate, and broadcast to all validators to submit the transaction to their local ledgers. When the validators receive this broadcast message, they commence to writing the transaction to their blockchain.

The leader selection process is initiated by each validator in the system in a round robin fashion where each validator broadcasts its recommended leader based on a random selection from the weighted list of validator IDs by current stake allocation. Each validator receives the request, then checks to ensure that the sender's ID exists in the system, and the claimed leader stake is what the sender reported. If any of these are incorrect, the validator will return false indicating it does not agree with the recommended leader. If the preliminary data is good, the validator processing the recommendation will select its recommended leader from the same weighted list of validator IDs. If its selected leader ID equals the recommended leader ID from the broadcast message, it will respond with a true value. If a validator can obtain a true value from more than half of the network, it will be granted the leadership role. Once a validator is selected as the leader, it is granted permission to broadcast the validated message to all validators indicating they can submit the current transaction block to their ledger.

Performance metrics are set up in the described simulation but the quantification and measurement of performance is discussed in more detail in the blockchain performance section.

- Average stake claimed per validator.
- Average and total times each validator was the leader.
- Total number of times a leader was selected as validator but did not have the highest stake amount.
- Average, max./min. iterations to find a leader.
- Average, max./min. time in milliseconds to make progress and extend the blockchain with a new block.

Simulation of a decentralized system has its challenges. The decentralized nature can be difficult because of the asynchronous properties, the potential resources or scalability, and the parallel processing of the distributed system. This can be accomplished in one of two ways. The simulation can be distributed in a parallel processing type of simulated environment. This is quite possible, where each object representing a peer runs as an individual thread or as a node on a multicore and multiprocessor hardware system. This creates a system closest to the real system where each peer can process simultaneously. If the resources are not available, then the modeler can always use round robin types of techniques. The round robin techniques.

13.5 Blockchain Simulation Introduction

Described in the prior section was an example of how a blockchain system can be implemented using the open source toolset Hyperledger Fabric, and through a simulated environment. The section focuses more on the idea of integrating a blockchain system that is real and not simulated (often this is referred to as live), with a simulation of an environment or system. The reason for doing this would be to see the effects that a blockchain would have on an existing system. Tests like this can be built to show how the performance of the blockchain would make a difference to the simulation. It also provides a means to demonstrate the effectiveness of a blockchain system. Before a blockchain system is implemented, it might be best to test the proposed system in a simulation of the environment or process that it will be working with. This is also a benefit to very large or costly systems as it allows for exploration of the benefits before a costly implementation.

13.5.1 Methodology

Of the different paradigms of modeling and simulation, the paradigms that have entity representation tend to be better suited for use with blockchain technologies. In addition to entity-based models and simulations, the more dynamic types of simulation also make more sense where there is a heavy influence of time on the system. These types of simulation systems tend to be agent-based models and simulations and discrete event models and simulation. Agent-based models and simulations (ABMS) are representations or an abstraction of reality in which there are entities that make decisions for themselves based on the environment variables around them. Discrete event simulations (DES) are representations or an abstraction of realty in which the action or timing of the simulation is based on significant events. The difference between these two paradigms comes down to the representation or the advancement of time and the amount of intelligence required for an entity. It would be possible to apply the effects of a blockchain system as a measure of rate to other M&S paradigms such as system dynamics or other types of models without simulation. This could be achieved by producing quantitative values for performance and security metrics that can be used as parameters, weights, or rates in static models or flow-based dynamic models.

13.5.2 Simulation Integration With Live Blockchain

The prior sections described blockchain examples that were simulated and real/functioning. The simulation integration can be set up to utilize either one. Simulation can integrate with an actual real time blockchain, Figure 13.22 shows where a simulation might integrate with a Hyperledger Fabric system. The major challenges or restrictions preventing the simulation and the blockchain to be integrated are the challenge of timing between the two and the ability to integrate communication between the two. Many simulations are not built by default with communication protocols outside of the simulation but do offer advanced programming interfaces (API) and ways to program this capability.

The timing issue might be the hardest challenge, especially if the simulation is to interact with a real-time, actual blockchain system and not a simulated one. In this case, the simulation might be performing faster than real time. In the DES paradigm, this can be throttled to advance in time based on events from the blockchain system when interacting with the blockchain. In the case of a time stepped simulation that runs faster than real time, it can also be throttled back to only advance until after its interaction with the blockchain. The result

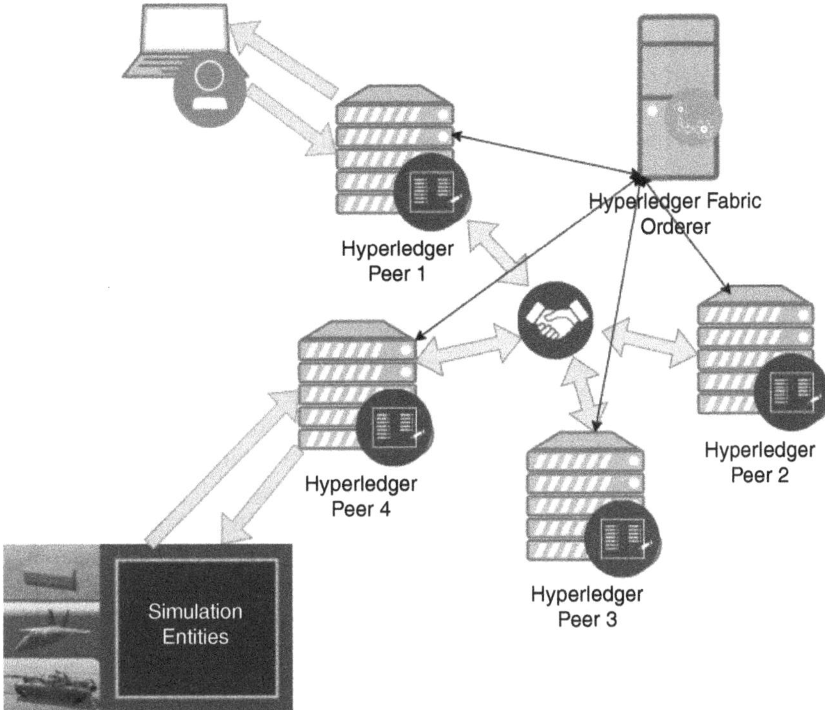

Figure 13.22 Illustration of a Hyperledger Fabric system connected and interacting with a simulated environment.

will be an overall slower simulation but should provide a successful integration of the real blockchain system with the simulation.

The actual integration might be an easier problem to solve, but this heavily depends on the ability of the simulator to communicate with systems outside of

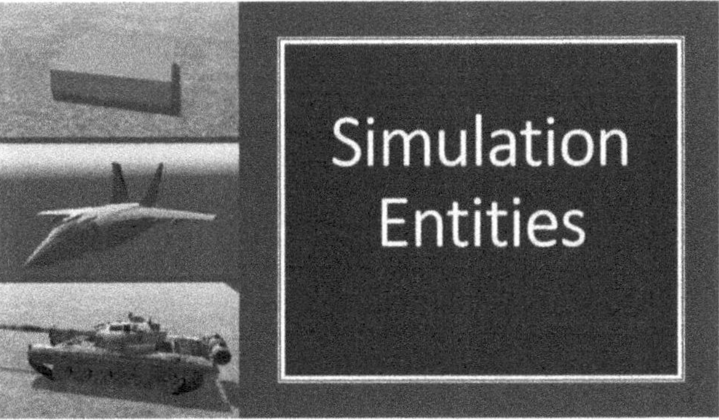

Figure 13.23 Image of the type of entities that are in the simulated world.

the simulation. If the simulator provides the ability program in these points of communication, the developers can simply program the messaging functions that are needed to interact with the blockchain using that API and any networking libraries that might be available to the language the API supports. The simulation can then be run, utilize inputs based on queries to the blockchain, and provide values and calls to the blockchain when state changes need to be recorded to the blockchain.

13.5.3 Simulation Integration With Simulated Blockchain

Simulation integration with simulated blockchain systems is a more natural combination as the timing and the communication can be tailored to be the same between both. If the modeler has access to the source code of the simulation, it is best to implement a blockchain representation within the simulation source code itself. Otherwise, the modeler will have to build a communication link between the simulation and the blockchain simulation. If a communication link is needed, the developer will need to make decisions on the implementation of the timing and communication in the same manner described earlier.

The biggest challenge will again come down to synchronization of the timing of the simulation and the blockchain simulation. For efficiency of the total system, it will be best to attempt to match the blockchain simulation time step scope with the simulation time step. Modeling a blockchain system in real time is clear as the representation of the communication flow and events are near real time. In the case of discrete event simulation, the blockchain does not necessarily need to model every aspect of the blockchain system. It should be modeled more as a queueing logistics problem. In order to achieve this, knowledge of transaction time metrics, bandwidth, and latency is needed. With this data, the interactions happening within the blockchain simulation will become actions based on values from distributions formed from the observed data. The queueing of messages and delay caused by the blockchain can still be simulated, but the details will be abstracted out to values of distributions. To extend the blockchain simulation to an even higher scope for flow-based models (for example system dynamics), the level of abstraction from the blockchain system will need to be further observed in higher level measures. This could simply be utilizing the measure of rates obtained from observations of the real blockchain system. The rates could reflect the average transaction time in various conditions, like bad network connectivity, bandwidth, and even the structure of the blockchain like number of peers, required computation of the smart contract, or consensus algorithm used.

13.5.4 Verification and Validation

It would be irresponsible to discuss the use of a simulation involving blockchain systems without mentioning the necessity of verification and validation of the models and simulations. Modelers must be aware of the inherent assumptions that exist when building abstractions of the real system. These assumptions can exist in how the data was generated, how the data was collected, and how the data was used in the actual modeling of the system. Once the blockchain simulation system is developed, it is strongly recommended that some time be dedicated to verification of the system or observation of the system's behavior to ensure that results of actions are behaving in the way that they were intended to.

It is also strongly recommended that the modeler dedicate data and time to validate the results of the blockchain simulation. An independent set of data should be recorded and stored for the intention of validation at the end of development. This independent set of data should not be used in the development of the model and simulation as this would be considered calibration; keep one set of data to be used to calibrate the model and a separate set of data to be used as a single check at the end to give a validation score. After the calibration process, score the model and simulation system with one of the many measures of error using the saved data set. This measure will let the modeler and any other party that uses the simulation have an idea of how well the blockchain simulation represents the real system from the perspective of the validation data set.

If the model and simulation is exploratory and is simulating a fictitious system in which a real system does not exist yet, the modeler might not have a data set that can be generated to perform validation. In this case, all checks must be made to the best of the modeler's ability to verify the actions, so that the simulation is what the developers, the users, and the modelers would intend it to be. This can be done using sensitivity analysis, where the modeler tests the extremes or ideal scenarios to see whether the results are realistic to the intentions of the subject matter experts.

13.5.5 Example

As an example, a simulation was built in Unity 3D of a simple battlefield. A blockchain network using the Hyperledger Fabric platform is started up on a network server. The blockchain can utilize any supported consensus algorithm that is implemented with Hyperledger Fabric; the example that was tested uses the Kafka consensus with three peer nodes, an orderer node, a client node, three Kafka nodes, and associated zookeeper nodes. This blockchain system can be simplified to use a solo consensus algorithm and fewer nodes. The simulation that was developed operates in near real time as a first-person shoot style simulation, where the user can move around the world freely and look around. Unity 3D is a game engine that is free to use in an academic sense but requires a license if it is used for commercial purposes. Unity provides many free models and has a fully capable physics engine that allows developers to quickly prototype simulations or games.

The simulation is simple in nature—there are tank entities, plane entities, and cube entities. A top down view of the world is provided in Figure 13.24. The

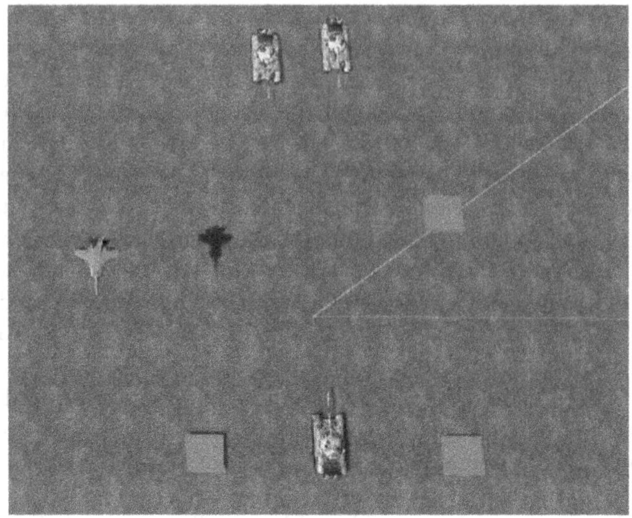

Figure 13.24 Top down view of the simulated environment.

cube entities represent locations hosting parts of the blockchain network, i.e. validating nodes, in this case peer nodes. The tank and air entities are associated with IDs that are maintained on the live blockchain.

When the simulation starts, the user is presented with a world that it can move around in a first person perspective as shown in Figure 13.25. In the top

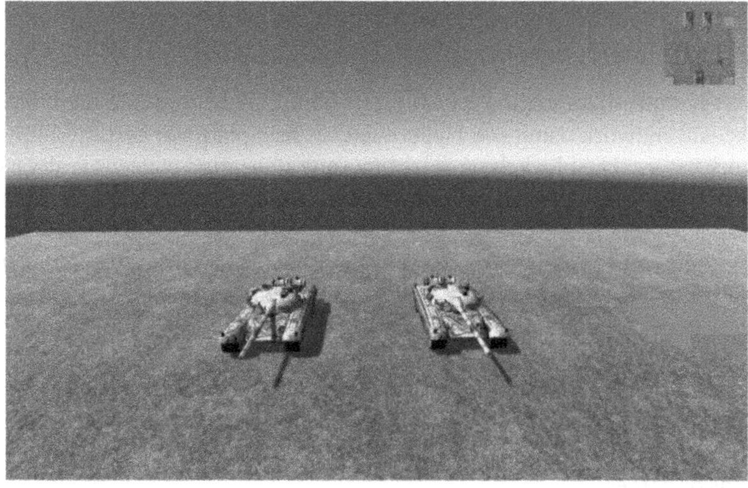

Figure 13.25 Game view of the simulated world with entities connected to the real blockchain system.

right corner there is a minimap; the minimap is a static camera above the battlefield that includes vision on the three cubes representing peer nodes. The minimap acts as a censor that utilizes the blockchain to determine whether the entity that is in view is friendly or unknown. The user will also notice that on the minimap is an air entity that is circling above; if the camera is moved to look up, the 3D jet will be in view and circling. Also on the minimap is a tank near the user's starting position; this tank acts as a static starting node for the user (think that the player stepped out of the tank and can move around). If the user maneuvers the character north, two other tanks will come into view, but are not within the range of the minimap sensor. Pressing spacebar will move the tanks within the range of the minimap as they advance south. The minimap reveals which entities are known friendlies that have been verified on the blockchain network by indicating a blue or green cube on the entities. If any entities are unknown and not verified on the blockchain, the minimap will show those entities with a red cube over them. Figure 13.22 shows the user's view, including the minimap with the colored cubes based on the entity IDs and their status on the blockchain.

In this example, the blockchain runs a chaincode that writes a simple data structure to the blockchain. The data structure contains the following values:

1. EntityID: string
2. EntityVal: string
3. Message: string

The chaincode queries the blockchain for the EntityID. If the EntityID does not exist or if the Message value is empty or null, then the entity is considered unknown. This chaincode allows privileged accounts to add entities to the blockchain or invoke new Messages and EntityVal strings. The blockchain is started and run using the JavaScript software development kit (SDK) for Hyperledger Fabric, to provide a cleaner interface between the clients and the peers hosting the chaincode. Once the blockchain network is started, the web service also starts listening to requests on a specific port from the server's IP address.

13.6 Conclusion and Future Work

Blockchain systems are very early in development and work continues to prove the theories that exist. Testing the theories in simulation or in an actual blockchain system is critical in understanding the true effects of the decisions made in the system. Discussing and thinking about how decentralized blockchain systems will work best is important but until proper tests show that these ideas work and provide a means for comparison, the technology will not be able to advance from paper to production.

Simulation of blockchain systems can be a very valuable tool when used appropriately. If decisions are to be made with simulations for real systems, developers should ensure proper verification and validation of the system that is being modeled and simulated. Even with this point, simulation offers a unique ability to test extreme variations of the system that can be expensive or impossible to implement.

The future is bright for open sourced blockchain systems as they will be better vetted by a large community and will offer opportunity for fast deployment. Additionally, they provide a means for developers to tailor the tools to work best for specific scenarios. Hyperledger Fabric provides a platform that is heavily supported and will be a great way for new developers to implement systems to build upon. Years beyond this book, the success of the platform will greatly be based on the community and where the developers choose to support and build on. When choosing a platform, look to see the quantity and the quality of developers that are supporting the tool to get an idea of the future of that platform.

Moving forward, the researchers of this book see a great deal of work in improving the scalability and performance of decentralized blockchain systems. Further work will be done on better understanding the best use cases for these types of systems. Early developers and researchers might quickly jump to try blockchain systems to solve many problems; this does not mean that blockchain will be great at solving all of these problems, but over time the success stories will rise to the top. Hopefully, stories of applications of blockchain systems to solve problems will be written for good use cases as well as bad use cases. There needs to be a better understanding of when blockchain works and when it does not work. Finally, there needs to be more documented evidence of the performance metrics and capabilities of these systems that are peer reviewed and vetted by the academic community, in addition to the open source community.

References

1 Hyperledger, "Hyperledger—open source blockchain technologies." [Online]. 2018. Available: https://www.hyperledger.org/.

2 Hyperledger Fabric, "A blockchain platform for the enterprise." [Online]. 2018. Available: https://hyperledger-fabric.readthedocs.io/.

3 D. Tosh, S. Shetty, P. Foytik, C. Kamhoua, and L. Njilla, "CloudPoS: A proof-of-stake consensus design for blockchain integrated cloud", in *IEEE International Conference on Cloud Computing (Cloud 2018)*, San Francisco, CA, July 2–7, 2018.

4 M. Castro and B. Liskov, "Practical Byzantine fault tolerance and proactive recovery," *ACM Transactions on Computer Systems (TOCS)*, vol. 20, no. 4, pp. 398–461, 2002.

14

Summary and Future Work

Sachin S. Shetty,[1] Laurent Njilla,[2] and Charles A. Kamhoua[3]

[1] *Old Dominion University, Virginia Modeling, Analysis and Simulation Center, Norfolk, VA, USA*
[2] *US Air Force Research Lab, Cyber Assurance Branch, Rome, NY, USA*
[3] *US Army Research Laboratory, Network Security Branch, Adelphi, MD, USA*

14.1 Introduction

Blockchain has attracted interest from a wide range of stakeholders, including those from finance, healthcare, utilities, real estate, and government agencies, as a potential way to address security challenges in distributed systems. As commercial, government, and military sectors become more comfortable with the technology, blockchain platforms will play a key role in cloud and Internet of Things (IoT) security. At the same time, it will be necessary to address security and privacy issues in blockchain platforms prior to integrating them with existing backend cloud and IoT systems.

The maturation of blockchain platforms will raise new concerns, such as trust, security, and privacy issues with the Internet of Battlefield Things (IoBT); performance assurance and security metrics; resilience to faulty and dishonest validation nodes in permissioned blockchains; incentive mechanisms to balance risk and reward; and security risk assessment. Academia and industry are collaboratively working to develop blockchain platforms that will address these pressing cloud and IoT security issues.

The preceding chapters of this book have suggested that blockchain platforms address security issues in cloud and IoT systems, as well as in the areas of cloud data provenance, information sharing, cloud storage, smart vehicles, IoT transportation security, attack surface analysis, double spending prevention, permissioned and permissionless platform security, fault-tolerant consensus protocols, simulation environments, and performance metrics. This final chapter summarizes our blockchain platform development insights and the remaining issues and obstacles in any mission-critical system deployment.

Blockchain for Distributed Systems Security, First Edition. Edited by Sachin S. Shetty, Charles A. Kamhoua, and Laurent L. Njilla.

14.2 Blockchain and Cloud Security

Cloud computing has been adopted by commercial entities and the military for supporting data storage, on-demand computing, and dynamic provisioning. Cloud computing environments are dynamic and heterogeneous. Because they involve several disparate software and hardware components that are manufactured by different vendors, they require interoperation capability. In Chapter 4, we propose blockchain-based solutions to secure cloud storage services.

Assurance of intracloud and intercloud data is crucial. Typical data assurance involves safeguarding the confidentiality, integrity, and availability of the data contents. Assurance of data ancestry (i.e. where it originated) is equally important, yet remains challenging in cloud environments. Blockchain-based solutions address these issues by gathering assured data provenance for services in cloud (data provenance provides data ancestry based on a detailed derivation of the data object). Blockchain-based provenance will be required to provide tracking of healthcare records and supply chain items.

We present a blockchain-based data provenance system to audit operations in the cloud storage service in Chapter 4; however, several concerns need to be addressed prior to deploying such a system. These include encoding operations in transactions at the appropriate granularity to balance transparency and overhead, real-time response, automatic incorporation of access control rules in smart contracts, choice of permissioned versus public blockchain, and consensus protocols.

14.3 Blockchain and IoT Security

The IoT has emerged as the primary platform seeking to maximize interconnectivity of the cyber and physical worlds, including but not limited to vehicles, infrastructures, home sensors, smart medical systems, and wearable electronics. Security is still the primary concern in IoT environments. Even though significant security assurance improvements have been made over the past few years in the area of communication engineering, application layer security (especially cross-domain and cross-scenario [heterogeneity] security schemes) remains an open topic for research.

A key IoT component is the Vehicular Communication System (VCS), a subsystem of the Intelligent Transportation System (ITS) that integrates advanced communications technologies into transportation infrastructure and vehicles. Two blockchain-based solutions that address VCS security issues are presented in Chapters 5 and 6.

Smart vehicles are increasingly connecting with other vehicles in close proximity, roadside infrastructures (e.g. traffic lights and overhead displays at motorways), and more generally to the Internet, qualifying them as IoT objects.

This high degree of connectivity introduces new sophisticated, personalized services for smart vehicle owners, as well as manufacturers, suppliers, and service providers (SPs) such as insurance companies. However, it also means that smart vehicles are very difficult to secure. Conventional security and privacy solutions used in smart vehicles tend to be ineffective due to centralization, lack of privacy, and safety threats.

A decentralized privacy-preserving and secure blockchain-based architecture for a smart vehicle ecosystem is presented in Chapter 5. Smart vehicles, original equipment manufacturers, and other SPs jointly form an overlay network, wherein they can communicate. Nodes in the overlay are clustered, and the cluster heads (CHs) are solely responsible for managing the blockchain and performing its core functions. These CHs are known as overlay block managers (OBMs). Transactions are broadcast to and verified by the OBMs, thus eliminating the need for a central broker. To protect user privacy, each vehicle is equipped with internal storage for sensitive privacy data such as location traces. The vehicle owner defines which data (and granularity) is provided to third parties in exchange for beneficial services and which to keep in the in-vehicle storage. Consequently, the owner has increased control over the disseminated data.

The security of a VCS depends heavily on the content of the exchanged messages, which are usually referred to as safety messages. The accuracy of the information in these messages (e.g. speed, direction, position, and vehicle size) determines whether or not ITSs operate in a regular and sustainable manner as they assist vehicles and infrastructures in interpreting the status of the surrounding environment. The integrity of safety messages can be ensured by encrypting them with predetermined secret keys. However, this extends the problem of VCS security into the reliable distribution or updating of these secret keys among all communicating participants, particularly in the timely delivery of the key to another security domain during the node handover process. Moreover, high mobility, a massive number of devices, and a wide range of vehicle activities present additional challenges to VCS centralized management and access point deployment. A distributed management structure will help the VCS achieve higher network management efficiency, reduce network manager burden, and lower infrastructure building cost.

A secure key management scheme in a VCS scenario using blockchain is proposed in Chapter 6. In this approach, blockchain is used to simplify the network structure so that the node handover processes experience fewer message handshakes and reduced delay.

The public ledger is maintained by all network participants instead of dedicated miners, which removes central key managers from the main body of the blockchain structure. Messages are broadcast to the network for nodes to authenticate. A new block is attached to the ledger if the authentication process determines that the messages are valid. This simplified structure can accelerate data propagation between security domains since the information is sent directly to the destination, bypassing central managers entirely. Moreover, the distributed structure of the blockchain network performs with better robustness under the single point of failure.

According to predictions, the IoT will eventually connect everything, including the details of human life. For this reason, personal information is threatened by malicious users in the IoT environment. Reliable privacy protection makes an adversary unable to focus their attack on any specific device. In order to address the privacy problem, future work will further consider these issues, including researching systems that provide both security and privacy.

14.4 Blockchain Security and Privacy

Blockchain platforms are susceptible to security and privacy attacks. This issue is addressed in several chapters by characterizing attack surfaces, pinpointing vulnerabilities in consensus protocols, discussing security and privacy threats to permissionless and permissioned blockchains, identifying methods of countering double spending, isolating effective defense measures taken by the blockchain technology or proposed by researchers to mitigate the effects of these attacks, and investigating ways to patch blockchain vulnerabilities.

> *The blockchain attack surface and the possible ways in which this technology can be compromised are explored in Chapter 3. We attribute attack viability in the attack surface to (i) blockchain cryptographic constructs, (ii) the distributed architecture of the systems using blockchain, and (iii) the blockchain application context. We outline several attacks for each of these contributing factors, including selfish mining and associated peer behaviors, 51% attack, Domain Name System (DNS) attacks, distributed denial-of-service (DoS) attacks, equivocation, consensus delay (due to selfish behavior or distributed DoS attacks), blockchain forking, orphaned and stale blocks, block ingestion, wallet thefts, and privacy attacks. We then explore the causal relationship between these attacks and show how one fraudulent activity can lead to the possibility of other attacks.*

In Chapter 8, we discuss two security design considerations and apply them to both permissioned and permissionless models. The first consideration is committee selection, where a large population of participants are narrowed down into a small, fairly sampled subset, thus limiting an attacker's presence. Committee selection applies equally well to both permissionless and permissioned blockchains, since it can improve performance by controlling participants' access. The second consideration is privacy. Blockchain applications often need to provide privacy guarantees for users if they involve, for example, sensitive information about financial transactions or the real-time location of IoT devices (cryptography can be employed for this purpose). If a high degree of trust exists among peers, as in a permissioned setting, secret sharing is natural, since it is assumed that the majority of peers will not violate confidentiality. On the other hand, in a context with less trust, zero-knowledge proofs allow clients to prevent peers from seeing protected data.

In Chapter 9, we analyze the impact of DoS attacks on blockchain, specifically focusing on a DoS attack variant that can be effectuated on the memory pools (mempools) of blockchain systems in general. To that end, we study such an attack and explore its effects on transaction fee structures of legitimate users. We also propose countermeasures (including fee- and age-based designs) that optimize the mempool size and thus help mitigate the effects from such an attack. We use simulations to evaluate our designs and analyze their usefulness in varying attack conditions. Our analyses can be extended to a wide variety of blockchain systems using proof concepts, where fees are provided as a participation incentive.

Dishonest mining strategies such as block withholding attack, selfish mining, eclipse attack, and stubborn mining have been proven to reduce the effectiveness of Proof-of-Work (PoW) protocols. As a result, it is necessary to regulate the mining process and hold miners accountable for any dishonest conduct. In Chapter 10, we model the block withholding attack prevalent in PoW-based mining pools to understand the strategy for appropriating pool members' rewards. Our results demonstrate that an attacker's access to additional computational power could disrupt the honest mining operation in the blockchain cloud. The attacker's strategy is analyzed based on two different pools with differing reward schemes. We demonstrate that a pay per last N shares (PPLNS) scheme is more useful than the proportional reward scheme in minimizing the impact of an attack. Future studies will apply our PoS-based blockchain cloud analysis to the real-time private blockchain platform.

In Chapter 11, we propose a new reputation-based framework for blockchain PoW computation that will help incentivize miners to conduct honest mining, while discouraging malicious activities against other mining pools. We illustrate the architecture of our reputation-based paradigm, explain the rewards or penalties given to miners, and provide game-theoretical analyses to show how this new framework discourages dishonest mining strategies. In our setting, a group of mining pool managers and miners repeatedly plays a game, during which the reputation of each miner or mining ally is continuously measured. At the beginning of each round, the pool managers send invitations to a subset of miners based on a nonuniform probability distribution defined by the miners' reputation values. Using our proposed solution concept, honest mining becomes the Nash equilibrium; in other words, it will not serve the miners' best interests to employ dishonest strategies, even if they gain a short-term utility in doing so. This is due to the consideration of a long-term utility in our model and its impact on the miners' utilities over time.

14.5 Experimental Testbed and Performance Evaluation

The emergence of several blockchain platforms in the market has created a need to evaluate the performance and security of the platform for cloud and IoT deployments. We address this in Chapter 12 by evaluating blockchain platforms that are best suited for IoT deployments. We also discuss the configuration and parameters to instrument the blockchain platform. We describe the implementation of two private blockchain configurations—blockchain-enabled gateways and blockchain-enabled end devices. We design experiments for the two configurations, implement them on a testbed composed of Raspberry Pi devices, and evaluate them on Ethereum and Hyperledger Fabric frameworks, respectively. In Chapter 13, we provide a simulated and experiential platform for the permissioned blockchain environment that would facilitate the evaluation of the algorithms and protocols presented in this book. The simulation environment provides the ability to quantify the performance of the protocols, as well as insight into the optimal blockchain platform to use in the experiential environment. For the experiential environment, we evaluate the scalability and resilience of the Hyperledger Fabric framework when subjected to realistic conditions.

14.6 The Future

Although there are multiple blockchain platforms on the market and considerable research and development on some blockchain features is ongoing, further research is required in the following areas:

- Public, private, or hybrid blockchain architecture
- Incentives
- Anonymity and data privacy

Public, Private, or Hybrid Blockchain Architecture—Public blockchain architecture provides a truly decentralized mechanism for performing transactions. However, commercial enterprises are skeptical of integrating public blockchain into their enterprise solutions due to data privacy, performance, and response concerns. Further research and development within the public blockchain platform is necessary to address these concerns.

In the meantime, commercial stakeholders are increasingly gravitating towards a private/permissioned/consortium blockchain architecture. This architecture varies according to the governance style, which ranges from a single member to a consortium overseeing the blockchain platform. These blockchain platforms have centralized components in the architecture, protocol, or the process in which the transactions are validated.

Incentives—In Bitcoin, the incentive to participate in the blockchain platform is monetary; in use cases such as provenance and identity management, the incentives are nonmonetary. The incentive structure needs to be incorporated within the protocol to ensure maximum participation. The incentive design mechanisms may be derived from use cases to ensure that the blockchain protocols are working toward maximizing the benefits for the use case. Although the blockchain platform's trust property may eliminate tampering or cheating, it is important for the design to include incentive mechanisms with properties that discourage cheating or unfairness. There is a need for theoretic models to capture the dynamics associated with incentivizing participants.

Anonymity and Data Privacy—The public availability of blockchain transactions makes it possible to use data analytics techniques to evaluate the vast quantities of data within them. This analysis could reveal valuable information, including the identity of participants and specific transactions they have performed. Several schemes address privacy issues in public blockchain platforms, including stealth addresses, homomorphic encryption, and zero knowledge proof. A combination of techniques is necessary to achieve the desired level of privacy.

Index

Blockchain for Distributed Systems Security, First Edition. Edited by Sachin S. Shetty, Charles A. Kamhoua, and Laurent L. Njilla.